Dealing with the Fragmented International Legal Environment

Turki Althunayan

Dealing with the Fragmented International Legal Environment

WTO, International Tax and Internal Tax Regulations

Springer

Turki Althunayan
King Saud University
P.O. Box 10022
Riyadh 11433
Saudi Arabia
e-mail: althunayan@gmail.com

ISBN: 978-3-642-04677-3 e-ISBN: 978-3-642-04678-0
DOI 10.1007/978-3-642-04678-0
Springer Heidelberg Dordrecht London New York

Library of Congress Control Number: 2009936789

Cover design: WMXDesign GmbH, Heidelberg, Germany

Printed on acid-free paper

Springer is part of Springer Science+Business Media (www.springer.com)

Contents

Part I The Problems

Part III The Future

Introduction

Taxation has become "the single most difficult substantive problem of international trade."[1]

The risk is that the pursuit of a more perfect globalization – more openness – endangers our imperfect, but still remarkable globalization by intensifying the conflicts that the system inevitably generates. (Rodrik 2007, p. 25)

Due mainly to the establishment of the World Trade Organization (WTO), the decline of trade barriers has been a major international accomplishment. In order to protect and enhance the liberalization of international trade, the WTO Agreements contain a fundamental obligation requiring WTO members to refrain from discriminatory or protectionist actions, including those using taxation instruments. However, one result of the unwarranted isolation of the independent tax and trade regimes has caused this policy of non-discrimination to be applied with less success in tax matters.

Even though there is a significant overlap in their objectives and effects, trade and tax regimes have been isolated from each other and have developed into two different legal schemas. Given the close relationship between trade and taxes, the continued sharp separation of the two regimes needs to be reexamined.

This study will search for a better understanding of the relationship between the two regimes within a historical context, and will explore the possibility of integrating international tax principles with international trade subjects. The continuing expansion and importance of international trade regulation and the relatively unchanged international income tax regime lead one to question the continuing validity of the separation of tax and trade regimes. This study will address the possibility of incorporating international tax principles into the WTO.

The fragmentation problem between international tax and trade issues emerges because there are "many parallels and overlaps between international trade and

[1] Professor John H. Jackson, discussing the Domestic International Sales Corporation (DISC) in 1978; this remains an issue. *See* Jackson (1978, pp. 747, 749).

taxation" (Warren 2001, pp. 131, 147–148). Over time, the two evolved into separate, non-collaborative legal regimes, although there is indisputable significant "overlap in their goals and effects" (Warren 2001, p. 148). Even the rationale for the two legal regimes is, according to Professor Alvin Warren, "basically the same, which is to reduce impediments to international commerce" (Warren 2001, p. 147).

The existing disconnects between the international trade and tax regimes poses serious challenges that could result in potential nullification of the WTO agreements. Warren writes that when tax and trade regimes are considered together, "no consistent principle explains the current dividing line" (Warren 2001, p. 158). Links between taxation and the international trading system, whether direct or indirect, are inevitable; thus, it is essential to establish guidelines for dealing with these links.

It is not as if taxation is unrelated to the GATT/WTO. The relationship is evident, for example, in a dispute over the US Federal Foreign Sale Corporate (FSC) income tax regimes, after which a WTO arbitration panel issued a decision allowing the European Union to impose $4.043 billion in trade sanctions against the USA,[2] and was also evident during the negotiations over the General Agreement on Trade in Services (GATS) treaty.[3] The relationship needs to be clarified, analyzed, and articulated in order to correct current mistakes and avoid future ones, or at least minimize the chances of conflict between the two regimes and manage those conflicts that do occur.

Reduced tax rates, tax holidays, or specific tax provisions to encourage exports, discourage imports, or otherwise discriminate against foreigners, or to protect local products and producers, or to achieve certain domestic policies (legitimate or otherwise), may be applied, either covertly or openly, to specific sectors or activities, possibly violating some of the WTO's rules. Manipulating some aspects of the tax base, such as depreciation schedules or deduction allowances, can achieve similar results.[4] Taxes can nullify WTO agreements, a possibility that is already a problem and needs to be confronted.

Tax and trade regimes sometimes clash. Although tax and trade share underlying goals, this should not discount the fact that taxes play major societal roles that are not necessarily based on economic considerations, and hence are not necessarily in harmony with international trade theory. Taxes are sometimes so fundamental to domestic systems that they are almost impossible to change, as when the tax system

---

[2] *See* United States-Tax Treatment of "Foreign Sales Corporations," WT/DS108/AB/R (Feb. 10, 2000). The WTO appellate panel upheld an earlier holding that the US FSC is a prohibited subsidy in violation of WTO rules. The FSC measure was subsequently repealed in the Extraterritorial Income Exclusion Act 2000, Pub. L. No. 106-519, which was also invalidated by the WTO. An Arbitration Panel imposed $4.043 billion in trade sanctions against US imported goods. *See also* Tax Analyst (2004).

[3] *See* Chap. 5, *infra*.

[4] Malaysia and Singapore exempt from taxation any shipping company income derived from the operations of ships owned by domestic companies, creating an incentive for the use of shipping services provided by resident companies. *See* Daly (2006, pp. 527–557).

is part of a nation's majority religion or is linked to another value deeply rooted in local communities, such as housing or farming. In such situations, people's tax contributions, deductions or subsidies to local mosques or churches, farms, social or homeownership programs, and the like, are difficult to deal with on a global level. Professor Warren writes that "[w]hatever one thinks about the relationship between trade and tax policies, an answer to the question of how free a country is to use its income tax to discriminate against international commerce requires consideration of both legal regimes" (Warren 2001, p. 149).

The Saudi Arabian tax system exemplifies the tension between religion, tax and trade, because tax has a role in the country's religion and is an essential part of its laws. The system subjects Saudi-Muslims to *zakat,*[5] a religious tax of 2.5% on wealth, while non-Saudis are subject to a "higher" income tax rate of 20% (flat rate) of their income. It is more difficult to decide this kind of tax case in Geneva,[6] since the effects of those decisions affect the religion of Saudi Arabians. There is a danger in the Geneva-based entity making decisions for people living in distant locations with regard to tax issues related to their local needs and wants.

Further, although many of the WTO agreements could potentially apply to national tax laws, because WTO agreements require national treatment and most-favored-nation status,[7] having implications on tax rules, some international tax scholars have expressed skepticism about the relevance and logic of combining both regimes. Common arguments that have been raised include: trade concepts are not analogous to tax policy (Rosenbloom 1994, p. 593); trade and tax serve different purposes, such as distribution of income[8] or encouragement of certain types of investments[9] and activities (Birde and Zolt 2003);[10] and tax is closely linked to nations' sovereignty (Green 1998, pp. 79, 131). Although these arguments might also apply to trade, they remain powerful and require careful consideration.[11]

Thus, there are two conflicting, strong points of view. From one perspective, taxation can affect trade so fundamentally as to nullify trade agreements. From the

---

[5] Zakat is an Islamic tax, discussed in details in Chap. 3, *infra*.

[6] It is interesting to note that changes usually resisted if coming from outside. Professor William P. Alford writes regarding China that respect for private property rights cannot be externally implanted (Alford 1995). After providing a historical account of copyright protection in China, he argued that the "institutions, personnel and values needed to undergird a rights-based legality" must support the laws themselves and not be imposed or forced on them; otherwise it would be of "limited value" (Alford 1995, p. 120).

[7] This issue will be discussed in Chap. 6, *infra*, The WTO Agreements.

[8] "What is the place of equity in comprehensive tax reform? The first goal ought to be to protect the lowest-income families in the society" (Gillis 1989, p. 167).

[9] "Many tax incentives have been employed to encourage investment" (Jorgenson and Landau 1993, p. 138).

[10] Birde and Zolt listed the following as possible objectives of tax laws: (1) Raising revenue; (2) Economic efficiency and the costs of taxation; (3) Fairness concerns; (4) Tax administration and tax policy; (5) Taxation and growth; (6) Taxation and decentralization; and (7) Using the tax system for non-fiscal objectives such as correcting market failures.

[11] *See* Chap. 4, *infra*, The Literature Review.

other point of view, tax is associated with deep local values that are hard to manage on an international level.

Consequently, there is a danger that countries with unchecked power to tax may use disguised taxes to purposely undermine the WTO agreements. To a large extent, tax and trade do overlap, but also clash in their objectives.[12] Tax does, to some extent, work as a barrier to the freedom of movement, with the potential to cause nullification of the WTO agreements. If tax rules continue to move in a direction incompatible with trade rules, trade liberalization cannot be implemented. There is a need to recognize the problems, and focus and put more effort into devising rules that can manage them, instead of proceeding with a market-opening agenda as if the problems were of little consequence or as if the market would solve them by default.

Therefore, there is a need for maintaining a delicate balance between local needs and international commitments with respect to taxation. The issue this study attempts to raise the complexity and difficulty of the tax issues, and cases addressed and/or litigated under the WTO. Cases are wrongly brought to the WTO, not wrongly decided. If they are to be brought, there must be a flexible infrastructure to offer countries the needed marginal freedom to move within acceptable levels in their own internal environment so that the WTO decisions are not viewed as threatening local interests.

The need is for more than exception. Due to this complex relationship, this author is of the opinion that tax issues need to be decided according to a different set of rules, a "soft" jurisdiction before a tax panel, where more understanding and more flexibility can foster respect for international rules while respecting local, deeply rooted values and interests. The ideal solution would be a flexible international tax agreement, which could provide a platform governing all tax-trade related issues on the one hand, while on the other hand leaving WTO members with as much freedom as possible to decide their own fundamental domestic tax issues.

This author strongly believes that the best resolution is not one single set of rules, but rather the establishment of a forum in the WTO designed to create a set of guidelines that would apply soft pressures implemented through dispute settlement mechanisms to achieve cooperation in tax matters, while at the same time offers WTO members the needed space to move as their internal pressures require. Professor Rodrik called this the "policy space" approach (Rodrik 2007, p. 26).

This study will attempt to fill the current gap in scholarship between the fields of trade and tax, taking into account both historical and religious factors. The analysis will be based on international trade, in particular WTO rules and policies, as well as on international tax policies. The author suggests a novel framework in which to resolve existing and potential tensions between international tax and international trade.

[12] Professor Reuven S. Avi-Yonah agreed that there exists some overlap. "The question is, how important is this area of overlap .... I would argue that it is extremely important ... perhaps the WTO is the most promising forum for finding a solution" (Avi-Yonah 2001, pp. 1683, 1692).

The goal of this work is to develop a practical proposal that takes into account historical circumstances as well as present needs and challenges, and to predict probable future circumstances and suggest potential resolutions. This work will take seriously two ideas. One is found in the GATS, Financial Annex, Article 4, which states that: "Panels for disputes on prudential issues and other financial matters shall have the necessary expertise relevant to the specific financial service under dispute."[13]

The second idea is found in the Appellate Body (AB) ruling, which states: "... we observe that many States have adopted bilateral or multilateral treaties to address double taxation ... In seeking to give meaning to the term 'foreign-source income' in footnote 59 to the *SCM Agreement*, which is a tax-related provision in an international trade treaty, we believe that it is appropriate for us to derive assistance from these widely recognized principles which many States generally apply in the field of taxation."[14]

Book Structure

The book is divided into three parts. Part I, entitled "The Problems," contains three chapters. Chapter 1 analyzes the problem of direct and indirect taxation. It is an issue that has fueled the tension between the USA and the EU, having different tax systems that rely on direct and indirect taxes. This chapter will attempt to show concretely the questionable foundation upon which this differentiation between direct and indirect taxes under the WTO is built. The meaning of each term varies greatly depending upon the source of the definition, so a variety of meanings are presented and analyzed. Scholars' views on the differentiation, both for and against, are also discussed.

Chapter 2 deals with existing problems illustrating the disconnect between the international trade and tax regimes, which can best be comprehended by examining and analyzing actual individual cases. The chapter is divided into two parts: part one covers tax-trade problems, presenting hypothetical cases that could arise; and part two discusses cases already litigated under the GATT/WTO involving tax issues that illustrate actual and potential conflicts.

Chapter 3 provides an investigation of taxation in the context of religion, which is another problem facing trade and tax when they interact. The chapter focuses on the Saudi Arabian tax system of zakat, specifically its religious aspects, to show situations in which the tax–religion relationship can be a barrier to international trade.

Part II, Analysis, begins with an examination of how other intellectuals have tackled this issue. Chapter 4 analyzes the existing literature regarding the

---

[13] WTO Annex on Financial Services, art 4.

[14] WTO Annex on Financial Services, art 4 ¶¶ 141–143.

incorporation of taxation into trade agreements. The scholarly works included represent the full spectrum of prior recommendations, from arguments against including any tax issues under the WTO to those that support the proposition.

Chapters 5 provides answers to major objections against including tax under the WTO, starting with the issue of sovereignty, including its meaning, applications, and relationship to the tax regime. The European Union Direct Tax Model is discussed in detail, with special attention paid to specific cases and the role of the European Court of Justice (ECJ). Then this chapter concludes with a summarized historical background of the tax and trade relation before proposing a suggested solution. The historic development of the GATT, for example, clearly indicates the political difficulties the negotiators faced. The failure to establish the International Trade Organization (ITO) is the strongest evidence of such a politically sensitive environment.

Chapter 6 investigates the tax issues in the most important agreements of the WTO: the General Agreement on Tariffs and Trade (GATT), the General Agreement on Trade in Services (GATS), and the Agreement on Subsidies and Countervailing Measures (SCM). A new and challenging construction will be proposed for some of the clauses, and the legal texts will be interpreted with the help of the Appellate Body decisions and other international sources.

Part III examines The Future. Chapter 7 proposes a new, workable tax model (the tax agreement option), designed to handle the relationship between tax and trade. The author proposes that such an option is particularly likely to succeed under the WTO; and discusses the particular factors that should be taken into account in order to avoid potential pitfalls. In addition, it is suggested that a "soft law" approach is the best fit for this option.

Chapter 8 concludes the study, providing recommendations based on the history and analyses covered throughout the work, and reiterating the advantages of the proposed tax agreement option, which is anticipated to help ease existing international tensions with respect to tax and trade, solve current problems, and avoid potential difficulties that could present a major barrier to international commerce.

References

Alford WP (1995) To steal a book is an elegant offense: intellectual property law in Chinese civilization. Stanford University Press, Stanford CA

Avi-Yonah RS (2001) Treating tax issues through trade regimes. Brook J Int'l L 26:1683, 1692

Birde R, Zolt E (2003) Introduction to tax policy design and development. A draft prepared for a WBI course on Practical Issues of Tax Policy in Developing Countries, April 28 – May 1, 2003

Daly M (2006) WTO rules on direct taxation. The World Economy 29:527–557. http://ssrn.com/abstract=896825

Gillis M (1989) Tax reform in developing countries. Duke University Press, Durham, NC

Green RA (1998) Antilegalistic approaches to resolving disputes between governments: a comparison of the international tax and trade regimes. Yale J Int'l L 23:79, 131

Jackson J (1978) The jurisprudence of international trade: the DISC case in GATT. Am J Int'l L 72:747, 749

Jorgenson DW, Landau R (1993) Tax reform and the cost of capital: an international comparison. The Brookings Institution, Washington, DC

Rodrik D (2007) How to save globalization from its cheerleaders. Working paper series RWP07-038. John F. Kennedy School of Government, Harvard University

Rosenbloom DH (1994) What's trade got to do with it? Tax L Rev 49:593

Tax Analyst (2004) Senate agrees to repel ETI; bill now heads to Bush. 2004 TNT 197-1, Oct 12, 2004

Warren AC Jr (2001) Income tax discrimination against international commerce. Tax L Rev 54:131, 147–148

Part I
The Problems

This part will deal with three sets of problems to illustrate the tension that can emerge from the separation of tax and trade. The first issue is the unsound differentiation between direct and indirect taxes, a theoretical problem that results in unnecessary, sometimes costly consequences and lasting costly disputes, starting with the Domestic International Sales Corporation (DISC), FSC, and Extraterritorial Income Exclusion (ETI). These cases are not isolated; they have been linked to other disputes. In fact, some have argued that the seeds of the FSC case "had nothing to do with tax policy and everything to do with the European search for 'bargaining chips' to trade against EU losses in the Bananas and Beef Hormone cases."[1] And the seeds of the Bananas and Beef disputes can be traced to the DISC. The list of trade disputes goes on. One benefit of bringing tax issues into the WTO would be to subject this divisive issue to scrutiny and reexamination with a new perspective, taking into account the lasting, consistent and costly trade disputes between the two major blocks, in addition to the unclear theoretical foundation.

The second chapter will discuss tax cases related to the WTO. Section 2.1 will discuss cases that have been litigated because of tax issues. They will illustrate the magnitude of this fragmentation. Many important tax issues have been litigated under the WTO. In fact, the tax cases brought were started early on, even before establishment of the WTO. Many of these cases have been previously discussed in the existing literature, and some are covered in other parts of this book. Some observers viewed "the DISC case as the largest and most conspicuous failure in the history of GATT's litigation procedure" (Hudec 1988, p. 1444). And the DISC came back wearing a different name, FSC, which the USA also lost. The US loss resulted in $4 billion. So, the issue of taxes under the WTO is not negligible.

---

[1] *See* Agnew (2000, pp. 139, 141); *see* Hufbauer (2001, p. 1555); discussing the timing of the FSC, Hufbauer writes that the "origins of the FSC case had nothing to do with tax policy and everything to do with the European search for 'bargaining chips' to trade against EU losses in the Bananas and Beef Hormone cases, and the prospective expiration of the agricultural 'peace clause' in 2003" Hufbauer (2001, p. 1563, footnote 20).

Discussing the cases makes the problem of separation, which begs for a solution, more visible.

Section 2.2 will discuss hypothetical cases that also can be envisioned. A brief survey of some tax rules reveals problems and conflicts just waiting to arise.

The third chapter of Part I will show the problems of tax and trade created when tax is linked or attached to deep social values in the society. Saudi Arabia's tax system, for example, has its roots in religion. Now that it is a WTO member, potential problems are not unlikely to occur when the Saudi tax system clashes with the WTO rules.

References

Agnew CL (2000) Overpriced bananas, bad meat, or foreign sales corporations: what is the EU really complaining about? Tax Notes Int'l 21:139, 141

Hudec RE (1988) Reforming GATT adjudication procedures: the lessons of the DISC case. Minn L Rev 72:1443

Hufbauer GC (2001) Income vs. consumption taxation: domestic and international reforms. Brook J Int'l L 26:1555

Chapter 1
Differentiation Between Direct and Indirect Taxes

Mr. King asked what was the precise meaning of direct taxation? No one answered.
(Max Farrand 1966, p. 350)

Taxation under every form presents but a choice of evils.
(Ricardo 1817, ¶ 9.29)

Tax issues are, at times, buried in the WTO under different names or misleading labels, and may be mishandled or mischaracterized because of historical misunderstandings that no longer apply. One issue, which this author believes has been interpreted incorrectly, is that of the distinction between direct and indirect taxation, and the treatment of the two under the GATT, a problem that emerges because of the fragmentation and isolation between the two fields, tax and trade. The fact that tax issues are handled outside the WTO has left the WTO with old foundations and unexamined bases for allowing outdated concepts to continue living under the WTO. It is very safe to state that the differentiation between direct and indirect taxes is a disputed issue within the tax community. Yet, it seems undisputed within the WTO. If there were a tax agreement, tax department, and tax staff, more attention would have been given to this issue and would have been reasonably addressed. The isolation between the two regimes has led to this sort of distortion. After presenting the relation of direct and indirect taxes to the WTO, this chapter will offer an overview of the literature and theoretical foundation behind the distinction between direct and indirect taxes.

1.1 Background

It is understood that the GATT applies only to indirect taxation, such as sales tax, rather than direct taxation (i.e., income tax), although "such an interpretation is implicit and is not clear from the language of the provision" (Brauner 2005, pp. 251, 274).

For many years, the discussion regarding direct and indirect taxes has not been focused on the classification of the taxes; rather, the emphasis has, in essence, been placed upon the implications of implementing one or both tax forms, or neither. Major themes of any discussion regarding the influences and effects of the GATT include the tax incidence, tax shifting, and the economic burden of taxation. In

T. Althunayan, *Dealing with the Fragmented International Legal Environment: WTO, International Tax and Internal Tax Regulations*,
DOI 10.1007/978-3-642-04678-0_1, © Springer-Verlag Berlin Heidelberg 2010

other words, who must pay the tax: the person or entity upon whom the tax is levied, or another to whom the former is able to "shift" the tax?

In a discussion of taxes, one problematic element is the use of the words "directly" and "indirectly". Therefore, any discussion of the GATT and taxes must touch upon the controversy surrounding the differences between direct taxes and indirect taxes. It is necessary to approach this specific tax problem in greater depth. In fact, it would be difficult to proceed with any further study of the relationship between taxes and the WTO without touching upon the issues surrounding direct and indirect taxation.

Addressing the specific problems of direct and indirect taxation is necessary for several reasons. One profound benefit of revisiting this subject is the ability to recognize its ultimate implications. If the GATT is only about indirect tax, then the income tax, a direct tax, will be not covered by the WTO unless it is included under the subsidies agreement. This is the case because income tax will be excluded from the GATT and, as the GATS is a "voluntary" agreement, income tax will not be applicable under most of the WTO agreements, which is an important result with significant implications. There is also a possibility that, with the removal or lessening of international trade barriers, more clever techniques will be developed in order to satisfy domestic special interests; for example, using direct taxation to provide benefits that are otherwise not allowed under the WTO. The WTO needs to be ahead of this movement in order to control any potential abuse.

Finally, in order to understand trade disputes, which have affected the GATT and are now affecting the WTO, one must know how, why, and where the real conflict evolved. Now infamous disputes, such as the DISC and FSC, have occurred because they are deeply rooted within the financial systems of the United States, not because the USA is enamored of the prospect of more conflict or with manipulating the international taxation system. In summary, one must understand the underlying principles of each party's claims in these disputes.

1.2 The Distinction Theoretically

Theoretically, under the GATT, the distinction between direct and indirect taxes is based on the assumption that producers will shift the cost of the indirect tax forward to the consumers as a component of the price of the goods sold. Such costs are added, in their entirety, to the consumer's costs for the goods. On the other hand, such forward-shifting will not theoretically occur with respect to direct taxes, because they are paid at the point of origin, usually out of profits. Since they are paid out of profits, the theory concludes, direct taxes do not, and should not, affect the final price of the product.

The consequence of this thinking is that only indirect taxes increase the domestic price, which places local producers on an unfavorable competitive footing *vis-à-vis* foreign producers who are subject to a direct tax system. As a result, the indirect taxes require an adjustment, which is the function of the VAT rebate for exported goods. The essence of this assumption is that indirect taxes are "always and wholly shifted forward into the final price of a product,"[1] while direct taxes, such as income tax "are always and wholly shifted backward to the factors of production."[2]

In other words, the reason for the distinction seems to rest upon the economic theory that distinguishes between direct and indirect taxes based upon the presumption of shifting tax incidence. This presumption was maintained during the 1950s and 1960s. Its basic assumption is that the economic burden of the income tax, and of direct taxes in general, cannot be shifted forward and, therefore, the burden of direct taxes falls entirely on the producers of goods. Since the economic burden of indirect taxes falls entirely and consistently on the purchasers of goods and services, the burden of indirect taxes is shifted to the consumers and reflected in the final price paid for products. As a result of this distinction, the GATT allows indirect taxes, such as VAT, to be rebated to producers after they export their goods because, presumptively, the tax will be paid and borne by the ultimate consumers of said products and services.

Direct taxes, on the other hand, are not shifted according to this old argument; thus, there is no need to rebate any tax, and any actual rebate would be considered a subsidy. Direct taxes are not exempt even when the income is generated from selling exported products. Thus, under the WTO, a country reliant on income taxes will not be able to rebate any tax to its exporters, whereas a country operating under the indirect tax system will be able to offer this benefit (subsidy) to its goods exporters.

The GATT also allows countries to exempt from taxes, or to provide rebates for taxes paid, those persons and entities subject to taxes imposed on their exported products, in order to allow them to compete on a level playing field with producers of domestically produced goods. This position is in accord with the GATT's most fundamental goals, but its foundation is not entirely accurate.

1.3 The Issue

Why is there a need to be concerned about the differences between direct and indirect taxes? Article III:2 of the GATT and the interpretative note to Article XVI of the GATT refer to "taxes on products", and scholars (Pitschas 1995, pp. 479, 485; see also Floyd 1973, pp. 489, 498) have, as a result, concluded that Article III targets only

[1]Staff analysis of issues raised by the General Agreement on Tariffs and Trade, 91st Congress, 2nd Session, prepared by the Staff of the Committees on Finance, US Senate, Russell B Long, Chairman (December 19, 1970), p. 5.

[2]Staff analysis of issues raised by the General Agreement on Tariffs and Trade, 91st Congress, 2nd Session, prepared by the Staff of the Committees on Finance, US Senate, Russell B Long, Chairman (December 19, 1970), p. 5.

indirect taxes (Pitschas 1995, p. 485) as the GATT concerns only with products. Indirect taxes include, for example, sales, excise, turnover, franchise, and value-added taxes (VAT). Therefore, Article III does not cover taxes that are not imposed on products, such as income tax and property tax. Thus, the GATT differentiates between direct and indirect taxes. The result of this distinction is that it allows adjustments by granting remissions, rebates or exemptions for indirect taxes, but not for direct taxes. Such adjustments may exist in the form of refunds or remissions of previously paid internal taxes on domestically produced products that are destined for export vs. domestic consumption. Exported products are relieved of taxation and imported products are subject to taxation at jurisdictional borders. In other words, the rebate of indirect taxes on exports, such as VAT, is not an export subsidy, whereas the rebate of direct taxes, such as income tax, is a prohibited subsidy.

These adjustments are regarded as "fiscal measures which put into effect, in whole or in part, the destination principle, which enable exported products to be relieved of some or all of the tax charged in the exporting country in respect of similar domestic products sold to consumers on the home market and which enable imported products sold to consumers to be charged with some or all of the tax charged in the importing country in respect of similar domestic products."[3] They are permitted only for indirect taxes, such as sales tax and VAT, but not for direct taxes, such as income tax. This is the primary reason that the USA, a major income tax country, has not accepted this distinction.[4]

In order to understand the consequences of the GATT–WTO distinction, it is important to know the differences between the two major tax systems as represented by the EU and the USA. The USA employs the worldwide tax system,[5] whereas the

[3]1970 Report of the Working Party on Border Tax Adjustments, BISD 18S/97.

[4]The issue was discussed among GATT members but was not decided. *See* the Border Tax Adjustment report, Report of the Working Party adopted on December 2, 1970, ¶ 22, stated in part, "The question was raised by some members why only indirect taxes should be eligible for adjustment since the economic basis for such a clear distinction between indirect and direct taxes for adjustment purposes has not been demonstrated. Most delegations stated, however, that in their opinion such a distinction was already justified by the fact alone that indirect taxes by their very nature bear on internal consumption and were consequently levied, according to the principle of destination, in the country of consumption, while direct taxes – even assuming that they were partly passed on into prices – were borne by entrepreneurs' profits or personal income. On the other hand, some members stated that while forward shifting of selective excise taxes could take place under most circumstances according to micro-economic approach, forward shifting in the case of general consumption taxes was, according to macro-economic approach, not possible unless one assumes either a sufficient increase in money supply or in velocity of money. Some further argued that market conditions including, for example, monopoly or imperfect competition, influenced the degree to which the shifting of taxes both direct and indirect could take place. Other members expressed their doubts about this thesis. They pointed out that forward shifting of indirect taxes is the rule and that in any case the relative importance of the degree of forward shifting of these indirect taxes in the light of the economic conditions does not constitute a determining criterion for the application of tax adjustments."

[5]Some would argue that the US system is not purely a worldwide tax system. *See* Goodspeed (2006, p. 143).

EU primarily uses a territorial tax system. A worldwide tax system means citizens and residents of the USA are subject to the income tax law on their income worldwide, regardless of the jurisdiction within which such income is earned.[6] The USA, in order to alleviate the occurrence of any double taxation as a result of its policies, offers a foreign tax credit, which provides for a dollar-for-dollar credit on taxes paid to a foreign nation.[7]

The territorial tax method, on the other hand, does not offer such relief; the tax under this system makes such relief unnecessary as it is assessed on a territorial basis, regardless of taxpayer status. Thus, taxes are imposed on all income generated within the borders of the country, while all income that is generated outside the nation's borders are exempt. In other words, persons and entities are taxed on their income generated from domestic sources. This basic principle, of course, sometimes makes it difficult to determine what is considered "within" a nation's borders and what is considered generated "outside." For example, "Think of a law firm in country A that provides advice on the legal implications of a merger of two multinationals whose parents are in countries A and B and whose operations are in 20 countries around the globe. What is the economic source of the law firm's income?" (Avi-Yonah 2004, pp. 483, 490).

The following example illustrates the issue. Suppose that there is a company, *Cor*, which manufactures televisions in the USA, and that its largest market is in France. Suppose further that a second company, *Fro,* manufactures radios in France for export primarily to the USA. France, which has a VAT tax of 10%, normally would tax *Fro* on its business at the point at which the company sells its products, for instance, in its store *Fro* (assuming for purposes of this illustration that it is an integrated entity), which collects a 10% VAT from its customers in addition to the purchase price it is asking for the product. According to the destination principle, for those products sold by *Fro* outside France (for example those sold in the USA), the French government would not impose any tax, because the products are to be consumed in a destination that is not under French jurisdiction. This would exempt (or remit or impose zero tax on) the exported radios from VAT, because they are to be consumed in the USA. Thus, France would make an adjustment by not imposing a tax upon the company *Fro* as it would normally do on those companies selling to domestic purchasers.

When one compares the previous scenario to one that involves a US company, such as the aforementioned *Cor*, it becomes clear why there is a problem and why the distinctions between direct and indirect taxes have created problems, both in the past and continue to do so at present. Assume that *Cor*, the US entity, sells televisions to French consumers for profit. However, because the USA does not subscribe to the destination principle (consumption tax) and, instead, follows the worldwide taxing system principle, *Cor* will be required to pay taxes on its profits to

---

[6]Staff of Joint Committee on Taxation, 108th Congress, United States International Tax Rules: Background and Selected Issues Relating to the Competitiveness of US Business Abroad, p. 2.

[7]Staff of Joint Committee on Taxation, 108th Congress, United States International Tax Rules: Background and Selected Issues Relating to the Competitiveness of US Business Abroad, pp. 2, 10–11.

the US government, because such profits represent income that is taxable under US law. In another words, the USA cannot make any border adjustments for its domestic companies. In addition, the US company will have to charge its consumers a 10% VAT remitted to the French government.

Thus, in theory, there is a conflict of jurisdiction between consumption taxes and income taxes. At *Cor*, the US company, US-produced goods bear both the US income tax and the French consumption tax. In other words, there are two taxes: one at home that cannot be rebated – by the order of the GATT – and another tax at the destination (with the possibility of a third tax if it is subject to the French income tax). In contrast, territorial systems, say in France, decline to tax foreign source income, so they are not subject to VAT, because it is consumed outside France and also not subject to income tax since the income is not generated inside France. In addition, consumption taxes are eligible for adjustment while income taxes are not. So, a country relying primarily on a consumption tax can easily subsidize its exports by border adjustments, while a country relying primarily on an income tax, especially one with worldwide jurisdiction like the USA, cannot. This creates an unfair preference for one tax system with no strong justification.[8]

The burden of the indirect tax in reality could be borne by the seller, producer, consumer, shareholder, or other production or market participant, or any combination of persons or entities, but certainly not by the product itself. An exemption from tax is, in reality, an offer of a benefit to the person or entity standing behind that product. For example, when Company A imports a product into France, Company A will be responsible for paying a tax on that product. That tax normally and naturally will be paid out of Company's profits; in the absence of such a system there would be no reason to conduct commercial transactions. The profit that is the source of the tax payment is subject to a pool of different factors, including advertisement, labor, the raw materials for the production of the product, and many others. Thus, there is no tax on a product *per se*; instead, every tax is paid out from profit generated from different factors or, most commonly, from a combination of factors. Thus, the product effectively acts as a collecting agency.

Thus there is no reason that "only indirect taxes should be eligible for adjustment since the economic basis for such a clear distinction between indirect and direct taxes for adjustment purposes has not been demonstrated."[9] Further, the differentiation between direct and indirect taxes is "based on assumptions which are now not accepted ... the assumption of full shifting of indirect taxes and no shifting of direct taxes is not a reflection of economic reality ... the present GATT rules favours countries which rely heavily on indirect taxes and discriminate against countries which rely predominantly on direct taxes."[10]

---

[8]Thanks to Professor Joel Trachtman for this note.

[9]Tax Board Adjustment Report, BISD § 18S/97-109 (1972), p. 6.

[10]Tax Board report (1969) p. 2, para 6. Repeated almost identically again in the 1972 report, BISD § 18S/97-109 (1972), p. 2, para 8.

In addition, with regard to the difference between direct and indirect tax, the USA asserted that "the GATT rules should be amended"[11] because they were "arbitrary,"[12] as the notion of allowing rebates or remissions (that is, the "border tax adjustments") was founded upon outdated assumptions that were not universal. The shifting of indirect taxes does not happen always. The shifting of direct taxes happens sometimes. Thus, there is no reason to allow one tax to be rebated and disallow the other.

Annex "A" to the 1968 meeting of the working party regarding tax border adjustments was prepared by the USA. In it, the USA clearly indicated that it believed it was at a disadvantage "because of the tax systems of some of our trading partners. Some nations give across-the-board tax rebates on exports which leave their ports and impose special border tax charges on our goods entering their country."[13] The US delegation went to visit different countries to convey the "urgent need for developing a new system whereby the differences between national tax systems could be harmonized with one another, with more equity than exists with present rules and understandings."[14]

The USA reiterated its grave and increasing concern with the "heightening and proliferation of the border tax adjustments" and expressed its concerns that GATT members were not cooperating and "that by ignoring the call for a standstill they automatically accelerated the pace of these deliberations."[15] The USA then warned the members that "the future may bring us unwelcome surprises"[16] if the border tax adjustments were not reexamined. *Unwelcome* surprises! The DISC, FSC, and ETI proved that the USA correctly anticipated the problems that were unwelcome.

1.4 Other Factors

With this theoretical background in mind, one must also be aware that there are other factors not related directly to this differentiation, but which have nevertheless contributed to keeping the differentiation in place. In fact, these factors have come into play consistently since the establishment of the distinction, and they have bolstered and supported retaining the distinction.

One such factor is the EU's influence over the GATT. Since its inception, the GATT has been subject to a great deal of influence at all levels by the European countries, one of the most important of which has been their influence upon tax levels. Excise and other border duties, which are indirect taxes, are the oldest taxes in the world, especially in EU countries (see James 2002, p. 137). These were the

[11]Working Party on Tax Adjustment meeting of October 8–11, 1968, p. 1.

[12]Working Party on Tax Adjustment meeting of October 8–11, 1968, p. 1.

[13]Report of 1968 meeting. At p. 21 the US delegation cited the US President.

[14]Report of 1968 meeting, p. 21.

[15]Report of 1968 meeting, p. 22.

[16]Report of 1968 meeting, p. 22.

"most important source of governments' revenue" (James 2002, p. 137) until they were overtaken by VAT and other taxes. Countries have been unwilling to give up this easy source of revenue, as such taxes are imposed on foreigners or foreign products, and importing governments were not willing to relinquish this financial and political benefit. This, combined with the notion that exporting countries somehow benefit from sales of their products, would have led to acceptance of the notion that a superior right to tax products lies with the importing countries, especially given the fact that if exporting countries were to tax their own exported products, they would hurt their own domestic products' competitiveness. As a result, exporting countries had to work out a mechanism to alleviate their tax burden and increase the competitiveness of their producers in order to facilitate exporting, taking into account that an export-oriented economy is considered beneficial to development. The solution was to exempt products being exported from taxes while taxing imported products.

Anything with the potential to alter this picture would have been made moot after the introduction of VAT, a French invention.[17] After the French introduced this new tax on net business income in 1948, which later came to be called value-added tax, many countries followed suit, and did so more quickly than they had with any other form of taxation.[18] However, VAT created the problem of double taxation, as each country, whether the importer or the exporter, would tax the transaction. The ultimate solution was that the tax would be imposed only once: at the destination point, where the goods were to be consumed (the destination principle). The French thus exempted exports from VAT and imposed the tax on imports. Destination-principle VAT imposes taxes on goods or services consumed in the taxing jurisdiction, regardless of where the goods are produced or the services rendered. Imports are taxed and exports are tax-free (Schenk 1998, pp. 207, 230).

It should also be noted that, from an administrative point of view, a rebate of indirect taxes is much easier to handle than a rebate of income tax. Sometimes, indirect taxes are not imposed until the consumer pays the tax, so in the case of exporting products, no tax is paid up front. Therefore, it is easy to rebate the tax. Indirect taxes generally are easy to determine because they are calculated based on the price paid for the goods or service, with no deduction or other matters taken into account. On the other hand, direct taxes, such as income tax, are not as easy to

---

[17]The VAT is defined as "a tax on the value added by a firm during the production and distribution process to the goods and services that it purchases from other firms." *See* James (2002, p. 74). Oldman and Alan defined it as a tax "limited to the value added by the labor and capital." *See* Oldman and Schenk (2001, pp. 3–5). Although the authors claim that consumption like-VAT tax existed previously, the VAT as we know it today is a French innovation in 1948; *see* Messere et al. (2003, p. 138). Oldman and Schenk (2001, p. 5), writes that the original idea was articulated by Dr. Wilhelm von Siemens, but other scholars claim otherwise. For example, in James (2002, p. 81), the issue is claimed to be raised and discussed by T.S. Adams, the father of US income taxation, who suggested as early as the 1920s that a VAT-like tax should be applied in the USA.

[18]Oldman and Schenk (2001, p. 1), agreeing with and quoting Alan Tait, who wrote of the VAT as being "the Mata Hari of the tax world." *See* Tait (1988, p. 3). *See also* James (2002, p. 82).

rebate, because there are usually both internal and external transactions that trigger the taxable income, making it more difficult to determine which part may qualify for a rebate. Although a direct tax rebate is not impossible, a rebate of an indirect tax is easier by comparison.

The failure of the ITO can also explain and shed light on the problem of differentiation. It may be that, during the negotiation of the GATT, nations made every effort to avoid any potential problems, especially the USA, which was most affected by such negative notoriety. Due to the failure of the ITO, no nation wanted another international agreement so easily destroyed.

In the aftermath of the ITO debacle, the GATT was created in order to codify international trade rules, including direct and indirect taxes, not only regionally, but internationally as well. The GATT was clearly influenced by the EC, and more specifically by its related organization, the Organization for Economic Co-operation and Development (OECD). The policy of differential treatment of indirect taxes was formally adopted in 1970 when a GATT Working Party codified "the ancient distinction between permissible border adjustments for direct and indirect taxes" (Hufbauer 2002).

1.5 Direct and Indirect Taxes: Basic Meaning

As is the case in a variety of contexts, a discussion of taxation definitions and issues can become confusing and misleading when those responsible for such discussion assume that their audience understands their meaning, especially when such understanding does not necessarily exist. Precisely what direct and indirect taxation actually means is not well established, even among scholars who have studied the subject in depth. This is surprising, because if one cannot identify what is being prohibited, it becomes difficult, if not impossible, to establish appropriate rules of law without such rules being based upon vague or nebulous understandings. Under the GATT, direct taxes cannot be rebated, whereas indirect tax rebates are so permitted; however, no definition of these terms is provided, therefore there is no way to establish with any certainty their meanings.

1.6 Tax Definition

Economists have no one definition of what constitutes a "tax" as a general term. In fact, most would consider any "imposition of costs on individuals or firms by the government" (Thuronyi 2003, p. 45) to be a tax. Public finance textbooks offer different definitions and give examples rather than providing a precise definition. This shows the perplexity and difficulty of ascribing an acceptable definition to the term. This is not a new issue; the meaning of *tax* is a subject addressed frequently and largely unsuccessfully in the past; this lack of clarity continues into the present. And this is why it needs to be brought and settled in the WTO.

To provide a background of the basic meaning, *Black's Law Dictionary* has defined "tax" as "a monetary charge imposed by the government on persons, entities, transactions, or property, to yield public revenue" (Garner 1999).

David Ricardo offers a different definition, asserting that "taxes are a portion of the produce of the land and labors of a country, placed at the disposal of the government; and are always ultimately paid, either from the capital, or from the revenue of the country" (Ricardo 1817, ¶ 8.1). Ricardo also claims that tax "necessitates a deduction from the wealth of the contributor, even though compensation may be indirectly brought about through its action" (Bastable 2003, ¶ III.I.7). Professor Thomas Cooley emphasized the nature of tax in the context of the importance of the government, asserting that tax can be any "burden that may be lawfully laid upon citizens by virtue of its [the State's] taxing power." He defined taxes as those amounts of money that "are enforced proportional contributions from persons and property, levied by the state by virtue of its sovereignty, for the support of government and for all public needs" (Cooley 1924, pp. 61–62). This definition of taxes, which is generally referred to as Cooley's definition, "has been quoted and endorsed or approved expressly or otherwise, by many different courts" (Cooley 1924, p. 62 n.4).

Tax is an inescapable, compulsory and obligatory payment imposed by government for some general public purpose, having no specified return for the contributor. These features – the compulsory, the non-contractual element, and the non-specific return elements – are common to any definition of tax, although not necessarily to all taxes themselves. For example, excise taxes are paid for specific reasons, such as for health reasons in the case of tobacco or for environmental reasons in the case of pollution related activities.

1.7 Direct and Indirect Taxes: Meanings[19]

As seen, tax in general is not easy to define, neither direct taxes nor indirect taxes are easily defined individually (Bastable 2003, p. 250). In fact, "unfortunately [they are] used in different senses, though with several points of connexion" (Bastable 2003, p. 250). No single agreed-upon non-controversial definition can be offered, because there are many elements composing each individual definition. In this book, definitions will be presented that represent various viewpoints, in an effort to explore, identify and extract general themes and ultimately to clarify, if possible, the distinction between direct and indirect taxes.

[19]The US Constitution creates "two classes: one 'direct' taxes required to be apportioned according to population, and the other 'duties, imposts, and excises' required to be uniform throughout the United States." *See* Cooley (1924, p. 244).

Black's Law Dictionary defines direct tax as: "a tax that is imposed on property, as distinguished from tax on right or privilege" (Garner 1999). Direct tax is levied on wealth or income (Bannock et al. 1998, p. 106), or may be imposed as a tax on the income and resources of individuals or organizations (Bannock et al. 1998, p. 106). It refers to those taxes that are to be collected from the same people or entities upon which they are imposed. Directness of the tax "implies that the levy is upon the person who is expected to bear the final incidence."[20] Wealth, which is comprised of income or a source of income, such as property, wages, and companies, or any person controlling such wealth (whether individuals or entities), is a common element of this definition of direct tax.

Indirect taxes, on the other hand, are "levied on expenditures"[21] or on things (Lipsey 1979, p. 433), or "when goods and service are exchanged" (Huber and Norman 2003, p. 277). Indirect taxes are taxes which are collected by an intermediary third party from those persons or entities who theoretically bear the ultimate economic burden of such taxes, or are taxes paid by those who are likely to be able to shift all or some of the burden of such taxes to others or who, in any event, are under no legal compulsion to pay such taxes. An indirect tax is a tax on a transaction rather than on a person (whether natural or corporate) although, of course, the person or entity subject to the tax actually pays it. However, the obligation to pay does not arise until goods or services change hands or are rendered. The most commonly recognized indirect taxes are sales taxes, value-added taxes (VAT), excise tax, and tariffs.

1.7.1 General Differentiations

As there is no conclusive definition of either direct taxes or indirect taxes that is satisfying or definitive, it is necessary to review the characteristics of the two types of taxes in order to try to define them more objectively and substantively, rather than by assigning arbitrary and artificial labels or by making distinctions that are mere formalities (that is, distinctions without real differences).

The literature has discussed the differences between direct and indirect taxes for a long time. The most common analyses focus on five features: directness, choices, transparency, fairness, and economic burden. Although this book has indirectly touched upon them previously, the following discussion will address each of the factors in detail.

---

[20]Buchanan (1999, Public Finance § 4.13.30). Retrieved September 5, 2006 from the World Wide Web: http://www.econlib.org/library/buchanan/buchCv4c13.html (Chap. 16's discussion of Specific Excise Taxation).

[21]This is the well-known definition by J.S. Mill cited by Bastable (2003, p. 250).

1.7.2 Directness

One of the differences between direct and indirect taxation lies in their very name. Direct tax is so named because it is levied directly on a taxpayer's income or property. In other words, there is no intermediary or agent between the government and the taxpayer. Due to this directness, the assessment of amounts to be paid takes into account the taxpayer's circumstances and allows for offsets through deductions, exemptions, and marginal rates, if applicable, which may differ according to individual circumstances. Direct taxes may typically be adjusted to take into account special circumstances, such as inflation or natural disasters, or specific situations, such as the necessity health care treatment or an individual's age (Gillis et al. 1996, pp. 725, 726).

Indirect taxes, on the other hand, are imposed on transactions. Sellers or service providers are obliged to pay the tax; in essence, this means that they are required to collect it or, of course, if they prefer, they can pay it out of their own profits. The taxes are "indirect" in the sense that they are not aimed at specific persons or specific income levels, but rather are aimed at the timing or the incidence of the exchange of goods or delivery of services. If a transaction does not take place, no tax is imposed.

1.7.3 Choices

Another key difference between direct and indirect taxation lies in the choices they offer to taxpayers. Indirect taxes are theoretically much easier to avoid (Jensen 1999, pp. 687, 695), at least in some instances. Indirect taxes offer consumers a choice as to whether or not to purchase a service or product, which means that a prospective buyer can choose whether or not to bear the burden of the tax, assuming that the tax is not hidden and is visible independent of the purchase price, or that the buyer is aware that the tax is embedded in the total purchase price and knows that the whole tax will be paid by the buyer. Thus, indirect taxes may be avoided by deciding to purchase fewer products or services subject to taxation. Alternatively, a conscious choice may be made to purchase no such taxed products at all in order to avoid paying any taxes altogether, although this is not a viable option given that the purchase of many taxed products is very difficult, if not impossible, to avoid.

As Mill notes, a citizen can indeed, for example, escape a wine duty by not consuming wine, but that "has the double disadvantage of depriving the State of revenue and of diminishing his own enjoyment" (Bastable 2003, § III.IV.25). In addition, some products or services are not avoidable at all, such as electricity or water, so there will be a tax anyway.

Income tax may also be avoided if one does not, by choice or otherwise, earn enough money or own enough property to be subject to taxation. For example, an individual who decides to stay home opts for free time in lieu of income-producing employment, and is in effect choosing to pay less tax; situations like this blur the distinction this thesis attempts to identify.

1.7.4 Transparency

With respect to transparency issues, indirect taxes may be problematic, because they tend to be less visible than direct taxes. Indirect taxes, when hidden within the price of a product, are "tolerated because those who pay them are not conscious of the burden" (Jensen 1999, p. 695). Indirect taxes are not immediately felt by the taxpayer (because one is less conscious of them) to the same extent as direct taxes, and "therefore cause him less annoyance" (Bastable 2003, p. 250). Indirect taxes, because they are less transparent, may be easily manipulated by governments. A government tends to create a "fiscal illusion and serves thereby to conceal from the taxpayer-voter the real weight of tax, and hence causes him to support a somewhat higher level of public spending" (Buchanan 1999, § 4.13.48) Without a high level of transparency and effective educational programs, "individuals are likely to be less informed about the costs that indirect taxes impose on them than they are about the costs of direct taxes" (Buchanan 1999, § 4.13.20).

Nevertheless, there are limits to how, and by how much, indirect taxes can be increased; indirect taxes contain some protections against their abuse. For example, indirect taxes cannot be increased indefinitely, and cannot be increased to too high a level without the risk of decreasing revenues due to a decline in consumption.

Direct taxes, specifically income taxes, are more transparent than indirect taxes. Taxpayers are responsible for the calculation of their own income, the determination of their personal deductions and allowances, and for the submission of their personal tax returns. All of these responsibilities increase taxpayers' awareness as to the exact amount that they are paying to the government. In addition, direct taxes are not increased by too much at one time, as the wealthy often use their political power to resist tax increases. In fact, increases in income tax rates are typically very difficult to affect unless a particular tax is targeting those taxpayers who are less powerful. Although less so than indirect taxes, direct taxes can also be manipulated by the government, for example by disallowing certain deductions and slowing down depreciation, which may prove an inequitable result for many people.

1.7.5 Fairness

Another difference between direct and indirect taxes is the fairness issue. Indirect taxes are, the mainstream would argue, more regressive than direct taxes, and thus, less fair (Fried 1992, pp. 961, 966). Indirect taxes bear down, with far greater weight, on the less affluent members of a taxpaying society than they do on the wealthy,[22] or to put it more bluntly, a "large use of indirect taxes will press severely on the poorer classes of society" (Bastable 2003, ¶ III.III.54). In addition, it is reasonable to expect a tendency to impose heavier or more indirect taxes on less expensive articles, such as salt or cigarettes, that are commonly used by all – but in greater quantity by the poor – than on more costly goods that are used only by the rich, because they offer "a wider basis for large revenues" (George 1892, ¶ VIII.10).

Indirect taxes affect people in low-income groups more than they do those in higher income brackets (Walsh et al. 2000, p. 93). The lower one's income, the larger the pro rata portion of one's available income will be paid in taxes. Hypothetically, if a share of food costs $10, with the imposition of a sales tax of 50%, then the total cost of the taxed food would be $15; someone with a weekly income of $100 would pay 15% of his income in tax to get the food, while someone with a weekly income of $1,000 would pay only 1.5% of his income in tax.

Of course, this depends on many diverse factors, including the elasticity of the taxed products. For example, a tax on electricity or soap, regardless of the level of income, will affect everyone, because all must consume and pay for these essential products, although they may change their levels of consumption in relation to their available resources, notwithstanding the fact that the governments can accommodate special needs to alleviate poverty by offering free social services and goods.

However, the above notion is not always true. The tax on the purchase of a diamond, airplane or yacht is less regressive than that on more commonly purchased goods, as one must already be in a high income bracket to afford such luxuries, and therefore must have relative wealth before being subject to such a tax. Furthermore, poor people are more likely to utilize public goods and services, such as public schools and welfare programs, than are wealthier people. Moreover, viewed from a lifetime perspective, some would argue that indirect taxes, specifically consumption taxes, tend to be proportional to lifetime income (see Graetz 1999, pp. 202–205; also see generally Atkinson 1983). Clearly, the fairness issue is also not beyond controversy.

Income tax, it is argued, is usually fairer if it is progressive and comprehensive, meaning that the burden on the taxpayer increases in relation to the taxpayer's income. The higher one's income, the heavier their tax burden. People in different income brackets pay different amounts in taxes. For example, suppose that income

[22]From George (1892, p. 79): "As much sugar is needed to sweeten a cup of tea for a working-girl as for the richest lady in the land, but the proportion of their means which a tax on sugar compels each to contribute to the government is in the case of the one much greater than in the case of the other. So it is with all taxes that increase the cost of articles of general consumption. They bear far more heavily on married men than on bachelors; on those who have children than on those who have none; on those barely able to support their families than on those whose incomes leave them a large surplus. If the millionaire chooses to live closely he need pay no more of these indirect taxes than the mechanic. I have known at least two millionaires – possessed not of one, but of from six to ten millions each – who paid little more of such taxes than ordinary day-laborers."

tax can be divided into three income tax brackets, 10%, 20%, and 50%, determined according to one's income. In country *XYZ*, having a tax rate that starts at 10% for income below $50,000, 20% for income above $50,000 but less than $100,000, and 50% for income above $100,000, taxpayer *A*, with an income of $1,000, would pay 10%, or $100, and taxpayer B with an income of 80,000 would pay 20%, or $16,000, and finally taxpayer *C*, with an income of $1,000,000, would pay 50% of his income in taxes, or $500,000.

1.7.6 Tax Incidence

The distinction between direct and indirect taxes has also been thought to depend upon impact and tax incidence (Sen 1963, p. 226), which is not an easy task because "economists frequently disagree about the shifting of the tax burden" (Graetz 1995, pp. 609, 641). Even Nobel Prize winners are in disagreement regarding the real consequences of introducing new tax policies and rules, or new taxes in general (Graetz 1999, pp. 180–181). This economic uncertainty and the ongoing debates make it "relatively easy for politicians or other policy advocates to find economic support for their proposal" (Graetz 1999, pp. 180–181). In fact, some have claimed that the "current state of the art in public finance ... may lead to a feeling that virtually any policy can be supported by selected reading of the existing public finance literature, especially since there is so much uncertainty regarding the value of several key parameters" (quoted in Graetz 1999, p. 182).

Economic theorists, however, have opined that because the distinction between the two tax forms is based on the unknown actual effect of direct and indirect taxes, referred to as the tax incidence, the GATT distinction between direct and indirect taxes is, if not simply artificial, not based on a sustainable foundation (see Dam 1977, p. 219). "Economists generally agree that exporters in indirect tax jurisdictions do not fully shift tax savings forward to consumers. Similarly, economists contend that exporters shift some direct tax benefits forward" (Sernau 1986, pp. 1181, 1184).

The economic burden of the tax can be handled in a variety of ways: it may be passed on to consumers, shared with consumers, absorbed by producers, passed on to workers by reducing their wages, passed to the properties' owner by reducing rent, or partially subsidized by the government, for example. The government, after imposing a tax such as income tax, can also participate, for example by allowing accelerated depreciation or increased deductions, or it can offer more subsidies through various methods, such as buying the taxed products at pre-set prices or giving increasingly generous tax deductions for the various components used in manufacturing the products.

The various approaches outlined above can change and shift from one to another, or in combination, for the long term as well as for the short term. For example, a store could increase the final sale price of the product by a percentage that is equal to the sales tax imposed by the government. For example, if *Person* goes to *Store* and buys a *Toy* for $10, *Store* would add to that amount the sales tax. Assuming for purposes of this example that the applicable sales tax is 50%, the total amount *Person* will pay for *Toy* will be $15. Alternatively, *Store* could reduce its profits to offset the increase, selling *Toy* for $12, with *Store* bearing $3 of the tax imposed. *Store* could also reduce its workers' wages or could renegotiate its lease rental agreement with its landlord for the property on which *Store* is located, all in an effort to distribute the tax burden so that it can keep selling *Toy* for $10 to prevent consumers from changing their purchasing behaviors. *Store* could also simply absorb the cost and offset it through changes in prices or production methods related to different products in order to remain in the retail market, or any other alternative. This sets in motion a cycle, the final outcome of which no one can predict with any certainty.

Direct taxes, on the other hand, are not classified as pass-through taxes, because they target an individual or corporation's ability to pay as measured by income or property. Unlike indirect taxes, direct taxes, it is argued, are those that cannot be shifted by the taxpayer to someone else, but this may actually be inaccurate or entirely untrue in many cases.

Also, there is no realistic way of ensuring that a direct tax will be paid out of the income of the targeted taxpayers because, in reality, some taxpayers are able to shift the tax burden to some extent to others, at least for a period of time. One cannot determine the true burden of a tax simply by looking at the individual against whom it is initially assessed, or by what it is called, or by who ultimately pays it. It depends on elasticity or "mobility", which is considered the "chief factor which controls shifting" (Ely and Adams 1923, p. 619) of taxes.

For example, if *Ali*, a lawyer, wants to end his calendar year with an income of $1 million, and the tax rate in his country of residence is 50%, he might attempt to generate his desired amount of net income by shifting the 50% tax to someone else, who may in turn shift it, or part of it, to someone else, and so on, until there is no one left to shift the tax to. *Ali* may need, for example, to increase his legal fees to make a gross income of $2 million in order to pay the 50% in taxes to the government and still retain the targeted $1 million for his own use. In a circumstance like this, there is no way to accurately predict where the shifting pattern ends. Thus, it seems that "the burden of taxation falls upon those with more inelastic demand and supply ... who run slowest" (Wessels 2000, p. 521).

This example illustrates the possibility to shift the income tax burden backwards or forward, not necessarily perfectly or permanently, but in such a way as to avoid the officially intended governmental goals. Taxes, by their very nature, have the ability to affect taxpayers' behavior by triggering economic and social changes, which, in turn, continually shift some, or even all, of the economic burden of a tax to other parties and thus alter people's behavior. The tax consequences impose additional costs on taxpayers that are not necessarily reflected in the simple dollar amounts represented as the taxes are collected (Entin 2004, p. 1).

1.8 Scholars' Views on the Differentiation

Professor Kenneth Dam claimed that historically, nations have accepted the distinction between direct and indirect taxes as a result of states' traditions (Dam 1977, p. 139). Dam noted that "governments relying heavily on turnover taxes have traditionally refunded those taxes in order to make export prices more competitive. Income taxes have been rarely refunded" (Dam 1977, pp. 139–140). This, in Dam's view, has created an international law based upon custom and practice, which was codified in the GATT. It is asserted, moreover, that the GATT drafters' intention was clearly intended to achieve this distinction.

However, According to Professor Jackson, further, the different treatment of the two taxes under the GATT was probably a result of the fact that "not too much thought was given to their potential impact in the future" (Jackson 1997, p. 220). Professor Michael Graetz claimed that the distinction between direct and indirect taxation, as employed by the WTO, is not correct because of its questionable economic foundation. James Buchanan has acknowledged that "for the more important indirect sources of revenue, such as general sales taxes, turnover taxes, value-added taxes, and corporation income taxes, where the incidence is in dispute even among experts, the ignorance of the taxpayer-voter must be great indeed" (Buchanan 1999, § 4.13.23).

1.8.1 Institutional Views

Governmental institutions do not generally consider the distinction between direct and indirect taxes an acceptable one. For example, a report on harmonization of indirect tax by the EEC noted that "indirect tax shifting does not have major support."[23] The US Congress, as far back as 1970, before any litigation under the GATT regarding income tax, expressed its disapproval of the distinction.[24] The report by the Committee on Finance stated about the distinction between direct and indirect tax: theory and practice is based on the assumption that "indirect taxes are always and wholly shifted forward into the final price of a product and that direct taxes are always and wholly shifted backward to the factors of production." This

[23]*See Report of the Fiscal and Financial Committee in The EEC Reports on Tax Harmonization* (1963).

[24]Staff analysis of issues raised by the General Agreement on Tariffs and Trade, 91st Congress, 2nd Session, prepared by the Staff of the Committees on Finance, US Senate, Russell B Long, Chairman (December 19, 1970).

theory, the Committee claimed, was "accepted two generations ago" (i.e., in the 1950s), but by 1970, was "widely questionable."[25]

Even the Border Tax Adjustments Report indicated disapproval of the distinction. Paragraph 8 states, in relevant part:

> There was general agreement that the main provisions of the GATT represented the codification of practices which existed at the time these provisions were drafted, re-examined and completed. Some members of the Working Party considered, however, that the main provisions of the GATT relevant to tax adjustments represent an attempt at the codification of a wide range of past practices based on assumptions which are not now universally accepted. In particular, they felt the assumption of full shifting of direct taxes is not a reflection of economic reality.
>
> They considered that the present GATT rules favour countries which rely heavily on indirect taxes and discriminate against countries which rely predominantly on direct taxes. Further, in their view, the present rules are ambiguous and lead to differing tax adjustment practices for similar types of taxes. They concluded that the current GATT provisions and tax practices are not trade neutral.[26]

The report continues by discussing the question of eligibility of taxes for tax adjustment under the then-present rules:

> The Working Party concluded that there was convergence of views to the effect that taxes directly levied on products were eligible for tax adjustment. Examples of such taxes comprised specific excise duties, sales taxes and cascade taxes and the tax on value added. It was agreed that the TVA, regardless of its technical construction (fractioned collection), was equivalent in this respect to a tax levied directly – a retail or sales tax. Furthermore, the Working Party concluded that there was convergence of views to the effect that certain taxes that were not directly levied on products were not eligible for tax adjustment. Examples of such taxes comprised social security charges whether on employers or employees and payroll taxes. It was generally felt that while this area of taxation was unclear, its importance – as indicated by the scarcity of complaints reported in connexion with adjustment of taxes occults – was not such as to justify further examination.[27]

In addition, even taxes that were remitted were not always easy to calculate. The report goes on to say:

> The Working Party noted that there were some taxes which, while generally considered eligible for adjustment, presented a problem because of the difficulty in some cases of calculating exactly the amount of compensation. Examples of such difficulties were encountered in cascade taxes. Other examples included composite goods which, on export, contained ingredients for which the Working Party agreed in principle it was

[25]Staff analysis of issues raised by the General Agreement on Tariffs and Trade, 91st Congress, 2nd Session, prepared by the Staff of the Committees on Finance, US Senate, Russell B Long, Chairman (December 19, 1970).

[26]Report of the Working Party adopted on December 2, 1970, Border Tax Adjustments, GATT Doc. L/3464, reprinted in The Contracting Parties To The General Agreement On Tariffs And Trade, Basic Instruments and Selected Documents 97, 99 (18th Supp. 1972) [hereinafter "Report"] ¶ 8.

[27]Report of the Working Party adopted on December 2, 1970, Border Tax Adjustments, GATT Doc. L/3464, ¶ 15(b).

administratively sensible and sufficiently accurate to rebate by average rates for a given class of goods.[28]

1.9 Concluding Observations

The meanings of the terms direct tax and indirect tax, as has been shown, can vary in different contexts, with potentially profound consequences. As a result, when one categorizes any type of taxation as direct or indirect, there is a real danger that certain important legal implications will follow, perhaps the most important of which, under the WTO, is allowing rebates for indirect taxes and disallowing rebates for direct taxes, even though both can produce the same effects. This becomes more complicated because the WTO is not defining direct taxes and indirect taxes, which leaves the door open to different possibilities.

Any definition of direct and indirect taxes should be viewed with caution if it is to be considered for adoption in WTO, especially if there is a conflict between the substance and the form on a critical element (see Adams et al. 1921, p. 57). As there is no consensus of agreement among scholars, governments, or international organizations as to the specific criteria for direct taxes and indirect taxes, the distinctions made between the two tax forms should be reevaluated and, if proven unacceptable, abolished. This can be done if there is a tax presence in the WTO, a tax agreement, or a tax department in which tax issues can be raised, negotiated and discussed. But if this distinction remains as an academic exercise, where only few examine the complexity of it, the issue will be outside the light even though its effects may be felt in major tax disputes.

It is therefore reasonable to conclude that there is no strong justification for treating direct and indirect taxes differently. All of the previously discussed distinctions do not justify different treatment under the two types of taxes by international organizations such as the WTO. Though income tax rebates can't be easily accomplished, the discussion is not about how to do it; the discussion is about whether or not it is legal. The functionality is secondary. With this analysis in mind, there is almost nothing to justify the implementation of a distinction that requires that the international community be compelled to treat direct and indirect taxes differently.

For that, it seems the time has come for the WTO to re-evaluate the issue of direct and indirect taxes. The best method for doing so is to introduce a tax presence within the WTO that can lead such a mission. A tax department is one possible venue by which this issue can be raised and examined thoroughly in this work.

---

[28]Report of the Working Party adopted on December 2, 1970, Border Tax Adjustments, GATT Doc. L/3464, ¶ 16.

References

Adams TS et al. (1921) The federal income tax. Columbia University Press, New York
Atkinson AB (1983) The economics of inequality, 2nd edn. Clarendon, Oxford
Avi-Yonah RS (2004) International tax as international law. Tax L Rev 57:483, 490
Bannock G, Baxter RE, Davis E (eds) (1998) Dictionary of Economics. The Economists Books. Wiley, New York
Bastable CF (2003) Public finance. Macmillan, London
Brauner Y (2005) International trade and tax agreements may be coordinated, but not reconciled. Va Tax Rev 25:251, 274
Buchanan JM (1999) Public finance in democratic process: fiscal institutions and individual choice. Collected works of James M. Buchanan, vol. 4. Library of economics and liberty, Indianapolis, IN
Cooley T (1924) The law of taxation, 4th edn. Callaghan, Chicago
Dam WK (1977) The GATT law and international economic organization. The University of Chicago Press, Chicago
Ely RT, Adams TS (1923) Outlines of economics. Macmillan, New York
Entin SJ (2004) Tax incidence, tax burden, and tax shifting: who really pays the tax? Center for Data Analysis Report, 04-12. The Heritage Foundation. http://www.heritage.org/Research/Taxes/upload/71440_1.pdf
Max Farrand (ed) (1966) The records of the federal convention of 1787, vol. 2. Yale University Press, New Haven
Floyd RH (1973) GATT provisions on border tax adjustments. J World Trade L 7:489, 498
Fried BH (1992) Fairness and the consumption tax. Stan L Rev 44:961, 966
Garner BA (ed) (1999) Black's law dictionary, 7th edn. West, St. paul, MN
George H (1892) Protection or free trade. Doubleday, New York
Gillis M, Perkins D, Romer M, Snodgrass D (1996) Indirect consumption taxes: common issues and differences among the alternative approaches. Tax L Rev 51:725–726
Goodspeed G (2006) Taxation and FDI in developing and developed countries. In: Alm J, Martinez-Vazquez J, Rider M (eds) The challenge of tax reform in a global economy. Springer, New York
Graetz MJ (1995) Paint-by-numbers tax lawmaking. Colum L Rev 95:609, 641
Graetz JM (1999) The US income tax: what it is, how it got that way, and where we go from here. W.W. Norton, New York
Huber B, Norman E (2003) Taxation in a global cconomy. In: Andersen TM, Molander P (eds) Alternatives for welfare policy: coping with internationalisation and demographic change. Cambridge University press, Cambridge
Hufbauer GC (2002) The FSC case: background and implications. Peterson Institute for International Economics. Washington, DC. http://www.iie.com/publications/papers/paper.cfm?ResearchID=451
Jackson JH (1997) The world trade system: law and policy of international economic relations, 2nd edn. MIT Press, Cambridge, MA
James SR (ed) (2002) Taxation: critical perspectives on the world economy. Routledge, London
Jensen EM (1999) Taxation and the constitution: how to read the direct tax clauses. J L Politics 15:687, 695
Lipsey R (1979) An introduction to positive economics, 5th edn. Weidenfeld and Nicholson, London
Messere K, De Kam F, Heady C (2003) Tax policy: theory and practice in OECD countries. Oxford University Press, Oxford
Oldman O, Schenk A (2001) Value added tax: a comparative approach with material and cases. Transnational, Ardsley, NY

Pitschas C (1995) GATT/WTO rules for border tax adjustment and the proposed European directive introducing a tax on carbon dioxide emissions and energy. Ga J Int'l Comp L 24:479, 485

Ricardo D (1817) On the principles of political economy and taxation. John Murray, London

Schenk A (1998) Value added tax: does this consumption tax have a place in the federal tax system. Va Tax Rev 7:207, 230

Sen SN (1963) Money, trade and public finance. The Bookland, Calcutta

Sernau RD (1986) The foreign sales corporation legislation: a $10 billion boondoggle. Cornell L Rev 71:1181, 1184

Tait A (1988) Value added tax: international practice and problems. IMF, Washington DC

Thuronyi V (2003) Comparative tax law. Kluwer, Deventer

Walsh M, Stephens P, Moore S (2000) Social policy and welfare. Stanley Thornes, Cheltenham

Wessels WJ (2000) Economics. Barron, New York

Chapter 2
The Cases

That separate development is itself undoubtedly related to the traditional separation of the tax and trade disciplines in practice, government, and the academy.

(Warren 2001, p. 158)

Custom duties were the only notable barriers to international trade.

(Gardner 1980, p. 58)

Tax issues sometimes are very hard to resolve, which can lead to nullify or modify trade agreements. Thus, there is a need for flexibility and an understanding of taxes within any organization that might encounter tax issues and disputes. This chapter is divided into two sections. The first discusses actual cases that arose in the past under the GATT and the WTO, where a tax, specifically income tax, was the subject of a dispute, such as the Domestic International Sales Corporation (DISC) cases. The second section includes several hypothetical cases that are presented to show the potential fallout if the problem is not dealt with.

2.1 Actual Problems: The Cases

The cases presented in this section have been disputed under the GATT/WTO. The focus and issue crucial to this study is whether or not tax and trade are related to an extent that it is appropriate to bring the tax regime under the WTO. Secondly, the focus is to show the context when trade and tax issues clash. The result of these cases may be legally acceptable according to the international trade as expressed in the WTO, but the issue this chapter attempts to raise the complexity and difficulty of the tax cases litigated under the WTO. These cases are wrongly brought to the WTO, not wrongly decided. If they are to be brought, there must be a flexible infrastructure to offer countries with the needed marginal freedom to move within acceptable levels in their own internal environment so that the WTO decisions are not viewed as threatening local interests.

Most tax disputes have involved indirect taxes, such as the sales tax or value added tax.[1] However, the ruling in a recent high-profile case involving direct

[1]Indirect taxes include taxes on alcoholic beverages (e.g., Chile taxes: Panel Report, *Chile – Taxes on Alcoholic Beverages*, WT/DS87/R, WT/DS110/R, adopted January 12, 2000, modified by Appellate Body Report, WT/DS87/AB/R, WT/DS110/AB/R, DSR 2000:I, 303), or Japan taxes

T. Althunayan, *Dealing with the Fragmented International Legal Environment: WTO, International Tax and Internal Tax Regulations*,
DOI 10.1007/978-3-642-04678-0_2, © Springer-Verlag Berlin Heidelberg 2010

taxation, initiated by the European Community, found that the US Foreign Sales Corporation (FSC) rules and their replacement, the Extraterritorial Income Exclusion (ETI), constituted a prohibited export subsidy in violation of the SCM. This case will "undoubtedly be of interest to Members as they formulate their domestic tax policies in the future, especially where such policies differentiate between export-oriented and domestically-oriented sectors, and may even move Members to reformulate these policies, as was the case with the US" (Daly 2006, p. 529).

2.1.1 The GATT Cases

The first dispute ever to arise under GATT during the First Session in 1948 concerned Cuba's alleged discriminatory consular tax[2] of 5% on imports from some countries and 2% on imports from others. The issue was not resolved fully during the first round of hearings, so during the Second Session the Netherlands delegation indirectly brought forth the issue again by requesting a ruling from the Chair, asking: "Did Article I (the most favored nation obligation) apply to consular tax?"[3] The answer was that with respect to consular tax, the Chairman ruled that such taxes would be covered by the phrase "charge of any kind,"[4] implying that a violation did exist with respect to the Cuban taxation scheme. Cuba agreed to remove the discriminatory element.[5]

The Belgium family allowance[6] tax was disputed during more than one session, and was finally resolved in 1952 after the Seventh Session. This case involved income tax issues, and warrants further attention:

on beverages: Panel Report, *Japan – Taxes on Alcoholic Beverages*, WT/DS8/R, WT/DS10/R, WT/DS11/R, adopted November 1, 1996, modified by Appellate Body Report, WT/DS8/AB/R, WT/DS10/AB/R, WT/DS11/AB/R, DSR 1996:I, 125; and sales taxes on automobiles as in Indonesia: Panel Report, *Indonesia – Certain Measures Affecting the Automobile Industry*, WT/DS54/R, WT/DS55/R, WT/DS59/R, WT/DS64/R and Corr. 1, 2, 3, and 4, adopted July 23, 1998, DSR 1998:VI, 2201).

[2]Ruling by the Chairman, The Phrase "Charges of any Kind" in Article I:1 in Relation to Consular Taxes, August 24, 1948, BISD II/12.

[3]Ruling by the Chairman, The Phrase "Charges of any Kind" in Article I:1 in Relation to Consular Taxes, August 24, 1948, BISD II/12.

[4]Ruling by the Chairman, The Phrase "Charges of any Kind" in Article I:1 in Relation to Consular Taxes, August 24, 1948, BISD II/12. *See also* Palmeter and Mavroidis (2004, p. 304).

[5]GATT Panel Report, *United States – Customs User Fee*, L/6264, adopted February 2, 1988, BISD 35S/245, Para 91, Footnote 13.

[6]Report of the Panel on "Belgium – Family Allowances," BISD 1S/59 (adopted on November 7, 1952).

2.1.1.1 Belgium Family Allowance

November 7, 1952, saw the first case concerning income tax issues governed under the "ad hoc" international trade organization, the GATT. Norwegian and Danish representatives submitted an objection regarding the application of a Belgian law levying a charge on foreign goods purchased by public bodies when those goods originated in a country whose system of family allowances and *income tax law* did not meet specific requirements as prescribed by Belgium's government. The government of Belgium was at that time imposing a tax on any goods coming from any country that did not have a similar or comparable *income tax system* to Belgium's system.

Adding to the complexity of this case, the Belgian government had granted exemptions from the tax to products originating in Luxemburg, the Netherlands, France, Italy, Sweden, and the United Kingdom, but the exemption was not extended to Norway or to Denmark. Pursuant to MFN, the exemption should have been granted unconditionally to all contracting parties.

After examining Belgium's provisions and the nation's application of a tax to goods from Norway and Denmark, the Panel found that the law was discriminatory and that it should be amended to eliminate its discriminatory effects. The Panel came to the conclusion that a 7.5% levy was collected only on products purchased by public bodies for their own use and not on imports as such, and that the levy was charged not at the time of importation, but at payment of the purchase price by the public body. The Panel held that "it would appear that the levy was to be treated as an 'internal charge' within the meaning of paragraph 2 of Article III of the General Agreement."[7]

The Panel also noted that "any advantage, favour, privilege or immunity granted by Belgium to any product originating in the territory of any country with respect to all matters referred to in paragraph 2 of Article III shall be granted immediately and unconditionally to the like product originating in the territories of all contracting parties."[8] Since the Belgian government had granted exemptions from the levy to products originating in Luxemburg and the Netherlands, as well as in France, Italy, Sweden, and the United Kingdom, "it is clear that that exemption would have to be granted unconditionally to all other contracting parties (including Denmark and Norway)."[9] The Panel found that "the Belgian legislation would have to be amended insofar as it introduced a discrimination between countries having a given system of family allowances and those which had a different system or no

---

[7]Report of the Panel on "Belgium – Family Allowances," BISD 1S/59 (adopted on November 7, 1952).

[8]Report of the Panel on "Belgium – Family Allowances," BISD 1S/59 (adopted on November 7, 1952), p. 3.

[9]Report of the Panel on "Belgium – Family Allowances," BISD 1S/59 (adopted on November 7, 1952).

system at all, and made the granting of the exemption dependent on certain conditions."[10]

The Panel concluded that "the Belgian legislation on family allowances was not only inconsistent with the provisions of Article I (and possibly with those of Article III, paragraph 2), but was based on a concept which was difficult to reconcile with the spirit of the General Agreement."[11] This heavily trade-oriented approach was reasonable at that time, given the early and uncertain stage of the GATT and the potential for creation of additional problems in attempting to use the GATT to challenge fundamental legal issues, such as the tax system.

This case demonstrated for the first time how direct tax can be under the preview of the GATT. It proved that GATT is not just about indirect taxes, even though the GATT's legal text stated "tax on products." As long as tax, direct or indirect, affects products directly or indirectly, the GATT has the power to decide the legality of the issue.

One final dimension of this case that needs to be mentioned is the fact that this kind of tax implemented in Belgium was not intended to be protectionist, but instead for legitimate social purpose, a social value held by this country. Though it was a social issue in the end Belgium followed the ruling of the GATT. This suggests that sometimes social issues, when related to taxation, can be changed. Sometimes, of course, these values would be hard to change. Sometimes politicians need an outsider to push for change. The dynamics are complicated, so value-related changes need to be carefully dealt with.

2.1.1.2 The Domestic International Sales Corporation

The "unwelcome surprise" the USA had warned about[12] finally came. The most important tax case arose in 1970s, in a time when the USA was seeing a growing trade deficit. In order to boost domestic business competition, the USA introduced a new tax regulation, the DISC.[13] This regulation allowed US companies to indefinitely defer taxes on their export profits. To increase DISC profitability, normal tax rules[14] concerning transfer pricing were drastically relaxed,[15] and no interest was imposed on the tax deferral, amounting to what was, essentially, "an interest-free

[10]Report of the Panel on "Belgium – Family Allowances," BISD 1S/59 (adopted on November 7, 1952).

[11]Report of the Panel on "Belgium – Family Allowances," BISD 1S/59 (adopted on November 7, 1952).

[12]*See* footnote 4 in Chap. 1. Working Party on Tax Adjustment meeting of October 8–11, 1968.

[13]Revenue Act of 1971, Pub. L. No. 92–178, 501–07, 85 Stat. 497, 535–53; *see* IRC 991–997 for current DISC rules.

[14]Internal Revenue Code (IRC 482).

[15]IRC 995(b)(2).

loan from the government" (McDaniel 2004, pp. 275, 277). The stated purpose was to soften the impact of the worldwide income tax rule as implemented by the USA (see generally, Hudec 1988, pp. 1443, 1448–1449).

The income tax laws of most countries permit exporters to reduce taxes on export income by adopting the "territoriality" principle, which taxes exporters just on transactions conducted within the territory of the country. The USA employs the worldwide tax system,[16] whereas the European Community (EC) primarily uses a territorial tax system. A worldwide tax system means citizens and residents of the USA are subject to the income tax law on their income worldwide, regardless of the jurisdiction within which such income is earned.[17]

In the territorial tax method, taxes are imposed on all income generated within the borders of the country, while all income that is generated outside the nation's borders are exempt. This basic principle, of course, sometimes makes it difficult to determine what is considered "within" a nation's borders and what is considered generated "outside."

The EC challenged the DISC under the GATT in 1973, arguing that it was an export subsidy, resulting in exports being taxed more favorably than domestic transactions, a scheme prohibited by the GATT. GATT Article XVI:4 prohibits granting subsidies on exports stating that "contracting parties shall cease to grant either directly or indirectly any form of subsidy on the export of any product other than a primary product which subsidy results in the sale of such product for export at a price lower than the comparable price charged for the like product to buyers in the domestic market."[18] In turn, the USA countered with three cases of its own against the tax systems of Belgium, France, and the Netherlands; the USA argued that the use of the exemption method by those countries constituted an export subsidy, resulting in exports being taxed more favorably than domestic transactions. It was a clash between two tax systems, the worldwide tax system and territorial tax system, systems that have been shaped by many factors, such as political, financial and cultural aspects.

There was a strong belief in the USA that the issue was merely equalization of disadvantageous tax border adjustments. Since the US Treasury Department "believed strongly in the legitimacy of this objective, it would defend DISC with an intensity considerably greater than governments normally expend on ordinary beggar-thy-neighbor trade measures. Indeed, the United States would never yield on the legitimacy of DISC's basic purpose" (Hudec 1988, p. 1449). The USA also insisted on having a tax panel deciding the case, instead of the usual trade lawyers (Hudec 1988, pp. 1454–1455).

A GATT panel decided in 1976 that all existing "tax cases" were in violation of the GATT, and concluded that the DISC was a prohibited subsidy, since no interest

---

[16] *See* Goodspeed (2006, 143). See footnote 14 in Chap. 1.

[17] Staff of Joint Committee on Taxation, 108th Congress, United States International Tax Rules: Background and Selected Issues Relating to the Competitiveness of US Business Abroad, p. 2.

[18] GATT XVI.

was charged on the deferral of tax on DISC income.[19] Since this exemption benefited US exporters by giving them the ability to reduce prices, increase export sales efforts, and realize increased profits from items that qualified for DISC benefits, the panel ruled that the DISC regime violated US obligations under GATT.[20]

As for three EU tax cases presented by the USA, the panel noted that the tax systems involved some elements of prohibited subsidies that violated the GATT, and found those schemes to be illegal as well.[21] And this is of great importance. The territorial tax system was ruled to be filled with prohibited subsidies as decided by a tax panel, a panel that understood the reality of taxation. Yet, trade officials disagreed and resisted that conclusion, because when they negotiated the trade agreements, everyone asserted that the tax systems in place were acceptable. The EC "never accepted the three findings of a GATT Article XVI:4 violation" (Hudec 1988, p. 1483).

The tax system was not, as in the worldwide system, purely confined to the territory of countries using this kind of taxation. Unsurprisingly, with broad support from GATT members, the three defendants rejected the panel ruling and proposed that the GATT Council set the reports aside. The USA blocked this suggestion until 1981, after which the decisions were disposed of by a Council decision (Hudec 1988, p. 1483).

The USA had very strong arguments. It insisted that the territorial tax system could generate tax savings with the same economic effect as any other export "prohibited" subsidy, equal if not superior than the saving realized under DISC; this argument and analysis "was difficult to refute" (Hudec 1988, p. 1483).

As in the worldwide tax system, a territorial tax system could be used to lower the taxation of export operations significantly below the taxation of identical domestic operations (Hudec 1988, p. 1483). "It was also clear that those tax savings would induce a greater allocation of resources to exporting than would otherwise be the case. Even if this were not the purpose of the territoriality principle, it was demonstrably its effect" (Hudec 1988, p. 1483). The European defendants "never made a serious effort to dispute the United States' economic argument" (Hudec 1988, p. 1484).

Their only real argument against the USA's position was based "primarily on the longstanding and widespread acceptance of the territoriality principle in world tax circles" (Hudec 1988, p. 1484). It was merely the old practice by GATT members that justified the territorial principle. Just an old practice. And since the US practice (that is, the DISC) was newly introduced, then this new creature must be wrong and disposed of, even if both practices have the same effects, with no substantive

[19]DISC Para. 71.

[20]DISC Para. 72.

[21]*See* Income Tax Practices Maintained by France, Nov. 12, 1976, GATT B.I.S.D. 114 (23d Supp. 1977); Income Tax Practices Maintained by the Netherlands, Nov. 12, 1976, GATT B.I.S.D. 137 (23d Supp. 1977); Income Tax Practices Maintained by Belgium, GATT B.I.S.D. 127 (23d Supp. 127 1977).

justification. The parties to the case were correct, in that "[t]here was not the slightest evidence that any signatory government even remotely envisioned such consequences" (Hudec 1988, p. 1484). But this should not mean that anything new aiming to correct a previous imbalance should be prohibited or be wrong. If the Europeans believed the territorial tax systems were acceptable, then anything that had the same or similar effects should also be acceptable unless proven wrong without a doubt. Otherwise, they both should be reexamined or both should be accepted

However, no resolution to end the disputes was reached until 1984. Before that time, the Tokyo Round (see, Jackson et al. 1984; see also Van Meerhaeghe 1998, p. 109) was taking place, from 1974 to 1979, and the need to solve this issue was recognized. The temporary settlement that resulted was based on four principles:

1. The distinction between allowing or disallowing direct and indirect tax adjustments was preserved.
2. The USA agreed to repeal DISC.
3. Avoidance of double taxation by the exemption method or credit method did not amount to a prohibited subsidy.
4. The arm's length pricing standard was to be observed in transactions between parent exporting companies and their foreign sales subsidiaries.[22]

This resolution and its foundation resembled an international tax settlement more than a decision regarding international trade; it was, in essence, an international tax understanding taken by the trade community. For example, principles 3 and 4 are both common in tax treaties; principle 3 deals with avoidance of double taxation, and principle 4 covers transfer pricing issues. The corresponding Articles in the tax treaties of the Organization for Economic Co-operation and Development (OECD) are 23a and 23b,[23] covering avoidance of double taxation by the

---

[22]The full understanding is:

> The Council adopts these reports on the understanding that with respect to these cases, and in general, economic processes (including transactions involving exported goods) located outside the territorial limits of the exporting country need not be subject to taxation by the exporting country and should not be regarded as export activities in terms of Article XVI:4 of the General Agreement. It is further understood that Article XVI:4 requires that arm's-length pricing be observed, i.e., prices for goods in transactions between exporting enterprises and foreign buyers under their or the same control should for tax purposes be the prices which would be charged between independent enterprises acting at arm's length. Furthermore, Article XVI:4 does not prohibit the adoption of measures to avoid double taxation of foreign-source income. GATT, BISD 114 (28th Supp. 1982).

[23]On the OECD, *see* Végh (2005, p. 141). OECD Article 23a provides in part:

> Where a resident of a Contracting State derives income or owns capital which, in accordance with the provisions of this Convention, may be taxed in the other Contracting State, the first-mentioned State shall, subject to the provisions of paragraphs 2 and 3, *exempt* such income or capital from tax.

exemption and credit methods, respectively, and 9,[24] regarding the transfer pricing issues.

The Tokyo understanding provided that countries would not provide prohibited subsidies in situations where they did not tax foreign source income, because they would be alleviating the burden of double taxation, even though such alleviation could potentially be characterized as an export subsidy in violation of the SCM.

The DISC cases provided several lessons. First, reaching the right solution to a difficult problem required legal work of the highest order. Improving the level of legal practice requires time. And finally, "one of the most important legacies of the DISC case in this regard was the creation of a separate legal staff within the GATT Secretariat" (Hudec 1988, p. 1487). Before the tax case, there was a policy within the GATT against having lawyers, or as Hudec called "the 'no lawyers' policy" (Hudec 1988, p. 1487). The way this policy was introduced is very important. It

---

Article 23b provides in part:

1. Where a resident of a Contracting State derives income or owns capital which, in accordance with the provisions of this Convention, may be taxed in the other Contracting State, the first-mentioned State shall allow:

a) as a *deduction* from the tax on the income of that resident, an amount equal to the income tax paid in that other State.

b) As a deduction from the tax on the capital of that resident, an amount equal to the capital tax paid in that other State.

Such deduction in either case shall not, however, exceed that part of the income tax or capital tax, as computed before the deduction is given, which is attributable, as the case may be, to the income or the capital which may be taxed in that other State.

[24]OECD Article 9 provides in part:

1. Where

a) an enterprise of a Contracting State participates directly or indirectly in the management, control or capital of an enterprise of the other Contracting State, or

b) the same persons participate directly or indirectly in the management, control or capital of an enterprise of a Contracting State and an enterprise of the other Contracting State, and in either case conditions are made or imposed between the two enterprises in their commercial or financial relations which differ from those which would be made between independent enterprises, *then any profits which would, but for those conditions, have accrued to one of the enterprises, but, by reason of those conditions, have not so accrued, may be included in the profits of that enterprise and taxed accordingly.*

2. Where a Contracting State includes in the profits of an enterprise of that State – and taxes accordingly – profits on which an enterprise of the other Contracting State has been charged to tax in that other State and the profits so included are profits which would have accrued to the enterprise of the first-mentioned State if the conditions made between the two enterprises had been those which would have been made between independent enterprises, *then that other State shall make an appropriate adjustment to the amount of the tax charged therein on those profits*. In determining such adjustment, due regard shall be had to the other provisions of this Convention and the competent authorities of the Contracting States shall if necessary consult each other. (emphasis added).

"had to be introduced very gradually" (Hudec 1988, p. 1487). This started with "just a legal advisor, a senior GATT official nearing retirement whose role was portrayed more like that of a historian-archivist than a lawyer. This was followed by a series of incremental changes in function and in personnel that eventually produced the present legal office, staffed now by four professionals who work with every panel" (Hudec 1988, p. 1487). This office had tremendous effect, "a major impact in raising both the quality of GATT panel decisions over the past decade and the quality of the legal practice before those panels. It may be the *most important* legacy the DISC case left behind" (Hudec 1988, p. 1487). The gradual change shows that things can be changed for the better.

2.1.1.3 Foreign Sales Corporation

The United States repealed the DISC, and enacted in its place the FSC in 1981. This enactment triggered a second round of similar conflicts, which are likely to continue until the core issues are resolved. These issues are diverse, and the system is one with many components (see Hudec 1993, p. 203) that cannot be easily solved through adjudication in Geneva.

In an attempt to get around the DISC holding, the United States changed its tax rules with the FSC "from a deferral system to a partial exemption system" (McDaniel 2004, p. 279). The new law established that a specified portion of foreign trade income would not be subject to US taxation.[25] The FSC, a wholly owned foreign subsidiary of a US corporation, was effectively a cover for continued prohibited action. In fact, more than 80% of FSCs are located in one of three so-called tax havens: the United States Virgin Islands, Guam, and Barbados (Hoekman and Kostecki 2001, p. 178). More than 7,000 American exporters have formed FSCs since 1984, when the FSC device was first introduced in the Tax Reform Act (Hoekman and Kostecki 2001, p. 178).

Professor Robert Hudec thought a dispute involving the FSC[26] was the "wrong" kind of case to bring before the WTO dispute settlement structure; he did intelligently note that the situation, with its unsettled legal questions, "presents a serious risk of further policy conflict" (see Petersmann and Pollack 2003, pp. 204–205). Professor Hudec recognized that tax cases between the USA and the EU have never been easy;[27] they have historically presented a serious problem, one that is still

[25]Joel P. Trachtman, *Decisions of the Appellate Body of the World Trade Organization* "United States – Tax Treatment for Foreign Sales Corporations – Recourse to Article 21.5 of the DSU by the European Communities," can be found at http://www.ejil.org/journal/curdevs/sr32.html.

[26]FSC Repeal and Extraterritorial Income Exclusion Act of 2000, Pub. L. No. 106-519, 2, 114 Stat. 2423, 2423; IRC 921-927 (before repeal in 2000).

[27]It is suspected that the EU's true purpose was not to deal with the tax issue, but to use the issue as a bargaining chip to achieve other goals such as: (a) beef hormones and potential biotechnology claims; (b) Section 201 restrictions on steel imports; or (c) agricultural subsidies. *See* Hufbauer (2002), Hufbauer (2001, p. 1555).

legally unresolved, because beneath the dispute lies a major divergence between the two traditional tax systems dominating the international community: the territorial system and the worldwide system. Moreover, income tax usually is related to a nation's internal political system in a very profound way that makes change difficult, especially if a given system is linked to deeply rooted national values. In addition, the FSC saw "massive support from the US business," the very people and entities paying taxes and voting for government decision-makers, making it very difficult to remove or reduce the impact of the FSC (Hudec 1993, p. 203).

Nevertheless, the case went to the WTO in 1998, after the EC asked the WTO to adjudicate the validity of the FSC regime. The dispute was lengthy and tortuous, and ultimately a judgment was issued for the EC. The Appellate Body (AB) heard the case, ruling in favor of the EU in an opinion that has been analyzed in depth by tax scholars.[28]

The FSC rules allow US exporters to claim an exemption from the USA worldwide tax system for a portion of their export income without changing the worldwide taxation concept (McDaniel 2004, pp. 279–280). Additionally, the FSC allows exporters to enter into agency agreements with a US parent or related subsidiaries[29] to operate within the USA. A portion of the income the FSC earned from "qualifying export transactions" with a US affiliate was considered for US tax purposes not connected with US trade or business and, as a result, not subject to US income tax law.[30]

In addition, an FSC was not subjected to treatment under Subpart "F" of the Code,[31] aimed to discourage US taxpayers from deferring payment of US taxes by accumulating income in foreign corporations. Consequently, the combined income earned by the FSC and its US affiliate from qualifying export transactions was subject to a lower tax rate, less than 30%, whereas a tax equal to 35% of this income would have normally been imposed on other types of income (Sheppard 2003, pp. 111, 114).

The Panel used a "but for" test to determine whether revenue was forgone; that is, would the taxpayer have paid increased taxes *but for* the FSC exemption? The Panel held that the FSC is a prohibited export subsidy, because there is revenue that is forgone, which is also linked to export.

This test is risky, because any "deduction-granting provision, including one for expenses incurred in a trade or business, results in the taxpayer paying less in tax than it would have paid in the absence of the provision" (McDaniel 2004, p. 291). Thus, misusing it, or structuring something that satisfies it, can nullify the intent of

---

[28]*See*, e.g., Stehmann (2000, p. 127); Clark et al. (2001, p. 291); McDaniel (2001, pp. 1621, 1629); Qureshi and Grynberg (2002, p. 979). Most scholars have come to the conclusion that the ultimate decision was correct in that the USA was violating the SCM, although they have criticized the decision in other aspects. *See*, e.g., McDaniel (2004, pp. 275, 277); *but see* Hufbauer (2001, pp. 1555, 1562), arguing that the FSC was "wrongly decided."

[29]I.R.C. 924(f)(1) (2000).

[30]I.R.C. 921(a) (2000).

[31]I.R.C. 951–964 (2000).

fighting the use of tax schemes to provide subsidies. Hypothetically, a country having no tax system at all could subsequently impose an exception to impose tax only in specific, limited circumstances, making the general rule the exception while keeping the exception looking as though it were the general rule. For example, the USA could create a tax law that taxes no one, then introduce an exception to tax income within the USA only, leaving export income free of taxation under the general rule, with more exceptions to ensure taxing the target income.

In February 2000, the WTO AB affirmed the Panel Report almost entirely, stating that because the FSC subsidies were contingent upon export performance, the scheme was considered a "prohibited export subsidy."[32] The AB stated that "whatever kind of tax system a Member chooses, that Member will not be in compliance with its WTO obligations if it provides, through its tax system, subsidies contingent upon export performance that are not permitted under the covered agreements."[33]

The AB rejected the Panel's "but for" test, because "it may not work in other cases,"[34] and suggested that the determination should instead be made by comparing the challenged measure against a normative benchmark, against which a comparison can be made between the revenue actually raised and the revenue that would have been raised "otherwise."[35] This conclusion is difficult to comprehend because there is no agreed-upon "normative benchmark," and the AB provided no explanation of the term.

2.1.1.4 The Extraterritorial Income Exclusion

Once the FSC regime was found to violate the WTO, the US Congress passed, in November 2000, the FSC Repeal and Extraterritorial Income Exclusion (ETI)[36] Act. The Act granted a partial exclusion for export income, allowing US exporters to "obtain the same net reduction in US tax under the ETI Act as under the previous FSC scheme" (Smith 2004, pp. 503, 525). This, too, was held invalid under WTO rules. The US view was that the ETI Act conformed to the AB's decision because: (a) revenue was no longer foregone (ETI income was no longer part of gross income subject to corporate tax), and (b) export earnings and foreign production earnings were similarly taxed under the ETI Act. However, two major similarities remained between the FSC and the new ETI. "First, the 50% domestic content requirement was continued. Second, the only income that could qualify was income from

[32]AB, on FSC, ¶ 180.

[33]AB, ¶ 179.

[34]AB, ¶ 91.

[35]AB, ¶ 90.

[36]FSC Repeal and Extraterritorial Income Exclusion Act of 2000, Pub. L. No. 16-519, 114 Stat. 2423.

foreign trade transactions" (McDaniel 2004, p. 286). The Act was still a subsidy that was export-contingent.

The EU didn't see the new law as much different and sued the USA in the WTO, claiming that (a) revenue was still foregone; (b) the export contingency remained, even if foreign production was, in some circumstances, covered; (c) the US content requirements for export earnings under ETI violated Article III; and (d) the FSC phase-out did not respect the first AB deadline, which was October 2000. For the "third"[37] time in the history of litigating US income tax rules, the USA lost. The WTO ruled that the US tax provisions violated the WTO rules, and the AB Report ruled as follows:

(a) Upholds the Panel's finding, that there the tax measure of the ETI involves the foregoing of revenue which is "otherwise due" and thus gives rise to a "financial contribution" as prescribed by the SCM.
(b) Upholds the Panel's finding, that the ETI measure includes subsidies "contingent ... upon export performance."
(c) Upholds the Panel's finding that the ETI measure, viewed as a whole, does not fall within the scope of footnote 59 of the *SCM Agreement* as a measure taken to avoid the double taxation of foreign-source income.[38]

In October 2004, the United States Congress passed legislation to repeal the FSC/ETI and to replace it with a new corporate tax law, which provides for the phasing out of the FSC by 2007. The replacement law would provide $138 billion in tax relief for domestic manufacturing, US multinationals, and a wide range of other industries and businesses. This new legislation, the American Jobs Creation Act of 2004, was signed into law by President George W. Bush on October 22, 2004 (Daly 2006, p. 541).

2.1.2 *Observations*

The USA insisted in introducing and re-introducing a tax scheme that aimed, from the US perspective, to re-balance the current equation between the worldwide tax system and the territorial tax system. It kept losing; nevertheless, it kept introducing the same sort of tax scheme. It brought "unwelcome" results from a US perspective. It is possible that there are huge benefits in creating a lobbying power that is strong enough to keep up the pressure to maintain this tax. It is more likely that, with or without special interests behind this taxing scheme, there is a conviction that the economic effects of the DISC/FSC/ETI are similar to the territorial system and

[37]DISC, FSC, ETI.

[38]World Trade Organization Appellate Body Report on US Tax Treatment for "Foreign Sales Corporations," WT/DS108/AB/RW (Jan. 14, 2002), ¶ 256.

there is no strong reason to differentiate the treatment. Equalizing the equation, leveling the playing field, is what the USA seemed to be attempting to achieve.

The internal pressure held for long time: from the enactment of the DISC in 1971 until 2007. That is, in another words, almost 40 years of an ongoing dispute, but under different names. This resistance tells the "wrong" aspect of this case. The USA has abided by the GATT, albeit reluctantly. "Four of the fourteen rulings of violation made against the United States ended with a negative outcome – two with a failure to comply and two with compliance only after the complainant had acceded to arm-twisting demands" (see Hudec et al. 1993, p. 40). But the USA seemed to have a stronger motivation to hold on for 40 years on the same issue and that wouldn't happen if it did not have a legitimate concern.

Finally, the recurrence of these highest-stake cases for such a long time, even if it was wrongly pursued by the USA, hurt the system's image as a whole. It is better for the system to allow exceptions for socially deeply rooted values and to keep moving forward. This is even truer if the matter is so crucial to a member that it keeps the issue alive for 40 years. The bitter fight between the USA and the EC doesn't do the system any good. These are inefficient, long-lasting and costly disputes that go nowhere. If an exception or a veto power was available to the USA, but because this case stayed alive in the system in full view of everyone, the message conveyed could have been an unfair one: that the organization is too weak.

2.2 Potential Hypothetical Problems

Several scenarios have been laid out by scholars hypothesizing how trade and tax can interact, as the following section will show. There is no way to tell whether or when these disputes might arise, but potential problems are evident.

Saudi Products in the USA

Suppose that S Corp., a Saudi company, exports products to the USA. Since there is no tax treaty between Saudi Arabia and the USA, the Saudi products will be subject to US tax laws as well as the relevant WTO rules. If the USA were to insist that the *producers* of the Saudi products pay 10% income tax[39] in addition to regular tariffs, and the tariffs were presumed to be the same for every nation, there would be no violation of any WTO agreement with respect to the tariffs.

But what about the 10% tax itself? Does it violate the GATT? In this scenario, accepting for the sake of argument that income tax issues could come under the GATT jurisprudence, there remains a potential violation with respect to the MFN.

[39]It could be done by imposing a withholding tax on the sellers, or additional tariffs, or other sanctions to force the producers to report the 10% income tax.

The USA in this hypothetical is treating the Saudi products unlike other members' products, subject to a special income tax of 10%, assuming there is no USA–Saudi tax treaty. If the Saudi products are identical to products imported from Egypt, for example, then there is a clear violation of the MFN. Article I of the GATT states clearly that any "advantage, favour, privilege or immunity granted by any contracting party to any product originating in or destined for any other country shall be accorded immediately and unconditionally to the like product originating in or destined for the territories of all other contracting parties."[40] Taxing Egyptian products, for example, more favorably than identical Saudi products clearly constitutes a violation of this article. Thus, there is an illegality illustrated by the unequal MFN treatment between Saudis products and other products.

A special income tax of 10% on persons selling those Saudi products also may violate the NT principle. Article III of the GATT[41] requires WTO's members to treat each other's products as they treat their own products once the products pass a member's borders, with a prohibition on subjecting them to any additional internal taxes or charges of any kind "in excess of those applied directly or indirectly, to like domestic products."[42]

Thus, if the USA imposes this special 10% income tax exclusively on (persons selling) Saudi products, it will be *affecting* the sales of the Saudi products, and since Saudi Arabia is a WTO member, this violates the requirement that WTO members should offer NT[43] to products of other members for like products. Here, the USA is treating Saudi products differently, though *indirectly*, by subjecting the persons dealing with them to this special income tax, Saudi products being indirectly burdened more than the like products. The text of the article states clearly that the Saudi products "imported into the territory of [the USA] shall not be subject, *directly or indirectly*, to internal taxes or other internal charges of any kind in excess of those applied, *directly or indirectly*, to like domestic products."[44] The word "indirectly," repeated twice, is an indication of the importance for understanding that this article is not only about direct application of tax on products; rather it is about a tax effect on the sales of products. The tax itself can take different forms.

[40]GATT, art. I.

[41]Art. III.2 states that "The products of the territory of any contracting party imported into the territory of any other contracting party shall not be subject, directly or indirectly, to internal taxes or other internal charges of any kind in excess of those applied, directly or indirectly, to like domestic products."

[42]GATT art. III.2.

[43]An additional problem would arise in a situation where the USA requires investors to pay income tax on worldwide as it requires from US individuals. The US government could theoretically impose a worldwide income tax on foreigners or foreign products by applying a literal interpretation of MFN and NT found in the GATT and GATS.

[44]GATT art. III.2. [emphasis T.al.].

2.2.1 WTO's Members Practices

In reality, WTO Members, including China and India, have provided corporate tax relief for income derived from exports or export activities (Daly 2006, p. 544). "In China, for example, foreign-invested enterprises which are exporting at least 70 per cent of their output qualify for a 50 per cent income tax reduction (or possibly more, if they are located in special zones) and a full refund of the income tax paid on the amount of their profits that they reinvest in export oriented businesses. The economic effect of such measures is not fundamentally different from that of levying a non-discriminatory corporate income tax combined with an export subsidy" (Daly 2006, p. 544).

It is an export subsidy very similar to the FSC. Yet, countries either do not understand the prohibition or they do understand it, but nonetheless choose to provide prohibited subsidies via the tax system, perhaps because the gain outweighs the cost or because there is no conviction of the prohibition logic. Whatever the reason, it seems that there is a blurred understanding surrounding the issue of taxation's interactions with trade rules to the extent that the same mistakes are repeated again and again by the same country, as the case of the USA in DISC and FSC, or by different countries as the case in China and India.

Other examples of provisions in US tax law that treat foreign taxpayers differently from domestic tax payers include IRC 168(g), which provides that property used predominantly outside the United States is subject to less favorable depreciation deductions than property used within the United States (Warren 1994, p. 613), and "the congressional proposal a few years ago that preferential tax treatment be extended to withdrawals from pension plans used to purchase US-made cars."[45] Preferring US-made cars over foreign produced cars is in direct conflict with the WTO national treatment principle.

Further, a US domestic corporation that qualifies and elects to be taxed under Subchapter S is generally not subject to an additional corporate tax; it is instead treated more favorably as a pass-through entity. In an "S" corporation, all business profits "pass through" to the owners, who report them on their personal tax returns, avoiding double taxation and enjoying limited liability. The possible illegality of this kind of company under international law appears because to form such a corporation and enjoy favorable tax treatment, shareholders must be resident aliens or US citizens,[46] so other WTO members cannot form "S" corporations. Thus, products or services produced by this kind of company will face a smaller tax

---

[45]Warren (2001, pp. 150, 157), citing Debate on Revenue Bill Continues, 92 TNT 210-99, Oct. 19, 1992. Other examples noted by Warren include: IRC 884 (taxation of certain branch profits), 243 (e) (the deductibility of interoperate dividends), 267(a)(3) (recognition of certain corporate transfers), 163(j) (deductibility of interest payments), and 1446 (withholding for foreign partners). *See also* Turro (1990, pp. 609, 612) (describing the view of foreign officials that excise taxes on "gas guzzler" and luxury automobiles would be disproportionately borne by imported vehicles).

[46]IRS Section 1366(a). *See also* CCH Incorporated, US Master Tax Guide at 152 (2004).

burden in the form of a single tax, whereas products produced by other forms of business entities are faced with double taxation. Products will not be treated similarly and thus NT will be violated. This is true even though under the GATS, at least in theory, other WTO members are entitled to this national treatment if no reservation is made,[47] and indeed no reservation made with respect to this corporation.

The religious tax of Saudi Arabia, which subjects Saudis to a 2.5% wealth tax, while imposing on non-Saudis a 20% income tax, illustrates a system with two sets of taxation rules, one for foreigners and another for domestic residents, departing from the GATS national treatment requirement that asks WTO members to offer service suppliers "of any other Member, in respect of all measures affecting the supply of services, treatment no less favourable than that it accords to its own like services and service suppliers."[48] If, for example, an American lawyer practices in Saudi Arabia, he will pay 20% of his income at the end of the fiscal year to the government, while his Saudi partner will be required to pay only 2.5% of the income from his practice. This appears to be a clear violation of the GATS, assuming no reservations have been made by the Saudis. Sure, Saudi Arabia can, and in fact did, make a reservation, but the fact remains that the national treatment is not offered to foreigners. What happens if an Islamic government obtains power (elected or otherwise) in any Moslem country, and introduces the Islamic tax? Will it be acceptable if it changes the scheduled commitment?

2.2.2 *Subsidies Confusion*

Subsidies present the clash of tax and trade most clearly. Subsidies and tax combine into an area so blurry that it is often difficult to determine what is a subsidy and what is a tax. Subsidies present problems similar to those associated with tariffs. From an economic perspective, the "main objectionable component of a tariff is its implicit subsidy to domestic producers" (Avi-Yonah and Slemrod 2002, pp. 533, 535).

[47]Interestingly, there appears to be no reservation made with regard to "S" corporations specifically. Research revealed only an indirect reservation with respect to the MFN under the GATS; it states that "sub-federal tax measures affording differential treatment to service suppliers or to services when the differential treatment is based on one of the following criteria: differ based on the size or income of the service supplier or on the scale or methods (including environmental and health and safety measures) of performance." *See* the US Schedule of Commitments under the General Agreement on Trade in Services (1998), available at http://hotdocs.usitc.gov/docs/pubs/332/GATS98.pdf. Since the "S" corporation is limited in size, it could be included under this reservation. Even with this inclusion, there is no reservation with respect to national treatment article. A similar reservation was made, however, for small business loans. Similarly, "[f]ederal Small Business Administration loans are restricted to US citizens or companies that are 100 per cent owned by US citizens and whose directors are all US citizens." http://hotdocs.usitc.gov/docs/pubs/332/GATS98.pdf.

[48]GATS art. XVII, 1.

Offering subsidies is the same as levying a non-discriminatory income tax in addition to imposing an export subsidy (Avi-Yonah and Slemrod 2002, p. 536).

Another potential problem arises when using direct tax to effectuate a protectionist policy, as for example the substitutability of production subsidies and tax incentives, both of which are subject to the WTO Subsidies Code. Direct taxes can be used to advance a domestic protectionist policy, "as when expenditures for inputs are deductible only when the inputs are domestically produced goods, a scheme parallel to allowing a deduction for all inputs, domestic or imported, and then levying an import tariff on imported goods" (Avi-Yonah and Slemrod 2002, pp. 536–537). Another potential equivalence is between a tariff and a consumption tax plus a production subsidy (Warren 2001, p. 148). This occurs where expenditures for inputs are deductible only if the goods are produced locally. This mechanism "is similar to allowing a deduction for all inputs, and levying an import tariff equal to the business tax rate" (Avi-Yonah and Slemrod 2002, p. 536).

2.2.3 GATS Potentiality

Under the GATS, there is also a potential for problems with respect to taxation, even though the GATS imposed limits on members' abilities to invoke Article XVII, the national treatment article, "with respect to a measure of another Member that falls within the scope of an international agreement *between them* relating to the avoidance of double taxation."[49] For a situation in which members do not have a tax treaty between them, as for example the case between Saudi Arabia and the USA, the GATS seems to be the organization which will decide the conflict that arises with respect to a tax disputed measure under the GATS.

The GATS goes on to say that "[i]n case of disagreement between Members as to whether a measure falls within the scope of such an agreement between them, it shall be open to either Member to bring this matter before the Council for Trade in Services. The Council shall refer the matter to arbitration. The decision of the arbitrator shall be final and binding on the Members."[50] Thus, according to this Article, the WTO is *the organization* to decide whether or not a measure is a tax and whether or not the measure falls within the scope of the tax treaty. A trade organization will decide whether a measure is a tax or not, an issue that should raise concern about whether the subject is suitable for handling under the WTO. Or maybe, the WTO needs to change a little by introducing a tax agreement, tax department, and staff with tax expertise to handle such an issue. Notice that the GATS seems to assume that every country has a tax treaty with the rest of the WTO members.

---

[49] GATS art. XXII.3 [emphasis T.al].

[50] GATS art. XXII.3.

2.3 Summary and Analysis

It should be noted that some "discrimination" or different treatment is acceptable if circumstances are different between local products and producers, and between foreign products and producers. Actions allowing limited discriminatory provisions "have been interpreted to permit differences in taxation of resident and nonresident portfolio investors, on the grounds that they are not in similar circumstances" (Warren 2001, p. 151). Since no mechanism exists to monitor how countries evaluate these circumstances, leaving the issue with no independent, objective third party is a risky course.

Another issue emerging from the above discussion is that tax problems do exist within the WTO actually (or potentially). As seen, taxation can be used to nullify the WTO agreements or goals. WTO members join the organization by agreeing to comply with a set of rules, including abstention from discriminatory practices that favor domestic production or producers, a principle highlighted by the NT and MFN principles. Violation can be found to occur either directly, by discriminating against foreign products or producers, or indirectly, through imposition of different rules or requirements on foreign products and producers via taxation. This problem can be expected to grow if it is not resolved quickly because, with tariffs and other direct trade protectionist policies under close scrutiny, it is logical to expect politicians to use non-traditional means to achieve political domestic gains.

Tax policies can be protected by sovereignty claims, and can be used to achieve trade goals, win the support of contributors, and gather votes of those who sympathize with arguments against globalization. Such use of tax rules can help politicians avoid WTO rules, satisfy their supporters, and achieve their ideological goals.

Moreover, a problematic feature with most of the scenarios discussed herein is that there is no way to guarantee the accuracy and objectivity of a given country's characterization of taxes affecting trade issues, such as subsidies, domestic or foreign income, similar situations or "circumstances"[51] when reaching its "own conclusion about whether such differential treatment is justified" (Warren 2001, p. 151). Even in bilateral tax treaty situations, protection against discrimination is more limited "in practice than might be suggested by the treaty language" (Warren 2001, p. 151). Thus, even a nation controlled by a tax treaty can misuse established tax rules to achieve its own goals, even if such misuse is in violation of the treaty. This results because contracting parties to bilateral tax treaties are not at all obligated to solve any problems that may arise other than to "endeavor"[52] to resolve a dispute by mutual agreement.

A third problem is that tax issues are handled already under the WTO umbrella by trade experts, which can be a risk. This is not the best possible approach, as illustrated by cases like those regarding DISC and FSC, described above, which involved a dispute between direct tax and indirect tax, and between the worldwide

---

[51]OECD art. 24.

[52]OECD art. 25.2.

tax system and the territorial tax system, an issue that is profoundly crucial to the dispute and needs to be settled by tax experts. Under the WTO, indirect taxes are favored; the US attempts have been to equalize direct tax and indirect tax.

A distinction between "direct" and "indirect" taxes was at first useful under the GATT border adjustment, when only two types of taxation were widely used: excise taxes (indirect taxes) and property taxes (direct taxes) (Hufbauer 2002). Direct tax and indirect tax can also be viewed as representative of the two major taxing systems, the worldwide system and the territorial system. The USA has claimed that the DISC,[53] FSC, and EIT were all analogous to territorial taxation, which was consistent with WTO rules, as it allowed countries to export products without subjection to taxation.[54]

WTO rules allow an exported product to be relieved of all indirect taxes, sales taxes, or value-added taxes (VAT) levied in the exporting country, thereby allowing relief that is not applied to direct taxes payable by the producing enterprise, for example border tax adjustments. The economic rationale for this rule arises from the old assumption that the indirect taxes burden can be shifted forward onto the product and thus can be reflected in the final price. On the other hand, direct taxes are not presumed to be shifted, but instead absorbed largely by the owners of the producing enterprise, so there is no sound reason to allow a rebate. Chapter 1 of this work discusses the issues of direct and indirect tax in greater depth to illustrate the problem of allowing the trade and tax regimes to develop in separate environments.

Another problem, discussed in further detail in the next chapter, occurs when tax serves a genuine domestic purpose, but happens to be in direct conflict with a trade rules. In Saudi Arabia, the current unemployment rate is by some estimates[55] as high as 30%, disastrous for what is regarded as an overall wealthy country. One method of easing this problem could be via the tax system, but any given method could *possibly unintentionally* conflict with the WTO rules. Of course, Saudi Arabia has different tools, but sometimes regulations are issued for legitimate internal concerns, and are also WTO-incompatible. Similarly, the USA encourages small business by offering favorable tax treatment to the "S" corporation, a benefit that is offered only to US citizens. Also, the USA encourages home ownership, a deeply rooted social/economic value in American society, by allowing interest deductions from taxable income; if these deductions are found in some way to violate a WTO rule, as an example, the policy would be considered unacceptable by Geneva, even where violation is unintentional and the internal goal is admirable. Any ultimate solution must allow domestic governments the flexibility they need to meet urgent demands without violating WTO agreements, as will be suggested in the tax agreement discussion in Chap. 7.

---

[53]Hudec writes: "Because the United States Treasury Department believed strongly in the legitimacy of this objective, it would defend DISC with an intensity considerably greater than governments normally expend on ordinary beggar-thy-neighbor trade measures. Indeed, the United States would never yield on the legitimacy of DISC's basic purpose." Hudec (1988, p. 1449).

[54]*See supra* Chap. 1.

[55]http://www.arabicnews.com/ansub/Daily/Day/030305/2003030513.html.

A related problem is that because the OECD is considered (perhaps wrongly) the most influential organization with respect to international tax matters, there is a risk that the Organization could fuel the tension between the fields of tax and trade by introducing concepts or ideas that are not entirely compatible with the international trade rules as administered by the WTO, taking also into account the fact that the OECD is a very small club. The need to integrate both regimes under the WTO requires a forum where more than the OECD countries can participate in shaping how international tax and trade remain interact.

There does not yet exist any coherent method for identifying acceptable tax rules that can pass trade standards where international trade and international tax come together. To achieve an acceptable interaction between the two regimes, the current fragmentation must be eliminated. What is needed to fix this problem is a "soft method" of resolving such issues, allowing governments the flexibility they require to administer their own tax policies that do not contradict WTO requirements and that are not intended to violate international trade rules, while allowing investors and traders to enjoy the predictability they desire and which is intended by the rules of the WTO.

References

Avi-Yonah RS, Slemrod J (2002) (How) should trade agreements deal with income tax issues. Tax L Rev 55:533, 535

Clark HR et al. (2001) The WTO ruling on foreign sales corporations: costliest battle yet in an escalating trade war between the United States and the European Union? Minn J Global Trade 10:291

Daly M (2006) WTO rules on direct taxation. The World Economy 29:527–557. http://ssrn.com/abstract=896825

Gardner R (1980) Sterling–dollar diplomacy, 3rd rev. edn. Clarendon, Oxford

Goodspeed G (2006) Taxation and FDI in developing and developed countries. In: Alm J, Martinez-Vazquez J, Rider M (eds) The challenge of tax reform in a global economy. Springer, New York

Hoekman BM, Kostecki MM (2001) The political economy of the world trading system: the WTO and beyond. Oxford University Press, Oxford

Hudec RE (1988) Reforming GATT adjudication procedures: the lessons of the DISC case. Minn L Rev 72:1443

Hudec RE (1993) Enforcing international trade law: the evolution of the modern GATT legal system. Butterworth, Salem, NH

Hudec RE, Kennedy DLM, Sgarbossa M (1993) A statistical profile of GATT dispute. Settlement cases: 1948–1989. Minn J Global Trade 2:40

Hufbauer GC (2001) Income vs. consumption taxation: domestic and international reforms. Brook J Int'l L 26:1555

Hufbauer GC (2002) The Foreign Sales Corporation drama: reaching the last act? International Economic Policy Brief, Number PB 02-10

Jackson JH, Louis J-V, Matsushita M (1984) Implementing the Tokyo round. University of Michigan Press, Ann Arbor

McDaniel PR (2001) Panel IV: the pursuit of national tax policies in a globalized environment: principal paper: trade and taxation. Brook J Int'l L 26:1621, 1629

McDaniel P (2004) The David R. Tillinghast lecture: trade agreements and income taxation: interactions, conflict and resolution. Tax L Rev 57:275, 277

Palmeter ND, Mavroidis PC (2004) Dispute settlement in the World Trade Organization: practice and procedure, 2nd edn. Cambridge University Press, Cambridge

Petersmann EU, Pollack MA (eds) (2003) Transatlantic economic disputes, the EU, the U.S., and the WTO. Oxford University Press, Oxford

Qureshi AF, Grynberg R (2002) United States tax subsidies under Domestic International Sales Corporation, Foreign Sales Corporation, and Extraterritorial Income Exclusion act legislation within the framework of the World Trade Organization. J World Trade 36:979

Sheppard HE (2003) Rethinking tax-based export incentives: converting repeated defeats before the WTO into positive tax policy. Tex Int'l L J 39:111, 114

Smith S (2004) Fishing for rainbows, the FSC repeal and Extraterritorial Income Exclusion Act. San Diego Int'l L J 5:503, 525

Stehmann O (2000) Foreign sales corporations under the WTO. J World Trade 34:127

Turro J (1990) Override articles may appear in future U.S. treaties, Morrison Warns; foreign officials discuss ADR. Tax Notes 49:609, 612

Van Meerhaeghe MAG (1998) International economic institutions. Kluwer, Dordrecht

Végh PG (2005) OECD model tax convention on income and on capital. OECD, Paris

Warren AC (1994) Alternatives for international corporate tax reform. Tax L Rev 49:613

Warren AC Jr (2001) Income tax discrimination against international commerce. Tax L Rev 54:131

Chapter 3
Tax and Religion: Saudi Arabia Tax System

Wealth and children are an adornment of the life of this world; and the ever-abiding, the good works, are better with your Lord in reward and better in expectation.[1]

3.1 The Dilemma

A difficult problem arises in situations where tax is used for religious reasons. There is a potential for a clash between religious tax and WTO rules. If trade rules are held as strictly as they are as applied currently, it could lead to a devastating effect. Such is the case with the Saudi Arabian tax system, which is based on religion. This religious tax has some discriminatory elements favoring Moslems. International tax law has allowed this result, being bilateral and subject to negotiation, bargaining, and diplomacy, and has not restrained religion-based discrimination. International trade law, on the other hand, if applied to this kind of religious discrimination, may (1) apply and make illegal this discrimination, and (2) be subject to stronger procedural arrangements.

This problem of fragmentation combines to cause a conflict between the tax and trade systems on an international level. The religious tax provides a good example of the fragmentation problem, where the tax regime accepts, even if unenthusiastically, a particular behavior, but the trade regime does not. It is an even more interesting fragmentation problem because it involves four systems: international tax law, international trade law, Islamic law, and Saudi domestic tax and constitutional law.[2]

This problem of the religious tax is not confined to Saudi Arabia.[3] It is an Islamic issue, having its root in religious texts. Therefore, any Islamic governments that

---

[1]Koran 18:46.

[2]Thanks to Professor Joel Trachtman for this comment.

[3]In fact, the problem of introducing foreign laws or modifying local laws that are based on different values is very complicated. Professor Alford writes, "Laws premised on the values and institutions of an economically advanced capitalist democracy will not generate identical results when transplanted to a different setting" Alford (1992, p. M5). This can be applied to different laws including tax, trade, etc.

T. Althunayan, *Dealing with the Fragmented International Legal Environment: WTO, International Tax and Internal Tax Regulations*,
DOI 10.1007/978-3-642-04678-0_3,

obtain enough political power to introduce new regulations could introduce Islamic taxation or similar versions of it, and thus, it could be the subject of the same dilemma. Consequently, the discussion in this chapter is about an abstract problem, but to make the matter as relevant as possible, Saudi Arabia's tax system is being used just to illustrate the problem and put it into context.

Even though several modern Islamic countries have adopted new commercial policies to meet the requirements of international trade reforms spearheaded by western nations, there remains one issue that has not been fully addressed at the governmental level: Islamic fiscal rules in business life that involve the taxation of non-Moslems. With the emergence of the WTO as the most important international global trade player, a crucial need in Islamic countries is either the creation of domestic rules and laws consistent with their commitment to the WTO agreements, or, alternatively, a better explanation or justification than currently exists for not following the rules as prescribed.

The dilemma for Islamic nations, which are theoretically obliged to follow Islamic principles, is that, because their governance has from the beginning been worked out along theocratic lines, and because the majority of these nations' populations consist of Islamic citizens, they feel they must base their tax systems on principles consistent with Islam. As a result, non-Moslems, whether or not they are residents of a given nation, are subject to different and higher taxes, and are treated differently and in a way that might be called inequitable. On the other hand, because zakat, the Islamic tax, is believed by Muslims to be imposed by God, all Moslems are supposed to pay or distribute their zakat to whomever deserves it (for example, the poor and the needy).

Zakat rules differ substantially among Islamic countries. Some countries have "established a complete incorporation of zakat as a regular tax of the Islamic state (Pakistan, Sudan, Saudi Arabia)," while "others utilize intermediary financial institutions to receive voluntary payments of zakat (Jordan, Egypt, Bahrain, Kuwait, Indonesia), and still others marginalize zakat to the individual's private conscience (Morocco, Oman)" (Salim 2006, pp. 683, 686). If Islamic nations were forced to adopt tax policies that were not structured according to Islamic principles, Muslims would believe they were required to pay zakat in addition to other required religion-neutral taxes, causing them to bear a greater burden than non-Moslems who are not required to pay zakat.

Saudi Arabia imposes different taxes on foreigners, rooted mainly on the historical concept that foreigners are normally non-Moslems and thus should be subject to different taxation schemes. The system is not very consistent with its old rooted concept, because the tax system taxes foreign Moslems and non-Moslems similarly according to income tax, and leaves Saudis to be subject only to zakat, without clear explanation[4] of the rationale for such a system. Some religious preachers have

[4]Dr. Al-Sultan, a prominent Saudi accountant, claimed that this is primarily an information issue; because the Saudi government cannot verify the personal information of non-Saudis, it cannot impose zakat on them. *See* Al-Sultan (1995, p. 158).

condemned the government for extending the income tax to "brother" Moslems, demanding they be treated like Saudis and be subject to zakat.[5]

This chapter will address the Saudi tax system. It begins with an overview of the zakat in general, with a summary of its social, economic, and religious goals, and a discussion of the rules and applications derived from that important framework, such as why zakat must not be imposed on non-Moslems or children. What follows is an examination of the application of the zakat in Saudi Arabia, and an overview of income tax in that nation. Finally, the author will discuss potential problems and possible solutions.

3.2 The Legal Texts

From the Koran, the holy book of Islam: "And in their (Moslems) wealth there is due share for the beggar and the deprived. The alms are only for the poor and the needy, and for those employed in connection therewith, and for those whose hearts are to be reconciled, and for the freeing of slaves, and for those in debt, and for the cause of Allah, and for the wayfarer."[6]

This rule from the Moslem holy book applies to Moslems; non-Moslems are subject to different rules of taxation. For non-Moslems under the control of Moslems, and who engage in a war with an Islamic state,[7] the Koran states the following: "Fight against those who believe not in Allah, nor in the Last Day, nor forbid that which has been forbidden by Allah and His Messenger and those who acknowledge not the religion of truth among the people of the Scripture, until they pay the Jizyah with willing submission."[8]

According to interpretations by Moslem scholars, there are two different sets of tax rules, which are likely to be stricter for non-Moslems and non-Moslems' products. This is in direct conflict with the plain meaning of the WTO; Article I, of which states:

> With respect to customs duties and charges of any kind imposed on or in connection with importation or exportation or imposed on the international transfer of payments for imports or exports, and with respect to the method of levying such duties and charges, and with respect to all rules and formalities in connection with importation and exportation, and with respect to all matters referred to in paragraphs 2 and 4 of Article III, any advantage, favor,

[5]In addition to preaching during Friday prayers, religious scholars have also conducted lessons during which they express some of their views. Most of this is, unfortunately, audiotaped in Arabic.

[6]The word *zakat* has been repeated 30 times, 27 of which were combined with the prayer in one sentence. *See* Alkrdawy (1994, p. 57) [hereinafter "Alkrdawy Islamic Zakat"]. For traditional views, *see* Abu Yusuf (1999).

[7]Interpretations have long been subject to debate; consider this contradictory verse: "Surely those who believe, and those who are Jews, and the Christians, and the Sabians, whoever believes in Allah and the Last day and does good, they shall have their reward from their Lord, and there is no fear for them, nor shall they grieve." Koran 2:62.

[8]Koran 5:29.

privilege or immunity granted by any contracting party to any product originating in or destined for any other country shall be accorded immediately and unconditionally to the like product originating in or destined for the territories of all other contracting parties.[9]

Article III of the GATT states:

1. The contracting parties recognize that internal taxes and other internal charges, and laws, regulations and requirements affecting the internal sale, offering for sale, purchase, transportation, distribution or use of products, and internal quantitative regulations requiring the mixture, processing or use of products in specified amounts or proportions, should not be applied to imported or domestic products so as to afford protection to domestic production.
2. The products of the territory of any contracting party imported into the territory of any other contracting party shall not be subject, directly or indirectly, to internal taxes or other internal charges of any kind *in excess of those applied*, directly or indirectly, to like domestic products. Moreover, no contracting party shall otherwise apply internal taxes or other internal charges to imported or domestic products in a manner contrary to the principles set forth in paragraph 1.

The conflict is clear: the WTO is advancing the concept of levelling the playing field, while Islamic jurisprudence has long felt that non-Moslems are to be taxed differently (and probably more heavily) than Moslems and their products.

3.3 Saudi Arabian Tax System

Background

Saudi laws, including tax laws, must either be derived from Islam or must not be in conflict with Islamic rules. The Saudi Basic Law, the Constitution, provides in its first Article that the official country religion is Islam. Further, Article Seven states that the rule in the Kingdom draws its authority from Islamic sources and, moreover, that all courts in the Kingdom must apply Islamic legal principles. In Saudi Arabia, the government must govern consistently with the Shari'a (Vogel 2000, p. 171), including the ruler, the King's[10] decisions. Although the new laws are not specifically expressions of traditional Islamic law, it is generally maintained that they are consistent with the *Shari'a* principles as long as they are not in conflict with the core principles of Islam.[11]

---

[9]GATT, I.

[10]The King has the supreme authority in the kingdom, supervising government operations, ratifying laws, ratifying death penalty punishments, approving budgets, and fulfilling other duties.

[11]Core principles vary, but all laws or rules must be designed to protect the five essential rights: the protection of life (i.e., prohibiting violence and killing), the protection of family (i.e., prohibiting adultery), the protection of the religion (i.e., prohibiting insulting or cursing religion), the

Saudi citizens and companies are normally subject to the religious tax, zakat,[12] and non-Saudi individuals or companies are always subject to income or company tax.[13] Generally, all individuals and business entities, whether Saudi owned or not, that operate and conduct business in Saudi Arabia, are required to submit income tax or zakat returns annually to the Department of Zakat and Income Tax (DZIT).[14]

3.3.0.1 Zakat

Zakat is applied in virtually all Islamic states in varying contexts. Most Islamic states follow zakat voluntarily, some compulsorily; a few have eliminated it from the system altogether. In Saudi Arabia, zakat is imposed on Saudis. In Pakistan, it is applied partially to bank accounts. The Islamic Affairs Councils of the various States and the Federal Territory of Kuala Lumpur have also organized the collection and distribution of zakat.

Zakat is also found in the international context; for example, Saudi Arabia's income tax treaty[15] with Austria has a provision concerning zakat.[16] Even in those countries which have eliminated zakat, there have been established non-government organizations that collect and spend it, including Thailand and the USA.[17] Thus, it is reasonable to expect this type of system to remain in force and, as such, the possibility must be considered that it could cause problems or difficulties in a globalized setting.

Since Saudi Arabia follows Islamic rules,[18] its government imposes zakat:[19] "all Saudi companies and persons: male, female, adults, minors or legally incompetent,

---

protection of wealth (i.e., prohibiting theft), and the protection of the mind or intellect (i.e., prohibiting alcohol). *See also* Hunter and Malik (2005, pp. 75–76).

[12]Saudi employees are subject to a social security tax. However, its name, "retirement payment," probably implies to Saudis that it is a retirement investment, rather than a tax.

[13]*See* Zakat and Income Tax Law, art. 2 [hereinafter "Tax Law"].

[14]The DZIT of the Ministry of Finance is the only governmental agency with authority to supervise tax and zakat matters, issue regulations, or handling litigations.

[15]Until recently, Saudi Arabia had only one income tax treaty, and that was with France. Recently, the Kingdom has executed several more tax treaties, and the list continues to grow. In all these treaties, zakat is treated as a tax. See footnote 35.

[16]Article III, 2 stated that: "3. The existing taxes to which this Convention shall apply are in particular: (a) In the case of the Kingdom of Saudi Arabia: i. the Zakat." Austria–Saudi Arabia, 2006 Income and Capital Tax Convention, March 19, 2006. Identical article found in tax treaties with China, India.

[17]The website for the Zakat Foundation of America, an international non-profit organization based in Chicago, USA, can be found at http://www.tzfa.org/a_abtus.html.

[18]Saudi Arabia follows the Hanbali Islamic School. *See* Nafisa Motleb, *Law and Social Change in Muslim Countries, the Concept of Islamic Law Held by the Hanbali School and Saudi Arabian Legal System* (1975) (unpublished SJD Book, Harvard University) (on file with the Harvard University).

[19]According to Islam, zakat, as well as other laws such as criminal and family laws, is a means for implementing God's words.

are subject to zakat after completion of one year under the provisions of Islamic Jurisprudence starting from 1/1/1370 H (corresponding to 13/10/1950)."[20] According to a Ministerial Resolution, the Saudi government collects zakat according to Islamic rules (*Shari'a*) at the end of each year at a fixed rate of 2.5% from all "Saudi companies and persons: male, female, adults, minors or legally incompetent, are subject to zakat after completion of one year under the provisions of Islamic Jurisprudence starting from 1/1/1370 H (corresponding to 13/10/1950)."[21]

Zakat covers nearly every aspect of the commerce life. It is "assessed on commercial goods, properties and financial belongings at estimated values at the end of the year in accordance with provisions of Islamic Jurisprudence."[22]

All zakat payers are required to offer proof of their assets and transactions to document their capital and expenditure. "All individuals and companies with industrial or commercial activity are required to keep organized books that show capital, receipts and expenditure relevant to their activity for each year to be used to assess their zakat. The books must be certified by commercial courts or, if not available, by notary publics."[23] Otherwise, assessments will be made "based on determination of value of zakatable goods, equipment, tools, belongings and properties at the end of the year; or based on estimation for zakatpayers with no apparent zakatable items."[24]

Finally, it should be noted that although Saudi Arabia imposes zakat on all companies,[25] the applicable rules are far from clear. A royal decree was issued in 1964, with only a brief statement stating that the zakat "shall be collected in full from all joint-stock and other companies, as well as from individuals who are liable to pay zakat. All amounts collected shall be remitted to the Social Security Department."[26] Rules created after this declaration were created by the DZIT, which itself has very few rules concerning zakat. The majority of the existing rules are found in a set of guidelines issued by the DZIT, which has little legal effect, because the Department has no authority to create new rules; it is authorized only to interpret or clarify existing rules, but not to create additional obligations.

---

[20]Regulation issued pursuant to Ministerial Resolution number 393, dated 6/8/1370 H (corresponding to 13/5/1950).

[21]Zakat By-Law was issued per Ministerial Resolution number 393, dated 6/8/1370 H (corresponding to 13/5/1950).

[22]Zakat By-Law was issued per Ministerial Resolution number 393, dated 6/8/1370 H (corresponding to 13/5/1950).

[23]Regulation art. 6.

[24]Regulation art. 7.

[25]All companies are subject to either zakat or income tax, depending on the nationality. The only exceptions are joint venture companies (sharikat al-muhassah) where partners remain unknown. This is similar to the German *still gesellschsft*, the Japanese *tokumei kumiai*, and the French *association commerciale en participation*. *See* Hanna (1997).

[26]Royal Decree No. 61/5/1, 1964.

3.3.0.2 Saudi Income Tax Law

In August 2004, a comprehensive new Saudi income tax law became effective. The Saudi Ministers Cabinet[27] approved a reduction in taxes on foreign investment, a move that can be fairly categorized as part of the Saudi government's efforts to speed up economic reform in the country.

While zakat is at its core an Islamic obligation, when foreign people, even Moslems, conduct business activities income tax applies. Thus, zakat is imposed based solely on nationality, even though its root is religion, though with resistance from religious scholars.[28] If a business entity is owned by both Saudi and non-Saudi persons, zakat is assessed in proportion to the equity interest of Saudis in the entity, while income tax is assessed in proportion to the equity interest of foreigners.

The new income tax law is unique in that it officially recognizes internationally accepted tax principles for the first time, and covers several areas that were not addressed by the old laws and regulations. One of its most noticeable features is the revocation of the progressive income tax and its replacement with a 20% flat tax rate. The law also introduces, for the first time, the transfer pricing principle, institutes an accelerated deduction mechanism, and provides for a research and development deduction, although its range is not clear. In addition, in a historic change, the new tax law is applicable to Saudis investing in the Kingdom who are residents of other countries.

In order to determine whether a person is subject to Saudi tax, sourcing income is the first thing to be considered. Saudi Arabian tax is based on a territorial concept. That is, the economic relationship between the income and the location from which the income is generated is the central concept on which Saudi legislators relied. The income tax is imposed on income that is generated in Saudi Arabia, regardless of the residency of the taxpayer.

Generally, all "profits and gains of any type and of any form of payment resulting from carrying out an activity, including capital gains and any incidental revenues, minus exempted income"[29] that are deemed to be sourced in Saudi Arabia will be subject to the new tax law, regardless of the place where the payment has been made. All forms of trade in goods or in service, or any similar activity aimed at deriving profit, including renting movable and immovable properties or generating royalties from intellectual properties, will be subject to the tax, as long as the profits are deemed Saudi-sourced.[30]

[27]Initially, in January 2004, the tax rate was to be set at 25%. However, after the bill was approved by *Majls A'Ashora* (Consultative Cabinet), the business community expressed its deep disappointment with the high rate and the government suggested a reduction of the tax rate to 20%. In May 2004, the lower rate was finally approved, but many businesses continue to request a further reduction of the tax rate.

[28]*See* for example, Alnoyam.

[29]Tax Law Art. 8.

[30]Tax Law Art. 5(a).

All tax obligations are imposed on net profit. Net profit is calculated after allowing specific deductions, such as technical and office expenses, incurred in earning such income.[31] Net profit is to be assessed based on a financial statement provided by the taxpayer. However, if DZIT finds the statement inadequate or incorrect, it has the right to declare at least 10% of income as profit.[32]

The subjects of the new law are:

(a) A resident capital company with respect to shares of non-Saudi partners
(b) A resident non-Saudi natural person who conducts business in the Kingdom
(c) A nonresident who conducts business in the Kingdom through a permanent establishment
(d) A nonresident with other taxable income from sources within the Kingdom[33]
(e) A person engaged in the field of natural gas investment
(f) A person engaged in the field of oil and hydrocarbons production[34]

It should be noted that for the first time ever in the Saudi history, an income tax is levied on Saudi citizens or companies owned by them. Article 2 of the new law stipulates that a natural person residing in the Kingdom is potentially taxable for a given year if he is deemed a resident; that is, if he has a permanent place of domicile in the Kingdom *and* is physically present in the Kingdom for not less than 30 days in aggregate during the taxable year.[35] If such person is Saudi, he will be subject to zakat. If he is non-Saudi, income tax will apply. If a taxpayer does not have a permanent place of residence in the Kingdom, he must be physically present there during not less than 183 days in a tax year to be considered a resident; a Saudi with a

---

[31]DZIT Regulation Chapter 3. *See* Albana (1982, p. 319); Al-Sultan (1995, pp. 264–266).

[32]Tax Law art. 34. *See also* Albana (1982, p. 343); *and see* Al-Sultan (1995, p. 382).

[33]According to the regulation,

> A non-resident person with no permanent establishment in the Kingdom who derives income from a source in the Kingdom is subject to tax as follows:
> (a) Income stipulated under Article 68 of the Law is subject to withholding provisions of that Article.
> (b) A capital gain derived from disposal of fixed and traded assets, or from disposal of shares in a resident company is subject to tax under general provisions of the Law. Reg. 1 (2).

Income under article 68 includes: (1) Rent, 5%; (2) Royalty or proceeds (bank interest), 15%; (3) Management fees, 20%; (4) Payments for airline tickets, air or maritime freight, 5%; (5) Payments for international telecommunications services, 5%; and (6) Any other payments specified in the Regulations, provided that the tax rate does not exceed 15%.

[34]Tax Law art. 2. It should be noted that the new law preserved the old tradition of not taxing the salaries of employees, a policy designed to attract experts from around the world to the Kingdom. This long-standing policy of exempting workers from taxation was challenged recently when it was suggested that workers earning more than SR 3,000 should be subject to a flat-rate tax of 10%. This suggestion was killed at the Majls. The majority of the Shura members rejected the proposal, a vote of 73 against 47. *See*, Janardhan (2006).

[35]This provision is potentially problematic, as there is no clear definition of "permanent residency."

presence of at least 183 days will be subject to zakat, but a Saudi present for less than 183 days will be subject to the income tax. The above reading was affirmed by a subsequent regulation stating that "[t]he provisions of the Law also apply to non-resident persons, natural or corporate, Saudi or non-Saudi, who conduct business in the Kingdom through a permanent establishment located in the Kingdom or who derive income from a source in the Kingdom."[36]

Subjection of Saudis to income tax law rather than to zakat is a major cultural shift and a deviation from old tradition for a society that has historically found zakat to be the only permissible financial levy[37] on Moslems. However, the fact that the income tax law is imposed only on Saudis who have a relatively weak relationship with the Kingdom probably will ease the acceptance of this law.

3.4 The Conflict with the WTO

There is a potential for problems between the Saudi tax law and the rules of the WTO, a conflict between trade and tax. When a non-Saudi individual forms a Saudi company by incorporating in the Kingdom to import products to Saudi Arabia, the company will be considered, for tax purposes, a non-Saudi resident company. Therefore, the company will not be able to obtain zakat treatment, but will be taxed at the higher income tax rate as a non-Saudi company. Arguably, in such a situation the Saudi internal tax system will have, by affecting the sales of products imported by the company in a negative way, discriminated against the company in comparison to a domestic company.

Products "imported into the territory of any other contracting party," Saudi Arabia in this case, "shall not be subject, directly or indirectly, to internal taxes ... in excess of those applied, directly or indirectly, to like domestic products."[38] The Saudi tax system is arguably subjecting imported products to higher taxes than domestic products, a 2.5% wealth tax applied to a Saudi limited liability company compared to a 20% income tax for a foreign company. Although the zakat can be seen to target the persons not the products, it affects the products indirectly. The case admittedly is weak in the products sector, the GATT, but it is still applicable indirectly, because there is an apparent favoritism granted to Saudis and products sold by Saudis. And this has a religious flavor.

This favoritism is clearer in the service industry. Consider, for example, two lawyers practicing in the Kingdom, one Saudi and one French. The Saudi will be

---

[36]Regulation art. 2.

[37]*See* Fourth Symposium on Zakat Contemporary Issues (Held in Bahrain Shawwal 17, 1414 A. H. / March 29, 1994 AD), an Islamic symposium in which a statement was issued calling on Islamic countries to impose zakat only and stating that, "imposing taxes is permissible only if there is a real need."

[38]GATT art. III.

subject to 2.5% zakat, while the French lawyer will be subject to the income tax of 20%, favoritism that is a violation of the GATS national treatment principle.[39]

If the Saudi tax system indeed protects domestic production, as seems to be the case, then it is inconsistent with the WTO agreements. This is indicated in the text of the Saudi negotiation group questions and answers during its WTO accession:

> Q 5: Saudi Arabia's corporate taxation system applies a different tax regime to businesses owned by citizens of Saudi Arabia and to foreign-owned or joint-venture businesses. As the Zakat is applied only to liquid assets and at a *rate sharply below* that applied to the income of non-Saudis, *it would appear that non-Saudis bear a higher tax burden than Saudi citizens.*
>
> (a) Is it correct to state that citizens of Saudi Arabia never pay the income tax? If not, what is the rate of income tax applied to the earnings of citizens of Saudi Arabia?
>
> Answer: (a) Saudi citizens are not subject to the income tax. However, they pay Zakat at an annual rate of 2.5% of the assessable amount.
>
> (b) Is it correct to state that foreign-owned firms that import goods are subject to a higher level of taxation on their earnings from this activity than importing or manufacturing firms owned by citizens of Saudi Arabia?
>
> Answer: (b) There are many cases where foreign partners would not pay a tax whereas Saudi partners are obliged to pay Zakat.
>
> (1) Companies in the process of being established. Saudi companies have to pay Zakat on their capital while the capital share of the foreign partner is not subject to any tax as long as the company is in the process of establishment and did not yet earn any taxable profits.
> (2) The foreign partner's share in a company incurring a loss is not taxable whereas the Saudi partner has to pay Zakat on the various components mentioned above.[40]
>
> (2) Though foreign companies are subject to a higher tax rate, this tax, however, is not necessarily bigger than Zakat payable by Saudi citizens. Only the share of the foreign partner of the annual profits is taxable, whereas the Saudi partner would pay Zakat on all his money in the company including net profit, which is only one of the aforementioned components.[41]

The question indirectly asked whether the Saudi income tax is less favorable than zakat. Saudi Arabia appeared to admit that a violation probably occur by affirming that non-Saudis are subject to a different tax, while not directly answering in the affirmative the question of whether discrimination is currently occurring. Instead, Saudi officials provided examples in which foreigners might be treated more favorably than Saudis, such as tax holidays[42] and tax incentives. The Saudi officials argued that because foreign firms will not generate a profit during the process of establishing a business, no tax will be imposed, while Saudis will be subject to the

[39]GATS art. 17.

[40]Saudi Arabia Accession Documents: World Trade WT/ACC/SPEC/SAU/3 (September 24, 1997) (Saudi Accession).

[41]Saudi Arabia Accession Documents: World Trade WT/ACC/SPEC/SAU/3 (September 24, 1997) (Saudi Accession).

[42]Tax holidays are abolished in the new tax law.

zakat even during establishment. This, however, is only true temporarily; in addition, almost all firms will conduct business only if there are profits, and the sooner profits are realized the better for the business. Foreign-owned firms will be treated differently once operations commence. The negotiators were arguing an exceptional case, not normal business treatment. Without entering into details, one factor remains true: a Saudi business has a different tax obligation, which most likely is less burdensome than the income tax imposed on non-Saudis.

The income tax burden may not necessarily be heavier than zakat, but it may be the case as indicated by the question, which stated that the zakat is *sharply* lower than the income tax. The last provision in this question, along with its answer, was this:

> Q. (c) Would Saudi Arabia please state for the record its position on the WTO consistency of this taxation system in light of Article III of the GATT 1994 and whether it believes that there are implications for national treatment and non-discrimination in the application of such a system?
>
> R (c) Non-Saudi business entities are subject to Income Tax while Saudi entities are subject to Zakat. The former is income-based while the latter is wealth-based. Thus, there is no automatic preference given to domestic interests in the area of taxation.

Saudi Arabia in its service commitment did reserve service-related zakat treatment for Saudis only. It did add the following text as a limitation to its national treatment duty stating that "Non Saudi business entities and foreign natural persons are subject to income tax while Saudi entities and Saudi individuals are subject to Zakat ... All modes of supply: In all respects other than Zakat, taxation measures will be applied in conformity with Articles II and XVII and all other relevant provisions of the GATS."[43]

Reading the Saudi response illustrates this important concept: a visible religious tax system, the zakat, has gone beyond domestic confinement to become an international concern.

3.5 Possible Solutions

There are several potential resolutions to the Saudi tax problem, as outlined below:

3.5.1 Ignoring International Practice

Saudi Arabia may ignore international practice and continue to act as it has been. This can be justified based on the sovereignty concept as well as on the practice of

[43]Saudi Arabia accession documents, GATS/SC/141 (March 29, 2006).

other nations. Saudi Arabian law, linked fundamentally to Islamic principles, is in fact in a difficult position where potential alterations in its current system could violate a constitutional provision as stated in the Saudi Basic Law.[44] Although equality in taxation would require a prohibition of tax discrimination against international commerce, the idea of sovereignty works to grant nations an independent judgment to evaluate whether to equalize domestic and foreign persons (Warren 2001, p. 167). Article 1 of the Basic Law (*See* Tarazi 1993, p. 258) of Saudi Arabia provides that "the Kingdom of Saudi Arabia is a sovereign Arab Islamic state with Islam as its religion; God's Book and the Sunnah of His Prophet, God's prayers and peace be upon him, are its constitution."[45]

Religious sovereignty also supports this approach. Some traditional Islamic scholars have argued that the only accepted fiscal obligation that can be imposed on Moslems is zakat, and that any alternative method of taxing Moslems is considered invalid (Alkrdawy 1994, p. 1035). Article 23 of the Basic Law says, "The state protects Islam; it implements its *Shari'ah*; it orders people to do right and shun evil; it fulfills the duty regarding God's call."[46] The Saudi government has a duty to implement Islamic law and principles, and since zakat is viewed as an obligation imposed by God, it is to be implemented by the government. Thus, it seems that non-Moslems should be subject to a tax system that is suitable to their beliefs other than zakat, or just what the Saudi government is doing: subjecting non-Saudi investors and traders,[47] who mainly are not Moslems, to different taxes.

This is the first line of defense: ignore and pay the price if there is a price to be paid. Assuming there is a violation, the Saudi can answer by welcoming any additional tariffs imposed on their products.

3.5.2 WTO Exception Articles

A more promising defense that may be raised by the Saudi government is applicability of the exception articles of the WTO. Article XX of the GATT provides that a member can violate the WTO rules by implementing measures that are not "applied in a manner which would constitute a means of arbitrary or unjustifiable discrimination between countries where the same conditions prevail, or a disguised restriction on international trade." These measures include the "adoption or enforcement by any contracting party of measures: (a) necessary to protect public morals."[48]

---

[44]Basic Law art. 1.

[45]Basic Law art. 1.

[46]Basic Law art. 23.

[47]Under some conditions Muslim foreigners, such as Gulf countries' citizens, are granted zakat treatment. Fundamentalists argued for granting zakat treatment to all Muslims trading or conducting business in the Kingdom. In fact, excluding them is viewed by the fundamentalists as a sign of Westernization. *See*, e.g., Yusuf (1999); *see also* Taymiyah (1999).

[48]GATT art. XX(a).

Article XIV of the GATS is almost identical, stating that "[s]ubject to the requirement that such measures are not applied in a manner which would constitute a means of arbitrary or unjustifiable discrimination between countries where like conditions prevail, or a disguised restriction on trade in services, nothing in this Agreement shall be construed to prevent the adoption or enforcement by any Member of measures: (a) necessary to protect public morals or to maintain public order . . . ."

The obvious question is whether or not zakat should be considered a public morals issue. Is implementation of different taxing systems necessary to protect public morals in Saudi Arabia? Two main issues must be resolved in order to answer this question: (1) the meaning of "public morals" and (2) the meaning of "necessary."

3.5.2.1 Public Morals

The concept of public morals[49] and their protection is problematic, because the goals of international organizations to promote "economic growth and wealth of states ... may not coincide with the 'public morals' of participating states" (Feddersen 1998, p. 75). The concept of public morals refers "to standards of right and wrong that can be described as belonging to, affecting, or concerning the community or nation."[50]

Public morals are an elusive concept, yet extremely important; in fact, the US State Department stated that retaining the moral exception in international treaties was "necessary" (Charnovitz 1998, pp. 689, 706). An objective determination of the concept's true meaning is difficult; any measures can possibly be characterized as public morals in order to avoid following rules. Surprisingly, such misuse has been limited; however, there is clearly a risk in leaving the subject uncontrolled, which could lead to misuse or overuse[51] and consequently overwhelm the WTO, which is why it is not invoked.

There is no accepted objective standard with which to evaluate the concept; in fact, this can happen even domestically, because of the differences among the locals where there must be a "prevailing system of public morals" (Cooley and McLaughlin 1898, p. 226) that must ignore some minorities. Some issues have gained universal agreement, such as the immorality of child pornography and

[49]Historically on grounds of public morals. *See*, e.g., Boyer (1978); Lynch and Loriaux (2000).

[50]US Gambling case, Report of the Panel ¶ 6.457.

[51]Commentators have already started arguing to include many issues, including women's and workers' rights. Howse (1999, p. 131) (arguing for inclusion of international labor standards in WTO through a public morals exception); Jarvis (2000, p. 219) (arguing for use of public morals exception to protect women's rights); Lopez-Hurtado (2002, p. 719) (discussing WTO compatibility of government-sponsored social labeling initiatives). *See* Rosas (2003, pp. 75, 78) (suggesting "certain cultural or religious traditions" as example of GATT drafters' original intent for inclusion of a public morals clause).

slavery, although how such acts should be punished will likely differ from country to country and from time to time. Most issues, however, must be determined locally, and it is these issues that are more likely to cause problems for the international trade regime. The crucial inquiry that arises is: on what basis should the WTO Panel evaluate a country's assertion that an issue is justified as "public morals," given that such interests are likely to be strongly "geographically localized"? (Marwell 2006, pp. 802, 805).

Some have argued that the drafters intended the vagueness of the term so that the terms could "evolve" with the society and international law, and be adaptable to the change in time and circumstances (Pauwelyn 2003, p. 267; *see also* McGee 1995; Baron and Dunoff 1996, p. 431; Armstrong 1975, p. 19). On the other hand, Charnovitz has argued that the meaning of "public morals" was known all along: "the negotiators knew what it meant... similar to those typically included in commercial treaties" (Charnovitz 1998, p. 702). He also noted that the meaning had "been admitted through long-established international practice, as recorded in a large number of commercial treaties, to be indispensable and compatible with the principle of freedom of trade" (Charnovitz 1998, p. 706). After examination of the history and preparatory work of GATT, he concluded that "there is clear evidence that opium, obscene photos, and lottery tickets were perceived as coming within the scope of the moral exception" (Charnovitz 1998, p. 707). In addition, he cited slavery, alcohol, narcotics, pornography, firearms, blasphemous articles, products linked to animal cruelty, prize fight films, and abortion-inducing drugs as within the context of public morals.[52]

Public morality has not been invoked under the WTO[53] until recently. Under the structure of GATT and GATS, the general exceptions clauses are invoked as a defense by a member state after a showing by the complaining state that the respondent state violated a trade obligation.[54] The US Gambling case[55] was the first case to center directly around the issue of public morality.

Any measure claimed to be related to public morals must meet the GATT Article XX test. It "must not only come under one or another of the particular exceptions paragraphs (a) to (j) – listed under Article XX; it must also satisfy the requirements

[52]Charnovitz (1998, pp. 705–713) (surveying historical evidence of contemporary understanding of morals clauses in bilateral and multilateral international trade agreements prior to GATT).

[53]Recent legal scholarship reviewed WTO Trade Policy Reviews and revealed that "products currently subject to morality-based import restrictions include alcohol and pornographic or obscene materials to name just a few" Marwell (2006, pp. 802, 817–818) (citing also child pornography, gambling equipment or games of chance, hate propaganda, illegal drugs, lottery tickets, non-kosher meat products, posters depicting crime or violence, stolen goods, treasonous or seditious materials, counterfeit money, automobile radar detectors, and videotapes and laser discs).

[54]Appellate Body Report, United States – Measures Affecting Imports of Woven Wool Shirts and Blouses from India 15–16, WT/DS33/AB/R (Apr. 25, 1997) (discussing the burden of proof imposed on a complaining party to establish an initial violation of WTO agreements).

[55]Appellate Body Report, United States – Measures Affecting the Cross-Border Supply of Gambling and Betting Services 5, 296, WT/DS285/AB/R (Apr. 7, 2005).

imposed by the opening clauses of Article XX. The analysis is, in other words, two-tiered: first, provisional justification by reason of characterization of the measure under XX(g); second, further appraisal of the same measure under the introductory clauses of Article XX."[56] The sequence of steps "indicated the fundamental structure and logic of Article XX."[57] Thus, to qualify for the exception, a measure must be on the referenced list and must also satisfy the requirements of the chapeau that the measure is justifiable and not arbitrary, as well as the least trade-restrictive measure.[58] Requiring that the chapeau be satisfied is "one expression of the principle of good faith. One application of this general principle, the application ... prohibits the abusive exercise of a state's rights."[59]

The AB also wrote that the "task of interpreting and applying the chapeau is, hence, essentially the delicate one of locating and marking out a line of equilibrium between the right of a Member to invoke an exception under Article XX and the rights of the other Members under varying substantive provisions...so that neither of the competing rights will cancel out the other and thereby distort and nullify or impair the balance of rights and obligations constructed by the Members themselves in that Agreement." This is difficult in practice, as use of the exception to violate the rules of the GATT by itself manifests the desire to deviate from the original bargaining between the country using the exceptions and other countries. The AB ultimately admitted that finding a balance is difficult, and offered the excuse that "the location of the line of equilibrium, as expressed in the chapeau, is not fixed and unchanging; the line moves as the kind and the shape of the measures at stake vary and as the facts making up specific cases differ."[60]

Article XIV of the GATS provides that measures that are not applied "in a manner which would constitute a means of arbitrary or unjustifiable discrimination between countries where like conditions prevail, or a disguised restriction on trade in services, nothing in this Agreement shall be construed to prevent the adoption or enforcement by any Member of measures: (a) necessary to protect public morals or to maintain public order ... ."

The Article was tested in the US Gambling case. In October 2004, Antigua and Barbuda brought a complaint against the United States, alleging that some of the US federal and state laws constitute a ban on the cross-border provision of Internet gambling services, allegedly a facial violation of US concessions for liberalization

[56]Appellate Body Report on US – Gasoline WTO Dispute Settlement Panel, United States Standards for Reformulated and Conventional Gasoline, WTO Doc., WT/DS2/R (Jan. 29, 1996) [hereinafter US-Gasoline].

[57]Panel Report, United States – Import Prohibition of Certain Shrimp and Shrimp Products, WT/DS58/R (98-1710), 15 May 1998, ¶ 7.28.

[58]WTO Appellate Body Report: United States – Import Prohibition of Certain Shrimp and Shrimp Products (Oct. 12, 1998), 38 I.L.M. 118, 123–24, ¶ 157.

[59]WTO Appellate Body Report: United States – Import Prohibition of Certain Shrimp and Shrimp Products (Oct. 12, 1998), 38 I.L.M. 118, ¶¶ 158–159.

[60]WTO Appellate Body Report: United States – Import Prohibition of Certain Shrimp and Shrimp Products (Oct. 12, 1998), 38 I.L.M. 118, ¶¶ 158–159.

of trade in services under GATS. In response, the United States invoked the "public morals" clause of GATS.

The Panel began its analysis by noting they "are well aware that there may be sensitivities associated with the interpretation of the terms 'public morals' and 'public order' in the context of Article XIV. In the Panel's view, the content of these concepts for Members can vary in time and space, depending upon a range of factors, including prevailing social, cultural, ethical and religious values."[61] In addition, "Members should be given some scope to define and apply for themselves the concepts of 'public morals' and 'public order' in their respective territories, according to their own systems and scales of values."[62]

The Panel then attempted to define "public morals," beginning with a literal meaning: "we turn to the *Shorter Oxford English Dictionary*. 'Public' is defined therein as: 'Of or pertaining to the people as a whole; belonging to, affecting, or concerning the community or nation.'[63] The word 'morals' (noun, pl.) is defined therein as: '[...] habits of life with regard to right and wrong conduct.'"[64] The Panel stated that it "considers the term 'public morals' denotes standards of right and wrong conduct maintained by or on behalf of a community or nation,"[65] that the term "refers to the 'preservation of the fundamental interests of a society,'[66] as reflected in public policy and law," and that these "fundamental interests can relate, *inter alia*, to standards of law, security and morality."[67]

The Panel referred to various examples of "supplementary means of interpretation,"[68] citing international law decisions;[69] examples from the WTO members which have at some point relied on "public morals" grounds[70] to justify measures such as in Israel and the Philippines;[71] and judicial rulings in other jurisdictions.[72] On this basis, the Panel concluded that "measures prohibiting gambling and betting services...could fall within the scope of Article XIV(a) if they are enforced in

[61]Panel Report, US-Gambling, ¶ 6.461.

[62]Panel Report, US-Gambling, ¶ 6.461.

[63]Panel Report, US-Gambling, ¶ 6.463.

[64]Panel Report, US-Gambling, ¶¶ 6.663–4.

[65]Panel Report, US-Gambling, ¶ 6.665.

[66]Panel Report, US-Gambling, ¶ 6.467.

[67]Panel Report, US-Gambling, ¶ 6.676.

[68]Panel Report, US-Gambling, ¶ 6.470.

[69]For example, the Panel cited two ECJ decisions regarding the right of member states to enact national legislation relating to gambling-related activities (specifically, cross-border access to lotteries and the operation of gambling equipment). *See* Panel Report, US-Gambling, ¶ 6.473.

[70]Panel Report, US-Gambling, 6.471.

[71]Israel prohibits the importation of lottery tickets and the Philippines restricts foreign ownership of gambling operations. *See* Trade Policy Review – Israel – Report by the Secretariat, WT/TPR/S/58, Table III.8 (1999) and Trade Policy Review – The Philippines – Report by the Secretariat, WT/TPR/S/59, Table III.11 (1999).

[72]Panel Report, US-Gambling, ¶ 6.473.

pursuance of policies, the object and purpose of which is to 'protect public morals'."[73]

The resolution of this case, "at least implicitly, suggests that states invoking a public morals defense will be expected to present evidence of similar practice by other states. Taken to an extreme, the Gambling doctrine might be read as implying that states cannot unilaterally define public morals" (Marwell 2006, p. 817).

3.5.2.2 Necessary

A measure violating the WTO rules must be necessary to implement the public morals. In the US Gambling case, the Panel and AB examined the issue of necessity by taking into account the *Korea – Beef* case.[74] In that case, the AB discussed the meaning of the term "necessary," concluding that is something "that cannot be dispensed with or done without, requisite, essential, needful."[75] The AB in that case concluded that "a 'necessary' measure is, in this continuum, located significantly closer to the pole of 'indispensable'."[76]

The Appellate Body also explained that "necessity" is "an *objective* standard."[77] In this regard, it said, while "a Member's characterization of a measure's objectives and of the effectiveness of its regulatory approach – as evidenced, for example, by texts of statutes, legislative history, and pronouncements of government agencies or officials – will be relevant in determining whether the measure is, objectively, 'necessary'," a Panel "is not bound by these characterizations . . . and may also find guidance in the structure and operation of the measure and in contrary evidence proffered by the complaining party." The Appellate Body then referred to its interpretation of this standard in *Korea – Beef*, in which it explained that "whether a measure is 'necessary' should be determined through 'a process of weighing and balancing a series of factors'."

The AB noted that there are "two factors that, in most cases, will be relevant to a panel's determination of the 'necessity' of a measure, although not necessarily exhaustive of factors that might be considered. One factor is the contribution of the measure to the realization of the ends pursued by it; the other factor is the restrictive impact of the measure on international commerce"[78] and that "the requirement, under Article XIV(a), that a measure be 'necessary' – that is, that there be no 'reasonably available', WTO-consistent alternative – reflects the shared

[73]Panel Report, US-Gambling, ¶ 6.474.

[74]Appellate Body Report, *Korea – Measures Affecting Imports of Fresh, Chilled and Frozen Beef*, WT/DS161/AB/R, WT/DS169/AB/R, adopted January 10, 2001, DSR 2001:I, 5.

[75]AB Korea, ¶ 160 (citing 2 The New Shorter Oxford English Dictionary 1895 [1993]).

[76]Appellate Body, Korea – Beef, ¶ 160.

[77]AB, p. 304.

[78]AB, p. 306.

understanding of Members that substantive GATS obligations should not be deviated from lightly."[79]

3.5.3 *Saudi Arabia and Public Morals*

Saudi Arabia can likely use public morality to justify its imposition of different tax rates on Saudis and on non-Saudis. First, the zakat system emerged from a religious value that is shared among the nation's people; in the Panel's view, the content of public morals "can vary in time and space, depending upon a range of factors, including prevailing social, cultural, ethical and *religious values*."[80] Zakat is a prevailing social and cultural value in Saudi Arabia, without a doubt. Saudi Arabia "should be given some scope to define and apply for [itself] the concepts of 'public morals' and 'public order' in [its] respective territory, according to [its] own systems and scales of values."[81] Zakat would be most likely considered a public moral issue. On this religious basis, the Panel most likely would conclude that "measures taxing [Saudis differently]. . .could fall within the scope of Article XIV (a) if they are enforced in pursuance of policies, the object and purpose of which is to 'protect public morals'."[82]

Is zakat the least restrictive measure? This question, and that of how to impose another tax system on non-Saudis, is controversial and difficult to answer. Equalizing tax burdens on both Saudis and non-Saudis would not be a violation of Islam, nor would it be a violation of any WTO agreements; in fact, it would be in line with the WTO rules prohibiting favorable treatment. The public morals exception will not shelter alternate taxing systems unless there be no "reasonably available," WTO-consistent alternative. What if Saudi Arabia imposes zakat-like on non-Saudis? Again, the issue seems to go back to the zakat/tax incidence; equalizing the burden is the critical factor in arriving at a satisfying result.

3.5.4 *Ignoring Zakat Alternative*

This approach would require imposing a modern tax system on Saudis and non-Saudis on an equal basis, for example, by imposing a uniform income tax. Zakat would be left to be distributed voluntarily by Saudis, after payment of income tax, with the possibility of allowing a deduction therefor. This system would be in conformity with international tax principles, and would facilitate Saudi

[79]AB, p. 308.

[80]Panel Report, US-Gambling, ¶ 6.461.

[81]Panel Report, US-Gambling, ¶ 6.461.

[82]Panel Report, US-Gambling, ¶ 6.474.

participation in the international tax community by helping accelerate the creation of new tax treaties while avoiding the discrimination issues designated by the OECD model. More importantly, the WTO requirement of implementing national treatment policy would be satisfied, although Saudi Arabia could still impose additional taxes on those who were in different circumstances, such as withholding taxes on interest or royalties, or special taxes on products that are not similar or like domestic products.

This approach lacks Islamic theoretical justification. It depends solely on government authority, or one which may be vaguely viewed by some liberal-religious thinkers as a *siyasah* approach. *Siyasah*, briefly, means that a ruler can make laws or regulations as long as they don't conflict with basic fundamental Islamic principles. It is agreed, however that *Fiqh*, which is the other part of the Islamic legal system and concerned mainly and arguably with private law, should be handled by only religious scholars.[83]

Additionally, because zakat is considered a form of worship, Moslems pay the tax not only because they are required to do so, but also because by not doing so they believe they are committing a sin. Any attempt to eliminate zakat entirely, therefore, would likely be impossible in Saudi Arabia, even if such action were accepted voluntarily. Well-known conservative Islamic scholars,[84] citing specific precedents, argue that the only compulsory fiscal obligation mentioned in the Koran is zakat, and that introducing new methods of taxing Saudi-Moslems, or eliminating such a tax, stands in conflict with this principle. Those scholars argued that collecting zakat is also a compulsory obligation on the State. Thus, the Saudi Arabian government, as any other government bound to Islamic rules and as stated in its constitution, is required to collect zakat, just as it is also required to determine the amount according to the Koran's zakat principles, which specify eight expenditure channels.

Finally, it is worth noting that, after the first income tax law was enacted in Saudi Arabia, it was supposed to apply to both Saudis and non-Saudis. Four months later following enactment, due to enormous pressure from Islamists, the tax law was modified to apply only to non-Saudis (Abdulaziz 1974, p. 549).[85] The regulation issued by the Ministry of Finance and National Economy stated that zakat would be imposed and enforced instead of the proposed income tax law.[86] Six years later, the law was again modified to state that income tax law is imposed on non-Saudis.[87]

---

[83]The distinction between *siyasah* and *fiqh* is a very controversial. *See*, e.g., Taymiyah (2000).

[84]There are numerous sources. *See*, e.g., Mohammed Al-Albany, lecture: Ruling on taxes under Islam, stating that one has no financial obligation except zakat except in urgent and unexpected circumstances, such as wars. http://audio.islamweb.net/audio/index.php?page=FullContent&audioid=109346. Also, Safer Alhowlaiy, a very conservative Saudi scholar, argues against taxation altogether. *See* http://www.alhawali.com/index.cfm?method=home.SubContent&contentID=4136&keywords=%D8%B6%D8%B1%D9%8A%D8%A8%D8%A9.

[85]This book is perhaps the only book documenting the tax history in modern Saudi Arabia.

[86]Mistrials Regulation No. 340 (1956).

[87]Old Tax Law art. 1.

3.6 Conclusion

Any resolution regarding what may be viewed as discriminatory tax treatment by a religiously affected tax system as the case in Saudi Arabia needs to be evaluated carefully in order not to upset the people who the law is supposed to serve. Three elements are important to succeed. First, if there is an internal change, there must be a religious argument, not an international trade liberalization argument, to defend a new system when a fundamentalist objection is raised. Second, the ultimately adopted tax system should be as consistent with international practice as possible. All of this can be done much more effectively if there are "soft" laws and some sort of international guidelines.

The main purpose of this chapter is to show that the deep values that are attached to, mixed with, and intermingled within the tax system of a WTO member, that is, the tax system of Saudi Arabia. This should show the difficulty facing the tax and trade relation under the WTO. Clearly, Saudi Arabia cannot amend the *Koran*, but it can try to work to influence the WTO.

The WTO and Islamic principles need to be examined together for the benefit of current and future governments. By the same token, without appreciation of the real issues facing Islamic nations, WTO members and agencies will not take into account the specific circumstances and levels of difficulty that Islamic nations face. A framework is needed that can assist WTO members and officials in understanding why they might need to ease requirements or take certain circumstances into consideration; this is religion, a deeply rooted value in the society, not a trade issue. WTO policy-makers will be in a better position to act fairly and implement policy wisely when they can assess the contradictions faced internally by Islamic nations.

References

Abdulaziz (1974) Allonym, ntham drab fe alislam and tatbegah fee alsuaid (Tax law in Islam and possible application in Saudi Arabia)

Albana M (1982) Ahkam and drab fe alsaudia (Zakat and tax rules in Saudi Arabia)

Alford WP (1992) Pressuring the pirate. LA Times (Jan. 12):M5

Alkrdawy Y (1994) Fiqh al-Zakat, Drasah Mokarnh l Ahkamha wa Falsfutha fe Dow A al-Koran and al-Sunna, 11th edn. Scientific publishing centre, King Abdulaziz University, Jeddah

Al-Sultan (1995) Tax and Zakat accounting

Armstrong CS (1975) American import controls and morality in international trade: an analysis of section 307 of the Tariff Act of 1930. NYU J Int'l L & Pol 8:19

Baron JB, Dunoff JL (1996) Against market rationality: moral critiques of economic analysis in legal theory. Cardozo L Rev 17:431

Boyer P (1978) Urban masses and moral order in America 1820–1920. Harvard University Press, Cambridge

Charnovitz S (1998) The moral exception in trade policy. Va J Int'l L 38:689, 706

Cooley TM, McLaughlin AC (1898) The general principles of constitutional law in the United States of America. Little Brown, Boston

Feddersen CT (1998) Substantive law in international economic relations: the public morals of GATT's article XX(a) and "conventional" rules of interpretation. Minn J Global Trade 7:75

Hanna C (1997) Initial thoughts on classifying the major Japanese business entities under the check-the-box regulations. S Meth Univ L Rev 51

Howse R (1999) The World Trade Organization and the protection of workers' rights. J Small & Emerging Bus L 3:131

Hunter S, Malik H (2005) Modernization, democracy, and Islam. Praeger, Westport, CT

Janardhan N (2006) Expatriates face a changing reality in Gulf countries. http://yaleglobal.yale.edu/article.print?id=8333

Jarvis LM (2000) Women's rights and the public morals exception of GATT Article 20. Mich J Int'l L 22:219

Lopez-Hurtado C (2002) Social labelling and WTO law. J Int'l Econ L 5:719

Lynch C, Loriaux M (2000) Law and moral action in world politics. University of Minnesota Press, Minneapolis

Marwell JC (2006) Trade and morality: the WTO public morals exception after gambling. NYU L Rev 81:802, 805

McGee RW (1995) The moral case for free trade. J World Trade 29

Pauwelyn J (2003) Conflict of norms in public international law: how WTO Law relates to other rules of international law. Cambridge University Press, Cambridge

Rosas A (2003) Commercial values and the world trade system: building on article XX. In: Kim Van der Borght (ed.) Essays on the future of the WTO: finding a new balance. CameronMay, London

Salim A (2006) The influential legacy of Dutch islamic policy on the formation of zakat (alms) law in modern Indonesia. Pac Rim L & Pol'y 15:683

Tarazi M (1993) Recent development: Saudi Arabia's new basic laws: the struggle for participatory Islamic government. Harv Int'l L J 34

Taymiyah I (1999) Fatawa al-kubra (The major rulings)

Taymiyah I (2000) Al-Siyasah al-shariyah fi islah al-rai wa-al-raiyah (Acceptable methods to improve the ruler and the ruled)

Vogel F (2000) Islamic law and legal system: studies of Saudi Arabia. Brill, Boston

Warren AC Jr (2001) Income tax discrimination against international commerce. Tax L Rev 54:131

Yusuf A (1999) Kitab al-kharaj (The revenue). Dar al Ma'rifah, Beirut

Part II
Analysis

Part II will analyze the problem of trade and tax separation, attempting to digest the conflicting issues in an attempt to draw a clear picture of how to go from the problem to any solution. Chapter 4 will review how scholars characterize the problem relationship between trade and tax. It will also examine how and what other scholars have contributed to solving this problem. As in any problem, people differ in approaching the core issues because of different perspectives, but their differences enrich this work significantly, because they suggest ways to go about tackling this issue. The trick is to avoid the drawbacks of these approaches and retain and build upon their strengths to develop a more comprehensive platform within which to operate to solve the problem of tax and trade issues.

Since scholars have raised serious concerns explicitly and implicitly regarding how to solve the problem of fragmentation, the remaining chapters will answer these concerns, or will, at a minimum, remove some doubts and challenge some objections in order to illustrate that the problem is solvable within the WTO.

Chapter 5 covers the possible objection that trade and tax issues are incompatible. It will start with the sovereignty issue, namely that tax decisions cannot be left to an international organization. It is a very legitimate concern, which this author shares in large part, so Chap. 5 does not attempt to argue otherwise. Instead, this chapter illustrates that the sovereignty issue can be, and has been, misused. Though sovereignty justifications still exist, their "voice" should be toned down. Recent international experience can also shed light on previous experiences, illustrating the notion that sovereignty is not absolute. EU's experience, with respect to income tax, will illustrate this point. Finally, to answer the compatibility concern, this chapter provides a historical background of tax treaties, attempting to show the commercial component behind the effort of their establishment. Then, the history addresses commercial treaties, in an attempt to show the tax implications, which were clearly visible. This chapter will show that tax and trade can be combined under one organization, because they have been combined within single treaties sometime in the past (and in the future as the WTO discussion will show).

Chapter 6 analyzes important WTO agreements to show the relation between tax and trade. It starts with the GATT, analyzing its legal texts and addressing some crucial problems emerging from the MFN and NT, the most important of which is the direct tax application to products. GATS is then covered. Though it is fundamentally different than GATT in that it is something of an optional agreement (countries choose what to commit themselves to with respect to the most important principles), it is remained to be an interesting agreement because of its implications for taxation. The subsidies agreement, SCM, will follow. In it, a discussion of the text, as well as some cases, will be presented to show the intermingling of tax and trade.

Chapter 4
Literature Review

A solution is necessary to the potential problem of how to treat income tax issues that can affect trade matters regulated by the WTO. Should tax issues be addressed within the WTO as part of a new agreement? Should tax issues be singled out, expressly excluded from the WTO and left to be dealt with by the OECD or other international organizations? Or should some tax issues be included and others excluded? If so, how should the determination be made, and why? Should a dispute including both tax and trade issues be resolved under the WTO dispute system, or should such be resolved diplomatically outside the WTO? No single answer exists to any of these questions, and most scholars who have dealt with these issues have differed in their opinions; in fact, some have changed their opinions over time.

This chapter will cover important scholarly works that represent the full spectrum from arguments for the exclusion of tax issues from the WTO to arguments for the inclusion of some or all tax issues under the WTO.

Notably, only few scholars have written about the tax-trade relationship at any length, because the issue arose recently and few scholars can understand trade and tax together, since most tend to focus only in one area or the other. Moreover, those few have tackled the issue of trade and tax issues only recently, so the subject has not yet been fully explored. The relationship is a relatively recent phenomenon, as before the WTO came into existence, the GATT included only limited implications for tax matters, especially with the understanding that only indirect taxes were subject to the GATT. After the WTO arose, specifically after the change in the legal dispute mechanism[1] and following the introduction of the SCM and the GATS, changes in legal issues led to the potential for an increase in conflicts and serious consequences arising therefrom.

Five major works will be discussed herein, prior to presenting the author's proposed recommendation. Virtually, all international tax experts are in agreement

---

[1]Previously, under the GATT jurisprudence, all decisions required the consensus of all parties, including the losing party. Under the WTO, dispute settlement rulings are binding unless there is a consensus not to implement them, and this consensus must include the prevailing party.

T. Althunayan, *Dealing with the Fragmented International Legal Environment: WTO, International Tax and Internal Tax Regulations*,
DOI 10.1007/978-3-642-04678-0_4, © Springer-Verlag Berlin Heidelberg 2010

that tax rules, in principle, are not in conflict with trade rules, since both sets of rules aim to serve the same or similar goals, with an ultimate view to benefiting the welfare of the people. However, scholars are not in agreement regarding how to deal with international taxation issues in a globalized world, especially when interacting with trade issues governed by the WTO.

There exist three major schools of thought as to the proper course of action: (1) exclusion of tax issues (Green 1998, p. 79) altogether from the WTO, with taxation addressed under the diplomatic umbrella;[2] (2) inclusion in the WTO of only those "pure" tax issues that affect the WTO (McDaniel 2004, p. 277); and (3) creation of a separate, independent tax organization (Brauner 2005, p. 268).

Professor Robert Green represents the first approach. He has suggested excluding tax issues from trade agreements, stating, "The legalistic GATT dispute settlement system is not an ideal model for the resolution of intergovernmental income tax disputes" (Green 1998, p. 139).

Professor Paul McDaniel leads the second school of thought. He divides tax issues into two categories based on his expenditure budget model: if a tax meets his criteria (i.e., if it is a subsidy), it is subject to inclusion under the trade treaty with its dispute settlement mechanism. If not, McDaniel argues, then the issue should resolved by a diplomatic approach.

The third school of thought is represented, most recently, by Professor Yariv Brauner, who argues that the optimal solution is to create an independent international organization to deal with tax issues, based on the contention that the WTO is too weak to handle them.

In addition to these three approaches, at one time Professor Reuven Avi-Yonah suggested that the overlap between trade and tax must be resolved, but provided no concrete guidance to resolve the dilemma (Avi-Yonah 2001, pp. 1683, 1692). Later, Avi-Yonah, with Professor Joel Slemrod, argued that the WTO may be equipped to deal with tax issues (Avi-Yonah and Slemrod 2002, pp. 533, 535). Professor Alvin Warren also agreed that there is an overlap and incoherent systematic conflict between international commerce and international taxation (Warren 2001, p. 131). He subsequently suggested, with Professor Michael Graetz, that the ECJ should not be involved in income tax issues (Graetz and Warren 2006, p. 1186), an argument that can be also applied to the WTO.

4.1 The Exclusion Approach

According to this school of thought, the diplomatic approach is the best possible practical option. Robert Green is credited with being one of the first scholars to discuss thoroughly the relationship between tax and trade issues advocating the diplomatic approach, and devoting an entire law review article, "Antilegalistic

---

[2]See Chap. 8, *infra*, for an argument that tax treaties are purely diplomatic.

Approaches to Resolving Disputes Between Governments: A Comparison of the International Tax and Trade Regimes" (Green 1998), to the analytical approach for the overlap between the two fields.

Green introduced his article by acknowledging that "international tax policy can have an enormous impact on international trade" (Green 1998, p. 78) and, moreover, that trade and tax are related, sharing the same "underlying goals, facilitating international trade and investment, and that they use similar means to achieve that goal" (Green 1998, pp. 87–88). Further, he observed that "a country can use discriminatory income tax measures directly to undercut the commitments it makes in international trade agreements" (Green 1998, p. 87).

Green's observation is crucial, because if trade and tax indeed share the same underlying goals, one might assume it is imperative that they be somehow coordinated, if not controlled entirely, by a single organization in order to ensure that the intended goals are achieved and that conflicts are prevented. In the absence of such a structure, there exists no safeguard against mismatched policies or abuse of uncoordinated systems. Yet, Green reached another conclusion.

Green noted that a number of proposals have been set forth involving the potential incorporation of income tax measures into a more sophisticated version of the GATT (Green 1998, p. 89). However, he chose to promote the option of excluding tax from any legalistic approach, emphasizing that tax treaties and trade agreements employ "radically different methods" (Green 1998, p. 79) of settling disputes. He agreed with the status quo with respect to the resolution of tax disputes diplomatically, by implementation of an "anti-legalistic approach." This is in contrast to the legalistic resolution of trade issues. Green's reasoning was that the cost is too high and the benefits too insignificant to justify a legalistic approach, arguing also that the need for the WTO to resolve trade disputes is based on two features that are typically lacking in the tax context: retaliation and lack of transparency.

Green continued by discussing non-technical tax policy issues (Green 1998, pp. 90–97). He admitted that the non-legalistic procedure, utilizing the competent authority mechanism in bilateral tax treaties, is a weak one for resolving fact-specific disputes, since the authority is only required to "endeavor" to resolve disputes, thus lacking any obligation to guarantee a successful settlement. Furthermore, Green pointed out that tax settlement is often based in such a regime upon political negotiation and compromise rather than on a neutral application of legal rules to the facts of the specific tax scenario.

Nevertheless, Green argued that this option is a better approach to tax issues for two primary reasons: unlike in the trade regime, in tax matters there is no need for a device to manage retaliatory strategies or for a tool to generate and disseminate information and increase transparency. Both can be useful, and indeed essential, in the trade regime, but are less crucial in the tax context. Trade needs to be governed by an organization using a legalistic approach in order to control retaliation and increase transparency, because in a trade regime the solution to the problems that disturb trust among nations is the development of a dispute settlement system that can interpret actions of countries as being either compliant or non-compliant with treaty obligations, and can control retaliation in cases where non-compliance occurs (Green 1998, pp. 108–109).

After discussing trade issues, Green focused on tax and highlighted the differences between the two areas. Green explained that there are two major implications associated with tax treaty violations as compared with international trade issues.

First, retaliatory strategies are likely less suitable to achieve and maintain cooperation in the tax context than with respect to trade, since as applied to trade the focus tends to be on specific industries, while tax issues cover a broader spectrum of affected parties (Green 1998, p. 118). This contention is, in the view of the author of the present study, not entirely accurate, because tax can be targeted to a particular industry or a specific country; for example, it is possible to tax only income from an exporting business, or only income from importing and exporting specific goods, such as cars, or only profits from business dealings with particular countries.

Second, Green argued, retaliatory strategies are less likely to be necessary in the tax context, because a government considering violation of a tax treaty knows that the violation would have a broad effect on foreign interests, and that any retaliation would be similarly broad-based, making tax treaty violations very risky (Green 1998, p. 118). Green then asserted, without presenting any actual numbers, that "the empirical evidence supports this conclusion: It is extremely rare for countries to retaliate in response to tax treaty violations" (Green 1998, p. 119)[3] and that retaliatory practices "are likely to be ineffective; indeed, they are seldom used in practice" (Green 1998, p. 130), diminishing the need for formal dispute settlement if the purpose of such a mechanism is to supervise retaliatory strategies.

Green then tested a hypothetical situation in which some income tax measures would be covered under trade agreements. This alternative, he argued, would create an explicit link between tax treaty obligations and trade agreement obligations, which could lead to more "narrowly targeted retaliation" (Green 1998, p. 123) and, in turn, make retaliatory strategies more effective in maintaining compliance with tax obligations (which seems to include tax under the WTO). He noted several potential problems associated with this approach, but suggested solutions for each of them, as outlined below:

[3]Empirically, it is very hard to prove that retaliation is rare. In fact, Green could not support that assertion. Citing a report saying nothing about empirical study, he stated the following: "As reported by the Federal Income Tax Project: While a partial termination [of a tax treaty] in response to a material breach is in theory possible, there is no reported instance in which this has been done with respect to an income tax treaty. Treaty partners have been understandably reluctant to take this action in light of the potentially disruptive effects on such terminations on the settled pattern of international tax relationships . . . ." *See also* OECD Committee on Fiscal Affairs (2000, p. 34). ("Member countries have so far refrained from taking retaliatory measures which all agree would not be conducive to better understanding in the international tax field against overriding legislation.") Green (1998, nn. 211, 213).

(A) Potential incompetence of the GATT (Green 1998, p. 123)[4] in dealing with tax issues – Green suggested that there exists no reason why the WTO would not be able to develop the international tax competence necessary for dealing with international tax issues.
(B) Potential perception in the WTO community that a trade retaliation against a tax obligation breach is less legitimate than retaliation against a trade obligation breach (Green 1998, p. 79) – Green wrote that "it is unlikely that trade retaliation against a breach of a tax obligation would be perceived to be as legitimate as trade retaliation against a breach of a trade obligation" (Green 1998, p. 79). This is the linkage issue, discussed extensively in the literature (see Trachtman 2002, p. 77), and even Green acknowledged that "trade retaliation that was approved by a decision of a third party panel or neutral appellate body might have greater legitimacy than unilateral tax retaliation" (Green 1998, p. 124).

Green raised the issue of legitimacy as well.[5] He admitted that an international adjudication system would not be able to provide the kind of political check on the outcome of a decision that domestic litigation allows (Green 1998, p. 133). More importantly, panel members are usually individuals from third countries; Green argues that those individuals "might have little understanding of the particular domestic norms and concerns of the countries that are parties to the dispute" (Green 1998, p. 134), and are thus less likely to be attuned than domestic judges to the will of the people. Focusing too much on domestic norms and concerns, Green seemed to downplay the need to uphold the international norms upon which WTO members have agreed.

There are additional points that serve to weaken Green's arguments. First, he stated that "notwithstanding this close relationship between international income taxation and international trade, international agreements historically have failed to link the two subjects." This contention is not entirely accurate; trade and tax have been linked before in a variety of ways, as illustrated in the history chapter of this work;[6] trade and tax were covered under one single treaty in many countries. The link has been acknowledged in the past through the granting of national treatment with regard to tax matters to citizens of a foreign contracting state. Specifically, the relationship was historically between trade and income tax, but its ramifications can be applied to the link between trade and tax in general. Green's statement was a general one, apparently contrary to the relationship, which he represented from a historical point of view, unless his intention was to refer to the more recent history of the two areas beginning in the 1920s.

[4]Avi-Yonah noted the same reason and suggested the same advice. *See* Avi-Yonah (2001, p. 1691).

[5]This was one of main reasons why Warren and Graetz rejected the inclusion of tax issues under the ECJ. *See* Graetz and Warren (2006, p. 1186).

[6]*See* Chap. 6, *infra*.

With respect to Green's basic arguments, it seems impractical to retaliate in trade only and not in tax. For example, hypothetically, increasing the income tax on American companies doing business in China by 80% would not pass undetected in the USA; a correction would have to be imposed or it can be expected that a tax war would begin and that the USA would impose similar tax burdens on Chinese companies investing in the USA. In fact, Green himself acknowledged the existence of tax retaliation. For example, he stated that violating or abusing tax rules can rarely trigger retaliation, and then proceeded to relate the stories of what happened between the USA and Canada, and the USA and the UK (Green 1998, p. 121), both situations which illustrated that retaliation is happening in the tax field.

Moreover, trade wars use taxation as a tool. Countries increase taxes on foreign products either as tariffs, or other tax forms to achieve trade goals. Thus, it could be stated that trade wars are in some way tax wars (see Conybeare 1987, p. 86; see also Ka Zeng 2004, p. 211). It should be noted that Professor Green returned to this issue, stating that there are "unpublicized tax disputes" between nations. Yet, he concluded that "the use of retaliatory strategies in the tax area, although not unheard of, is extremely rare" (Green 1998, p. 138). It is necessary to identify what Green meant in using the terms "extremely" and "rare," because the combination of both terms indicates that retaliatory strategies do not commonly exist, which by Green's own admission is not the case.

As to the transparency argument, trade is not the best example of transparency, as Green's article might lead one to believe. WTO agreements still include ambiguities and problems, and a major concern arises when more demand is placed on the WTO to increase the transparency of its decision-making process (Jackson 1996, pp. 511, 517).[7] One of the main weak points of the GATT was its secrecy.[8] The existence of non-transparent decision-making processes "has been an enormous weakness of international organizations and structures, partly from several centuries' history of diplomatic discourse, which has strongly stressed negotiation in a context of secrecy, and, in some cases, secrecy in order to prevent their home constituencies from learning what they are doing" (Jackson 1996, p. 517). Lack of transparency has been a major cause for frustration recently, which is why some countries have proposed opening up the WTO doors to more transparency; for example, the USA asked for increased transparency "by urging that some of the WTO council and committee meetings be opened up on an experimental basis to the public, just as the plenary sessions of the Ministerial Conference have been opened to observers."[9]

---

[7]*See also* Robert Keohane and Joseph Nye, *Between centralization and fragmentation: the club model of multinational cooperation and the World Trade Organization: problems of democratic legitimacy*, February 2001 (mimeograph); Stephan (1996, p. 681).

[8]*See* Nichols (1996, p. 295); Charnovitz (1996, pp. 331, 343–346); Debevoise (1998, p. 817); Schleyer (1997, p. 2275).

[9]WTO Transparency Debate, at http://www.thunderlake.com/wtotrans.html. *See also* Transparency Summary, available at http://www.cid.harvard.edu/cidtrade/issues/transparency.html.

Tax rules are themselves not always transparent. Green relied on the US tax laws and regulations example. In the USA, the laws and regulations might be characterized as transparent, but the same is not necessarily true for the rest of the world.[10] In fact, even in the USA this argument cannot be considered completely flawless; for example, some IRS dealings are kept private, including the privately issued Advanced Pricing Agreement (APA),[11] as well as the complexity of the code which can hinder achieving a high level of transparency.

Nevertheless, transparency is important and it should be a condition for tax laws. Tax affects trade, and more specifically affects FDI, which many countries struggle to attract. Without announcing relevant rules very clearly and transparently, it would be hard for any country to attract FDI, because foreign capital, goods, and persons would not risk their assets in a market where regulations are too vague. Clear rules are imperative, and the most important of these are tax rules. Thus, in theory, trade (or tax) rules can never be totally secretive if countries are willing to engage in international relations, so the importance of the WTO making them transparent could be deemed a mere statement of the obvious. Trade rules must be known if countries are to import or export goods, services, or capital; otherwise, the simple deduction is that countries do not want trade, since producers would not send their products abroad without knowing the rules of the recipient nation.

Despite these reservations, Green's article supporting the exclusion of tax issues from the WTO does make sense in the context of local values and the strict legal enforcement under the WTO. As religion and culture cannot be governed by one globalized international organization, it may be argued that tax is a very localized issue. Tax serves major goals, such as redistribution of income, guidance of the national economy, and the provision of social insurance for local people; this strengthens the argument that tax decisions should not be made by the WTO. It is also up to each government individually, as a matter of "sovereignty," to decide its own budget and how to fund it. It may be further argued that the WTO is at risk of being destroyed because of its involvement in local issues and its disregard for legitimate national regulatory policies. It is certainly within the realm of possibility, and even likely, that the WTO will act improperly, especially with respect to a very sensitive issue like tax. Even though tax and trade have common goals, they approach those goals differently. The best approach towards a resolution of the current dilemma is to have tax matters resolved under an anti-legalistic system. This is the thrust of Green's suggestion, regardless of his specific reasoning. This author agrees that it is important to maintain some flexibility with respect to tax issues, but not outside the WTO, as will be described later on.

Green's opinion subsequently seems to change (Green 2002, p. 107).

---

[10]In Saudi Arabia, for example, tax cases are not published.

[11]The IRS maintained that the content of APA was privileged taxpayer information subject to confidentiality under I.R.C. § 6103. For a general overview, *see* Ring (2000, p. 143). *See also* Turro (1992, p. 709).

He suggested that "[i]f tax measures were brought under the scope of trade and investment agreements to a greater extent, the explicit linkages between tax issues and non-tax issues would be increased. This could have the beneficial effect of expanding the possibilities for agreement, since countries could trade non-tax concessions for tax concessions (and vice versa). It could also expand the possibilities for retaliation of compensatory concessions in the event of treaty breaches" (Green 2002, p. 112). The only disadvantage he mentioned is that such a link "could make it more difficult for negotiating countries to reach a stable bargain. Finally, the increased salience of linkages could cause non-tax related trade and investment disputes to spill over into tax regimes" (Green 2002, p. 113).

It should be noted that in his recent article, Green either changed his mind or the forum for the latter was not conductive to a deeper expression or analysis of the issue. In any case, Green has done the best work in documenting the negotiation process of the GATS and income tax, and he is the first to explore directly the possibility of incorporating tax under the WTO. Although he was against such incorporation in his first article, he subsequently leaned toward including at least some income tax issues under the WTO.

4.2 Partial Tax Inclusion Approach

The Partial Tax Inclusion approach to tax and trade is aimed at striking a balance between trade and tax rules affecting trade regimes. Professor Paul McDaniel supports this idea, most recently in his article "Trade and Taxation, & The David R. Tillinghast Lecture: Trade Agreements and Income Taxation: Interactions, Conflicts, And Resolutions" (McDaniel 2004, p. 275).

Subjecting tax rules affecting trade agreements to the trade regime is an excellent approach to dealing with this sensitive subject. It is a compromise between ignoring tax issues altogether from the perspective of trade and including all tax issues blindly under the trade regime. The only problem with this approach is its practicality, in that it is very difficult, if not impossible, to identify factors according to which "pure tax" could be separated from disguised tax. Part of this problem stems from the fact that the focus tends to be on the US tax system and like systems, disregarding other tax systems which are fundamentally different.

McDaniel, relying on his previous work (McDaniel 2001, p. 1621), reached three main conclusions:

1. A normative income tax structure and free trade principles are not in conflict with one another.
2. A nation's tax system should have normative provisions that are outside the scope of trade agreements and governed exclusively by bilateral tax treaties.
3. Subsidies provided through a normative tax system, or tax expenditures, should be scrutinized by trade agreement regimes in the same way as are direct subsidies (McDaniel 2004, pp. 275–276).

Six crucial factors distinguish the normative tax structure from disguised subsidies. If a tax system were to meet those six factors, then it would be beyond the jurisdiction of the WTO or any other international organization; otherwise, some taxes could actually be disguised subsidies, which the author called "tax expenditures," and which he argued should be subject to scrutiny. Accordingly, to identify the normative tax system, there are six normative provisions, distinguishing real tax from disguised tax:

1. What is the tax base?
2. What are the tax rates?
3. Who is to pay the tax (the taxable unit)?
4. When is the tax to be paid (accounting rules)?
5. How is the tax to be applied in cross-border transactions?
6. How is the tax to be administered?[12]

For McDaniel, there are rules that should be beyond the reach of the WTO legalistic system, and those include rules that define the tax base, establish the tax rate, determine the taxable unit, establish accounting rules and methods, determine the tax treatment of cross-border flows of trade and investment; and provide the rules necessary to administer the tax (McDaniel 2001, p. 1622).

All of the above factors, McDaniel contended, should be "outside the scope of trade agreements and procedures." Moreover, he argued that those factors should be governed by domestic rules or diplomatic-bilateral tax treaties. Finally, and most importantly, he admitted that there exists an overlap between principles concerning tax provisions and trade issues. He acknowledged potential conflicts with the following factors: tax rates, taxable units, accounting rules, cross border transactions, and tax administration issues (McDaniel 2001, p. 1624). Thus, only one factor remains that will not interact with trade issues: the tax base. In conclusion, with reference to the EC experience, McDaniel stated that it is true that "many, perhaps most, items are relatively easy to classify as subsidies under both the current EC and the normative or benchmark approaches" (McDaniel 2001, p. 1640).

The last point is arguably the most important. The listed factors are useful in determining real domestic concerns, but any overlap with trade issues results in a return to the "first corner." The factors can provide guidance when disputes erupt, but are not determinative, because they can be misused to achieve trade goals when disguised in tax form. The main argument is certainly open to debate.

This is particularly true when noting that McDaniel offered no explanation as to how to distinguish between the true tax provisions and disguised tax, or what he

[12]McDaniel (2001, p. 1622). For example, for tax rate he acknowledged that "fiscal and trade rules may come into conflict;" for the taxable unit he wrote "there is a potential for conflict between fiscal and trade policies;" for the accounting factor he stated that there is "the potential for interaction between fiscal and trade policies;" for cross border transactions he admitted, "interactions of trade and fiscal rules can create conflict," and for tax administration rules, he stated, "interferences with trade rules are possible" (McDaniel 2001, p. 1622).

called tax expenditure. In addition, McDaniel provided no guidance as to what course of action would be required should an overlap exist. By failing to provide any clarification regarding how to differentiate between trade and tax in the event of an overlap, McDaniel cannot expect others to fully comprehend his argument or how his suggestion would be implemented.

Since overlap does exist, it would be arbitrary to identify one factor as a pure tax. For example, it is almost impossible for an accounting method to have a pure tax application with no overlapping affect on trade issues, such as requiring more documents or adhering to certain regulations for foreign investors, which would always be both a trade and a tax issue. If a dispute changes the competitive balance between local and foreign producers, what body should provide a dispute resolution structure? Should such a dispute be decided under the WTO because it affects trade in goods or services, or should it be a matter for a bilateral tax treaty to resolve? Clearly, the overlap is hard to pinpoint; therefore if the pure six factors are not evident, then it is difficult to qualify disputes as being exclusively the subject of bilateral tax treaties.

Additionally, bilateral tax treaties are developed according to criteria different from those concerning agreements like the WTO, including the commercial and political circumstances of the nations that are parties to a given treaty. For example, a tax treaty between Saudi Arabia and neighboring countries like Kuwait and Qatar would be quite different from a tax treaty between Saudi Arabia and China.

The six factors are helpful guides and can be utilized for different goals, but it would be hard to make them decisive factors. If the factors are hard to separate from other trade issues because of overlap, then any attempt to keep them out of trade-related legal dispute mechanisms, as well as keep them the subject of bilateral tax treaties, would fail.

In a later article (McDaniel 2004), Professor McDaniel discusses whether or not the WTO has developed a normative standard that adequately identifies trade subsidies which are provided through the income tax system of a particular nation and, if it has not done so, what standard should be followed by WTO dispute resolution bodies in evaluating whether there is revenue due as a result of a given tax provision. He notes that the FSC Dispute Panel specifically rejected the possibility of applying a normative standard, and instead adopted a "but for" test, which asks whether a United States company that utilizes an FSC would pay less in taxes than it would *but for* the existence of the FSC regime. This author supports McDaniel in his criticism of this approach; McDaniel correctly argues that all deduction-granting provisions will normally result in the taxpayer paying less in taxes than would be required as payment in absence of the provision, which could lead to characterizing the provision as prohibited subsidies. McDaniel insisted that such an approach requires classification of provisions as either tax expenditures or provisions necessary to develop a structural component of an income tax.

McDaniel cites two main issues that can assist the WTO in the classification of disputed tax provisions. The first is based on the GATT requirement that every nation submit by June 30 of each year a list of subsidies that it employs, along with an identification of the form taken by each subsidy, such as a tax exemption

(McDaniel 2004, p. 292). The inclusion by a country in its submission of a tax subsidy limits any related dispute to whether or not that subsidy can be considered a prohibited export subsidy. McDaniel cautions (McDaniel 2004, p. 293), however, that the benefit of such lists is limited by each nation's individual assessment of whether a particular provision is a subsidy or not, a subjective matter which could lead to misuse and concealment violations.

The second source (McDaniel 2004, p. 293) cited by McDaniel is the tax expenditure account,[13] published annually by countries. A country's classification of a particular provision as a tax expenditure in its own published account should end the subsidy question, but the author noted that "again, inclusion or exclusion of an item from a country's tax expenditure list can be a politically charged issue" (McDaniel 2004, p. 293).

Accordingly, McDaniel argued that tax expenditures should be subject to WTO law and the WTO dispute settlement process, while other income tax measures should be immune from it. This suggestion is a weak one in practice. Although it looks useful as presented by Professor McDaniel, this approach is difficult to implement in reality,[14] since not every country has this "tax expenditure" categorization. McDaniel assumed that countries have such a division in their fiscal systems, but this is not true for all countries (Brauner 2005, p. 298). Even in the USA, there is no consensus on this issue: "[D]uring the making of the tax expenditure budgets one can see that the Treasury and the Joint Committee on Taxation (JCT) publish separate and different versions of the budget based on different benchmarks" (Brauner 2005, p. 297). McDaniel's idea is therefore theoretically conceivable, but in practical terms it is impossible to implement the model internationally.

4.3 International Tax Organization Approach

With the relative success of WTO, as well as the European Union approach to tax matters, as background, this third option might best serve the international community. Without involving adjustment issues under WTO, such an organization can be built from the bottom up with support from the international community. Since globalization has affected many aspects of international relations, one can anticipate creating international organizations dealing with international needs, one of the most important of which is taxation affecting international communities. Establishing collaboration between this new organization and WTO will serve the interests of the international community. Additionally, both can join in a dispute resolution process upon request to decide a case involving the two organizations.

---

[13]For more on this subject, *see* Surrey (1973); *see also* Surreu and McDaniel (1985).

[14]*See* Brauner (2005, p. 260), criticizing McDaniel's model as not "practically workable."

A variety of suggestions have been offered by several scholars for how to approach the creation and maintenance of such an organization. One solution suggested by a variety of scholars since the emergence of the international tax system, is an international multilateral tax convention. The first study to this effect was published in 1895 by German scholar, Ludwig von Bar, who suggested the establishment of an international tax court (see Lindencrona and Mattsson 1981, p. 89 n.1); in 1899, Italian Scholar Alessandro Garelli also proposed such an international tax court (Altman 2006, p. 75). Thomas Adams suggested the establishment of an international multilateral tax treaty (Hudson and Turner 1994, p. 131), as did a report prepared by a committee of technical experts on double taxation and tax evasion, which stated that "it would certainly be desirable that the states should conclude collective conventions."[15]

In his article "International Trade and Tax Agreements May Be Coordinated, But Not Reconciled" (Brauner 2005, p. 252), Yariv Brauner discusses a recent FSC WTO case that held United States export tax subsidies to be inconsistent with its WTO obligations. In addition to proving that even the world's largest economic superpower is not immune to the requirements of the WTO, the case revealed, as Brauner pointed out, the tension that exists between the international trade and tax regimes and the "difficulty of applying WTO law to income tax measures" (Brauner 2005, p. 253). Brauner suggested that the use of tax systems as a protectionist measure to shelter domestic interests is likely to "increase as a result of economic globalization" (Brauner 2005, p. 253), enhancing the likelihood that individual nations will attempt to use income tax measures and other alternative techniques to accomplish protectionism beyond the scope of what the WTO can monitor and enforce.

Brauner wrote that "although the international trade and tax regimes cannot be simply reconciled or meshed together, their policies could (and should) be coordinated, with some adjustments made to the present legal constructs" (Brauner 2005, p. 254). This should be done institutionally; such an organization, Brauner suggested, should be the result of "establishment of an international tax organization" (Brauner 2005, p. 254),[16] an entirely separate entity from the WTO with independent responsibility for "making the evolving international tax regime more compatible with the trade regime" (Brauner 2005, p. 254). This independent international tax organization is needed, he contended, because of the WTO's "different focus, lack of

[15] *Double Taxation and Tax Evasion*, Report by the Committee of Technical Experts on Double Taxation and Tax Evasion, 8, available at http://www.law.wayne.edu/Faculty/Fac_web/mcintyre/text/Treaty_Class/League_Tech_Experts.pdf.

[16] Brauner, in another article, writes that, "the OECD's experience leading the recent global think tank on taxation of electronic commerce, after the practical concession of all the nation states that they could not deal with it alone, proved the necessity of a forum for global tax coordination. This experience also singled out the OECD as the most appropriate and practical institution around which a tax harmonization effort could be built, due to its expertise and experience in coordinating international tax cooperation. More specifically, I envision that the OECD would take the lead in designing a multilateral treaty, which would not be restricted to its members. Such a treaty should include a full set of international tax rules, as embedded currently in tax treaties, following the example of the OECD Model Treaty and commentaries" (Brauner 2003, pp. 259, 261).

tax expertise, political vulnerability, and insufficient compatibility" (Brauner 2005, pp. 258–259).

Most nations, he argued, do not coordinate their individual trade and tax regimes (Brauner 2005, p. 262). Brauner identifies two major potential conflicts facing the coordination of the two regimes (Brauner 2005, p. 262).

First, the legal constructs differ in format (Brauner 2005, p. 262). Unlike multilateral WTO agreements, income tax treaties are bilateral, normally following the model of the OECD and the US model (Brauner 2005, pp. 263–262). Second, conflict is likely to arise from nondiscrimination obligations (Brauner 2005, p. 266); WTO law focuses on such obligations, attempting to minimize domestic barriers through two requirements: the MFN and the NT (National Treatment). On the other hand, the international tax regime "typically only forbids discrimination against foreigners as compared to domestic persons. Moreover, the prohibition applies separately to each set of bilateral treaty partners" (Brauner 2005, p. 266). This prohibition is limited to the extent that is agreed upon by the parties to a specific bilateral treaty, so there is no MFN obligation and different bilateral treaties entered into by a particular nation may have drastically different provisions from the nation's other obligations. Some treaties contain provisions that have effects similar to those of an MFN provision, such as the bilateral tax treaty between the United States and Canada. However, the norm is to exclude MFN obligations from bilateral tax treaties, the absence of which "may be explained by the treaties' bilateral natures" (Brauner 2005, p. 267). The national treatment requirements of the WTO, according to Brauner, do not significantly affect direct taxation in the United States.

Brauner's article examines the potential effect of clashes between tax and trade regimes from a United States perspective. If a national treatment obligation is applied to direct taxation, Brauner pointed out, certain provisions of the existing United States Internal Revenue Code may be considered potential violations. Examples include a standard deduction, not available to non-residents; and branch profit taxes and excess interest rules that apply only to foreigners (Brauner 2005, pp. 286–287).

Brauner also discusses possible approaches that may be employed to alleviate the tension and reduce the incongruity between the international tax and trade regimes. One alternative cited by the author is the adoption of a dividing-line jurisdiction, initially promoted by Professor Paul McDaniel, which would act to assign and divide jurisdiction over contested tax measures, with pure tax measures being exempt from WTO law while all other matters, such as tax expenditures, would be fully and exclusively subject to such law. Brauner is of the opinion that such a solution model is "unsatisfactory and undesirable" for a variety of reasons.[17]

[17]Brauner challenged McDaniel's article, arguing that the assumptions therein are unrealistic. Those assumptions, in Brauner's opinion, are: (1) Every nation has an easily identifiable, non-controversial income tax system that could be used as a benchmark for the proposed jurisdictional division; (2) Deviations from such a benchmark will in most cases be easily identifiable; (3) Such deviations are included in every nation's tax expenditure budget; (4) Disparities between the different benchmark systems will not result in a destabilization of the international tax regime; and

Brauner concludes his article by stating, "this article doubts the feasibility of reconciling the current international tax and international trade regimes. Maintaining the current status quo, however, is risky, and is not the only available option, since the policies of these two dynamically evolving international regimes could be coordinated in a manner that should prevent serious conflicts" (Brauner 2005, p. 303). Although Brauner "does not attempt to provide a detailed prescription for such coordination" (Brauner 2005, p. 303) his article did offer guidelines.

First, Brauner suggested the incorporation of certain international trade-related standards into international tax policies, most notably the introduction and enforcement of national treatment (Brauner 2005, p. 310). He noted that in the current political climate, MFN provisions are unlikely to be incorporated, but the effects of such provisions can be replicated by incorporating similar measures, such as "minimum and maximum rates provisions, harmonization, setting a capped range of possibilities, thresholds, and preferred rates" (Brauner 2005, p. 310).

Brauner's article, finally and most importantly, argued for an independent international tax organization, because the WTO is not the most effective organization to handle tax issues. Although he admitted that at some point "there is no complete escape from WTO law and jurisprudence," he nevertheless suggested that the WTO should not be involved in solving the tension between trade and tax regimes.

One of the weaknesses of his suggestion is that it ignored the fact that the tension between the two regimes requires a solution from within rather than from the outside. In a situation where another organization was given responsibility for issuance of a decision on a tax issue relating to trade matters, without WTO cooperation the decision would be very ineffective. Also, such a scenario presents a choice-of-law dilemma; in an issue such as subsidies, it is unclear whether the WTO or the newly formed independent tax organization should be responsible for resolution. The suggestion of a coordination of efforts underestimates the potential conflict that could emerge between international organizations.

In another article (Brauner 2003), Brauner offered a different set of arguments against the WTO. He wrote that the WTO is not the venue for resolution of tax issues related to trade matters because "politically, the WTO already has the smell of a hated and unwelcome international government" (Brauner 2005, p. 316). This is sometimes true, but the political explanation is linked mainly to timing issues, which are temporary. Regard, or lack thereof, for an organization such as the WTO can presumably change, although there is no way to test this assertion. For example, it could be argued that since its membership is increasing, the WTO is an attractive organization; if it were not, it would be politically costly to join or to continue to participate actively in it.

Brauner offered support for the OECD, claiming "that the prime mover should be an organization that has current, proven expertise in tax" (Brauner 2005, p. 316).

---

(5) Strengthening the role of the WTO by explicitly widening its jurisdiction over direct taxes is desirable (Brauner 2005, pp. 292–295).

This is a legitimate concern against the WTO, but it weighs against his other argument calling for a new international organization. Finally, in support of the OECD, there is a risk that trade negotiations would cross paths with tax negotiations, which could increase the inefficiencies arising from the treaty negotiation process. Mixing trade and tax at the negotiation table may worsen this inherent problem, a reality that's part of the game, as with service and goods negotiation.

On the other hand, devoting a resource is a matter of will; if WTO members are willing to introduce tax issues, they will support the organization. Focus is an important issue. This author contends that the appropriate solution should be achieved through a mechanism that is purely voluntary, and by an organization that is larger in scope than that represented by the members of the OECD. And it should be an organization that already has proven success and is related to tax issues. The WTO fits the bill.

4.4 Undetermined Approaches

4.4.1 Treating Tax Issues Through Trade Regimes

Professor Reuven S. Avi-Yonah began his commentary by agreeing with McDaniel, claiming that trade law and tax law (the partial tax inclusion model) are areas with little overlap (Avi-Yonah 2001, p. 1683). However, Avi-Yonah admitted that this overlap is true to a large extent, given that "the goal of trade law is to facilitate trade, while the goal of tax law is to raise revenue" (Avi-Yonah 2001, p. 1683). This statement is not, in this author's opinion, entirely accurate; tax law, in fact, has two main goals, affecting economic as well as social and political policies (see Smith et al. 2005, pp. 1–22), in addition to the goal of raising revenue. Avi-Yonah essentially contended that there is some overlap between the two, and his commentary aimed to show such overlap.

He first discussed this overlap in the context of the GATT. According to Avi-Yonah, all possible interpretations of Article III of the GATT, which prohibits the application of discriminatory internal taxes to protect domestic production, lead to the conclusion that compliance results in a situation in which taxes cannot be used as a tool to protect domestic production (Avi-Yonah 2001, p. 1684); Avi-Yonah explained that this is because it is too difficult to design income tax provisions with enough particularity to apply exclusively to foreign-produced goods (Avi-Yonah 2001, p. 1684).[18] Further, Avi-Yonah discusses Article XVI of the GATT,

[18]The author of this work respectfully disagrees with this contention, and proposes that a tax system could be designed in which only foreigners were subject to the "discriminatory" tax. In Saudi Arabia for example, only non-Saudis are taxed based on their income, while Saudis are taxed differently, according to their wealth.

which deals with the subsidies issue. Both Article III and Article XVI of the GATT demonstrate the overlap between trade and tax law.

Avi-Yonah went on to discuss the GATS, explaining that even more significant (Avi-Yonah 2001, p. 1686) overlap between trade and tax issues occurs in the context of services, because foreign direct investments are frequently involved, even though there are provisions which do not permit the application of the GATS (Avi-Yonah 2001, p. 1686).

Avi-Yonah devoted a large part of his commentary to discussing the relationship between tax havens and the trade regime. He identified three types of tax havens and discussed the application of the GATT rules thereto:

1. *Production Tax Havens*. A production tax haven, according to Avi-Yonah, is a tax benefit, or "holiday scheme," that is set up in an effort to attract foreign investors to a host country for the purpose of establishing production facilities therein. Production tax havens "are invariably 'ring fenced,' i.e., they are designed to foster exports and, therefore, are separated from the domestic economy" (Avi-Yonah 2001, p. 1688). In other words, tax havens are the equivalent of prohibited export subsidies under the GATT (Avi-Yonah 2001, p. 1687).
2. *Traditional Tax Havens*. Avi-Yonah defines a traditional tax haven as a jurisdiction with a low or non-existent income tax, a situation that is likely to attract foreign investors and providers of financial services (Avi-Yonah 2001, p. 1687). The case here is "harder" (Avi-Yonah 2001, p. 1687) than that associated with production tax havens. The lack of income tax in such havens means there is no traditional "tax expenditure," but for those taxes that are collected, such havens often grant exemptions to foreign sectors; in addition, other benefits are provided to foreigners, such as provisions for intangible goods (Avi-Yonah 2001, p. 1687). Avi-Yonah interprets the allowance of this type of activity as also falling into the category of export subsidies prohibited by the GATT (Avi-Yonah 2001, p. 1687).
3. *Headquarters Tax Havens*. A headquarters tax haven is described by Avi-Yonah as a regime that is designed to attract the headquarters of multinational enterprises with the promise of no (or deferred) income taxation on income that comes from foreign subsidiaries. Avi-Yonah notes that, in addition to pure investment activity, which can be legally acceptable, such schemes often involve additionally the transfer of intangibles and/or the sale of goods to foreign subsidiaries, activities which would cause the provisions allowing them to be considered export subsidies (Avi-Yonah 2001, p. 1688).

Avi-Yonah concluded his commentary with an evaluation of whether or not the WTO is the appropriate forum in which to address harmful tax competition, comparing it to leaving the handling of the issue to the OECD. Leaning toward entrusting the WTO to handle the issue rather than delegating responsibility to the OECD, Avi-Yonah offered the following reasoning:

1. *Membership.* The OECD has only 29 members, so its ability to enforce tax competition rules on non-member nations is questionable. On the other hand, the WTO has a much broader membership, with 149 members, a list that continues to grow.
2. *Trustworthiness.* The OECD, Avi-Yonah explains, has made efforts to include non-member countries in planning tax competition rules, but developing nations are still suspicious of the intentions of the OECD and may not trust the organization to act in their best interest, especially after the blacklist of the tax heavens. The WTO, on the other hand, includes in its membership developing countries, and these countries relatively have a real say, and therefore increased confidence, in WTO policies.
3. *Extent of Coverage.* The OECD is limited in terms of what its tax competition policies cover. Furthermore, for the areas it does cover, the OECD does not have any binding adjudicative power. The WTO already has in place policies that prohibit many types of harmful tax competition.

Despite the clear advantages of leaving tax-governance to the WTO, Avi-Yonah also cited several objections to this structure, and then proceeds to offer solutions to said objections. First, he notes that many feel the WTO does not have sufficient tax expertise, a point previously raised by Professor Green (Avi-Yonah 2001, p. 1690); the proposed solution advanced by Avi-Yonah is to hire a sufficient number of tax professionals to sit on WTO panels as participants and advisors (Avi-Yonah 2001, p. 1690).

In addition, there is the prospective problem of nations being wary of giving up their sovereignty (Avi-Yonah 2001, pp. 1691–1692), leading to potential non-compliance with any imposed tax regulations, an issue this author disagreed with elsewhere. Avi-Yonah suggests that the solution to this threat of non-compliance and sovereignty concerns may lie in changing the structure of the old GATT; unlike the WTO, which automatically makes all dispute settlement rulings binding unless there is a consensus *not* to implement them, the GATT requires all decisions to be reached by consensus, including the agreement of the member nation whose regime stands to be affected, thereby allowing a nation to veto a proposed decision if it feels that a threat to its sovereignty looms.

He concluded essentially by stating that the overlap between tax and trade law, while limited in extent, certainly carries significant weight, and by explaining that the WTO is "the most promising forum for finding a solution" (Avi-Yonah 2001, p. 1692).[19]

[19] Brauner disagreed, stating that the OECD is "the most appropriate and practical institution around which a tax harmonization effort could be built, due to its expertise and experience in coordinating international tax cooperation." *See* Brauner (2003, p. 263).

4.4.2 *(How) Should Trade Agreements Deal with Income Tax Issues?*

Avi-Yonah subsequently discussed the relationship between multilateral trade agreements and international tax regimes in the above-referenced article, co-authored with Professor Joel Slemrod. The aim of the article was to answer three fundamental questions:

1. Why are distinctions between trade, investment, and tax agreements becoming increasingly blurred?
2. Do current trade, investment, and tax policies complement or conflict with one another?
3. What is the current relationship between trade and tax agreements? (Avi-Yonah and Slemrod 2002, p. 533)

The authors explained that trade agreements cannot ignore tax issues, because a multilateral agreement that covers tariffs only would not be sufficient to achieve the goal of free trade. They described in detail the two primary non-tariff barriers to trade: subsidies and taxes (Avi-Yonah and Slemrod 2002, p. 534).

With respect to subsidies, they claimed that from an economic perspective, the "main objectionable component of a tariff is its implicit subsidy to domestic producers" (Avi-Yonah and Slemrod 2002, p. 535). They compared the policy expressed in the GATT to the levying of a non-discriminatory income tax in addition to the imposition of an export subsidy (Avi-Yonah and Slemrod 2002, p. 536). Direct taxes, they argued, can also be used to advance a domestic protectionist policy, as when expenditures for inputs are deductible only when the inputs are domestically produced goods, a scheme parallel to allowing a deduction for all inputs, domestic or imported, and then levying an import tariff on imported goods (Avi-Yonah and Slemrod 2002, pp. 536–537).

The authors then identified several differences between trade and tax regimes. First, they noted that trade policy operates in a system of border protectionism; income taxation, on the other hand, "may involve another kind of protectionism that we refer to as 'ownership protectionism' within a country's borders" (Avi-Yonah and Slemrod 2002, p. 541). Second, they noted that there is a difference in the basis for duties as applied to tariffs and taxes: the basis for tariff policy is the value of the transaction, while that for income tax policy is the measure of income (Avi-Yonah and Slemrod 2002, p. 542). Given that tax rates vary widely among countries, tax havens force nations with relatively high tax rates to establish a strict enforcement structure of their tax policies and to monitor income shifting (Avi-Yonah and Slemrod 2002, pp. 543–544).

The article continued by addressing the shortfalls of bilateral tax treaties (Avi-Yonah and Slemrod 2002, p. 544). Although the goal of such treaties to avoid double or zero taxation is consistent with a free trade system, the authors claimed that policies of non-discrimination or national treatment are not sufficient to prevent trade distortion. They argued that there are "aspects of taxation that on the face of things appear to be discriminatory, because they differentiate tax liability depending on residence" (Avi-Yonah and Slemrod 2002, p. 548). Further, there is the threat of what they refer to as "predatory tax protectionism" (Avi-Yonah and Slemrod 2002, p. 548), a situation in which countries construct domestic tax systems so as to attract tax liability from other countries, whether or not real resources follow.

The authors then raised their most important point: "Fundamentally, the principal limitation of the current set of bilateral tax treaties stems directly from their bilateral nature, which in turn follows from the principle of reciprocity" (Avi-Yonah and Slemrod 2002, p. 549). A further crucial issue is that bilateral tax treaties are ill-equipped to adequately deal with distortions caused by production havens or by tax havens (Avi-Yonah and Slemrod 2002, p. 552).

Slemrod and Avi-Yonah suggested that the ideal solution to the problem of the disconnect between tax and trade regimes is "a multilateral treaty, similar to the GATT" (Avi-Yonah and Slemrod 2002, p. 552), that can address tax and trade issues, and that will be applicable "to subsidies for services as well as goods" (Avi-Yonah and Slemrod 2002, p. 552).

However, the authors asked how, since "[we] do not have – and are not likely to have soon – a broad multilateral agreement, should trade agreements distinguish between apparently discriminatory tax practices that are not protectionist, and those that are?" (Avi-Yonah and Slemrod 2002, p. 553). They offered the following general rules for how trade agreements should distinguish between apparently discriminatory tax practices that are protectionist and those that are not. They conclude that "trade agreements should

1. Accept bilateral tax agreements designed to generate, and allocate between the taxing jurisdictions, a single layer of taxation.
2. Not accept situations in which the direct tax system is merely the vehicle for otherwise proscribed actions, such as tariffs or export subsidies.
3. Accept statutorily uniform source-based factor taxes, even if the effective tax on factors, by sector, is relatively higher for import-intensive sectors.
4. Accept anti-evasion provisions that deal with predatory tax protectionism, even if they discriminate, as long as these provisions do not effectively levy more than a single layer of taxation." (Avi-Yonah and Slemrod 2002, p. 553)

Finally, the authors concluded that a "multilateral instrument devoted specifically to taxes is a more appropriate way to handle these issues. Whether, in the future, the WTO might be the institutional vehicle for negotiating such a tax instrument is a tactical question we leave open for now" (Avi-Yonah and Slemrod 2002, p. 553).[20]

The last part of the article is the most applicable to this present study. From the article, it is clear that the authors agree there is a potential problem that may emerge

[20]Compare with Avi-Yonah's previous article, stating that, "the WTO is the most promising forum for finding a solution" (Avi-Yonah 2001, p. 1692).

from the relationship between trade and tax. . For example, they advised that the WTO should not accept situations in which the direct tax system is "merely the vehicle" for prohibited actions. This is more easily said than done; the distinction is a difficult one to make without further elaboration. For example, in a situation where by the nature of the tax action, the tax allows for something prohibited, as where a tax exemption leads to increase exports, such as in the territorial system or the FSC, the proper course of action is unknown. This is a crucial and most difficult issue, and simply stating that the issue should be dealt with adds little to the resolution of the problem.

Avi-Yonah and Slemrod were reluctant to determine whether the WTO is the most appropriate organization to deal with international tax issues on a multilateral basis, but their analysis implies that currently the WTO is the only qualified candidate, even if it is not the best possible one.

This article is helpful in admitting the existence of the problem, in pointing out the existing and potential issues involved in the trade and tax relationship, and in suggesting a broad solution for trade agreements in general. Avi-Yonah and Slemrod are proponents of solving the problem by any means, including under the WTO umbrella, although they believe that there are some issues which should not be included under the WTO.

4.4.3 Income Tax Discrimination Against International Commerce

Professor Alvin C. Warren's article argues that with respect to international tax "the current distinction between permissible and impermissible discrimination is incoherent" (Warren 2001, p. 131). Warren analyzed the potential for discrimination against international commerce given the constraints that are imposed on national income tax systems by international tax and trade treaties. Warren also attempted to identify a "coherent" norm to explain the distinctions between trade and tax regimes, and concluded that in the current international climate, such a norm is unavailable.

According to Warren, two legal regimes impose constraints on national income tax systems: international tax law and international trade law (Warren 2001, p. 131). With respect to trade law, he explained the traditional division of the tax base, which has historically delegated to the source-country jurisdiction to tax corporate business income, and to the residence-country the jurisdiction to tax investment income (Warren 2001, p. 132). This division is a result of the combination of domestic tax laws of individual countries and bilateral tax treaties between pairs of countries. Warren further noted that in some cases, there may be more than a single source-country, with several countries participating in the production of income and dividing the source-country tax base among jurisdictions.

Warren next examined the relationship between international trade law and international tax law. He noted that the main differences between tax and trade regimes include that the tax treaties are bilateral, require national treatment, and are subject to diplomatic dispute resolution, while the trade treaties are "multinational, require most-favored-nation as well as national treatment and are subject to binding dispute resolution procedures. On their face, many of the trade treaties potentially apply to national tax laws, but the international tax community has insisted on broad exemptions for income taxation in recent trade negotiations" (Warren 2001, p. 147). Nevertheless, Warren insisted that the two legal regimes have essentially the same goal – a "reduction of impediments to international commerce" (Warren 2001, p. 147).

In addition, Warren examined how a free country uses its income tax structure to discriminate against international commerce. He presented three ways in which a country might achieve such discrimination:

1. Favoring domestic producers over foreign producers
2. Favoring domestic production over foreign production
3. Favoring domestic products over imported foreign products, including services (Warren 2001, p. 149)

Warren then analyzed the different scenarios that could occur in each of the three situations. He warned that because no international dispute-settlement body exists to monitor international tax actions involving potential discrimination against international commerce, a source country is essentially given free rein in reaching "its own conclusion about whether differential treatment is justified" (Warren 2001, p. 151). Moreover, Warren argued that the absence of most favored nation treatment requirements in international tax law is an open invitation to discriminate against foreign producers (Warren 2001, p. 153).

Warren's overall idea was that international trade and tax law both, in principle, prohibit discrimination by source countries based on taxpayer identity; both international tax and trade law, in principle, permit discrimination by residence countries on the basis of production location; and international trade law alone limits discrimination by importing countries on the basis of whether a good or service is domestic or foreign, a limit which tax law does not impose (Warren 2001, pp. 157–158).

The author posed the question of whether the current blurry distinction between permissible and impermissible discrimination may be justified as implementing a norm that is applicable both in the tax context and in the international trade context. He considered efficiency, competitiveness, and equality.

Warren concluded that when the tax and trade regimes are considered together, "no coherent principle explains the current dividing line between prohibited and permitted income tax discrimination against international commerce" (Warren 2001, p. 168). He explained that "the distribution of jurisdiction between the tax and trade disciplines seems best understood as an accidental byproduct of the separate historical development of those disciplines" (Warren 2001, p. 168). He also suggested that a fundamental reexamination of the income tax system is required so that the international community can come to a point where it is in a position to accurately consider how much weight should be given to the ideas of efficiency, competitiveness, and equality. Warren emphasized that such a reexamination would require careful consideration of the appropriate relationship of income taxation to the overall international trade regime.

The most important remark Warren offered was this: "the time has come for a fundamental reexamination of the international income tax system ... Subsequent developments, including the GATT and WTO, as well as corporate tax integration, threaten to render the old regime obsolete, if it is not already so" (Warren 2001, p. 196).

Warren's analytical approach to both the permissible and impermissible discriminations involved in trade and tax regimes is extremely articulate and well-reasoned. He pointed out the dangers of leaving the situation as it currently stands, but he stopped short of suggesting solutions, although some ideas for resolution can be extracted from his analysis. Warren's proposal that the international tax regime needs to be re-examined, and his linkage thereof to the development of the WTO, indicates that Warren's main concern is the link between international trade and international tax.

4.5 Concluding Remark

As discussed above, some scholars have mixed concepts, or have attempted to build multiple concepts precariously on assumptions that remain poorly defined. However, these scholars, despite any weakening in their arguments, have at least tackled this issue and analyzed it systematically in a way that increases an understanding of the real danger of leaving the issue unresolved. The success of solving any problem starts with the knowledge and admission that a problem does exist. The actual resolution of the problem is another, separate step.

References

Altman ZD (2006) Dispute resolution under tax treaties. IBFD, Amsterdam

Avi-Yonah RS (2001) Treating tax issues through trade regimes. Brook J Int'l L 26:1683, 1692

Avi-Yonah RS, Slemrod J (2002) (How) should trade agreements deal with income tax issues. Tax L Rev 55:533, 535

Brauner Y (2003) An international tax regime in crystallization. Tax L Rev 56:259, 261

Brauner Y (2005) International trade and tax agreements may be coordinated, but not reconciled. Va Tax Rev 25:251, 274

Charnovitz S (1996) Participation of nongovernmental organizations in the World Trade Organization. U Pa J Int'l Econ L 17:331, 343–346

Conybeare JAC (1987) Trade wars: the theory and practice of international commercial rivalry. Columbia University Press, New York

Debevoise W (1998) Access to documents and panel and appellate body sessions: practice and suggestions for greater transparency. Int'l Law 32:817

Graetz MJ, Warren AC (2006) Income tax discrimination and the political and economic integration of Europe. Yale L J 115:1186

Green RA (1998) Antilegalistic approaches to resolving disputes between governments: a comparison of the international tax and trade regimes. Yale J Int'l 23:79

Green R (2002) The interaction of tax and non-tax treaties. Canadian tax J 50:107. Reprinted in Bul Int'l Fiscal Documentation 56:254

Hudson DM, Turner DC (1994) International and interstate approaches to taxing business income. In: Dunning JH (ed) United Nations library on transnational corporations: international business and the world. Routledge, London

Jackson J (1996) The institutional and jurisdictional architecture: reflections on constitutional changes to the global trading system. Chi-Kent L Rev 72:511, 517

Ka Zeng (2004) Trade threats, trade wars: bargaining, retaliation, and American coercive diplomacy. University of Michigan Press, Ann Arbor

Lindencrona G, Mattsson N (1981) Arbitration in taxation. Kluwer, Deventer

McDaniel PR (2001) The pursuit of national tax policies in a globalized environment: principal paper: trade and taxation. Brook J Int'l L 26:1621

McDaniel PR (2004) Trade agreements and income taxation: interactions, conflicts, and resolutions. Tax L Rev 57:275

Nichols PM (1996) Extension of standing in World Trade Organization disputes to nongovernment parties. U Pa J Int'l Econ L 17:295

OECD Committee on Fiscal Affairs (2000) Model tax convention on income and on capital. OECD, Paris

Ring DM (2000) On the frontier of procedural innovation: advance pricing agreements and the struggle to allocate income for cross border taxation. Mich J Int'l L 21:143

Schleyer GT (1997) Power to the people: allowing private parties to raise claims before the WTO dispute resolution system. Fordham L Rev 65:2275

Smith EP et al. (2005) Federal taxation: basic principles. Commerce Clearing House, Chicago

Stephan P (1996) Accountability and international rulemaking: rules, rents, and legitimacy. Nw J Int'l L & Bus 17:681

Surreu S, McDaniel P (1985) Tax expenditures. Harvard University Press, Cambridge, MA

Surrey S (1973) Pathways to tax reform: the concept of tax expenditures. Harvard University Press, Cambridge, MA

Trachtman J (2002) Institutional linkage: transcending "trade and...". AJIL 96:77

Turro J (1992, April 6) United States: IRS official says no APA disclosure, but generic information to be provided (quoting IRS Associate Chief Counsel International Robert E. Culbertson). Tax Notes Int'l 4:709

Warren AC Jr (2001) Income tax discrimination against international commerce. Tax L Rev 54:131–431

Chapter 5
Sovereignty

One of the principle objections that can be raised against including tax under the WTO is the sovereignty objection. This chapter is an answer to the arguments that can be invoked by suggesting that taxes be governed by any international organization. It answers the claim first, by reviewing the concept itself. Second, it relies on practical current EU experience. Finally, in identifying the answer to the incompatibility, this chapter will provide an historical overview of tax and trade interrelations.

5.1 Sovereignty Basic Meaning

Sovereignty[1] is an extremely serious issue that has affected available tax models and prevented the creation of uniform international tax rules. Sovereignty is a critical concept, yet it is "elusive" (Shinoda 2000, p. 1), in a way that is more true today than ever before. It is the most powerful concept with an impact on shaping national policy everywhere, and therefore undeniably affects international affairs. However, for all of its importance, sovereignty remains a surprisingly unclear concept. Professor Henkin stated that the meaning of "sovereignty is confused" (Henkin 1999, p. 1), that it "has not aged well," and that its use has at times been unjustifiably used for the promotion of "destructive human values." Henkin wrote: "It is undeniable that the centuries-old doctrine of absolute and exclusive sovereignty no longer stands, and was in fact never so absolute as it was conceived to be in theory" (Henkin et al. 1993, p. 18, citing Boutros Boutros-Ghali).

[1] *See* Krasner (1999); Goldsmith (2000, pp. 959, 967); Heller and Sofaer (2001, p. 31); Fulton (1911); Lee (1997, p. 241); Simpson (1996, pp. 255, 282); Fowler and Bunk (1995); Rabkin (1998).

T. Althunayan, *Dealing with the Fragmented International Legal Environment: WTO, International Tax and Internal Tax Regulations*,
DOI 10.1007/978-3-642-04678-0_5,

5.1.1 Why Is It Important to Study the Issue of Sovereignty?

The short answer to the question of why a study of the sovereignty issue is important is that that the concept has been, and continues to be, misused because it is unclear. The term "sovereignty" itself is commonly used in a way that is more rhetorical than legal, which is an easy way to distort arguments and debates. Even within academia, there is no uniform understanding of the definition and implications of sovereignty. One well-known scholar, Stephen D. Krasner, described the concept as "organized hypocrisy" (Krasner 1999).

The problem, however, is that there is no clearly defined concept of what sovereignty means. Sovereignty is certainly an issue that should be acknowledged, but at times, especially with respect to tax issues, it has been misused in a way that makes rational discussion on the subject meaningless, as much of the discussion is based on a faulty foundation rather than on clear understanding of the concept. Therefore, the concept of sovereignty needs to be clarified, or at least to be put into a framework within which one can identify its main elements.

Sovereignty has its roots in the relationship that existed between a nation's king or queen and his or her subjects when monarchies were prevalent; the social and political construct was such that the monarch had absolute power and unfiltered authority over all of his or her subjects. Although the concept stems from the sixteenth century, it is still alive today because it has a deeper root. Nonetheless, Henkin thinks that the concept of "sovereignty" is out of date and that the "S word" should be eliminated. If complete elimination is not possible, Henkin suggests that it is necessary to "decompose" the sovereignty concept, and to identify which elements of the concept are "appropriate and desirable for a state in a system of states at the turn of the twenty-first century" (Henkin 1993, p. 10).

All nations have some internal control over subjects located within their borders – an internal sovereignty. This is the power to govern and control a nation's own affairs, a collection of internal rights necessary for a country to function by controlling its own legislative, executive, and administrative matters. But this type of control is not absolute sovereignty; there are many limitations on such internal control, and here begins the controversy. Absolute sovereignty is impossible; it is an illusion which does not exist. No person or governing body, for example, can control the air inhaled by a nation's people, or the books they read, or the ideas they believe, let alone the sovereignty of outside space, even if they try and can do it for short time.

It would likely be disastrous for a given country to claim absolute sovereignty. Hobbes eloquently wrote that if men were to hold on to all of their rights and be free to do as they wished without restrictions, such a global society would lead inevitably to war or anarchy. Peace can be achieved only when there is a mutual "laying down of rights for mutual benefits." This becomes even more true in the international tax context; "the ultimate consideration which lies at the heart of all the striving to eliminate international direct tax distortions – the efficient allocation of revenue between countries inuring to the benefit of taxpayers" (Jeffery 1999, pp. 21–22). Countries must mutually give up some rights to achieve mutual benefits, as reflected in the prisoner dilemma story.

5.1.2 *The Meaning of "Sovereignty"*

Some scholars have attempted to identify the meaning of sovereignty. The meaning of sovereignty was first articulated by Jean Bodin in 1576 as "the supreme authority in a political community" (Murphy 2005, p. 3). Bodin referred to sovereignty as the perpetual power of a government, which clearly indicates that he considered sovereignty to be infinite (Bodin 1992, p. 1),[2] assigned to the state "without limitation of time" (Schulze 1996, p. 50). Thomas Hobbes similarly felt that sovereignty must be concentrated in one person, an indication of the original meaning of sovereignty (Wendt 1999, pp. 206–207). However, Hobbes also stated that sovereignty cannot be absolute, but rather that some must be given up in order to achieve peace.

Internally,[3] sovereignty can be generally defined with little controversy as the ability to have a supreme authority within a defined territory, where "supreme" does *not* indicate "absolute." Sovereignty is "undoubtedly territorial in character" (Mann 1999, p. 4). Another understanding is that sovereignty refers to a "bundle of rights and competencies which go to make up the nation state" (Jeffery 1999, p. 26). From a negative perspective, sovereignty means that no nation is responsible for what happens in territories that it does not control (Rabkin 1998, p. 39); alternatively, "it is the power to act without being subject to the legal control of another" (Rabkin 1998, p. 13, citing Hugo Grotius).

Externally, no single meaning of sovereignty exists. States have limited sovereignty depending on different variables, which is natural, because no one state can exist forever without any limitation on international affairs, and "most if not all sovereign governments have very seriously limited choices in the exercise of their supposedly sovereign competence because their theoretically important areas for decisions are much restricted and hemmed in by treaties, customary international law, and by the consequences of the sheer interdependency of all states nowadays" (see Sir Jenning 2002, p. 31).

One reason why there is no consensus as to a single definition is that there is no international authority which has undertaken the task of identifying an acceptable and accurate definition. In his article on sovereignty and international law, the Hungarian international law scholar László Valki concluded that "international law has never produced a definition of sovereignty; even the international legal documents signed under the umbrella of the UN, which are supposed to infringe it, only define it in a

---

[2]Hobbes and Bodin "were both driven by a desire to provide an intellectual rationale for the legitimacy of some one final source of authority within the state." Their goal was to provide a legitimate ground for the King, the notion being that "no final and absolute authority exists elsewhere." *See* Krasner (1999, p. 11).

[3]*See* Thomson, p. 219; Hall, p. 17; Jackson and James, p. 13.

negative way, saying what sovereign states cannot do, i.e., what sovereignty is not. For instance, states have to respect other states as equals, must not endanger the territorial integrity of other states and cannot use force to resolve conflict."[4]

5.1.3 Sovereignty Applications

As of January 2006, a simple search in the UN website about multilateral treaties returned 517 multilateral treaties. In addition, there are more than 158,000 bilateral treaties recorded at the United Nations. Treaties imply giving up some presumed rights, or define them bilaterally or multilaterally. Applications of sovereignty have changed in different ways in different parts of the international arena; "exclusive and absolute" (Goldsmith 2000, p. 959) sovereignty:

> appears to have diminished significantly in the past half century as a result of economic globalization, transportation and communications advances, the rise of nongovernmental organizations (NGOs), and the spread of international human rights law. NATO's bombing of Yugoslavia, the extraordinary increase in the velocity of capital and information flows, Great Britain's denial of General Pinochet's immunity claims ... and the United Nations' occupation of East Timor, among many other things appear to confirm UN Secretary General Kofi Annan's assertion that 'state sovereignty, in its most basic sense, is being redefined'. (Goldsmith 2000, pp. 959–960)

After the Second World War, three important institutions were created: the United Nations (UN), the World Bank, and the International Monetary Fund (IMF). Each of the three has affected international relations, as each organization has some legal authority that, even when not enforceable under domestic constructs, carries weight. After the failed attempt to create the ITO, the GATT was created in 1949 and has been regulating tariff rates ever since until the creation of the WTO in 1994; this movement affects the meaning of sovereignty.

There are numerous examples of sovereignty being relinquished. In 1948, the Universal Declaration of Human Rights was signed; in 1976, the Convention on Political and Civil Rights, and the Convention on Social, Economic and Cultural Rights were signed. The financial sector provides a notable example of relinquishing sovereignty. The International Organization of Securities Commissioners (IOSCO),[5] which emerged in 1984, is another example; this was followed in the

---

[4]Lack of definition is common in international law; for example, definitions of direct and indirect tax under the WTO consist of mere examples rather than statements identifying the concepts.

[5]The member agencies currently assembled together in the International Organization of Securities Commissions have resolved as follows: to cooperate together to promote high standards of regulation in order to maintain just, efficient and sound markets; to exchange information on their respective experiences in order to promote the development of domestic markets; to unite their efforts to establish standards and an effective surveillance of international securities transactions; and to provide mutual assistance to promote the integrity of the markets by a rigorous application of the standards and by effective enforcement against offenses. *See* http://www.iosco.org/about/ (April 26, 2007).

1990s by the creation of the International Association of Insurance Supervisors (IAIS), a nonprofit corporation incorporated in Illinois.

In addition, the Basle Committee[6] on Banking Supervision was created by the central-bank Governors of the Group of Ten countries at the end of 1974. It "does not possess any formal supranational supervisory authority, and its conclusions do not, and were never intended to, have legal force. Rather, it formulates broad supervisory standards and guidelines and recommends statements of best practice in the expectation that individual authorities will take steps to implement them through detailed arrangements – statutory or otherwise – which are best suited to their own national systems."[7]

National security seems an unlikely subject for external supervision. Nevertheless, this is precisely what has happened. One example of such a situation is an individual nation's right to develop and maintain nuclear power. Opened for signature on July 1, 1968, and signed by the USA, the UK, and the former USSR, among others, the Nuclear Nonproliferation Treaty[8] is a major treaty that has absolutely changed the meaning of sovereignty. It entered into force in 1970, and commentators called it the "most widely subscribed and successful arms control treaty in history, with one hundred eighty-nine states parties" (Jonas 2005, pp. 417, 418). The treaty limited the transport of nuclear material for military purposes by agreement to prevent non-nuclear nations from getting or making nuclear weapons. In 1995, the treaty was extended indefinitely. Despite the sensitive nature of the issue, 189 countries participated. This is clearly an illustration of the magnitude of limitations on sovereignty.

The Organization of Economic Cooperation and Development (OECD) itself is an example of sovereignty surrender, regulating informally a variety of issues ranging from taxes to environment to labor, with sometimes serious consequences, such as the identification of tax havens and the blacklisting of any country that does not comply with its evaluation. It functions more as a forum "to convene government officials in specific issue areas for the purpose of addressing a common problem and making recommendations or promulgating a model code for its solution."[9]

---

[6]Members are the central banks or monetary authorities of Algeria, Argentina, Australia, Austria, Belgium, Bosnia and Herzegovina, Brazil, Bulgaria, Canada, Chile, China, Croatia, the Czech Republic, Denmark, Estonia, Finland, France, Germany, Greece, Hong Kong SAR, Hungary, Iceland, India, Indonesia, Ireland, Israel, Italy, Japan, Korea, Latvia, Lithuania, the Republic of Macedonia, Malaysia, Mexico, the Netherlands, New Zealand, Norway, the Philippines, Poland, Portugal, Romania, Russia, Saudi Arabia, Singapore, Slovakia, Slovenia, South Africa, Spain, Sweden, Switzerland, Thailand, Turkey, the United Kingdom and the United States, plus the European Central Bank.

[7]*History of the Basel Committee and its Membership*, http://www.bis.org/bcbs/history.htm (April 4, 2006). *See also* Zaring (1998, pp. 281, 287–291).

[8]Treaty on the Non-Proliferation of Nuclear Weapons, opened for signature July 1, 1968, 21 U.S. T. 483, 484, 729 U.N.T.S. 161, 169. *See* Williamson (1995, pp. 71, 77); Carmody (1994, p. 229).

[9]Anne, p. 1050.

5.1.4 Existence of Sovereignty

The above discussion is not intended to suggest that sovereignty is a myth; rather, it aims to show that the concept has been misused, overstated, and overused. The above examples are also intended to show that the concept is diminishing in value and importance. Nevertheless, nations do retain some sovereignty. National flags, national anthems, languages, educational and healthcare systems, constitutions, and many other aspects of life in a particular country are all within sovereign powers for most nations.

However, although nations do have some sovereignty, its strength can be challenged when there arises a possible spillover effect on other nations. As an example, national police operations are within the sovereignty of an individual state, including what types of vehicles police forces will use, how much officers will be paid for their services, rules of conduct, and the like; police operations are, therefore, normally run without any external interference. However, this is true only until some line is crossed that concerns or has an effect on outsiders,[10] as when a nation's domestic officers use force in a brutal way against civilians of other nations, or against the nation's own citizens in a way that constitutes a violation of international human rights standards.[11]

5.1.5 Sovereignty and Tax

Professor John Jackson, focusing on international economic law, stated that "national government leaders and politicians as well as special interest representatives too often invoke the term 'sovereignty' to mislead needed debate" (Jackson 2007, p. 59). He further stated that "the concept of sovereignty sometimes is extremely, and perhaps purposefully, misleading, and a crutch to politicians and media to avoid the tough and very complex thinking that should be taken up about real policy issues that are involved" (Jackson 2007, p. 69). It is indeed a controversial concept; in fact, it is "difficult to find a political notion more controversial than sovereignty" (Shinoda 2000, p. 1).

If there are issues where sovereignty is strong, such as selection of a national flag, and those where sovereignty is less strong, such as human rights violations, where do tax issues stand? Should tax issues be included under a regime of internal sovereignty, with little or no outside interference allowed, or should they be handled within the context of external sovereignty, with other countries able to have a say the structure of tax rules? It seems reasonable to expect that for internal tax matters, such as setting a tax rate or establishing a tax base, the answer should be

[10] This could trigger international reaction to the extent of waging war; the bombing of Serbia is an example of intervening militarily.

[11] The ongoing genocide in Darfur serves as an example.

strongly in favor of domestic sovereignty. For external tax matters, those that overlap with multinational issues or that are related in some way to foreign people and entities inside and outside national borders (for example transfer pricing issues and taxation of foreigners inside a nation's geographical territory), the issue becomes more appropriately associated with some level of international control.

It is easy to contend that a country has absolute sovereignty to tax its citizens as it wishes; Martin Norr stated that no rules of international law exist "to limit the extent of any country's tax jurisdiction" (Norr 1962, p. 431).[12] Norr explained that it is "logical to expect that as long as there are states serving populations with common purposes and interests, such states will wish to retain a degree of sovereignty over the tax treatment" (Musgrave 2001, pp. 1335, 1336–1337). Nations "wish" to retain as much power as possible, but is it possible or even desirable to do so, compared with the benefits of laying down their taxing powers?

The most obvious problem is that although a given country has the sovereign power to tax as it wishes (and it can disallow people or goods from entering its territory), the idea would be harder to accept with regard to the ability to tax people who are not residents, citizens, or entities organized within that country. In addition, it is important to remember that no country can tax foreigners 100% of their profits unless it wants to drive away all foreign presences – another powerful illustration of the limitation on sovereignty.

In addition, when countries sign an international agreement concerning taxation, they explicitly agree to give up some of their individual taxing power, relinquishing to some extent their sovereignty. Such agreements are obligatory contracts; states can withdraw from them or disobey if they anticipate greater benefits from such withdrawal whether or not the action is legal. Realistically, it would be impossible to find a country committed to a treaty which imposes upon that country a burden disproportionate to the benefits; a nation would find a way to ease its obligations.

As previously discussed herein and illustrated by Avi-Yonah, there are clear indications that there exists a set of international tax laws, customary in nature (see Avi-Yonah 2004, pp. 483, 490; see also Ault 1992, p. 565; Rosenbloom and Langbein 1981, p. 359; Wang 1945, p. 73), such as the informal proscription against double taxation and discrimination, and the concepts of source and residence. Further, the concept of reciprocity forces nations to follow certain rules with regard to international taxation; "source, residence, and citizenship are the currently existing bases for the imposition of an income tax" (Kaufman 1998, pp. 145, 148).

Avi-Yonah further argued that:

> to those who doubt the existence of the international tax regime, let me pose the following question: Suppose you were advising a developing country or transition economy that wanted to adopt an income tax for the first time. How free do you think you would be to write the international tax rules for such a country in any way you wanted, assuming that it wished to attract foreign investment? I would argue that the freedom of most countries to adopt international tax rules is severely constrained, even before entering into any tax

---

[12] *See also* Rhoades and Langer (1985, § 1.11, 1–3), stating that no rule of international law limits the US power to tax.

treaties, by the need to adapt to generally accepted principles of international taxation. (Avi-Yonah 2001a, pp. 170–171)

International judicial opinions provide further support for some limitation on tax sovereignty. The German court, for example, acknowledged in 1983 that the taxing power of a state is unlimited regarding its own citizens, but limited by public international law with respect to the taxation of aliens (Meessen 1996, p. 27).[13] The ECJ, for example, also argued firmly that the tax laws of a Member State must be consistently in compliance with the general principles of the economic community as laid down in the Treaty of Rome[14] and its relevant provision relating to tax issues.[15] Members of EU, further, are no longer free to establish individual structures for their specific direct taxation issues, internally and internationally.[16]

Finally, the mere existence of the current international tax regime proves that "despite each country's claim to sovereignty in tax matters, it is possible to reach an internationally acceptable consensus that will be followed by the majority of the world's taxing jurisdictions" (see Graetz and O'Hear 1997, pp. 1021, 1106–1107). This observation provides powerful support in an argument against absolute sovereignty over international tax issues. The current system has proven effective for 70 years; even with its shortcomings, countries are willing to give up some of their taxing power under the current system. The mere fact that countries have accepted and respected an agreement that orders them to give up their tax sovereignty over some issues, regardless of the underlying reasons for such acceptance and respect, is of great importance.

5.1.6 Is Sovereignty an Acceptable Excuse?

This author's opinion is that individual nations do not have absolute and unfettered rights of tax sovereignty, but rather that rights are influenced and ultimately determined by both internal and external factors, the most important of which is the interaction of international law, treaties in particular, with national law (Jeffery 1999, p. 25). This is the very responsibility of what is called international tax law, which is "concerned with defining the tax sovereignty of states" (Daniels 2001, p. 2). International tax law includes rules regulating the application of bilateral tax

---

[13]Meesen also cited another Turkish and US example, acknowledging the limitation on taxing non-citizens.

[14]*See* Treaty Establishing the European Economic Community (Rome, March 25, 1957), also known as the Treaty of Rome.

[15]Article 87 in part refers to "[a]ny aid granted by a Member State through State resources in any form whatsoever which distorts competition or threatens to distort competition by favoring certain undertakings or the production or certain good, insofar as it affects trade between Member States." This provision can be used in answering Warren's and Graetz's argument against the involvement of the ECJ (Graetz and Warren 2006, p. 1186).

[16]*See* Pistone (2002); *but see also* Graetz and Warren (2006, p. 1186), disagreeing with the ECJ approach and arguing for less involvement by the EU in income tax issues.

treaties. Further, the OECD also plays "an important role in establishing and applying tax treaties" (Daniels 2001, p. 2).

The globalization of the market economy, advancements in technology, decreasing costs of transportation, and other factors have all resulted in a further reduction of the importance and applicability of the sovereignty concept. In sum, the basic concept of sovereignty is changing "by the forces of globalisation and international co-operation" (Annan 1999, p. 49). The clear suggestion is that internal sovereignty is by no means an absolute term; rather, it is affected by other international forces.

In reality, nations obey international law most of the time; Henkin famously argued that "almost all nations observe almost all principles of international law and almost all of their obligations almost all of the time" (Henkin 1979, p. 47). Therefore, presentation of a sovereignty argument should be received with caution, especially with respect to international law matters, where issues subject to dispute cross national borders and affect not just domestic residents, but non-residents as well. Admittedly, sovereignty is an elusive concept which can "mislead us if we keep on using it" (Maritain 1951, pp. 29–30; see Bradley 1999, p. 87; Jackson 2007, p. 69). Nevertheless, it must be acknowledged and kept in mind when setting any new plan. The tax agreement option suggested at the end of this study should give nations the cushion they feel is needed to deal with international supervision.

5.2 The EU Income Taxation Integration Experience

The EU experience with tax issues provides a good answer for the sovereignty proponents. The EU is the best institutionalized example for demonstrating the possibility of bringing tax and trade under one organization. Thus far, the EU has been successful despite certain difficulties. The EU is a special case, with commonalities among its members, including a shared geography and mutual political aspiration, such as minimization of the potential for wars and an increase economic interdependence, primarily through increased trade between these member states (Graetz and Warren 2006, p. 1188).

However, it is important to acknowledge first that EU members have different languages, different economic needs, different infrastructures, and different customs. Reaching an agreement among such a diverse group is no easy task, and the nations' ultimate treaty is impressive, covering important issues including taxation affecting cross-border transactions. With this achievement in mind, the articles of the Rome treaty are analyzed, followed by a discussion of the role of the ECJ.

The European Council can adopt European tax rules only on the basis of unanimity,[17] so there is no way to force any country to change its laws or rules

[17]Demands continue to intensify for tax decisions within the EU to be made by a strong majority rather than unanimously, a more pressing concern as the EU continues to increase its membership. *See* Kaye (1996, pp. 109, 126).

without that nation's prior approval. Therefore, the EU does not have exclusive jurisdiction over direct tax laws, and tax directives can only be issued unanimously (Andersson 2000, p. 6), although the Union does have jurisdiction to decide whether a particular nation's rules conflict with the Rome treaty or not. Moreover, once a consensus is reached, no country is allowed to deviate from adopted tax rules without the consent of all of other Member States. The designers of Europe apparently did believe that the tax system was a critical factor within the various Member States. "[T]his Treaty is more than an agreement which merely creates mutual obligations between the contracting States." Instead, "the Community constitutes a new legal order of international law for ... which the states have limited their sovereign rights ... ."[18]

5.2.1 The Role of the ECJ

The EU is sometimes "wrongly assumed to have a sovereignty exception for income taxation." In fact, it does not. Several cases have made it obvious that the EU allows for basic rights to free movement and non-discrimination, which are capable of overriding national tax measures of member states (van Thiel 2001, p. xi).

The ECJ was established in 1957 by the Treaty of Rome, and was given the power to adjudicate EU related disputes.[19] Under the Treaty of Rome, ECJ rulings are binding upon the member states.[20] "Today, the ECJ has no rival as the most effective supranational judicial body in the history of the world, comparing favorably with the most powerful constitutional courts anywhere" (Warren 2001, n.22). Eric Stein summarized the work of the ECJ as follows: "the Court of Justice of the European Communities has fashioned a constitutional framework for a federal-type structure in Europe" (Warren 2001, n.23). The role of the ECJ in resolving EU income tax disputes serves to demonstrate that governments have agreed in the past, in at least this limited context, to have tax disputes adjudicated by an international court.

The ECJ's decisions are not imposed on EU members arbitrarily. First, the ECJ applies the Treaty of Rome, an obligatory international contract, and the conditions of which EU member nations are aware. Second, the fact that application of the Treaty may entail some change in domestic legislation does not mean that the ECJ is interfering with local laws; rather, the ECJ is upholding a treaty intended to be superior to local laws. Also, without interpreting and imposing its rules, the treaty will be become meaningless. It is created by the EU and staffed by the EU

[18]Case 26/62, *Van Gend en Loos v. Nederlandse Administratie Der Belastingen*, 1963 E.C.R. 1, 9–10.

[19]*See* Treaty Establishing the European Economic Community (Rome, March 25, 1957); also known as the Treaty of Rome. For a discussion of the role of the European Court of Justice, *see* Art. 7, 68, 220–245.

[20]Treaty of Rome, art. 228 (consolidated version), *see also* Kaye (1996, p. 126).

governments for the EU members regarding the EU agreements, so it's run by people who understand the current affairs of the surrounding environment.

One sign of success of this structure is the fact that EU members are reacting favorably to decisions of the ECJ. When the ECJ consistently interprets the Treaty in a non-discriminatory way, its actions are well received, and "as a result legislative changes have been introduced in several Member States" (Teixeira 2006, p. 51). For example, the Greek government was "quick" in implementing ECJ decisions with respect to income taxation (Brokelind 2007, p. 369).

5.2.2 The Cases

The basis for ECJ consists of the fundamental "four freedoms": free movement of workers,[21] freedom of establishment,[22] freedom to provide services,[23] and freedom to move capital.[24] These are considered the primary source of and powerful driving force behind the ECJ's involvement with income taxation of the EU members, and

[21]Treaty of Rome, art. 39.

[22]Treaty of Rome, art. 43.

[23]Treaty of Rome, art. 49.

[24]Art. 56 of the Treaty of Rome states:

> 1. Within the framework of the provisions set out in this chapter, all restrictions on the movement of capital between Member States and between Member States and third countries shall be prohibited.
>
> 2. Within the framework of the provisions set out in this chapter, all restrictions on payments between Member States and between Member States and third countries shall be prohibited.

Article 58 then provides that taxing different people is not prohibited, saying:

> 1. The provisions of Article 56 shall be without prejudice to the right of Member States:
>
> (a) to apply the relevant provisions of their tax law which distinguish between taxpayers who are not in the same situation with regard to their place of residence or with regard to the place where their capital is invested;
>
> (b) to take all requisite measures to prevent infringements of national law and regulations, in particular in the field of taxation and the prudential supervision of financial institutions, or to lay down procedures for the declaration of capital movements for purposes of administrative or statistical information, or to take measures which are justified on grounds of public policy or public security.
>
> 3. The measures and procedures referred to in paragraphs 1 and 2 shall not constitute a means of arbitrary discrimination or a disguised restriction on the free movement of capital and payments as defined in Article 56.

Note the language similarities between this article and the GATT or GATS versions, specifically with respect to "arbitrary" and "disguised restriction." Another article is the fiscal State aid in Article 87.1 stating that: "Any aid granted by a Member State through State resources in any form whatsoever which distorts competition or threatens to distort competition by favoring certain undertakings or the production or certain good, insofar as it affects trade between Member States."

are mostly based on the non-discrimination principle (Teixeira 2006, p. 50). The ECJ began "very cautiously" (Andersson 2000, p. 30), dealing with the issue of income tax discrimination as far back as 1986, when the first direct tax case came before the ECJ.

The *Avoir Fiscal* case[25] was a simple case of nondiscrimination, based on the traditional EU concept of freedom of establishment. It concerned foreign insurance companies with branch offices in France that were denied tax benefits which French insurance companies received. The ECJ held that for general tax purposes, French branches of foreign companies should be treated similarly to domestic ones, refusing to apply domestic provisions infringing on the non-discrimination principle. The Court held that a national tax law that refused a dividend imputation tax credit to permanent establishments of foreign nonresident companies while granting it to resident companies was in conflict with Community law. The ECJ "has constructed the freedom of establishment as meaning that tax benefits accorded to resident companies must be accorded in the same way to branches (permanent establishments) of non-resident companies if these branches are otherwise subject to corporate tax in the same way as resident companies, irrespective of their differences between branches and subsidiaries in other areas of law" (Brokelind 2007, p. 79). The Court's determination was appropriate and not unexpected; it merely reinforced the idea that tax laws of a member state must comply with the general principles of the economic community as expressed and agreed upon in the Treaty.

Since the 1990s, the ECJ has more firmly ensured that direct income taxes on individuals or companies must not conflict with EU rules, stating that "although direct taxation is a matter for the member states, they must nevertheless exercise their direct taxation power consistently with the community law."[26] For example, in *Biehl* (1990), a German national had lived and worked in Luxembourg for ten years before returning to Germany in 1983. Too much tax had been deducted from his salary, but he could not get a refund because he was not among those entitled to a refund, a benefit limited to those who had lived for the entire tax year in Luxembourg. The Court found this to be in conflict with freedom of movement of persons, and refused to allow such discrimination.

Similarly, *Archer* (1996) involved a Dutch citizen who was an active partner in a Dutch partnership and lived in Belgium. According to Dutch tax rules, anyone living in Holland was subject to a 35% income tax within a particular income bracket, of which 13% was tax proper and 22% was a social security contribution. This contribution was required of people residing abroad (such as Archer), but such individuals had no right to social security benefits. The tax rate for foreigners, however, was 25%. Holland explained that the difference between the two rates, 13% and 25%, was an attempt to avoid taxing foreigners at a far lower rate than

[25]*EC Commission v. French Republic*, C-270/83 (1986).

[26]Schumaker, ECJ in ECR (1995), I-225, Para 21.

Dutch residents. The ECJ decided that this structure was discriminatory and made it more expensive for a foreigner to establish a business in Holland than a resident.

These cases demonstrate the ECJ's firm commitment to the policy that "[no] Member State remains safe if it has tax regulations that favour its own citizens. Both overt and covert discrimination can be struck down. This action by the EC Court of Justice is welcome in that it prevents Member States from adopting and maintaining direct tax regulations that diverge from legality" (Andersson 2000, p. 30). However, the Court does attempt to be reasonable and limit its involvement. For example, the ECJ has found there is no violation of Union rules when a Member State discriminates against its own citizens, even if they live outside the country. In *Werner* (1991), a German national operated a dental practice in Germany, his only source of income, but lived in Holland. He was taxed in Germany as a foreigner and consequently lost the right to certain deductions, resulting in a heavier tax assessment. This was found by the Court to be an internal German affair, indicating the Court's willingness to stop short of infringing upon the internal sovereignty of the members states.

5.2.3 *Opening Pandora's Box*

The Court's effort to strike down income tax provisions and resolve tax disputes is not without controversy. Willem Vermeend, The Netherlands Secretary of Finance, criticized the Court as follows: "ECJ loses sight of the fact that it is dealing with delicate issues .... [I]t would be wrong to underestimate the complexity of national direct taxation, and the difficulty of non-fiscal experts in understanding it .... The Court's decisions can sometimes be read as the 'Alice in Wonderland' of fiscal legislation" (see Altman 2006, p. 32, citing Vermeend 1996, p. 55).

A.H.M. Daniels also criticized the court for being too involved in tax issues in spite of "the absence of European harmonization and the unanimity principle," arguing that "many believe that the Court opened Pandora's box. ... The Court of Justice's own rulings also have the appearances of a Pandora's box .... This uncertain evolution implies the risk that rulings of the ECJ will shoot holes in Member States' tax systems and budgets ... Those holes may confront Member States with serious problems" (Daniels 2001, p. 8).

5.2.4 *Warren and Graetz*

American academics Warren and Graetz joined the debate, arguing that the danger of the ECJ overstepping its boundaries outweighs the benefits of the Court's involvement. They examined cases relating to income tax discrimination and concluded that "the court has developed a jurisprudence of nondiscrimination that goes beyond such requirements in international trade or tax treaties" (Graetz and

Warren 2006, p. 1253) and is "creating not only legal uncertainty, but ultimately doctrinal incoherence" (Graetz and Warren 2006, p. 1254).

The professors begin by stating that "countries are generally free under the international trade and tax treaties to favor domestic production over foreign production by their own companies. The ECJ, on the other hand, has invalidated many provisions of this type, particularly in recent years" (Graetz and Warren 2006, p. 1203). This claim is not entirely true. For example, the GATT has struck down an Italian[27] tax deduction that was imposed on machines produced in Italy, not allowing domestic production to be favorably treated as compared to foreign production once the relevant foreign machinery had passed the Italian border.

The professors continued by writing that "[a]t the same time, the ECJ's jurisprudence is restricting member states' flexibility over their own fiscal policies in a manner that conflicts sharply with the member states' retention of the power to veto any European income tax legislation."[28] They argued that "it is unnecessary to restrict member states' ability to use tax incentives to stimulate their domestic economies."[29] However, the ECJ is not acting without authorization; the text not only permits but requires the Court to give effect to the Treaty and prohibits it from being inactive.

Notably, the fact that countries have been following the Court's rulings indicates an acceptance of the role of the Court. Mistakes may occur, simply because perfection cannot and should not be expected. The EU judiciary is "responsible for upholding a minimum set of rights which entitles Community economic operators to move their products and production factors freely in the various geographical and decentrally regulated parts of the market" (van Thiel 2001, p. 3). The Court may potentially step outside the bounds of what is acceptable at times when interpretation is required regarding an unclear issue, but the alternative is leaving tax issues entirely uncontrolled, and it seems EU members have chosen the former option.

Regarding the effect of the ECJ on the USA, the professors write that "if the US Supreme Court were to become convinced that the ECJ's interpretations are appropriate for the United States, the Court might impose new constraints on the flexibility of our states to enact tax incentives promoting local investments" (Graetz and Warren 2006, p. 1254). If the Supreme Court is convinced that ECJ efforts are appropriate, acceptance of the Court's actions will be bolstered.

Warren and Graetz offered another argument to exclude the Court from the realm of income tax, claiming that reliance "on corporate income taxes as an important source of government revenues could be threatened." Disregarding an absence of empirical studies, this claim would only be true if the Court's involvement was significant enough to effect the base, but the cases show that the ECJ

[27]GATT Panel Report, *Italian Discrimination Against Imported Agricultural Machinery*, L/833, adopted October 23, 1958, BISD 7S/60.

[28]GATT Panel Report, *Italian Discrimination Against Imported Agricultural Machinery*, L/833, p. 1254.

[29]GATT Panel Report, *Italian Discrimination Against Imported Agricultural Machinery*, L/833, p. 1255.

involves itself only when there is a cross-border transaction or when there is a dispute about a rule in the treaty concerning discriminatory treatment, which is not true of all disputes.

The professors continue their argument by writing that "the tax decisions of the ECJ, spurred by the tax policy objectives of the European Commission, conflict directly with the member states' retention of veto power over issues of direct taxation" (Graetz and Warren 2006, p. 1255). This argument is an exaggeration; the ECJ does not and cannot create new rules that have not been previously agreed upon by the member states, or create rules that are strikingly in a direct conflict with a fundamental right, such as the veto power – after all, the courts are comprised of judges from the EU, experienced and very familiar with the treaty's rights.

Regarding sovereignty, Warren and Graetz wrote that "to be sure, greater federalization may require giving up this autonomy. If that is to occur, however, we believe that such change should come through democratic processes, with the critical decisions made by elected representatives rather than by appointed judges" (Graetz and Warren 2006, p. 1255).

Elsewhere, they write also that the EU member states "have held on fiercely to their sovereign right to impose income taxes even as they have integrated economically in their treaties through free trade and the free movement of workers, residents, goods, services, and capital (and through the monetary union)" (Graetz and Warren 2006, p. 1193). Although possibly, the ECJ has no power to force its interpretations on the members; nations domestically elect to implement them.

"Our point is that making nondiscrimination the sole criterion for the choice necessarily suppresses considerations of efficiency, fairness, and administrability that should inform difficult tax policy decisions" (Graetz and Warren 2006, p. 1212), the academics write. This is true; tax issues are structured domestically based on the expressed criteria. Although there is no guarantee, it is likely that if countries accepted a ruling, or at least did not "fiercely" reject it, it must at least to some extent be considered acceptable by the nations concerned.

5.2.5 Lessons Learned

There are several lessons to be learned from the EU experience. The first is that structuring and handling international income taxation using a multilateral approach is possible. The EU, with a diverse multi-national group having different flags, cultures, histories, and traditions, has managed to accept multilateral tax rules. Second, despite the aforementioned criticisms, EU members seem willing to follow their agreed-upon rules and to have a positive regard for rulings of the ECJ. This is a direct response to the sovereignty objection. This has been the case since 1986, which began a 20-year period during which the countries had more than ample opportunity to express their views, objections, or concerns regarding any alleged infringement of their tax sovereignty, yet no serious tax sovereignty claims have been raised.

Since the EU is a special case, however, its experience is not necessarily directly applicable in a larger context such as, for example, the WTO. Furthermore, there will continue to be critics, those who object to multinational tax policy harmonization. One way of avoiding critics like Warren and Graetz may be to insert a clause into future suggested agreements offering countries the right to veto the ruling of any applicable court, as well as the right to modify and express reservations so that nations can join an international tax agreement with minimum fear of unexpected consequences or of potentially losing sovereignty.

5.3 History of the Interaction Between International Trade and Tax

History without analyzing is just one damn fact after another.[30]

Background

An answer to the tax and trade compatibility question lies also in history. The historical record provides a rich source for bringing tax and trade under one umbrella. The relationship between trade and tax has long been a "familiar subject in international commercial arrangements" (Wilson 1960, p. 156). The beginning of inter-actional tax treaties had the commerce environment in mind. The commercial treaties also impeded tax provisions. The intersection of the two regimes is expected, since tax can have a tremendous effect on commercial relationships and cross-border transactions among nations. It can affect the movement of goods, persons, services, capital, and other commercial elements from different regions. Understandably, nations have commonly included provisions dealing with tax discrimination, tax favor, tax burden, or other tax concepts in their commercial treaties, demonstrating the close relationship between the two fields.

The fact that this relationship has worked in the past does not mean it was flawless; it did function during the old days *with* some problems, but since international tax law, especially related to income tax, was in its infancy, it was logical and natural to have and be satisfied with a system with some problems, as long as it could solve most of the current problems and evolve to solve newly occurring problems. It did solve the original problems, but was not as successful as hoped with respect to new problems.

Trade treaties existed long before the emergence of tax treaties. They were the result of the commercial relationships between pairs of nations (see McCulloch 1883, p. 81; Neufeld 1971). Trade exists between nations for many reasons, one of which is

[30] Source unknown.

to take advantage of the different prices for commodities, which are based on different comparative advantages (see Kenwood and Lougheed 1999). The expansion of innovations makes trade among nations, advanced or not, a continuing process.

The most common characterization of commercial treaties included the concepts of "Friendship, Commerce, and Navigation."[31] Trade among nations generally began on a reciprocity basis. With advances in technology, increases in production, and other factors, treaties grew over time to reflect the more sophisticated and complicated relationships and transactions among nations.

History offers insight into the potential for combining the two fields of tax and trade. A look at the history of commercial treaties reveals that tax and trade issues have in the past co-existed under a single treaty for an extended period of time; it could mean that there would be no substantial conflict if the two were to be combined. Sharing a mutual and common background would certainly facilitate the conclusion of any given international treaty.

Furthermore, there are also other benefits from reviewing the recent history of commercial treaties, because history sheds light on events that have impacted the development of international law. Richard Gardner observed that the setting of international policies is sometimes done in an unorganized way, because particular circumstances are not suited to optimal choices,[32] so there is a need to understand its original setting to be able to grasp the difficulty and complexity of any given issue.

The first part of this chapter will cover the origin of the tax treaties, including the International Chamber of Commerce and the League of Nations' efforts. Next, the work done after World War II by the OECD and the UN will be covered, concluding with several observations. The chapter's second part will cover the commercial treaties, or the so-called Friendship, Commerce, Navigation treaties, by examining several treaties such as the US treaties with the UK and with France. This examination will cover commercial treaties in different times as well as different ideologies. Since it is impossible to cover all commercial treaties,[33] the selection of these treaties will be limited. Although the purpose of the survey is to show the existence of the tax issues in commerce treaties, to maintain maximum objectivity, the author has selected treaties for analysis that represent *different time periods* and *different geographical regions*, as well as those between nations that *differ in their ideology* and culture. Regardless of the different varieties of treaties, this study reveals that tax issues were present in most, if not all, of the treaties.

---

[31]It seems a logical combination. Other names are Treaty of Amity and Commerce, Treaty of Amity and Commerce, Treaty of Peace and Friendship, Treaty of Amity, Commerce and Navigation, for a general historical overview see, Vandevelde (2005, pp. 157, 159).

[32]Gardner, writing that international policies "must be made piece by piece – the pieces not always fitting very neatly together" (Gardner 1980, p. 423).

[33]The UN publication, 1946–2003, "contains the texts of over 158,000 records of bilateral and multilateral treaties and subsequent treaty actions in their authentic language (s), along with a translation into English and French, as appropriate." http://untreaty.un.org.ezp2.harvard.edu/English/access.asp visited April 3, 2006.

Thirdly, the post-Bretton Woods Era will be investigated, including analysis of tax related provisions under the Havana Charter. Finally, some historical lessons will be highlighted, followed by concluding remarks.

5.3.1 I. The Origin of Tax Treaties

Introduction

Tax issues are nearly universal. Nearly 2,000 years ago, Caesar Augustus even sent a decree that the entire world should be taxed (Kitto and Alexander 2003, p. 602). As with respect to income tax, "although personal incomes were occasionally taxed in medieval Italian cities, the income tax is essentially a modern form of taxation" (Lagasse et al. 2000, Income Tax). The Dutch Batavian Republic levied the first important income tax in 1797. Then, from 1799 to 1816, Great Britain levied a tax in order to raise funds for wars. Britain finally adopted a permanent income tax in 1874. The United States imposed its first income tax in 1864. Introduced during the Civil War, it was discontinued in 1872; a permanent income tax was subsequently introduced in 1913 following a series of constitutional battles. Several European countries, along with Australia, New Zealand and Japan, adopted regular income taxes during the latter half of the nineteenth century (Lagasse et al. 2000).

Cross border taxes are more difficult to trace (Seligman 1928, pp. 32–58; see also Herndon 1932, pp. 10–19). Several examples are illustrative:

- During the early days of the Islamic states, a resolution that tariffs be calculated on a reciprocity basis was issued. Thus, if a neighboring state showed an interest in having low tariffs, the Islamic state would be willing to lower its tariffs, and vice versa.
- Prior to the thirteenth century, France and Germany (Seligman 1928, p. 32) negotiated a new form of tax that had international features.[34]
- In 1490, Judge John Bertachinus in Siena wrote a "leading treatise" on the subject of indirect taxation, in which he argued that foreigners' duty to pay taxes was dependent on their nationality (Seligman 1928, p. 35).
- In 1819, the Netherlands exempted foreign ships from business-license taxes on a reciprocity basis (Carroll 1927, p. 1).[35]
- In 1870, a federal law in what is now Germany articulated that any German citizen would only be subject to direct taxes, except in the state of his domicile. In the event that there is no state of domicile, direct taxes would be based on the state of residency (Seligman 1928, p. 38).
- In 1899, as a result of a newly imposed income tax in several European nations, a simple bilateral income tax treaty was signed by Austria and Prussia on June 21,

[34]The issue during that time was whether a woman who was married to a man from a different village was liable for payment of property taxes in both locations (Seligman 1928, p. 33).

[35]*See* also a short story about this issue cited in Herndon (1932, p. 11).

1899,[36] which provided that a national of either state should be liable to income tax only in the state of domicile.
- In 1921, the first multilateral tax treaty was signed in Rome by Austria, Hungary, Italy, Poland, Yugoslavia, and Romania (Graetz and O'Hear 1997, pp. 1079–1080).

Although it is difficult to pinpoint exactly when international tax history began, it is reasonable to believe that before the First World War, income tax laws were new and their rates were very low (Brownlee and Hamilton 2004, p. 14),[37] so their effect on international commerce was minimal, and they did not act as trade barriers (Carroll 1941, pp. 793–794). In fact, "the conceptual basis for modern tax treaties developed in the period between the First and Second World Wars" (Ault 1992, pp. 567–568). This makes early income tax history less relevant to this study.

Following the First World War, there was an effort to expand domestic businesses and to "free international business from exterritorial and discriminatory taxation and also from double taxation in general" (Carroll 1939, p. 9). This study will focus on income tax history after 1920.

The International Chamber of Commerce

The emergence of tax treaties first began in the period between the two World Wars (Ault 1992, p. 567). Pressure from international businesses led to the establishment of an institutional mechanism to solve the problem of double taxation because at that time, international economic relations were developing rapidly, but cross-border transactions were impeded by overlapping tax claims (Braithwaite and Drahos 2000, pp. 96–97). The business community was at risk because of tax issues; specifically, after the First World War, "the business campaign against double international taxation became more institutionalized" (Picciotto 1989, p. 22). This occurred through the establishment of the International Chamber of Commerce (ICC), following the signing of the Versailles Treaty (Herndon 1932, p. 19).

The ICC put the matter of double taxation on its agenda as "among the most important subjects" (Seligman 1928, p. 114) and "called the attention to the paralyzing effect of multiple tax burdens on international trade" (Carroll 1939, p. 10). Beginning in the 1920s, the ICC studied the impeding effect of double taxation

---

[36]Herndon (1932, p. 16). *See also*, Carroll (1927, p. 2). Though Carroll claimed this to be the first early treaties, his claim can be disputed. Take for example the treaty between the USA and Nassau concluded in 1846, entitled: Convention for the Mutual Abolition of the Droit d'Aubaine and Taxes on Emigration Between the United States of America and his Royal Highness the Duke of Nassau; May 27, 1846. *See* Avalon project at Yale Law School. http://www.yale.edu/lawweb/avalon/diplomacy/germany/nas1846.htm last visited (1/12/2006).

[37]*Also see*, K. Julius, *Forward in* Carroll (1927, p. II), stating that the tax rates were "in general so low that having to pay taxes in two countries on the same income didn't constitute a burden on trade. But rate mounted during and after the war." *Also see*, Herndon (1932, p. 7). *See also*, Rosenbloom and Langbein (1981, pp. 359, 361).

through a committee that included members from Belgium, France, Great Britain, Italy, the Netherlands, and the United States. In a statement issued in Paris, in 1921, the committee proposed desired solutions to dealing with double income taxation:

> 1. With regard to the tax on income earned and collected within the country, from whatever source derived ..., without prejudice to the question of super-tax ... on income, each country should accord similar treatment to all taxpayers, both citizens and foreigners, whether resident in country or not. (Carroll 1939, pp. 21–22)

This was a proposal for *national treatment* of all taxpayers, regardless of their citizenship or residency. It was more liberal a proposal than could be applied today, when at best a modified "national treatment" might be extended to citizens of a treaty country, though not to all taxpayers. It is remarkable that in the year 1921, six officials from different countries requested from a respected international organization a provision that could be considered irrational by today's international taxation standards:

> 2. With regard to tax on incomes earned and collected abroad, from whatever sources derived ... without prejudice to super-tax ... on income, *a nation should accord similar treatment to all taxpayers subject to this tax (i.e., citizens or foreigners resident in the country or citizens resident abroad).* If this class of income cannot be entirely free from liability to taxation, it should be the object of a considerable rebate in consideration of the tax on such income already levied in the country of origin. (Herndon 1932, p. 23)

This proposed solution to the problem of double taxation suggested that, should a tax be levied abroad, the country of residence should be aware of the magnitude of that tax on its people or businesses and should, accordingly, offer some relief or rebate to anyone liable for payment in order to avoid double taxation. Similar requests were made around this time, all striving towards an agenda that was to prohibit "discrimination among taxpayers because of their nationality" (Herndon 1932, p. 25) because double taxation "constitutes burdens so heavy that they paralyzed the development of international trade and consequently threaten to endanger the prosperity of nations" (Herndon 1932, p. 30). Since the ICC was representing the business community, it was not authoritative on this matter. This led the business community to seek another venue to alleviate double taxation more effectively: The League of Nations.

The League of Nations

Like the ICC, and sometimes in cooperation therewith,[38] the League of Nations aimed to achieve the same goal of alleviating the effect of double taxation because

[38]Cooperation could be seen from using similar concepts and asking for similar solutions. Take for example, the urgent request to define important concepts like residency. The report by the League of Nations stated that "in order to avoid double taxation, domicile or habitual residence must everywhere be interpreted alike for the purposes of taxation." *See* League of Nations, Economic and Financial Commission, Report on Double Taxation, submitted to the Financial Committee of the League of Nations, prepared by Professors Bruins, Einaudi, Seligman and Sir Josiah Stamp,

of its effects on commerce. Its first subcommittee was composed of four well-known economic experts assigned the task of studying international double taxation from a different prospective. Its report was published in 1923:[39]

> The terms of reference given to these four experts were fixed in March 1922 by a Sub-Committee of the Financial Committee (Doc. E.F.S. 253. A. 152); they were as follows:
>
> (1) What are the economic consequences of double taxation from the point of view:
> (*a*) of the equitable distribution of burdens;
> (*b*) of interference with economic intercourse and with the free flow of capital?
>
> (2) Can any general principles be formulated as the basis for an international convention to remove the evil consequences of double taxation, or should conventions be made between particular countries, limited to their own immediate requirements? In the latter alternative, can such particular conventions be so framed as to be capable ultimately of being embodied in a general convention?
>
> (3) Are the principles of existing arrangements for avoiding double taxation, either between independent nations (e.g., the Rome Convention) or between the components portions of a federal state, capable of application to a new international convention?[40]

Experts responded by stating that "[d]ouble taxation will be either a burden or an interference."[41] The subcommittee's first objective was to study "the economic consequences of double taxation" (Seligman 1928, p. 115). The diverse economic interests and tax principles involved (Hewitt et al. 2002, p. 51) made it difficult for the subcommittee to reach a conclusion, yet the group cleared the path for construction of an international taxation system, and provided a platform through which crucial international taxation problems could be addressed.

It is not easy to establish a new field in an international setting, especially after a major war such as the First World War, but the subcommittee managed successfully to deal with the issues. It did not try to enforce one ideology, and did not try to side with one view; rather, it articulated the issues based on well-supported theories. Many concepts used by this subcommittee were shared and known beforehand, but the importance of the subcommittee's work was that it was for the first time done officially and internationally by a public institution run by government officials, unlike the ICC.

E.F.S. 73, F. 19 (Geneva, April 3, 1923), p. 26. The report by the ICC stated that "there must be a international agreement as to the meaning of domicile, applicable to individuals and corporations." *See* Herndon (1932, p. 25).

[39]League of Nations, Economic and Financial Commission, Report on Double Taxation, submitted to the Financial Committee of the League of Nations, prepared by Professors Bruins, Einaudi, Seligman and Sir Josiah Stamp, E.F.S. 73, F. 19 (Geneva, April 3, 1923). *See* Graetz and O'Hear (1997, pp. 1066–1077).

[40]League of Nations, Economic and Financial Commission, Report on Double Taxation, submitted to the Financial Committee of the League of Nations prepared by Professors Bruins, Einaudi, Seligman and Sir Josiah Stamp, E.F.S. 73, F. 19 (Geneva, April 3, 1923), p. 2.

[41]League of Nations, Economic and Financial Commission, Report on Double Taxation, submitted to the Financial Committee of the League of Nations prepared by Professors Bruins, Einaudi, Seligman and Sir Josiah Stamp, E.F.S. 73, F. 19 (Geneva, April 3, 1923), p. 3.

Technical Experts Committee

Another committee was appointed by the League of Nations to study the matter from a practical and administrative point of view[42] and to develop more practical suggestions for solving international double taxation in collaboration with the ICC committee, a delegation to convey the views of the business community:[43] the Committee of Technical Experts,[44] a group of seven high-level tax officials from Belgium, Czechoslovakia, France, Italy, the Netherlands, Switzerland, and the United Kingdom.

After several meetings, this committee reached different conclusions than the theoretical committee. While the 1923 report had "allocated personal taxes to residence and divided up impersonal taxes between source and residence, the Technical Experts allocated personal taxes to residence and impersonal taxes exclusively to source" (see Graetz and O'Hear 1997, p. 1080). The technical experts were "torn" by conflicting considerations (Seligman 1928, p. 145). On the one hand, there was a conflict between theoretical standards and practical political difficulties; on the other, there was a more fundamental conflict between capital importing countries and capital exporting countries. Capital exporting countries desired jurisdiction over income wherever it was located as long as there was a connection between the country and the income. As a result, "conflicting economic interests were soon apparent."[45]

The Tax Conventions Models

The committee met many times between 1924 and 1927 in an attempt to agree on a tax treaty model. After failing to agree on a multilateral treaty (Picciotto 1989, p. 25) or failing even to agree on one model,[46] progress was finally made in Geneva in 1927, when four bilateral tax model conventions were prepared for further discussion.[47] The conventions and their commentaries were sent to various governments. The League ultimately issued another report containing three tax convention models in 1928.[48] Draft (1a) was similar to the 1927 draft and consisted of impersonal taxes with a flat rate on some types of income and a personal income

[42]Mitchell, p. 697.

[43]Mitchell, p. 689.

[44]When "technical experts came together, their concern was to enter into some arrangements which would be politically agreeable to their respective countries." (Seligman 1928, p. 143).

[45]Hancher and Moran, p. 23.

[46]For an excellent discussion of what occurred, *see* Graetz and O'Hear (1997, pp. 1083–1090).

[47]Bilateral Convention for the Prevention of Double Taxation in the Special Matter of Direct Taxes, dealing with income and property taxes; Bilateral Convention for the Prevention of Double Taxation in the Special Matter of Succession Duties; Bilateral Convention on Administrative Assistance in Matters of Taxation; and Bilateral Convention on [Judicial] Assistance in the Collection of Taxes.

[48]Mitchell, p. 699, see also Wang (1945, p. 90).

tax subject progressive rate, illustrating the French and Italian position. Draft (1b) illustrated the US and UK position, and proposed that no distinction be made between personal and impersonal taxes, and that the credit method be employed to avoided double taxation. Draft (1c) made no distinction between the types of taxes and had a scope similar to that of Draft (1a), but permitted residence-based taxes on investment income such as interest and dividends.[49]

Post-World War II

The formation of tax models to satisfy different needs provided a framework for negotiation of a network of bilateral tax treaties internationally. The USA, for example, negotiated its first tax treaty with France in 1932 (Wang 1945, p. 107). The first new suggestions set forth by the committee were multilateral conventions called *Plurilateral Conventions,*[50] but were ultimately unsuccessful attempts. A fourth meeting took place in 1933, during which the committee first established the arm's length standard[51] and reemphasized the importance of the permanent establishment concept as described in the first League report (Wang 1945, p. 78).

After WWII, a regional conference was organized and held in Mexico in 1943 during which "Latin and South American countries were heavily represented, and they brought an economic perspective very different from that of the United States and the industrialized countries of Europe" (Hudson and Turner 1984, pp. 707–708). The conference favored taxation of international income in the source country, since most of the participants were capital exporting countries.[52] Capital exporting countries were not satisfied, and the conflict between the two taxing methods continued. At a subsequent tax convention held in London in 1946, it was suggested that there be a strong preference toward capital exporting countries, in favor of the residence principle.[53]

Organization of Economic Cooperation and Development

In late 1948, a new organization called the Organization of (European) Economic Cooperation and Development[54] (OEEC, which became the OECD in 1961) was

[49]Mitchell, p. 699.

[50]Report to the Council on the Work of the Third Session of the Committee, League of Nations Doc. C.415 M.171 1931 II A, pp. 3, 13–16 (1931). *See also* Hudson and Turner (1984, pp. 562, 571).

[51]The principle requires related countries to deal with each other, for tax purposes, as if unrelated. *See* Rosenbloom and Langbein (1981, pp. 359, 367).

[52]Mitchell, p. 708.

[53]Mitchell, p. 708.

[54]The OEEC's main goal was to rebuild Europe by administering the Marshall Plan for the reconstruction of the continent following the war. *See* Salzman (2005, p. 189).

created in the midst of World War II. Charged with studying and developing a solution to the problem of double international taxation, the Organization took over the development and supervision of model international tax treaties from the League of Nations by creating a Fiscal Committee (later the "Committee on Fiscal Affairs").

The first task of this committee was to study the possibility of creating *a multilateral tax treaty* (Rosenbloom and Langbein 1981, pp. 367–368). In its first report, the committee suggested that while it was important to form such a treaty, the starting point should be a draft, bilateral in nature, which would be applicable to all members (Rosenbloom and Langbein 1981, p. 368). It appeared that the committee felt it was too early and too much to start working on a multilateral basis, rather, it aimed at establishing a network of bilateral tax treaties that shared the same underlying principles and concepts, which in the end would constitute and develop as a multilateral tax treaty in effect, if not in fact.

The committee then published a series of thirty tax treaty articles in five installments (Rosenbloom and Langbein 1981, p. 368), which resulted in a final Report issued in 1963 entitled "Draft Double Taxation Convention on Income and Capital." This report, also known as the OECD draft of 1963, went through a series of revisions, starting in 1977 and ending in 2005.

One of the Report's recommendations was development of greater harmonization among tax conventions "in accordance with uniform principles, definitions, rules and method."[55] The goal of providing a means for settlement on a uniform basis of double taxation problems remains the most significant work of this organization, with the greatest effect on the international tax community since the publication of the first Report of the League of Nations.

This OECD model established the framework within which countries could begin negotiations with one another, and was a great success for the OECD as evidenced by the number of treaties that have followed its guidance. In 1939, there were only 20 treaties between OECD members; the number had jumped to 85 in 1963, 179 in 1977, 475 in 1995, and 740 by 2005. The model treaty has become the blueprint for virtually all bilateral tax treaties between industrialized countries. Another measure of the model's success is the reliance on it by major courts around the world. The Commentaries on the provisions of the Model Convention have become "a widely-accepted guide to the interpretation and application of the provisions of existing bilateral conventions."[56]

Other works of the OECD have also had major effects, and some have generated controversies. Transfer pricing agreements,[57] dealing with the prices charged by

[55]OECD, Report by the Committee on Fiscal Affairs, Model Double Taxation Convention on Income and Capital (April 11, 1977), Introduction at par. 5.

[56]OECD, 2005 Model Convention, note 15.

[57]OECD, Transfer Pricing Guidelines for Multinational Enterprises and Tax Administrations (1995).

associated enterprises,[58] have been a success for the OECD, even though these issues have been subject to debate since the publication of the League report.[59] In 1979, the OECD published transfer-pricing guidelines,[60] which endorsed the arm's length principle. This was followed in 1995 by a major revision in the form of the Transfer Pricing Guidelines,[61] which addressed all aspects of transfer pricing, including issues related to intangible property. More recently, the OECD published an extensive analysis of the application of transfer pricing rules to calculate the income of permanent establishments. The OECD Transfer Pricing Guidelines are arguably the most significant recent development in harmonization (Lowell and Briger 2002, p. 725; see also, Lester 1995, p. 283; Ring 2000, p. 143; Gordon and Mackie-Mason 1994).

A more controversial issue was the publication of the OECD report on tax havens and harmful preferential tax regimes.[62] The OECD asked each member country to perform a self-review to identify any aspects of its tax system which would constitute a preferential tax regime according to the criteria formulated by the Committee in 1998.[63] It stated that governments will not "stand back while their tax bases are eroded" by other countries' tax systems that "offer taxpayers ways to exploit tax havens and preferential regimes to reduce the tax that would otherwise be payable to them."[64] It identified and targeted some countries with relatively small economies, which have only their tax systems to attract foreign investments;

[58]OECD, Draft Discussion on Transfer Pricing (OECD, Paris, 1994).

[59]Legislation designed to combat such manipulation originated in Regulation 41, articles 77 and 78, of the War Revenue Act of 1917, which gave the Commissioner authority to require related corporations to file consolidated returns "whenever necessary to more equitably determine the invested capital or taxable income." T.D. 2694, 20 Treas. Dec. Int. Rev. 294, 321 (1918). Since 1921, the USA has been active in fighting the transfer pricing issue, and in 1968, section 482 authorized the United States Tax Commissioner to reallocate income among controlled enterprises using the arm's length principle. I.R.C. § 482 (1988). *See* Fuller (1990, p. 421); Loengard (1991); Wickham (1991, p. 1).

[60]OECD, Transfer Pricing and Multinational Enterprises (1979).

[61]OECD, Transfer Pricing Guidelines for Multinational Enterprises and Tax Administrations (1995).

[62]OECD, Harmful Tax Competition: An Emerging Global Issue (1998), available at http://www.oecd.org/dataoecd/33/0/1904176.pdf (visited Feb. 11, 2006). *See also* Littlewood (2004, p. 411), suggesting that "the OECD's manner of operation has been opaque and in some respects arbitrary" and that its approach to the "identification of tax havens seems flawed." Littlewood further argues that, "the OECD's approach to the identification of preferential regimes seems unsatisfactory as does the distinction that the Organization draws between 'harmful' and 'harmless' preferential regimes."

[63]A harmful preferential tax regime is essentially a targeted tax incentive; a country might operate a normal tax system, but exempt specified classes of income from tax (or subject them to tax at lower rates than apply to other forms of income). The report establishes four criteria that, if met, would indicate a nation is applying harmful tax practices: (1) no effective exchange of information; (2) lack of transparency; (3) no substantial activities or ring-fencing from domestic activities; and (4) simultaneously offering low, non-existent, or nominal tax rates.

[64]Harmful Tax Competition Report (1998), p. 37.

this understandably created conflict between the OECD and those targeted, unsatisfied small countries.[65] Overall, the OECD works were not always without controversies, perhaps because of the organization's membership limitation.

Nevertheless, the OECD is the leading international tax entity; no other organization yet has similar support of wealthy nations, abundant resources, extensive expertise, or diverse experiences in the field of international taxation. The OECD has established a strong foundation upon which it has established its model, reports, and commentaries as trustworthy in the international community. The major problem with the OECD, among other issues, is that it is a close network with no outside representation, an issue that becomes critical in the consideration of solutions to the tax-trade relationship dilemma.

United Nations

Believing that the tax treaty model issued by the OECD showed strong preference for capital-exporting countries, developing countries asked that the United Nations participate in the matter to ensure those nations' concerns were represented. In response, the United Nation Economic and Social Council issued a resolution in 1967 that emphasized the need for a tax treaty promoting productive investment between developing and developed countries.[66]

An ad hoc group of experts was appointed to study this old conflict between capital importing and exporting countries. The group was comprised of a total of 18 delegates from developing and developed countries.[67] In addition, observers from different countries[68] and from other international organizations[69] were present and allowed to listen to the discussion. Sessions were held in Geneva in 1968, and a

[65] *See* Ault (2002, p. 1); Biswas (2002); Schon (2003); Avi-Yonah (2001b, p. 1395); Avi-Yonah (2000, p. 2841); Carlson (2002, p. 163); Horner (2001, p. 179); Salinas (2003, p. 531); Stewart (2002, p. 139); Margalioth (2003, pp. 161, 175–180).

[66] *See* E.S.L. Res. 1273,. 43 UN. ESCOR, Supp. (No. 1) 5, U.N. Doc. E/4429 (1967), in United Nations, Department of Economic and Social Affairs, Tax Treaties Between Developed and Developing Countries, Part I, Annex 1, U.N. Doc. E/4614, ST/ECA/110 (New York, 1969).

[67] The countries originally represented were Argentina, Chile, France, Federal Republic of Germany, Ghana, India, Israel, Japan, Netherlands, Pakistan, Philippines, Sudan, Sweden, Switzerland, Tunisia, Turkey, United Kingdom, and the United States. A Representative from Sri Lanka was added in 1972, and a representative from Brazil in 1973.

[68] Austria, Belgium, Finland, the Republic of Korea, Mexico, Nigeria, Spain, Swaziland, and Venezuela. *See* United Nations, Model Taxation Convention Between Developed and Developing Countries, 85 TNI 41-66 (December 1, 1979), Introduction, Part A, Origin of the United Nations Model Convention.

[69] International Monetary Fund, the International Fiscal Association, the Organization for Economic Co-operation and Development, the Organization of American States and the International Chamber of Commerce. *See* United Nations, Model Taxation Convention Between Developed and Developing Countries, 85 TNI 41-66 (December 1, 1979), Introduction, Part A, Origin of the United Nations Model Convention.

preliminary report was submitted in 1969, subsequently superseded by the 1979 guidelines for the negotiation of tax treaties between developed and developing countries. In 1980, the United Nations published a model convention.[70]

Other attempts were unsuccessful. For example, Latin American countries opposed the OECD Model, arguing for exclusive taxation of income in the source country from their perspective as primarily capital importing countries. In 1971, the Andean Group[71] presented a tax convention that emphasized the principle of exclusive taxation at the source; however, capital exporting countries were not prepared to accept the territorial principle espoused by the Andean Model,[72] and the attempt failed to gain popularity outside of Latin America (Hausman 1975; see also Forgione 2003, p. 513).

Observations

Several fundamental observations may be drawn from the above summary of the history of international taxation. First, the concept of double taxation instills fear, as reflected in the actions of the ICC, the League, the OEEC, the OECD, and the UN. Although double taxation is a difficult problem, there were sincere efforts to resolve it, and promising signals that a solution could be achieved. For example, there was a call to make national treatment available to all taxpayers. It was feared because of its effects on international businesses, and that's one reason that this subject was discussed between trade and tax specialists.

Second, there did not emerge during this history any concern for loss of sovereignty due to the provisions of a tax treaty. It is true that differences between countries and their unwillingness to change their existing tax systems could be interpreted as a preservation of sovereignty, but countries showed a strong willingness to negotiate and to compromise on tax issues, realizing that they might need to give up some of their "rights" and adapt their traditional systems to new economic factors in order to raise revenue and achieve cooperation in the tax context.

Let us not forget that for the first time in modern history there was recognition of the danger of double international taxation and the need to counter it internationally and institutionally. The solution began, as all solutions do, by facing difficult circumstances and conflicting views. Let us also not forget that the timing of these initiatives was not particularly opportune; however, satisfactory solutions were still able to emerge.

Due to OECD members' military, technological, and economic superiority, including production of approximately two-thirds of the world's goods and services, and because the members support and implement its tax model, the OECD's

---

[70]United Nations, Model Taxation Convention Between Developed and Developing Countries.

[71]The Andean Group is also known as the Latin American Free Trade Association.

[72]The Model Convention for the Avoidance of Double Taxation Between Member Countries and Other Countries Outside the Subregion.

recommendations, practices, and guidelines have had, and will continue to have, a major impact on the rest of the world with respect to international tax matters.

Although the international tax regime is likely to cling to its "outdated concepts and inadequate principles" (see Graetz 2001), the historical efforts described herein were undoubtedly successful, resulting in the formation of the first popularly accepted tax treaty model and the beginning of a revolution in the international tax community. Responsibility for further changes and improvements in the regime should today be delegated to the international tax community to ensure consistency, objectivity, and proven success.

5.3.2 II. International Commerce and Tax: Friendship, Commerce, and Navigation Treaties

Now, let's turn to the other face of coin, the existence of the commercial treaties, and examine the tax element. The main obstacle to investment "is the reluctance of foreign countries to grant same treatment to foreigners for a wide variety of economic activities as they grant to their nationals, our important principle, the national treatment,[73] can be found in the friendship, commerce, navigation treaties, (FCNTs), which apply to goods, persons, and vassals" (Wilson 1960, p. 2).[74] One objective of the aforementioned treaties was, and continues to be, to provide investors with "national treatment for the enterprise in matters such as taxation, which directly affect its operations."[75] The first non-discrimination requirement in a treaty appeared in 1654, interestingly, in an agreement between Portugal and Great Britain, which provided that people from each nation "shall enjoy the same privileges and exemptions."[76] Since that time, the avoidance of discrimination has been a goal incorporated into almost all commercial treaties between nations. Following is an examination of some of these treaties.

---

[73]The Most Favored Nation (MFN) principle is also very important in tax matters. Addressing just one of these central principles would be enough from a historical point of view. To take an example, the treaty between the USA and Prussia of 1785 stated in articles 2 and 3 that: "The subjects of his majesty the king of Prussia, (citizens of the United States of America) may frequent all the coasts and countries of the United States of America, and reside & trade there in all forts of produce, manufactures and merchandise; and shall pay within the said United States no other or greater duties, charges or fees whatsoever than the most favored nations are or shall be obliged to pay; and they shall enjoy all the rights, privileges and exemptions in navigation & commerce, which the most favored nation does or shall enjoy; submitting themselves, nevertheless to the laws and usages there established, and to which are submitted the citizens of the United States, and the citizens and subjects of the most favored nations." Avalon Project Yale Law School, http://www.yale.edu/lawweb/avalon/diplomacy/germany/prus1785.htm.

[74]*See also* US Department of State, Office of Public Affairs, Commercial Treaties and US Economic Foreign Policy (1950), p. 3.

[75]US Dept. of State, Office of Public Affairs, Commercial Treaties and US Economic Foreign Policy (1950), p. 4.

[76]II Hertslet Treaties and Conventions 8, 10 (1840), cited in Bischel (1978, p. 421, footnote 8).

The US Treaty with the UK

The United States' first commercial treaty was the Treaty of Amity, signed with France in 1778.[77] The Treaty was simple, narrow in scope and concerned only with the protection of merchant shipping during wartime (Wilson 1960, p. 2).[78] In 1794, the USA formed a Friendship, Commerce, and Navigation Treaty (FCNT) with the United Kingdom, in which the principle of national treatment was emphasized. Article III of this treaty states:

> "All Goods and Merchandize whose importation into His Majesty's said Territories in America, shall not be entirely prohibited, may freely, for the purposes of Commerce, be carried into the same in the manner aforesaid, by the Citizens of the United States, and such Goods and Merchandize shall be *subject to no higher or other Duties* than would be payable by His Majesty's Subjects on the Importation of the same from Europe into the said Territories." And also it stated that "No higher or other Tolls or Rates of Ferriage than what are, or shall be payable by Natives."

It is worth noting that the USA/UK FCNT was executed prior to the emergence of the theories advocating for international trade benefits, which argued for a greater exchange of goods and services based on Adam Smith's theory (Smith 1970) or on the comparative advantage theory advanced by Ricardo (Ricardo 2004). Although these theories are by no means conclusive, and do not have universal agreement, they have changed the attitudes of the Americans and Britons toward international trade. Thus, it is striking not only to notice that countries have realized the effect of higher duties, tolls, and other charges, but also that they have given up some of their sovereignty and revenue during a time when the concept of sovereignty was at its peak, and have concluded international agreements to deal with its effect.

The US Treaty with Argentina

The US shares historical and cultural characteristics with the UK, but not as much as with South American countries. Nevertheless, the USA executed an FCNT with Argentina in 1853, which contained an article dealing with tax discrimination.

The central premise of that Treaty was the MFN principle, as demonstrated in Article IV:

> No higher or *other duties* shall be imposed on the importation into the territories of either of the two contracting parties of any article of the growth, produce or manufacture of the territories of the other contracting party, than are, or shall be, payable on the *like article of any other foreign country*; nor shall any *other or higher duties or charges* be imposed in the territories of either of the contracting parties on the exportation of any article to the

[77]US Department of State, Office of Public Affairs, Commercial Treaties and US Economic Foreign Policy (1950), p. 2.

[78]*See also* US Department of State, Office of Public Affairs, Commercial Treaties and US Economic Foreign Policy (1950), pp. 2–3.

> territories of the other, than such as are, or shall be, payable on the exportation of the *like article to any other foreign country*; nor shall any prohibition be imposed upon the importation or exportation of any article of the growth, produce or manufacture of the territories of either of the contracting parties, to or from the territories of the other, which shall not equally extend to the like article of any other foreign country.

Article III extends the MFN principle to goods, and offers such treatment to citizens of both nations that are party to the treaty:

> [T]he two high contracting parties agree that *any favor, exemption, privilege or immunity whatever*, in matters of commerce or navigation, which either of them has actually granted, or may hereafter grant, to the *citizens* or *subjects* of any other government, nation or state, shall extend, in identity of cases and circumstances, to the citizens of the other contracting party, gratuitously. . . .

The text of this Article indicates that if the USA were to offer a tax exemption to the citizens of Canada, for example, it would also have to extend that same treatment to the citizens of Argentina. This shows the relevance of taxation to the commercial environment even if this tax is on persons not on products. This treaty was also concerned with the personal tax to which individual citizens may be subject. Article X states:

> The citizens of the United States residing in the Argentine Confederation, and the citizens of the Argentine Confederation residing in the United States, shall be exempted from all compulsory military service whatsoever, whether by sea or by land, and from all forced loans, requisitions or military exactions; and *they shall not be compelled, under any pretext whatever, to pay any ordinary charges, requisitions or taxes, greater than those that are paid by native Citizens of the contracting parties respectively.*[79]

Non-US Treaties

Although the USA has had a major impact on the international community, and many initiatives have been either undertaken or dropped as a result of US support or opposition, respectively, it is necessary to examine other treaties regarding tax and trade to develop a more complete international view.

Treaty of Friendship, Establishment, and Commerce Between the Hawaiian Islands and the Swiss Confederation

Article I of the 1864 Treaty between Hawaii and Switzerland requires adherence to the MFN principle by stating that both nations:

> shall not pay on account of their commerce or industry in any of the towns, or places of the said States, whether they be there established or temporarily residing, any duties, taxes or imposts of whatever denomination they may be, *other or higher than those paid by natives*

[79]The USA and Argentina.

> *or citizens of the most favored nations* and the privileges, immunities or other favors whatever, which are enjoyed in the matters of commerce or industry by the citizens of either of the contracting States shall be common to those of the other.

The treaty also covers the national treatment principle. Article IV requires that "in no case shall [the parties] pay on the value of such property any impost, contribution or charge, other or greater than that to which natives are subject." Although this provision is applicable only to property tax, the inclusion of non-discriminatory principles over a century ago was in and of itself an impressive measure, particularly at a time when sovereignty was a much more sensitive issue.

Commercial Convention Between the United Kingdom of Great Britain and Ireland and Egypt[80]

The inclusion of MFN and national treatment was also extended to treaties to which Middle Eastern nations were party. Although much of the Middle East was under the control of the Ottoman Empire for more than 700 years, by the end of the 1800s the Ottoman Empire (see Ziegler 2004, p. 338) was unsteady and about to fall apart. Furthermore, although this treaty with Egypt could specifically serve a political purpose, every treaty contained political goals used to spread "influence of the major powers" (see Sornarajah 2004, p. 210) as well as commercial ones. In the Treaty between the UK and Egypt, which entered into force on January 1, 1890, Article II implements the MFN principle at every possible level:

> No *other or higher duties* shall be imposed on the importation into the United Kingdom of Great Britain and Ireland of any article, the produce or manufacture of Egypt, from whatever place arriving, *and no other or higher duties shall be imposed on the importation into Egypt of any article*, the produce or manufacture of the United Kingdom of Great Britain and Ireland, from whatever place arriving, than on the like article produced or manufactured in any other foreign country; nor shall any prohibition be maintained or imposed on the importation of any article, the produce or manufacture of either of the Contracting Countries, into the other, from whatever place arriving, which shall not equally extend to the importation of the like article being the produce or manufacture of any other foreign country.

Article III further states that "[n]o other or higher duties or charges shall be imposed in the United Kingdom of Great Britain and Ireland or in Egypt respectively on the exportation of any article to the other Contracting Country than such as are or may be payable on the exportation of the like article to any other foreign country . . . ."

In addition, a residual article was inserted to protect further expectations. Article IV states that:

> The Contracting Governments agree that in all matters relating to commerce and navigation, *any privilege, favor or immunity whatever* which one Contracting Party has actually

[80]Cairo, October 29, 1889; Entry Into Force [UK/Egypt] January 1, 1890.

granted, or may hereafter grant, to the natives of any other State shall, on the demand of the other Contracting Government, be immediately and unconditionally extended to the natives of the other Contracting Party.

Changing Times

Commercial treaties have increased in number over the years, presumably because of the positive effect they have on the business community and their association with the spread of peace and friendly relations among nations. These treaties have, however, changed over time to expand in scope and include provisions that recognize changing world economies and international relations.

The US Treaty with France

The USA entered into a treaty with France, more sophisticated and broader in scope than the UK treaty. The new treaty covered a variety of new topics, including both companies and natural persons, citizens, residents, and non-residents. Article IX addressed the persons to whom the treaty would be applicable:

1. The following categories:

   (a) *nationals* of either High Contracting Party *residing within the territories* of the other High Contracting Party,

   (b) *nationals* of either High Contracting Party *not residing within the territories* of the other High Contracting Party *but engaged in trade or other gainful pursuit within such territories, whether or not through a permanent establishment or a fixed place of business,*

   (c) *companies* of either High Contracting Party *engaged in trade or other gainful pursuit within the territories of the other High Contracting Party, whether or not through a permanent establishment or a fixed place of business,*

   (d) *associations* of either High Contracting Party that are engaged in scientific, educational, religious or philanthropic activities within the territories of the other High Contracting Party, whether through a fixed place of business or otherwise, *shall not be subject to any form of taxation or any obligation relating thereto, within the territories of such other High Contracting Party, which is more burdensome than that to which nationals, companies and associations of such other High Contracting Party in the same situation are or may be subject.*

2. Nationals, companies and associations of either High Contracting Party, not falling within one of the categories specified in paragraph 1 above, *shall not be subject, within the territories of the other High Contracting Party, to any form of taxation or any obligation relating thereto which is more burdensome than that to which nationals, companies and associations of any third country in the same situation* are or may be subject.
3. [...]
4. The nationals, companies and associations of either High Contracting Party referred to in paragraph 1 (b), (c), and (d) of the present Article shall not be subject, within the territories of the other High Contracting Party, *to any form of taxation upon capital, income, profits or any other basis,* except by reason of the property which they possess within those territories, the income and profits derived from sources therein, the business in which they are there

> engaged, the transactions which they accomplish there, or any other bases of taxation directly related to their activities within those territories.[81]

The national treatment principle is covered in the Article's Point (1), and the MFN principle in Point (2). The treaty indicates applicability to a diverse range of subjects, including the citizens of both countries, whether resident or not, as well as those who engage in commercial conduct in either of the countries' permanent establishment. In addition, this treaty covered social, educational, and religious associations, and companies without regard to their residency, as well as a broad spectrum of taxes, including those imposed on income, profits, and capital.

The existence in this early treaty of a permanent establishment concept indicates that such commercial treaties shaped the structure of modern tax treaties, which commonly include such provisions.

US and Yemen Friendship and Commerce Treaty (1946)

The 1946 US Treaty with Yemen illustrates the expansion of the inclusion of anti-discrimination provisions to include Arab nations, which shows that the pattern to conclude such a treaty with such provisions was spreading out in every direction in the globe. The most important article to our discussion is Article IV. It states that:

> In all matters relating to *customs duties and charges of any kind* imposed on or in connection with importation or exportation or otherwise *affecting commerce* and navigation, *to the method of levying* such duties and charges, to all rules and formalities in connection with importation or exportation, and to transit, warehousing and other facilities, each Party *shall accord unconditional and unrestricted most-favored-nation treatment* to articles [related to] the growth, produce or manufacture of the other Party, from whatever place arriving, or to articles destined for exportation to the territories of such other Party, by whatever route. Any advantage, favor, privilege or immunity with respect to any duty, charge or regulation affecting commerce or navigation now or hereafter accorded by the United States of America or by the Kingdom of the Yemen to any third country will be accorded immediately and unconditionally to the commerce and navigation of the Kingdom of the Yemen and of the United States of America, respectively.

It is interesting to note that not only did the MFN principle apply to duties and levies imposed on products or articles, it was also extended to cover the procedures one was supposed to follow in order to fulfill governmental requirements.

Different Ideology: Germany and Kingdom of Siam Friendship Treaty (1928)

The 1928 friendship treaty between Germany and the Kingdom of Siam contained provisions that would be considered very liberal by today's standards with regard to taxation issues. Article II states that "[t]he citizens or the subjects of the High

[81]France–United States. *Convention of Establishment, with Protocol and Joint Declaration*. Paris, November 25, 1959.

Contracting Parties shall not be compelled to, in the territory of the other, to pay any charges or taxes other or higher than those paid by nationals or the citizens or subjects of the most-favored-nation."[82] At this time, before Adolf Hitler rose to power with his own extreme discriminatory beliefs, a friendship treaty with the Kingdom of Siam was deemed be beneficial to Germany and worth relinquishment of some of Germany's sovereign powers related to taxation.

Observations

The most noticeable feature that can be extracted from the above discussion is the clear presence of the tax issue in commercial treaties. Regardless of many important elements, including timing, ideology, geography, or culture closeness, commercial treaties were concluded among a variety of nations with diverse backgrounds in different time periods. Most, if not all, included a tax issue somehow, whether it was called a levy, a charge, a duty, or a tax. A revenue-generating unit was given up based on reciprocal approach.

It should be clear by now that during the early days of commercial treaty protocol development, nations were willing to treat foreigners the same as their own citizens. Since the international commerce arena is never static, changes did, and will continue to occur. Tax issues were included under this type of treaty without any reluctance by the nations.

Moreover, this friendly attitude showed that tax issues were dealt with under commerce treaties and not separately. Commercial treaties were in some ways similar to the WTO agreements, specifically the WTO-mini-agreement. Naturally, the volume of goods, services and investments were less than they are today, but still they were neither negligible nor easily dismissible taking into account their potential affect on the relationship between countries.

Again, this short overview should not and does not mean that every commercial treaty has always included a tax issue, or that every country has a treaty with all other countries. The point is that different countries have concluded commercial treaties containing tax matters with other countries in different time periods frequently enough that such treaties can't be considered the exception; rather, they can be considered the norm to a large extent.

This summarized history of the commercial treaties is necessary background to keep in mind when discussing the trade and tax relations as they stand nowadays. It is not easy to discuss these complex relationships without knowing the past. Omitting the history could be fatally harmful to our understanding.

Thus, history informs us of what we should avoid, what we should do better, what should expect and how we should react in case something happens. It is an informative tool that is very rich; hence, it is included in this study. With that in

[82]Treaty of Friendship, Commerce and Navigation and Protocol Concerning the Provisional Economic Arrangement Between Germany and Siam Signed at Bangkok, April 7, 1928.

mind, it is time to move to another, and more recent, commercial development: the Bretton Woods era.

5.3.3 III. Bretton Woods Era

The world climate changed dramatically following WWII, with peace among nations recognized as an essential element for prosperity that could be accomplished in various ways, including the development of strong commercial ties and low tariffs (Hudec 1990, p. 6). Treaties encouraging investment and securing a more favorable environment for international investors spread all over the world, with Americans and Britons taking the initiative to plan this next phase of international relations.

Immediately following the war, an effort was made to encourage trade liberalization to counteract the protectionist measures that had emerged, most notably high tariffs. The original intention was to create international multilateral institutions, called "Bretton Woods" institutions. Following the successful creation of the International Monetary Fund (IMF) and the World Bank (WB), the key pillars of post-World War II reconstruction and economic development, a third institution was necessary to handle the trade aspects of international economic cooperation.

The history of the International Trade Organization (ITO) (see also Van den Bossche 2005, pp. 13–14) can be traced to two programs, one with its roots in the USA and the other in the UK. The US program was led by Cordell Hull, who dreamed of drafting a comprehensive commercial code that would govern the conduct of world trade. In the UK, James Madeade, a member of the economic section of the War Cabinet Secretariat, drafted a complementary plan on commercial policy known as the Commercial Union. In 1943, the Americans and Britons met informally in Washington, DC (Hudec 1990, p. 9). to discuss their plans regarding the creation of a commercial union and the "multilateral convention on commercial policy" to develop international trade rules aimed at facilitating global commerce. This meeting, in which participants recognized the importance of a commercial convention "supplemented by an international trade organization, to interpret the convention and investigate complaints and settle differences between members" (Hudec 1990, p. 104), resulted in the first draft of the ITO.[83]

The USA proposed a "Suggested Chart" (Hudec 1990, p. 12), and subsequently submitted a proposal to the Economic and Social Council (ECOSOC) of the United Nations regarding the establishment of an international trade organization that was to be named, accordingly, the International Trade Organization (ITO). The idea behind the ITO was to create the first commercial attempt to institutionalize and globalize commerce. The ECOSOC held an international conference[84] in 1946 to consider the US and UK proposals, and as a result, a UN Preparatory Committee

[83]Final Act of the United Nations Conference on Trade and Employment: Havana Charter.

[84]United Nations Conference on Trade and Employment (1946).

drafted the ITO Charter, which, in 1948, was approved in Havana. What came to be known as the "Havana Charter" was the first step toward multilateral institutionalization not only of trade matters, but also of the relationship between trade and tax. Income tax rules and issues were articulated in Articles 11, 18, and 72 of the Charter.

Article 11: Means of Promoting Economic Development and Reconstruction

Article 11 is a policy article. It discusses a number of issues, including the following:

> 1. Progressive industrial and general economic development, as well as reconstruction, requires among other things adequate supplies of capital funds, materials, modern equipment and technology, and technical and managerial skills.

There is a clear emphasis on easing the movement of, or facilitating access to, capital, goods or raw materials, technology, and services. The Article goes on to state:

> Accordingly, in order to stimulate and assist in the provision and exchange of these facilities:
>
> (b) no Member shall take unreasonable or unjustifiable action within its territory injurious to the rights or interests of nationals of other Members in the enterprise, skills, capital, arts or technology which they have supplied.

This general requirement is broadly inclusive, encompassing, among other things, tax measures imposed by a given member nation if such were to cause injury to other members:

> Article 11 continues with a list of possible ways to achieve the stated goal:
>
> 2. The Organization may, in such collaboration with other inter-governmental organizations as may be appropriate:
>
> (a) make recommendations for and promote bilateral or multilateral agreements on measures designed:
>
> (i) to assure just and equitable treatment for the enterprise, skills, capital, arts and technology brought from one Member country to another;
> (ii) to avoid international double taxation in order to stimulate foreign private investments[.]

Concern with the potential for double taxation emerges herein. Section (a), above, provided that the ITO be empowered to administer bilateral or multilateral agreements dealing with double taxation, in collaboration with other international organizations. This section further listed equitable treatment in (i) just prior to double taxation clause in (ii). If it was not done intentionally, it seemed that this was a logical organization, because double taxation as well as discriminatory taxation could not be characterized as fair.

This Article, in Section (b), also permits the ITO to "make recommendations and promote agreements designed to facilitate an equitable distribution of skills, arts, technology, materials and equipment, with due regard to the needs of all Members."

The drafters clearly intended that the ITO should promote agreements aimed at protecting the equitable distribution of capital, goods, services, and technology.

Article 18: National Treatment on Internal Taxation and Regulation

Article 18 is almost identical to Article III of the GATT, which was initially intended to be part of the ITO. (Indeed, many of the articles are closely similar to the GATT provisions.) This article has had a tremendous effect on taxation. Looking at the title and provisions within the article, it is interesting to notice that each time the word internal taxation comes up, it is followed by, "and regulation." It does not seem that tax was considered in the eyes of the drafters as part of the regulation, although it could mean that they felt internal taxation deserved more attention. Furthermore, it seems that internal taxation and internal regulation shared certain elements in that they could be used to discriminate against foreign productions. Also, their scope overlaps considerably in being the most effective means to produce favorable results, some of which can be discriminatory:

1. The Members recognize that internal taxes and other internal charges and laws, regulations and requirements affecting the internal sale, offering for sale, purchase, transportation, distribution or use of products, and internal quantitative regulations requiring the mixture, processing or use of products in specified amounts or proportions, should not be applied to imported or domestic products so as to afford protection to domestic production.
2. The products of any Member country imported into any other Member country shall not be subject, directly or indirectly, to internal taxes or other internal charges of any kind in excess of those applied, directly or indirectly, to like domestic products. Moreover, no Member shall otherwise apply internal taxes or other internal charges to imported or domestic products in a manner contrary to the principles set forth in paragraph 1.
3. [...]
4. The products of any Member country imported into any other Member country shall be accorded treatment no less favourable than that accorded to like products of national origin in respect of all laws, regulations, and requirements affecting their internal sale, offering for sale, purchase, transportation, distribution or use. The provisions of this paragraph shall not prevent the application of differential internal transportation charges which are based exclusively on the economic operation of the means of transport and not on the nationality of the product.

   ...

   8.

(a) [...]
(b) The provisions of this Article shall not prevent the payment of subsidies exclusively to domestic producers, including payments to domestic producers derived from the proceeds of internal taxes or charges applied consistently with the provisions of this Article and subsidies effected through governmental purchases of domestic products.

Article 72: Functions

In Article 72, the Charter again emphasized the importance of dealing with potential double taxation, delegating to the ITO the job of undertaking studies to promote bilateral or multilateral agreements to achieve the Organization's objectives, of which avoiding double taxation is one. The Article reads as follows:

> 1. The Organization shall perform the functions attributed to it elsewhere in this Charter. In addition, the Organization shall have the following functions:
>
> ...
>
> (c) to undertake studies, and, having due regard to the objectives of this Charter and the constitutional and legal systems of Members, make recommendations, and promote bilateral or multilateral agreements concerning measures designed
>
> (i) to assure just and equitable treatment for foreign national and enterprises;
> (ii) to expand the volume and to improve the bases of international trade, including measures designed to facilitate commercial arbitration and the avoidance of double taxation ....

The intention of the drafters was clearly to include tax issues within the authority delegated to the international organization. Had this organization been established, it would have participated in the formation of all tax treaties.

The Charter was redrafted three times before the final Charter was signed by 54 nations in Havana in March of 1948 at a UN Conference on Trade and Employment. However, ratification proved difficult, as many nations waited for the USA to first approve the Charter. When the USA announced in 1950 that it would not seek Congressional ratification of the Havana Charter, the ITO was effectively dead. However, the commercial section of the Charter survived, and later became the GATT, which was forced to take on an expanded role as a multilateral trade mechanism (Brown 1994, pp. 347, 351).

A History Lesson: Why Did the GATT Succeed and the ITO Fall Short?

The GATT lacked many fundamental components, such as administration and institutional structure, because it had been expected to be included under the ITO. Nevertheless, the GATT functioned relatively well as an international organization for many years despite its shortcomings, with perhaps its greatest success illustrated by the birth of the WTO.

Comparing the failure of the ITO to the success of the GATT can offer valuable insight into how to approach the creation of such organizations in the future. A number of issues are instructive regarding why the broader organizational structure failed while the GATT survived to shape modern international tax and trade policies. Studying the history of the ITO and GATT[85] is essential to understanding those reasons, because the circumstances during that time and the issues raised can appear again in other issues, such as bringing international taxation to the forefront. Thus, extracting the most important lessons can be beneficial in avoiding similar pitfalls in the future because the ITO, and later the GATT, was the first attempt at

[85]For a complete history, *see* Wilcox (1949); Hudec (1990); Dam (1970); Jackson (1969).

institutionalizing the commercial regime internationally and multilaterally. Any objection to institutionalizing international tax multilaterally has been already raised by the GATT. This does not mean that if we solve the old problems we will be free to adopt a multilateral international tax system. Though tax issues share similar characteristics with trade matters, there are still distinctive features which cannot be resolved with one solution.

The failure of the ITO, in contrast to the success of the GATT/WTO, can further illustrate the circumstances and conditions needed for success. Success in completing such an enormous project is not easy; it needs the right subjects, timing and circumstances. If we can point out the critical components of the failure of the ITO, we will thus have a benchmark according to which we can evaluate the possibility of success for any proposal relating to multilaterally institutionalizing the international tax regime. This section addresses those conditions needed to maximize the possibilities of success.

Broad Coverage

The broad ITO extended beyond the trade issues to include rules on employment, living standards, increased real income, development of developing countries, access to markets and restricted business practices, international investment, tax agreements, labor (Eres 2004, pp. 597, 605), human rights (Bal 2001, p. 62), and the service sector, some of which were only remotely linked to the core of the commercial regime as perceived during that period. Even today, some of the aforementioned subjects, such as labor and human rights issues, lack a close connection with the core of the trade area.

The first Article of the Charter illustrated this over-broad scope, stating that countries would:

> pledge themselves, individually and collectively, to promote national and international action designed to attain the following objectives:
>
> 1. To assure a large and steadily growing volume of real income and effective demand, to increase the production, consumption and exchange of goods, and thus to contribute to a balanced and expanding world economy.
> 2. To foster and assist industrial and general economic development, particularly of those countries which are still in the early stages of industrial development, and to encourage the international flow of capital for productive investment.
> 3. To further the enjoyment by all countries, on equal terms, of access to the markets, products and productive facilities which are needed for their economic prosperity and development.
> 4. To promote on a reciprocal and mutually advantageous basis the reduction of tariffs and other barriers to trade and the elimination of discriminatory treatment in international commerce.
> 5. To enable countries, by increasing the opportunities for their trade and economic development, to abstain from measures which would disrupt world commerce, reduce productive employment or retard economic progress.
> 6. To facilitate through the promotion of mutual understanding, consultation and co-operation, the solution of problems relating to international trade in the fields of employment, economic development, commercial policy, business practices and commodity policy.

With its wide coverage, the ITO would be ill-equipped to handle all issues at once. The ambitious goals of the Charter were more than a single trade organization could possibly accomplish, especially after the war.

Exceptions as Rules

In a failed attempt to satisfy everyone, the ITO Charter was "riddled with exceptions and escape clauses" (Aaronson 1996, p. 68) that rendered it a poor and inappropriate solution to the dilemmas at hand. Since the Charter included subjects that were beyond the ITO's normal jurisdiction, exceptions were necessary. Rather than codifying the actual rules of trade that would open up world markets (Aaronson 1996, p. 68), the Charter codified the exceptions, but the exceptions were too numerous to make the Charter workable. According to Professor Robert Hudec, it had so many gaps that "nothing" would have been better than to have it as such (Hudec 1990, p. 53).

The resulting Charter was a conglomeration of the exceptions that could not be reconciled into one document. Nations were unimpressed with the structure of the Charter, and businesses, including the American businesses that played significant behind-the-scenes roles, felt that the ITO was unpredictable, worrying that it would "prove too bureaucratic, too tolerant of exchange and trade restrictions, and too much a forum for developing and debtor countries" (Lovett et al. 1999, p. 59). In fact, Mr. Campbell of the US chamber of commerce stated that the chamber would accept the ITO if it contained only the commercial issues, contained in Section IV (Aaronson 1996, p. 125), which was the GATT.

The ITO contained concepts that "please[d], but also offend[d], nearly everybody."[86] The combination of too many subjects forced the ITO Charter to compromise on important issues, weakening it to the point that countries viewed it as unreliable and could not commit themselves thereto.

US and UK Conflicts

Perhaps the most difficult issue facing the ITO was that each country had its own priorities, some of which conflicted with the priorities of other countries. The major conflict came from the original planning countries, i.e., the USA and the UK. Although the two nations shared a goal of a uniform multilateral commercial treaty, each wanted the resulting product to be based on its own needs and visions.

Trade officials in both countries worked towards improving their *own* plans. Even though they were working together to create a multilateral commercial organization, each country was following its own, and sometimes totally different, agenda and objectives. For example, the USA wanted to remove high and

---

[86]Grander, p. 364.

discriminatory taxes,[87] to allow more free trade policies, to reduce tariffs and restrictions, and to make the system less rigid with regard to subsidies to the agriculture sector (Hudec 1990, p. 65). In addition, the USA wanted to eliminate the preferential treatment the UK enjoyed with so-called Commonwealth countries. Meanwhile, the UK desired a reduction in the high US tariffs and achievement of full employment (Goldstein 1993, p. 216). In the end, US officials, determined to succeed at any cost, allowed the British to retain their imperial preferences, which was perceived poorly in the USA. The negotiators should have reported to Congress that their negotiations with the British failed instead of achieving only a 5% elimination of imperial preferences (Gardner 1980, p. 360). Since the negotiators did not do this, there was a misconception that the ITO was killed mainly by the USA and not by the US negotiators. After all, it was the negotiators that raised the expectation of Congress (Gardner 1980, p. 350) that imperial preference would be eliminated, while keeping all of the US anti-free trade issues intact.

Conflicts Among Other Countries

The failure of the ITO could have been foreseeable, in retrospect, because the negotiations were between only the USA and the UK. The ITO negotiation was an international gathering of representatives from 55 countries, including China, Syria, Cuba, the UK, and the USA. In a group so diverse, each participant approached the negotiation with its own concerns and independent methods of solving problems, which proved to be an unworkable scenario. With such different ideologies, backgrounds, and agendas,[88] which differed from the rest of the world's (see Hudec 1992, pp. 67, 71; Kale 1988, pp. 291, 292), negotiating fundamental issues like MFN, national treatment, tariffs, and subsidies became first a formidable task, and within a short time became an impossible one.

A further problem was the lack of inclusion of other countries' concerns in the process of developing the proposals from their inception. After three years of negotiation, the USA and the UK finally invited under-developed countries (as they were called at that time) to come and participate in the process. These countries insisted on including issues that had not been extensively studied (Weiss 2002). They did manage to insert their issues. In the end, this could have contributed to the breakdown of the ITO when those nations' issues proved not to have been sufficiently studied.

[87] Thomas, p. 133.

[88] Dam (2005, p. 709), stating "[I]t went well beyond trade negotiations to include a full range of economic chapters ranging from commodity agreements to economic development and even to employment. When one considers the socialist thinking – nationalizations and central planning that were so much the vogue in the late 1940s – we are perhaps fortunate that it failed."

Too Much Too Soon

New concepts need time to develop before they can be gradually accepted, particularly in the international arena, where different ideologies and circumstances prevail. This was not the case during the introduction of the ITO; it seemed as though "making history" at any expense was the most important goal. For example, Will Clayton said, "This is a day for history." "Few" international commercial agreements have affected "[so] many vital economic interest[s] of so many states" (Gardner 1980, p. 368). The major players appeared to want to "make history" at the expense of devoting the necessary time and caution to potentially sensitive issues. Unlike advocates of the United Nations, the IMF, and the World Bank, proponents of the ITO never mounted an effective appeal for public support (Aaronson 1996, p. 42). In light of the establishment of the IMF and WB, officials overestimated their chances of success despite a lack of support and planning.

Special Interests

Public choice theory (Buchanan and Tullock 1962) teaches that officials will attempt to protect their own interests and powers from being minimized; in other words, politicians are motivated by self-interest. Trade, tax, labor, and diplomatic officials are no exception. Thus, when the Charter came into life, having been negotiated mainly by trade officials (Hudec 1988), participants from different interest groups clashed in an effort to protect their own regimes. Tax officials wanted to keep tax matters under their own control; labor departments wanted to keep labor issues under their own control. No group was willing relinquish control.

If other officials feel superior to trade officials, the situation is much harder. And this was what, to some extent, happening behind the scenes. Finance or treasury department officials thought of themselves, and of the work done by their departments, as superior to others, including trade people. This feeling complicated matters and made it more difficult to achieve meaningful results. If trade people, being the architects, structure an international agreement under an international organization, in essence eliminating the role of finance people, that means declaring war with everybody else. Ultimately, they can't fight everyone; hence, the ITO failed.

Trade matters are similar to tariffs, sales contracts, shipping, and so on. When added to Havana Charter issues like employment, tax, social development, and the needs of developing countries, people in other departments balked. No one, except probably the trade officials themselves, believed that the trade people were best equipped to manage these complicated subjects. International trade and diplomatic officials were running the show in the ITO and afterward in the GATT. Therefore, it is not difficult to see why other officials in other departments would be not very happy with the ITO's work because it excluded them, or at least made working under the trade officials seem unattractive.

Hudec writes: "In the United States government, as in most others, a jurisdictional line exists between matters that belong to the finance ministry (the Treasury Department) and those which belong to the trade ministry (the Office of the United States Trade Representative). Trade ministries have jurisdiction over trade measures, and they deal with their problems in GATT. Finance ministries deal in the more elite area of fiscal and monetary matters and take their problems to international fora, such as the Organization for Economic Cooperation and Development (OECD) or the International Monetary Fund (IMF). Finance ministers tend to outrank trade ministers and so tend to dictate where the jurisdictional line is drawn" (Hudec 1988, pp. 1553–1554).

This observation was reflected during the DISC clearly. During the dispute, the Treasury officials (that is, the tax people), "did not need the GATT to tell them how to do their job" (Hudec 1988, p. 1454). Later on, the Treasury Department eventually had to bow to the government's international obligations under the GATT, but "did so only grudgingly, however, and only on its own terms, making the sort of demands on GATT that finance ministries usually make when dealing with trade ministries" (Hudec 1988, p. 1454). Then, within the GATT, the Treasury officials insisted "on making the GATT adjudication procedures measure up to finance ministry standards" (Hudec 1988, p. 1555), by demanding that all four tax cases "be treated as one case" (Hudec 1988, p. 1555). Not only that, but an attitude of superiority surfaced when the Treasury insisted, "that the panel include at least one tax expert – someone with the capacity to understand the finer points of international tax policy" (Hudec 1988, p. 1555).

The GATT Creation

Many of the mistakes that occurred during the creation of the ITO were avoided during the creation of the GATT. The GATT managed to alleviate tensions and to produce results by controlling countries' behaviors, impressive successes that led ultimately to the creation of the WTO, negotiated by 114 nations. On July 27, 2007, just 12 years following its creation, the WTO had more than 151 members.[89]

GATT negotiators, coming from the State Departments of the USA and the UK (see Swinbank and Tanner 1996, p. 2; see also Zeiler 1999, p. 1; Resnick 2003, pp. 72–57), had similar backgrounds and similar goals: to reduce tariffs and limit trade barriers. In addition, participant nations wanted to begin a new post-war phase (even though some might argue that the GATT was about American politics, values and security, see Zeiler 1999, p. 2)

With only 23 countries participating in the negotiations, the environment was conducive to an appreciation for the sensitivity of certain issues, and many special interest pressures could be avoided. Hudec notes that the success of the GATT was likely due to "caution and low visibility" (Hudec 1990, p. 55), an

[89]http://www.wto.org/english/thewto_e/whatis_e/tif_e/org6_e.htm.

approach followed both during and after the GATT negotiations that was absent during consideration of the ITO. Also, there was an urgent need to negotiate tariffs – thus, there was hardly any room for negotiations to include double tax issues (Graetz and O'Hear 1997, pp. 1051–1052).

5.4 Observations

The first issue that can be seen throughout the history of trade treaties is the prominence of tax issues. Signs of tax issues have clearly always been present in commercial treaty culture. This is to be expected, given that taxation can affect the purposes and the goals of commercial relations, or can nullify treaties entirely. However, the role of tax in trade treaties should not be overstated; careful analysis reveals that most of the tax provisions discussed herein were merely policy issues rather than technical in nature. Negotiating countries requested inclusion of MFN or national treatment provisions, but did not provide details, since the treaties served primarily trade goals. It is also important to recognize that many tax-related issues are recent and were not yet of crucial importance at the time these treaties arose.

Finally, the most noticeable trend we can observe is the fact that taxation was not a very sensitive issue. While it was included in ITO discussions, many of the opponents of the ITO were more concerned with other issues, such as the tariffs and preferential areas. All of this has changed, especially since World War II.

References

Aaronson SA (1996) Trade and the American dream: a social history of postwar trade policy. University Press of Kentucky, Lexington

Altman ZD (2006) Dispute resolution under tax treaties. IBFD, Amsterdam

Andersson E (2000) EC court of justice combats income tax discrimination. Merita Bank UNITAS Econ Rev 72(4):24–29

Annan K (1999) Two concepts of sovereignty. The Economist 352:49

Ault HJ (1992) Corporate integration, tax treaties and the division of the international tax base: principles and practices. Tax L Rev 47:565

Ault HJ (2002) Tax competition: what (if anything) to do about it? In: Kirchhof P et al. (eds) International and comparative taxation: essays in honour of Klaus Vogel, vol 26. Kluwer, London

Avi-Yonah RS (2000) Tax, trade, and harmful tax competition: reflections on the FSC controversy. Tax Notes Int'l 21:2841

Avi-Yonah RS (2001a) Treating tax issues through trade regimes. Brook J Int'l L 26:1683, 1692

Avi-Yonah RS (2001b) Tax competition and e-commerce. Tax Notes Int'l 23:1395

Avi-Yonah RS (2004) International tax as international law. Tax L Rev 57:483, 490

Bal S (2001) International free trade agreements and human rights: reinterpreting article XX of the GATT. Minn J Global Trade 10:62

Bischel JE (ed) (1978) Income tax treaties. Practising Law Institute, New York

Biswas R (2002) International tax competition: globalization and fiscal sovereignty. Commonwealth Secretariat, London

Bodin J (1992) On sovereignty. Cambridge University Press, Cambridge

Bradley O (1999) A modern Maistre: the social and political thought of Joseph de Maistre. University of Nebraska Press, Lincoln, NA

Braithwaite J, Drahos P (2000) Global business regulation. Cambridge University Press, Cambridge

Brokelind C (eds) (2007) Towards a homogeneous EC direct tax law. IBFD, Amsterdam

Brown BS (1994) Developing countries in the international trade order. N Ill U L Rev 14:347, 351

Brownlee WE, Hamilton LH (2004) Federal taxation in America: a short history. Cambridge University Press, Cambridge

Buchanan JM, Tullock G (1962) The calculus of consent: logical foundations of a constitutional democracy. University of Michigan Press, Ann Arbor, MI

Carlson K (2002) When cows have wings: an analysis of the OECD's tax haven work as it relates to globalization, sovereignty, and privacy. J Marshall L Rev 35:163

Carmody S (1994) Balancing collective security and national sovereignty: does the United Nations have the right to inspect North Korea's nuclear facilities? Fordham Int'l L J 18:229

Carroll MB (1927) Double taxation relief, discussion of conventions drafted at international conference of experts 1927 and other measures. US Bureau of Foreign and Domestic Commerce, Trade Information Bulletin No. 523.

Carroll MB (1939) Discriminatory and extra-territorial taxation. Delivered at the Lawyers Club, New York City, March 21, 1935

Carroll MB (1941) Development of international tax law in the Americas, law and contemporary problems. Hemispheric Trade 8(4):793–794.

Dam KW (1970) The GATT: law and international economic organization. University of Chicago Press, Chicago

Dam KW (2005) Cordell Hull, The reciprocal trade agreements act and the WTO. NYU J L Bus 1(3):709

Daniels AHM (2001) Sovereign affairs. Intertax 29(1):2

Eres T (2004) The limits of GATT article XX: a back door for human rights? Geo J Int'l L 35:597, 605

Forgione A (2003) Weaving the continental web: exploring free trade, taxation, and the internet. NAFTA L Bus Rev Am 9:513

Fowler MR, Bunk JM (1995) Power, and the sovereign state: the evolution and application of the concept of sovereignty. Pennsylvania State University Press, University Park

Fuller JP (1990) Section 482: revisited again. Tax L Rev 45:421

Fulton TW (1911) The sovereignty of the sea. William Blackwood, London

Gardner R (1980) Sterling–dollar diplomacy, 3rd rev. edn. Clarendon, Oxford

Goldsmith J (2000) Sovereignty, international relations theory, and international law. Stan L Rev 52:959, 967

Goldstein J (1993) Creating the GATT rules: politics, institutions, and American policy. In: Ruggie JG (ed) Multilateralism matters: the theory and practice of institutional reform. Columbia University Press, New York

Gordon R, Mackie-Mason J (1994) Why is there corporate taxation in a small open economy? The rule of transfer pricing and income shifting. National Bureau of Economic Research Working Paper No. 4690

Graetz MJ (2001) The David R. Tillinghast lecture: taxing international income – inadequate principles, outdated concept, and unsatisfactory policy. Brooklyn J Int'l L 26:1357

Graetz MJ, O'Hear MM (1997) The "original intent" of US international taxation. Duke L J 46:1021, 1106–1107

Graetz MJ, Warren AC (2006) Income tax discrimination and the political and economic integration of Europe. Yale L J 115:1186

Hausman JS (1975) The Andean pact model convention as viewed by the capital exporting countries. In: Atchabahian A et al (eds) Fiscal harmonization in the Andean countries. International Bureau of Fiscal Documentation, Amsterdam
Heller TC, Sofaer AD (2001) Sovereignty: the practitioners' perspective. In: Krasner SD (ed) Problematic sovereignty: contested rules and political possibilities. Columbia University Press, New York
Henkin L (1979) How nations behave. Columbia University Press, New York
Henkin L (1993) The mythology of sovereignty. Am Soc'y Int'l L Newsl 1993:10
Henkin L (1999) That "S" word: sovereignty and globalization, and human rights, et cetera. Fordham L Rev 68:1
Henkin L, Pugh RC, Schachter O, Smit H (1993) International law: cases and materials, 3rd edn. West, St. Paul
Herndon JG (1932) Relief from international income taxation: the development of international reciprocity for the prevention of double income taxation. Callaghan, Chicago
Hewitt P, Lymer A, Oats L (2002) History of international business taxation. In: Lymer A, Hasseldine J (eds) The international taxation system. Kluwer, Norwell
Horner FM (2001) Do we need an international tax organization? Tax Notes Intl 24:179
Hudec RE (1988) Reforming GATT adjudication procedures: the lessons of the DISC case. Minn L Rev 72:1443
Hudec RE (1990) The GATT legal system and world trade diplomacy, 2nd edn. Butterworth, New Hampshire
Hudec RE (1992) GATT and the developing countries. Colum Bus L Rev 1992:67, 71
Hudson DM, Turner DC (1984) International and interstate approaches to taxing business income. NW J Int'l L Bus 6:562, 571
Jackson JH (1969) World trade and the law of GATT. The Michie, Charlottesville, VA
Jackson JH (2007) Sovereignty, the WTO and changing fundamentals of international law. Cambridge University Press, Cambridge
Jeffery RJ (1999) The impact of state sovereignty on global trade and international taxation. Kluwer, The Hague
Jonas DS (2005) Variations on non-nuclear: may the "final four" join the nuclear nonproliferation treaty as non-nuclear weapon states while retaining their nuclear weapons? Mich St L Rev 2005:417–459
Kale K (1988) The principle of preferential treatment in the law of GATT: toward achieving the objective of an equitable world trading system. Cal W Int'l L J 18:291, 292
Kaufman NH (1998) Fairness and the taxation of international income. Law Pol'y Int'l Bus 29:145, 148
Kaye TA (1996) European tax harmonization and the implications for US tax policy. B C Int'l Comp L Rev 19:109, 126
Kenwood AG, Lougheed AL (1999) The growth of the international economy 1820–2000. Routledge, New York
Kitto J, Alexander WL (2003) Encyclopedia of biblical literature, Part 2. Kessinger, Whitefish, MT
Krasner SD (1999) Sovereignty: organized hypocrisy. Princeton University Press, Princeton, NJ
Lagasse P, Goldman L, Hobson A, Norton SR (eds) (2000) The Columbia encyclopedia, 6th edn. Columbia University Press, New York
Lee S (1997) A puzzle of sovereignty: sovereignty either is or is not. Cal W Int'l L J 27:241
Lester EE (1995) International transfer pricing rules: unconventional wisdom. ILSA J Int'l Comp L 2:283
Littlewood M (2004) Tax competition: harmful to whom? Mich J Int'l L 26:411
Loengard RO (1991) The section 482 pot boils on: comments on recent developments. Tax Forum No. 469
Lovett WA, Eckes AE, Brinkman RL (1999) US trade policy: history, theory, and the WTO. M.E. Sharpe, Armonk, NY

Lowell CH, Briger PL (2002) Adequacy of international dispute resolution mechanisms. Geo Mason L Rev 10:725
Mann FA (1999) Further studies in international law. Clarendon, Oxford
Margalioth Y (2003) Tax competition, foreign direct investments and growth: using the tax system to promote developing countries. Va Tax Rev 23:161, 175–180
Maritain J (1951) Man and the state. University of Chicago Press, Chicago
McCulloch JR (1883) A treatise on the principles, practice, and history of commerce. Charles Knight, London
Meessen KM (1996) Extraterritorial jurisdiction in theory and practice. Kluwer, Deventer
Murphy JB (2005) The philosophy of positive law: foundations of jurisprudence. Yale University Press, New Haven
Musgrave PB (2001) Revisiting the theory of international income taxation: principal paper: sovereignty, entitlement, and cooperation in international taxation. Brook J Int'l L 26:1335, 1336–1337
Neufeld H (1971) The international protection of private creditors from the Treaty of Westphalia to the Congress of Vienna. Martinus Nijhoff, Leiden
Norr M (1962) Jurisdiction on tax and international income, Tax L Rev 17:431
Picciotto S (1989) Slicing a shadow: business taxation in an international framework. In: Hancher L, Moran M (eds) Capitalism, culture, and economic regulation. Clarendon, Oxford
Pistone P (2002) The impact of community law on tax treaties: issues and solutions. Kluwer, The Hague
Rabkin JA (1998) Why sovereignty matters. American Enterprise Institute, Washington, DC
Resnick SA (2003) Japan postwar economic recovery and Anglo-Japanese relations 1948–1962. Routledge, London
Rhoades R, Langer M (1985) Income taxation of foreign related transactions. Matthew Bender, New York
Ricardo D (2004) On the principle of economy and taxation. Dover, New York
Ring DM (2000) The frontier of procedural innovation: advance pricing agreements and the struggle to allocate income for cross border taxation. Mich J Int'l L 21:143–234
Rosenbloom HD, Langbein SI (1981) United states treaty policy: an overview. Colum J Transnat'l L 19:359
Salinas J (2003) The OECD tax competition initiative: a critique of its merits in the global marketplace. Hous J Int'l L 25:531
Salzman J (2005) The emergence of global administrative law: decentralized administrative law in the organization for economic cooperation and development. Law Contemp Prob 68:189
Schon W (2003) Tax competition in Europe. International Bureau of Fiscal Documentation, Amsterdam
Schulze H (1996) State, nations and nationalism: from the middle ages to the present. Blackwell, Cambridge
Seligman ERA (1928) Double taxation and international fiscal cooperation. Macmillan, New York
Shinoda H (2000) Re-examining sovereignty, from classic theory to the global age. St. Martin's, New York
Simpson GJ (1996) The diffusion of sovereignty: self-determination in the postcolonial age. Stan J Int'l L 32:255, 282
Sir Jenning R (2002) Sovereignty and international law. In: Kreijen G (ed) State, sovereignty, and international governance. Oxford University Press, Oxford
Smith A (1970) The wealth of nations. Penguin, Harmondsworth
Sornarajah M (2004) The international law on investment. Cambridge University Press, Cambridge
Stewart M (2002) Global trajectories of tax reform: the discourse of tax reform in developing and transition countries. Harv Int'l L J 44:139
Swinbank A, Tanner C (1996) Farm policy and trade conflict, the Uruguay round and cap reform. University of Michigan Press, Ann Arbor, MI

Teixeira G (2006) Tax systems and non-discrimination in the European Union. Intertax 34(2):51.
Van den Bossche P (2005) The law and policy of the world trade organization: text, cases and materials. Cambridge University Press, Cambridge
van Thiel S (2001) EU case law on income taxation. IBFD, Amsterdam
Vandevelde KJ (2005) A brief history of international investment agreements. U C Davis J Int'l L Pol'y 12:157, 159
Vermeend W (1996) Editorial: the court of justice of the European communities and direct taxes. ECtax Rev 1996:55
Wang KC (1945) International double taxation of income: relief through international agreement, 1921–1945. Harv L Rev 59:73
Warren AC Jr (2001) Income tax discrimination against international commerce. Tax L Rev 54:131
Weiss F (2002) WTO decision-making: is it reformable? In: Kennedy DLM, Southwick JD (eds) The political economy of international trade law: essays in honor of Robert E. Hudec. Cambridge University Press, Cambridge
Wendt A (1999) Social theory of international politics. Cambridge University Press, Cambridge
Wickham DW (1991) The new US transfer pricing tax penalty: a solution, or a symptom of the cause, of the international transfer pricing puzzle? Int'l Tax J 18:1
Wilcox C (1949) A charter for world trade. Macmillan, New York
Williamson RL Jr (1995) Law and the H-bomb: strengthening the nonproliferation regime to impede advanced proliferation. Cornell Int'l L J 28:71, 77
Wilson RR (1960) United States commercial treaties and international law. Huser, New Orleans
Zaring D (1998) International law by other means: the twilight existence of international financial regulatory organizations. Tex Int'l L J 33:281, 287–291
Zeiler TW (1999) Free trade, free world: the advent of GATT. University of North Carolina Press, Chapel Hill, NC
Ziegler K-H (2004) The pace treaty of the ottoman empire with European Christian powers. In: Randall Lesaffer (ed) Pace treaties and international law in European history from the late middle ages to world war one. Cambridge University Press, Cambridge

Chapter 6
WTO Agreements

This chapter will explore the current relationship between trade and tax under the WTO agreements, discussing the WTO agreements most relevant to the tax issues: the GATT, the GATS, and the SCM. Accordingly, this chapter will be divided into three sections, each section shedding light on how taxation has already commingled with trade issues.

Section 6.1 discusses taxation under the GATT. Section 6.2 discusses the GATS, including the negotiating history and the US resistance to the inclusion of income tax under the GATS. The subsidies agreement then will be considered.

6.1 I. The GATT

6.1.1 Introduction

Having offered an overview of direct and indirect taxation, this chapter will highlight the tax elements of the agreement and discuss its implications. In dealing with the texts and cases, vague terms and conflicting concepts arise, in legal domestic settings as well as under the WTO jurisprudence. Under the WTO, there are different approaches to understanding, interpreting, and explaining the legal texts. Approaches "range from those that are restrained and highly deferential to the consent of members, to those that suggest more expansive judicial lawmaking" (Steinberg 2004, p. 258).

T. Althunayan, *Dealing with the Fragmented International Legal Environment: WTO, International Tax and Internal Tax Regulations*,
DOI 10.1007/978-3-642-04678-0_6,

6.1.2 The Vienna Convention

The Vienna Convention on the Law of Treaties is a useful starting point to begin a discussion of the legal texts.[1] The relevant provisions of the Vienna Convention are Articles 31 and 32, which read as follows:

Article 31: General rule of interpretation

(1) A treaty shall be interpreted in good faith in accordance with the ordinary meaning to be given to the terms of the treaty in their context and in the light of its object and purpose.
(2) The context for the purpose of the interpretation of a treaty shall comprise, in addition to the text, including its preamble and annexes:
   (a) any agreement relating to the treaty which was made between all the parties in connection with the conclusion of the treaty;
   (b) any instrument which was made by one or more parties in connection with the conclusion of the treaty and accepted by the other parties as an instrument related to the treaty.
(3) There shall be taken into account, together with the context:
   (a) any subsequent agreement between the parties regarding the interpretation of the treaty or the application of its provisions;
   (b) any subsequent practice in the application of the treaty which establishes the agreement of the parties regarding its interpretation;
   (c) any relevant rules of international law applicable in the relations between the parties.
(4) A special meaning shall be given to a term if it is established that the parties so intended.

Article 32: Supplementary means of interpretation

Recourse may be had to supplementary means of interpretation, including the preparatory work of the treaty and the circumstances of its conclusion, in order to confirm the meaning resulting from the application of article 31, or to determine the meaning when the interpretation according to article 31:

(a) leaves the meaning ambiguous or obscure; or
(b) leads to a result which is manifestly absurd or unreasonable.

From these two provisions, one can draw a framework aiding the interpretation of the WTO texts. The primary goal of any interpretation is to determine the intention of the drafters (Lennard 2002, p. 21); this approach is called the "intention approach," and uses any available means to find out the true intentions (or a close approximation thereof) of the treaty negotiators. This approach places a great deal of emphasis on the text itself as a starting point for interpretation, an interpretation method referred to as the textual method. It looks to "determine the intent of the negotiators through analyzing what they said in the text, which is presumed to be the final, authentic and most reliable expression of their intent, and only looks beyond the text ... in limited cases, such as where the text leaves the question unanswered" (Lennard 2002, pp. 20–21). If the text itself is not helpful, another

[1]This approach has been approved by the WTO AB. Appellate Body Report, United States – Standards for Reformulated and Conventional Gasoline, 25, WT/DS2/AB/R (Apr. 29, 1996), at 17 (stating that article 31 "has attained the status of a rule of customary or general international law").

approach is used. The teleogical method which "begins with a broader consideration of the object and purpose of a treaty and then interprets the text in a way viewed as best adapted to fulfilling that object and purpose" (Lennard 2002, p. 21).

Implementing this general rule, it is also necessary to take into account the history of the WTO. The political history of the WTO suggests that the main "intended function of WTO dispute settlement was to help ensure the faithful application of the rules agreed upon in the Uruguay Round negotiations, even if those rules were incomplete, not optimally efficient, or considered inequitable" (Steinberg 2004, p. 250).

6.1.3 GATT Text

There are three primary GATT articles relating directly to taxation. Article I, the MFN Article, states that WTO members are required to grant most favored nation status to all WTO members in situations relating to importing or exporting like products, with the specific provision that "any advantage [or] favor ... granted by any contracting party to any product originating in or destined for any other country shall be accorded ... to the like product ... of all other contracting parties."[2]

Article III of the GATT states that "internal taxes ... should not be applied to imported or domestic products so as to afford protection to domestic production."[3] In Part 2, Article III goes on to explain that the products "of the territory of any contracting party imported into the territory of any other contracting party shall not be subject, *directly or indirectly*, to *internal taxes or other internal charges of any kind in excess* of those applied, directly or indirectly, to like domestic products."[4]

Article XVI relates to subsidies, an issue covered independently in this work.

These two articles are considered to be the foundations of the GATT-WTO (Trebilcock 2004, p. 1) because they are the core anti-discrimination, equal treatment, and level-playing-field principles according to which the international trade has been built in order to ensure its efficiency.

6.1.4 Most Favored Nation[5]

6.1.4.1 Article I: Most-Favored-Nation Treatment

With respect to customs duties and charges of any kind imposed on or in connection with importation or exportation or imposed on the international transfer of payments for imports

---

[2]GATT Article I.

[3]GATT Article III, 1.

[4]GATT Article III, 2.

[5]*See* Lansing and Rose (1984, p. 329); Snyder (1948, p. 10). Mintz (2001). *See* O'Brien (1978, p. 545). Also *see* Rädler (1998). It was also present in the first American commercial treaty,

> or exports, and with respect to the method of levying such duties and charges, and with respect to all rules and formalities in connection with importation and exportation, and with respect to all matters referred to in paragraphs 2 and 4 of Article III, any advantage, favor, privilege or immunity granted by any contracting party to any product originating in or destined for any other country shall be accorded immediately and unconditionally to the like product originating in or destined for the territories of all other contracting parties.

Meaning and Purpose

The MFN clause "prohibit[s] discrimination among like products originating in or destined for different countries."[6] Generally speaking, this clause explains the overall original goal of the GATT, ensuring that there is an equal opportunity offered to all members.

"Charges"

The GATT does not define the words of its legal texts. Some words are interpreted by the dispute settlement body, by panel, or by the appellate body, but others are never interpreted at all or their meanings never questioned, as is the case for terms that have never been disputed, or those the meaning of which have been taken for granted even when they are ambiguous. One such word particularly relevant to tax issues in this Article, is "charges." In the first case ever to arise under the GATT,[7] the question arose whether "charges of any kind" should cover consular tax. The answer was yes, that "any charges" included any advantage, favor, or privilege with respect to internal taxes.[8]

The word "charges" could also be interpreted to mean financial liability. It is reasonable to assume that all types of charges that are connected to products are to be included in this definition. These charges reasonably include fines, fees, tariffs, and, most importantly, taxes.

"In connection"

Another point that commands examination is the phrase "in connection," a very general term that could potentially include any rule, even if remotely related to the importation or exportation of products. There is no discrete interpretive line and no objective criteria from which it is possible to know what exactly is "in connection" and what is not, but what is certain is that taxes affecting the exportation and

---

Article II–IV, Treaty of Amity and Commerce signed on February 6, 1778 between the USA and France. 8 Stat 12, TS No. 83; *see* also Lidstone (1962, pp. 537–538), Gifford (1978, p. 51).

[6] Appellate Body Report on Canada – Autos, Para. 84.

[7] Ruling by the Chairman, The Phrase "Charges of Any Kind" in Article I:1 in Relation to Consular Taxes, August 24, 1948, BISD II/12.

[8] Ruling by the Chairman, Consular Taxes (1948), II BISD 12.

importation of products are not merely a remote factor, but rather affect the price of products and the transaction itself fundamentally.

"With respect to the method of levying such duties and charges"

The above phrase is related to another aspect surrounding the issue of importing and exporting products. The phrase seems to aim at administrating applicable duties and charges. The plain meaning should require similar administrative procedures, unless there is a reason to differentiate the treatment and no unnecessary burden is imposed. For example, if a person imports a car, after paying applicable tariffs they should not be subject to an additional unnecessary tax burden that could be considered arbitrary or unjustifiable. It would be reasonably acceptable, however, to recognize the need for filing additional tax forms or doing more tax paperwork because the car in question is not domestically produced.

"With respect to all rules and formalities in connection with importation and exportation"

The above is a catchall clause. Its plain meaning seems to cover everything not covered by the previous parts of the Article. The clause could apply to anything new that might arise that wasn't anticipated by the drafters at the time of the writing of the Article.

"And with respect to all matters referred to in paragraphs 2 and 4 of article iii"

This phrase is a crucial inclusion under the MFN. The cross-reference to Article III, which deals, *inter alia*, with offering national treatment relating to internal taxes, is an indication that tax issues are not excluded from MFN treatment, and clearly relays that information to the public. Although it would have arguably been a stronger approach to state in the MFN article a clear reference to internal taxes, the cross-reference nevertheless established a link between MFN and internal taxes. It is further important to recognize that under Article III, in addition to a reference to internal taxes, there is also a reference to "internal regulation." Internal regulations affecting imported products, although their application seems to be very broad, seem reasonably to include taxes on products. Thus, this makes clear that all taxes that can affect the exporting and importing of goods, regardless of type, are subject to this article.

"Any advantage, favor, privilege or immunity granted by any contracting party to any product originating in or destined for any other country shall be accorded immediately and unconditionally to the like product originating in or destined for the territories of all other contracting parties"

The above is a very broad clause. Particularly noticeable is the use of the word "any" four times. The references apply as follows: the first "any" refers to any benefit offered or given; the second refers to any member, with no exceptions relating to the actor/giver of the favor; the third refers to any product; and the fourth refers to any receiver of the benefit. The language leaves no room for an exception for any products, any givers or recipients, or any benefit, since all can obviously affect the balance of competition. In light of this, the first goal of the GATT remains an attempt to make sure that the rules do not adversely modify the conditions of competition between domestic and imported products in the internal market.[9]

Another issue related to taxation with regard to the above-referenced clause is that when individual national governments offer tax holidays or participate in tax favoritism that affects the importation and exportation of any product, they should, in theory, offer the same "privilege" to all WTO members importing or exporting goods to the same country. Assume for example, that country X offers a tax "favor," such as a lower income tax rate, for profits generated from goods produced in country Y. In principle, X should extend that same offer to all MFN-eligible nations. In other words, the offer should be extended to all like products imported from other countries. In fact, a similar scenario occurred during the early days of the GATT. The Belgian government imposed a tax on goods that were purchased from public entities when those goods were imported from countries whose system of family allowance did not meet certain specific standards that were required by the Belgian government. Simultaneously, the government did not impose taxes on goods coming from countries that did meet the stated requirement. The GATT[10] determined this to be a discriminatory tax, which did not conform with the MFN requirement, and asked the Belgian government to cease the practice.[11]

6.1.5 Further MFN Difficulties

The author supports the contention of Professor Avi-Yonah that Article I, the MFN article, "applies to any taxes that affect imports and exports. Conceptually, it is therefore plausible to apply Article I to income tax measures that affect imports or exports. One must remember, however, that GATT applies only in the context of 'like' products, and therefore application of GATT to income tax measures is limited to the extent that such measures affect imports or exports of like products. Other than that, GATT contains no specific limitations or carve-outs for income tax measures" (Brauner 2005, pp. 251, 268).

Theory aside, in practice it becomes clear that tax issues, specifically income tax issues, are not easy to implement in compliance with the MFN clause. It is hard to imagine a typical scenario where income tax is the subject of a dispute relating to

[9]Panel Report, Italian Discrimination Against Imported Agricultural Machinery, adopted October 23, 1958.

[10]GATT Panel Report, *Belgian Family Allowances*, G/32, adopted November 7, 1952, BISD 1S/59.

[11]*See* Belgium Family Allowance, adopted November 7, 1952. See Chap. 2.

MFN under the GATT. For example, if Saudi Arabia offers a favorable tax treatment to French manufacturing companies, perhaps by exempting them from Saudi income taxation, it would be difficult to hold the Saudis liable under the GATT agreement or to require them to offer the same treatment to Canadian companies for several reasons.

First, the tariffs imposed on the companies of both nations are the same. The tax imposed after the products enter the country is not sales tax, but rather income tax, imposed on the profits of selling the final products, including the price paid for raw materials and other business-related expenses, such as marketing and management. If the tariffs are the same on all materials imported as required by the GATT, then even if subsequent treatment favors France, the issue is murky, because there is no more tax on pure "goods." Tax treatment for both French and Canadian companies will be applied to services performed by the companies, but taxes on services are not under the supervision of the GATT. It could, however, be argued that the ultimate result of a tax on services affects the sales of the products, and the GATT aims to guarantee the same treatment for Canada's products as for those from a French company, even when tax charges affect the sales indirectly. Is there enough evidence to support the "indirectness" effect? This is the ultimate question, the answer to which is necessary for determining the result of such a case.

Other practical problems arise. First, there exists a difficulty in reality: it is not traditional to impose income tax in a way that violates MFN with regard to products, at least not directly. As a result, it seems less likely that this concept can be applied under the GATT. As the Rust Conference[12] has illustrated, many tax officials from different countries – but not all of them – have expressed doubts on MFN applicability to tax treaties. Tax treaties do not apply generally and are inapplicable to international trade in goods. As a result, they are commonly agreed upon bilaterally, and there is therefore an assumption that there should be minimal interference, and that instead such treaties should be left to the governance of the involved nations, especially if there is no clear reference to amendment or modification of their scope. Since there is no clear direct deviation from the established international practice, MFN reasonably should not be interpreted to nullify that tradition.

Second, applying Article II, rigidly could potentially lead to a disturbance of the bilateral tax treaties under which income tax issues are usually treated. Tax treaties are normally bilateral, "ignoring other countries' interests and concerns" (Brauner 2005, p. 267). MFN is not applicable to bilateral income agreements "since these agreements are based on mutual concessions between two states" (Luja 1999, p. 211). Their bilateral nature makes tax treaties take into account each party country's circumstances, factors, and relations with respect to the other negotiating party country. Agreements can cover a variety of topics, including foreign investment volume, citizens of one party nation working in the other country, friendly or hostile relations, politics, and the like. It can be argued that this method of dealing with tax issues is an international customary law that has been developing for as

[12]WTO and Direct Taxation, p. 23.

long as 57 years,[13] and should be respected in its present form, because there is a "mutual practice of the contracting parties which indicates an implicit agreement that the GATT MFN clause should be interpreted as carving out tax treaties, in very much the same way as the GATS clause."[14]

In conclusion, it is difficult today to envision an income tax that triggers MFN in practice, but it is essential that international rules not be limited in structure to satisfy only current needs and problems. Instead, they should be set to fulfill current as well as future foreseeable needs to the greatest extent possible. No constructive result can be achieved by insisting on excluding the MFN from application to income taxation laws entirely. Keeping in mind that the major purpose of the GATT is prohibiting discrimination, and reading the text as plainly as possible, it seems safe to state that any charges or privileges of any kind should conform to the GATT-WTO goal of providing an equal and fair competitive environment after the goods cross the borders for the import and export of products. Thus, any measure that does not fall legally within the accepted exceptions should not be immune outright, and should be recognized as running the risk of violating the MFN, and therefore the GATT.

6.1.6 National Treatment on Internal Taxation and Regulation

6.1.6.1 Analyzing the Legal Text

Article III, the National Treatment on Internal Taxation and Regulation, reads as follows:

1. The contracting parties recognize that internal taxes and other internal charges, and laws, regulations and requirements affecting the internal sale, offering for sale, purchase, transportation, distribution or use of products, and internal quantitative regulations requiring the mixture, processing or use of products in specified amounts or proportions, should not be applied to imported or domestic products so *as to afford protection to domestic production.*
2. The products of the territory of any contracting party imported into the territory of any other contracting party shall not be subject, directly or indirectly, to *internal taxes* or other *internal charges* of any kind *in excess* of those applied, directly or indirectly, to *like* domestic products. Moreover, no contracting party shall otherwise apply internal taxes or other internal charges to imported or domestic products in a manner contrary to the principles set forth in paragraph 1.
3. [. . .]
4. The products of the territory of any contracting party imported into the territory of any other contracting party shall be accorded treatment no less favorable than that accorded to like products of national origin in respect of *all laws, regulations and requirements* affecting their internal sale, offering for sale, purchase, transportation, distribution or use . . ..

   Ad. Article III

   Any internal tax or other internal charge, or any law, regulation or requirement of the kind referred to in paragraph 1 which applies to an imported product and to the like

[13] WTO and Direct Taxation, p. 23.

[14] WTO and Direct Taxation, p. 23.

> domestic product and is collected or enforced in the case of the imported product at the time or point of importation, is nevertheless to be regarded as an internal tax or other internal charge, or a law, regulation or requirement of the kind referred to in paragraph 1, and is accordingly subject to the provisions of Article III.

The general rule presented in Article III is that internal taxes and regulations must treat imports no less favorably than like domestic products. If a domestic regulatory measure is found to discriminate against imports in violation of Article III, the regulating government can seek to justify that discrimination by proving it is necessary to the achievement of some legitimate regulatory purpose. GATT article XX defines this exception (Hudec 1998, p. 619).

GATT Article III is the other imperative pillar of the GATT. For tax purposes, this is the Article that has been at the center of many disputes since the inception of the GATT. It requires each member nation to grant national treatment to other member nations, which means that member nations must treat foreign products as they treat their national or local products. It also requires WTO members to extend this action to "all the other members with respect to all laws ... affecting the internal sale ... or use of goods." The major significance of the Article is that it is designed to ensure that no measures, whether in the form of a law or an administrative action (including taxation issues), be applied which are designed to afford protection to domestic production, but which are not equally applied with respect to imported or domestic products.

This "national treatment" rule has two main themes. First, it prohibits discriminatory taxes by providing that "the products of the territory of any contracting party imported into the territory of any other contracting party shall not be subject, directly or indirectly, to internal taxes or other internal charges of any kind in excess of those applied directly or indirectly, to like domestic products."

Second, in those instances in which imported products and domestic products are "directly competitive or substitutable," a much broader characterization than "like" products, the GATT rule prohibits protective taxation by providing that a member nation's internal taxes and other charges affecting the sale or use of products "should not be applied to imported or domestic products so as to afford protection to domestic production."

It should be noted that the reference to internal taxes in Article III is in contrast to import duties or tariffs, which are imposed at the border. This distinction highlights the importance of differentiating between the two types of events, even though they may have similar effects. This Article ensures non-discriminatory tax treatment of goods after they have already crossed a country's border, and protects the expected anticipated benefits of lower tariffs so that they are not nullified by other tax measures.

6.1.6.2 Purpose

The fundamental purpose of Article III is to avoid protectionism in the application of internal tax and regulatory measures (Choi 2002, p. 107). The AB states that the "broad and fundamental purpose of Article III is to avoid protectionism in the application of internal tax and regulatory measures."[15] In this regard, the Appellate Body has made clear that the scope of Article III is not limited to those products that are the subject of tariff concessions under Article II. The Appellate Body has repeatedly stated that the "fundamental purpose of Article III of the GATT 1994 is to ensure equality of competitive conditions between imported and like domestic products."[16]

Under the national treatment rule, the members of the GATT are not permitted to enforce discriminatory treatment between imports and "like" domestic products once the imported products cross the border. The national treatment principle requires member nations to treat "imported products in the same way as the like domestic products once they had been cleared through customs."[17] This is a logical approach to prevent countries from offsetting the effects of reducing their tariffs through non-tariff measures, the most important of which are domestic direct and indirect taxes, and/or other regulatory requirements and policies. This Article ensures that "an imported product is treated in the same way in terms of taxation and regulatory treatment as a 'like' domestically produced good after that imported product has cleared customs" (Tsai 1999, pp. 26, 28). For example, when Saudi Arabia reduces its tariff on radios from 20% to 2%, it can effectively offset that reduction by imposing a sales tax of 18% on imported radios. This Article prevents such a scenario and levels the playing field in line with the intent of the GATT by prohibiting other measures to be "used as protectionist measures that would defeat the purpose of the tariff binding" (Jackson 1997, p. 213).

Finally, Article III is not intended to intervene with members' laws and regulations. It does not aim to harmonize members' laws against their wishes; it is instead a completely legitimate way to ensure compliance with international rules while retaining the power of individual nations to set domestic rules and policies according to their local needs and wishes. The focus of the Article is on how to "ensure equality of competitive conditions between imported and like domestic products."[18] The primary Article III goal is to prevent "contracting parties from using fiscal and regulatory powers for purpose other than to afford protection to domestic production."[19]

The Article's purpose is to "ensure that internal measures not be applied to imported or domestic products so as to afford protection to domestic production." The purpose can alternatively be stated as an attempt to combat any domestic measures that present barriers to trade among WTO member countries; this can be most effectively accomplished by requiring the equalization of treatment

[15]GATT Panel Report, *Japan – Customs Duties, Taxes and Labelling Practices on Imported Wines and Alcoholic Beverages*, L/6216, adopted November 10, 1987, BISD 34S/83, Para 16.

[16]Appellate Body Report on Canada – Periodicals, p. 18.

[17]Panel Report on Italy, "Discrimination Against Imported Agricultural Machinery," adopted October 30, 1958, Para. 6.

[18]Appellate Body Report on Canada – Periodicals, p. 18.

[19]Panel Report on the United States, "Measures Affecting Alcoholic and Malt Beverages," adopted June 19, 1992, Para. 5.25.

between local and imported products with respect to applicable laws, regulations, and any other internal measures. Domestic taxes and regulations are "hidden barriers to trade" that lack both transparency and predictability, which means that they have a large trade-distortion impact.

This Article is generally viewed as relating to only "indirect taxes," as opposed to direct taxes. Indirect taxes are not usually defined in the relevant literature, but where they are mentioned, the author found that they were identified through examples. The most typical examples presented are sales, excise, turnover, value-added, franchise, stamp, transfer, and inventory and equipment taxes. Direct taxes usually include property, payroll, wealth, and most significantly, income tax.

6.1.6.3 Internal Taxation and Direct Taxation

From the perspective of Article III, definitions of direct and indirect taxes, and a determination of the difference between them, can best be garnered from a very specific textual-contextual reading. Unlike MFN, under which an income tax dispute is unlikely, under this Article, tax disputes have been the subject of several cases relating to income tax as well as other taxes, such as the DISC and FSC.

This Article covers many issues relating to taxation. It covers all type of taxes, since no exception to its application is indicated by the inclusion of the words "charges of any kind." The "method of levying" any taxes that can affect the sale of taxable products is also relevant. "Rules and formalities" according to which such taxes are employed, must also be compliant with the concept of national treatment. This Article manifests itself as an acknowledgment that tax of any kind, including income tax, as well as rules and procedures associated with the tax in question, can have a protectionist policy (Avi-Yonah and Slemrod 2002, p. 536).

Article III says nothing about direct tax and indirect tax. The Article is limited in scope to a discussion of charges or duties affecting "the internal sale, offering for sale, purchase, transportation, distribution or use of products."[20] Nevertheless, proponents of the distinction between direct and indirect taxes rely too much on the word "product" as mentioned in this Article. The mere fact that the subject of the provision was a "product" does not necessarily mean that the Article excludes direct taxes from its application. A consideration of the pure text and plain meaning indicates no word relating to the claimed distinction. The understanding of the scope of applicability by one person or entity can be easily disputed by another person or group reading the text in a different way as influenced by a different background.

Direct and indirect taxes as they relate to Article III have been addressed under the WTO dispute mechanism, but not with particular clarity. In fact, in one case there arose a conflicting view from the same dispute resolution panel. In *Argentina – Hides and Leather*, the Argentinean government argued that "since an income tax

[20] Article III, 1.

is not a tax on products, its measure establishing the collection regime for such a tax ('RG 3543') could not be subject to the provisions of Article III:2."[21] The panel responded by saying that "income taxes are not excluded *per se* from the scope of application of Article III:2."[22] The Panel went on to say that "ordinary income taxes fall outside the scope of Article III:2 because they apply to all income, irrespective of the source, rather than to income derived from the sale of goods only. For that reason, it is assumed that they are not passed on into the prices of the products. That assumption, however, is not justified in the case of the «advance» IG, which is collected whenever a product is imported."[23]

The confusion begins with the uncertainty of what "ordinary income taxes" means in the given situation. The Panel's reasoning was incoherent: it first stated that income tax was not excluded, and subsequently went on to state that "ordinary income taxes" fell outside the scope of the Article. The phrase "ordinary income taxes" has no basis in tax law, and thus no applicable meaning whatsoever. The Panel did not explain the meaning of the word "ordinary." In addition, an old assumption arose: the backward and forward tax incidence, which, as previously discussed, has no ascertainable basis in economics. The Panel was unable to support its argument with any authoritative sources. The report was thereby confusing, and was made weaker by the FSC report which followed it in 2002, which addressed the issue of income tax law as described below.

The Panel Report on the FSC/ETI makes it very clear that income taxes fall within the scope of GATT Article III, which means that GATT covers both direct and indirect taxation. This interesting notion requires elaboration. The USA argued in the FSC that Article III:4 was never intended to apply to income taxes according to the historical background of the Article. The Panel's answer to the US argument was as follows:

> We take note of the preparatory work for the Havana Charter referred to by the United States in these proceedings. According to the United States, the Reports of the Havana Convention at which Article 18 of the Havana Charter[24] was drafted, specify that "neither income taxes nor import duties fall within the scope of Article 18 which is concerned solely with internal taxes on goods."[25] This statement in the preparatory work of the Havana Charter *does not change our view that the scope of Article III:4 of the GATT 1994 includes measures conditioning access to income tax* advantages in respect of certain products.

---

[21]Panel Report on Argentina – Hides and Leather, Para 8.26.

[22]Panel Report on Argentina – Hides and Leather, Para 8.26.

[23]Panel Report on Argentina – Hides and Leather, Para 8.26.

[24]Final Act of the United Nations Conference on Trade and Employment, March 24, 1948 [original footnote].

[25]In its response to Panel Question 18, the United States cited the Interim Committee for the International Trade Organization, Report of Committees and Principal Sub-committees, Report of Sub-committee A of the Third Committee on Articles 16, 17, 18 and 19, E/CONF.2/C.3/59, Para. 44, p. 63, Geneva 1948 [original footnote]. The WTO analytical notes that "during the discussion in Sub-committee at the Havana Conference which considered article 18 of the charter, it was agreed that neither income taxes nor import duties cam within the scope of Article 18 since this Article refers specifically to internal taxes on products" [original footnote].

> While seemingly framed in general terms, this statement appears in a section containing comments on paragraphs 1, 2 and 3 of Article 18 and thus seems to relate to what would later become Article III:2 of the GATT. It therefore would not be decisive concerning the scope of Article III:4, in any event. Moreover, the statement was made in relation to the withdrawal of a specific proposal by Peru dealing with a situation materially different than the one currently before us (not deeming as "in opposition to" Article 18 the exemption of import duties on equipment or materials and exemption from income taxes granted for a limited time to enterprises created for the establishment of "economically sound industries").[26] However, even if the statement was meant to refer more generally to what would later become Article III as a whole (including Article III:4), if taken literally, it would entirely exclude an area that was explicitly covered by Article 18 of the Havana Charter, and now Article III:4 of the GATT: i.e., internal regulation (it suffices here to recall that Article III of the GATT 1994 is entitled: "National Treatment on Internal Taxation and Regulation"), which would amount to a result that clearly runs counter to the object and purpose of Article III and of the *GATT 1994* in general. Therefore, the statement in the preparatory work of the Havana Charter does not change our view that Article III:4 of the GATT 1994 applies to measures conditioning access to income tax advantages in respect of certain products.[27]

In a footnote, the Panel continued to explain its position, stating that:

> In accordance with the customary rules of interpretation of public international law as codified in Articles 31 and 32 of the Vienna Convention on the Law of Treaties, Recourse may be had to supplementary means of interpretation, including the preparatory work of a treaty . . . in order to confirm the meaning resulting from the application of article 31, or to determine the meaning when the interpretation according to article 31:
>
> (a) leaves the meaning ambiguous or obscure; or
> (b) leads to a result which is manifestly absurd or unreasonable.
>
> Here, we do not consider that the ordinary meaning of the text of Article III:4, in its context and in light of the object and purpose of the GATT 1994 and the WTO Agreement to be "ambiguous or obscure" or that our interpretation of that provision "leads to a result which is manifestly absurd or unreasonable". We are therefore of the view that it is not necessary to refer at all to the preparatory work.[28]

The Panel not only rejected the US interpretation, but the report clarified the historical background by explaining that this historical comment concerned only Article III:2, and that regardless it was not, in the Panel's view, acceptable to adhere to that comment, because it would run "counter to the object and purpose of Article III." The panel affirmed that the historical background of this comment was not a determining factor or "decisive" in deciding whether there should be a distinction between direct tax and indirect tax under Article III. The Panel's result, in this author's opinion, was correct.

Although Article 18 of the ITO and Article III of GATT are almost identical, this similarity is not determinate. This committee, discussed in the mentioned FSC Panel Report, footnote was a discussion about an Article of an agreement (that is the

---

[26]Third Committee: Commercial Policy, Revised Annotated Agenda for Chapter IV, Proposed Amendment by Peru, E/Conf.2/C.3/6/Add. 2, December 17, 1947 [original footnote].

[27]FSC-Panel report, para 8.145.

[28]FSC-Panel Report footnote 257, para 8.145.

ITO) that has never materialized. Also, the ITO was a broader discussion, taking place in 1940s, and included a number of other issues. Therefore, it was taking place in an environment very different from that surrounding the negotiations of the GATT/WTO in 1994. Although it is useful to understand the history of the GATT Articles, their history is by no means binding, and imposes no obligation to follow the reasoning and results that were discussed during that time; instead, they can at best be considered preparatory work for an international organization that never came to life. This must be viewed in combination with the fact that there is nothing in the plain language of the provision specifically excluding income tax measures.

More importantly, this Committee[29] note emerged during a discussion of the relationship between Article 25, the subsidies article, and Article 18, the national treatment article, both of which could potentially conflict with each other, since Article 25 covered the permitting of subsidies and Article 18 covered national treatment as related to taxation. As a result, it was apparently a concern that Article 18 would effectively stop Article 25 from being utilized, and that the tension between the two could force a country to offer the same subsidies to other foreigners. To clarify the issue, the Committee stated that "exemption from income taxes would constitute a form of subsidy permissible under Article 25 [XVI] and therefore [was] not precluded by Article 18." This made it clear that the major concern was whether Article 18 would prevent the functioning of Article 25, offering subsidies via exemption of income taxes. The question that emerged was whether territorial tax systems were compatible with Article 18, and the answer was that "neither income taxes nor import duties fall within the scope of Article 18 which is concerned solely with internal taxes on goods." This was undoubtedly done to ensure the contracting parties that subsidies through exemption from income taxes were not within the scope of this Article.

Some GATT/WTO cases have dealt with direct and indirect taxation, even though the case has not addressed them directly. For example, when the USA granted special tax treatment to wine and beer producers, Canada objected. The matter was disputed under the GATT. The Panel in *US Malt Beverages*[30] found that a preferential federal excise tax plan for small US brewers, and numerous tax rules and distribution practices in more than 40 states, were "inconsistent" with international trade rules.[31] The Panel held that Article III's purpose is to ensure that internal taxes are not used to nullify tariff reductions and agreements.[32] The Panel also found that offering tax credits on domestic wine and beer is not

[29]Interim Committee for the International Trade Organization, Report of Committees and Principal Subcommittees, Report of Subcommittee "A" of the Third Committee on Articles 16, 17, 18 and 19, E/CONF.2/C.3/59, Geneva 1948.

[30]GATT Panel Report, United States – Measures Affecting Alcoholic and Malt Beverages, DS23/R, adopted June 19, 1992, BISD 39S/206.

[31]GATT Panel Report, United States – Measures Affecting Alcoholic and Malt Beverages, DS23/R, adopted June 19, 1992, BISD 39S/206. *See* also Lachica (1992, p. A8).

[32]GATT Panel Report, United States – Measures Affecting Alcoholic and Malt Beverages, DS23/R, adopted June 19, 1992, BISD 39S/206, para 5.71.

consistent with Article III:2. This case demonstrated that, although indirect taxes were imposed on products, those taxes had the effect of benefiting mainly *local taxpayers* involved in producing the beer and wines in the USA. Thus, it had the effect of directly impacting the competitive relationship between foreigners and locals through the use of tax regulations, which is a level of involvement that the GATT should avoid.

Professor Avi-Yonah asserts that "even if the article is interpreted as referring to direct taxes as well, it seems unlikely that the income tax in particular can be used as an instrument for protecting domestic production because of the difficulty of designing income tax provisions that will apply only to foreign production" (Avi-Yonah 2001, p. 1684).

Avi-Yonah's opinion appeared to change later on. He and Professor Slemrod wrote that "tax and trade agreements share similar nondiscrimination and national treatment provisions" (Avi-Yonah and Slemrod 2002, p. 534). Later, regarding Article III, they affirmed that "the presumption has always been that direct taxes, in particular income taxes, are not in its purview. In principle, however, a protectionist policy can be affected via the direct tax system" (Avi-Yonah and Slemrod 2002, p. 536). It seems, therefore, that the issue of national treatment as applied to tax issues, and income tax specifically, has been resolved.

Finally, Michael Lennard summarized the issue well, writing that Article III, specifically part 2, is "directed at measures which directly or indirectly have sufficient *effect on*, or *linkage to*, the product to disturb competitive conditions" (Lennard 2005, p. 98, emphasis in original).[33] Although there is likely to be some argument regarding the exact meaning of the word "sufficient," this author's opinion is that this represents the best possible analysis of this issue. Income tax cannot be a tax on a product directly, but can be imposed indirectly by affecting or having a traceable link to the product – for example, through the allowance of a deduction for locally manufactured products or disallowance of the same for foreign products, negatively impacting fair competition. Such a scenario would be sufficient to subject it to the policies of the GATT. Thus, income tax law is generally covered by the GATT Article III. However, the issue of whether any specific issue of income tax is subject to GATT Article III will be determined case by case, by the Panel based on whether a given action has (or is likely in the future to have) a sufficient impact on the sale and international trade of goods.

[33]Lennard later stated that "the great majority of direct tax measures sufficiently affect products so as to afford products so as to be regulated by article III" (p. 101). He fluctuates between two ideas: that the GATT covers, or does not cover, income tax measures, a clear indication that the issue is hard to determine. In his latter argument, he uses the term "the majority." This word leaves the reader with uncertainty as to what could be included and excluded under this characterization.

6.1.6.4 The Article Wording

"Internal taxation and other internal charges"

The first paragraph begins by referring to "internal taxes and other internal charges." This demonstrates the importance of the word "taxes." The text is simultaneously very specific and very general, covering all taxes and other charges while singling out taxes among other charges to ensure that they are indisputably covered by the Article. The provision reflects a concern with all charges that could be used to violate the agreement, but in particular with those that are most important and potentially the most controversial: "taxes."

If taxes were not particularly important in this context, it would have been sufficient to simply state "internal charges," which would include "taxes." Apparently, however, the drafters felt a need for additional emphasis and specificity to make sure that "taxes" are treated as a distinctive issue that should be identified as presenting a potential problem. Finally, it must be noted that the phrase "other internal charge" would be less meaningful if expressed alone, but when combined with laws and regulations, it is more obvious that the intent was to cover all aspects of financial charges by any means, regardless of the source.

"And laws, regulations and requirements"

Next, the drafters added "laws, regulations and requirements ..." Again, the drafters aimed to cover all possibilities and bridge any potential gaps that could be (mis)used to manipulate the environment within which products are traded. Since tax laws and regulations can affect the trade agreements, they have been singled out to ensure that they are covered by the agreement. This is a result of the need for an authorization to extract money from people and entities. Thus, words such as decrees, acts, statutes, laws, regulations, or any synonym would be adequate to convey the meaning, in the event that the actual naming is different among countries.

"Affecting the internal sale, offering for sale, purchase"

If a tax or any law does not affect a sale or its surrounding circumstances (offers for sale, related purchases and other expenditures, transportation, and the like), it would be acceptable to impose whatever rules or regulations a given country wishes; the WTO does not exist to govern local matters. But if taxes or charges have an effect on the internal sale of products with international ties, they must conform to the Article III requirement of national treatment for all if the affected products are alike. The Appellate Body has reinforced this concept, saying that all WTO members "are free to pursue their own domestic goals through internal taxation or regulation so long as they do not do so in a way that violates Article III."[34]

The major problem in this phrase is the word "affecting." First, many factors can be said to affect "the internal sales, offering for sale . . ." The plain meaning of this word has the potential to give rise to arguments that the effects of other even remotely non-trade issues are sometimes much stronger than those of trade issues. For example, the educational and legal systems in a developed country like the USA have a strong effect on the way Americans conduct business and trade inside the USA and abroad. Would these systems be a factor that must be dealt with under the trade umbrella? Or is that taking the scope too far? Where should the line be drawn?

One way to solve the mystery of this word is by adopting the "aim-and-effects" test. In *Japan – Alcoholic Beverages II*, Japan argued that the Panel should "examine the contested legislation in the light of its aim and effect in order to determine whether or not it is consistent with Article III:2."[35] The United States also argued for the use of this test, saying "that, in determining whether two products that were taxed differently . . . for the purposes of Article III:2, the Panel should examine . . . whether the aim and effect of that distinction, considered as a whole, was to afford protection to domestic production."[36] The Panel rejected accepting this test as determinative in deciding the case, and subsequently, the Appellate Body was very explicit in likewise rejecting the "aims-and-effects" test, saying that "no one approach to exercising judgment will be appropriate for all cases."[37] Nevertheless, the aim and effects test is without a doubt a very useful tool (Choi 2002, p. 46) to be used, if not as a determinative test, as a guide to ensure that the "affecting" does not result in the discriminatory protection of domestic products.

"Should not be applied to imported or domestic products"

The above prohibition is aimed not only at imported products, but also at domestic products. Thus, offering a tax favor, such as allowing tax deduction acceleration for the use of domestic goods, should fall under the jurisdiction of this Article, even though imported products are not explicitly covered by this particular law. Moreover, this part of Article III "informs the rest of Article III and acts as a guide to understanding and interpreting the specific obligations contained in the other paragraphs of Article III."[38]

[34]Appellate Body Report on Japan – Alcoholic Beverages II, p. 16.

[35]Japan Alcohol case, Para. 6.15.

[36]Japan Alcohol case, Para. 6.15.

[37]Japan Alcohol case, Para. 6.15.

[38]EC-Asbestos para 94.

"So as to afford protection to domestic production"

This is "the broad and fundamental purpose of Article III":[39] to protect the environment of trade from protectionism "in the application of internal taxes and regulatory measures."[40] It requires WTO members to offer "equality of competitive conditions"[41] between foreign and local products. The wisdom behind this condition is subject to debate, but its value is for economic and policy makers to decide. In this thesis, the main concern is the applicability of this provision to tax matters, and in particular its applicability to income tax measures. There is no doubt that tax can be used to effectuate protectionism.

Article III:1 establishes the general principle of not affording protection to domestic production by using internal taxes and regulatory measures. It is a guideline to "understanding and interpreting the specific obligations contained under Article III:2."[42] This, of course, does not mean that the other provisions are meaningless, but it does seem to be an umbrella under which other Articles should operate.

6.1.7 Article III:2

> The products of the territory of any contracting party imported into the territory of any other contracting party shall not be subject, directly or indirectly, to internal taxes or other internal charges of any kind in excess of those applied, directly or indirectly, to like domestic products.

The general requirement of Article III:2 is that member nations must not apply *internal taxes in excess* of those applied to domestic products; it is a prohibition on the use of internal taxes or other internal charges to discriminate between imported goods and "like" domestic goods, as well as between imported goods and directly competitive or substitutable products, a broader concept than that of "like" products. The aim is to protect the "expectation of the contracting parties as to the competitive relationship between their products and those of other contracting parties."[43] Internal charges include any financial responsibility imposed on any legal person, as stated by the Panel, which asserts that the "term 'charge' denotes, *inter alia*, a 'pecuniary burden' and a 'liability to pay money laid on a person.'"[44]

---

[39]Japan – Alcohol Beverage II, pp. 16.

[40]Japan, p. 16–17.

[41]Japan, p. 16–17.

[42]Japan – Alcohol Beverages II, p. 111.

[43]Panel report on Unites States – Taxes on Petroleum and Certain Imported Substances, adopted June 17, 1987, Para 5.2.2.

[44]Panel Report on Argentina – Hides and Leather, Para. 11.143.

The most important aspect of this chapter, however, is its potential application in the area of taxation in general. The terminology of this Article includes the words "directly" and "indirectly," which usage is likely to be problematic or "ambiguous" (Lennard 2005, p. 96). It should be noted that these words do not "refer to direct tax and indirect tax" (Dam 1977, p. 124); they refer instead to the entire phrase, including measures and regulations. The GATT Analytical Index states that "the word 'indirectly' would cover even a tax not on a product as such but on the *processing* of the product."[45] Even the process of producing such a product would be covered by this Article, with the inclusion of taxation for environmental protection purposes or relating to social issues. Therefore, any measures regulating the processes of producing products that are considered "like" or in competition would be covered by Article III:2.

Under the plain meaning of this provision, neither direct nor indirect taxes should be applied to imported products by (a) directly imposing the taxes, or (b) indirectly imposing taxes in a way that ultimately affects the products in question, as, for example, taxes imposed on import licenses.

"In excess" means any amount, and it has been established that even "the smallest amount of 'excess' is too much."[46] This is in line with the AB reasoning that member nations should provide equality of competitive conditions.[47] "Equality" means most plainly that all member nations should be treated in the same manner to the greatest extent possible. This does not mean that they must necessarily be treated identically, because in some cases the goal of equality will require that they be treated differently. For example, requiring a lawyer to know French before he or she can secure employment as a lawyer in France, even if the work does not require that, is a requirement that, while natural for a French lawyer, could be unjustifiably difficult to meet for a Chinese lawyer.

> ... no contracting party shall otherwise apply internal taxes or other internal charges to imported or domestic products in a manner contrary to the principles set forth in paragraph 1

This second sentence of Article III:2 broadens the scope of Article III by referring back to paragraph 1, which says that "the contracting parties recognize that internal taxes and other internal charges, and laws, regulations and requirements affecting the internal sale, offering for sale, purchase, transportation, distribution or use of products, and internal quantitative regulations requiring the mixture, processing or use of products in specified amounts or proportions, should not be applied to imported or domestic products so as to afford protection to domestic production."[48] A familiar principle arises: there should be no effect on the competitive

[45]EPCT/A/PV/ p:19; EPCT/W/181, p. 3 as cited by Lennard (2005, p. 95).

[46]Appellate Body Report on Japan – Alcoholic Beverages II, p. 23.

[47]Appellate Body Report on Canada – Periodicals, p. 18.

[48]Article III, 1.

environment between domestic and imported products, regardless of the means, whether by internal taxes, internal regulations and laws, or any other requirements.

It is important to note that the second sentence of Article III:2 directly references Article III:1, whereas the first sentence does not, a puzzling difference, because there seems to be no reason to distinguish between them. Furthermore, the scope of the second sentence of Article III:2 is limited by an Interpretive Note ad Article III, paragraph 2, which defines appropriate application as limited to "directly competitive or substitutable" products (Tsai 1999, p. 29). The ad Article states as follows:

> A tax conforming to the requirements of the first sentence of paragraph 2 would be considered to be inconsistent with the provisions of the second sentence only in cases where competition was involved between, on the one hand, the taxed product and, on the other hand, a directly competitive or substitutable product which was not similarly taxed.

This note interpreting Article III:2 adds another dimension, covering competing products even if they are not alike. Thus, with regard to internal taxes, the second sentence of Article III:2 states, in effect, that differential taxes based on product distinctions between "not-like" but directly competitive products are also not accepted, and are not in accordance with the GATT if the tax difference results in any protection of domestic production (Hudec 1998, p. 619).

Here, the reference to tax is stated differently, with reference to products "not similarly taxed" rather than the first sentence requirement of taxes "in excess of." This difference has been interpreted by the AB to indicate different meanings between the two phrases. The AB offered an analysis of what the two concepts are likely to mean:

> To give due meaning to the distinctions in the wording of Article III:2, first sentence, and Article III:2, second sentence, the phrase 'not similarly taxed' in the Ad Article to the second sentence must not be construed so as to mean the same thing as the phrase 'in excess of' in the first sentence. On its face, the phrase 'in excess of' in the first sentence means any amount of tax on imported products 'in excess of' the tax on domestic 'like products'. The phrase 'not similarly taxed' in the Ad Article to the second sentence must therefore mean something else. It requires a different standard, just as 'directly competitive or substitutable products' requires a different standard as compared to 'like products' for these same interpretive purposes.[49]
>
> There may be an amount of excess taxation that may well be more of a burden on imported products than on domestic 'directly competitive or substitutable products' but may nevertheless not be enough to justify a conclusion that such products are 'not similarly taxed' for the purposes of Article III:2, second sentence. We agree with the Panel that this amount of differential taxation must be more than *de minimis* to be deemed 'not similarly taxed' in any given case. And, like the Panel, we believe that whether any particular differential amount of taxation is *de minimis* or is not *de minimis* must, here too, be determined on a case-by-case basis. Thus, to be 'not similarly taxed', the tax burden on imported products must be heavier than on 'directly competitive or substitutable' domestic products, and that burden must be more than *de minimis* in any given case.[50]

[49]Appellate Body Report on Japan – Alcoholic Beverages II, p. 26.

[50]Appellate Body Report on Japan – Alcoholic Beverages II, pp. 26–27 This "de minimis" standard was endorsed by the Appellate Body in Canada – Periodicals (Appellate Body Report

This analysis is too narrow, because it focuses too much on the "amount" or "quantity" of taxes imposed on products, and ignores other possibilities. For example, it excludes the fact that "similarly taxed" could also mean issues other than the amount of taxes imposed. Also, it could mean potentially different methods of taxation, such as collecting a tax based on speculation about foreign products while allowing local products to be taxed based on actual data and facts, which can affect the level of equality between the products. Alternatively, the meaning could include situations in which imported products are subject to one tax system, such as the VAT, while local products are subject to a different tax system, such as sales tax; although the tax systems may be to some extent similar, this differentiation could nevertheless satisfy the phrase "similarly taxed."

In addition, it seems that the AB has mistakenly rejected the finding of a violation if a tax is found to be not more than *de minimis* following a case-specific determination. This is not entirely accurate, because the AB is in effect making new rules beyond its intended role. This ruling is an addition or a modification to the original legal texts. If the drafters wanted to set a *minimum* threshold for the finding of a violation, they would have stated that intent at least abstractly if not explicitly; in fact, they added nothing, referring only to "similarly taxed," a phrase which could include anything that would change the level of the playing field between the products or the necessary "equal competitive conditions."

Further, there is no reason to believe that the drafters meant something substantially different by inserting two different phrases, as understood by the AB. The AB understood that since the drafters applied different words, there must be a different meaning, and that difference must be related to the amount of taxes. The AB interprets "in excess" to mean something that is related to the amount of taxes, while finding that "similarly taxed" means something more relaxed. The AB's addition of a threshold does not seem to be supported by any evidence.

"In excess" seems instead to be narrower, but not substantially different than "similarly taxed." "In excess of" indicates amounts or quantities when comparing two situations – one when taxing local products and the other when taxing imported goods. But "similarly taxed" is a more expansive reading, and this phrase could include a variety of issues, such as the amount of taxes, methods of taxation, and any other factor relevant to the process of imposing a tax on products that could affect the competitive environment.

This understanding is reinforced by looking at the context in which both phrases have been mentioned. In the first sentence, "in excess of" is mentioned when dealing with two like products, which normally should be taxed in a like manner – identically or to a very large extent. Thus, it is reasonable to expect the text to assert that the tax imposed on one product should not be "in excess of" that imposed on the other product.

on Canada – Periodicals, p. 29); in Chile – Alcoholic Beverages (Appellate Body Report on Chile – Alcoholic Beverages, para. 49). Also, the Panel on Indonesia Autos followed it. Panel Report on Indonesia – Auto, para. 14.115.

On the other hand, the second sentence, as modified by the ad Note, refers to products which are not necessarily alike, but which are competing against each other or are substitutable for one another. The products being not alike leaves open a possibility that they are not "similarly taxed." The drafters likely did not expect these different products to be taxed identically or even substantially similarly, but they did want to ensure that the products would be treated and affected by the tax factor, regardless of its nature, similarly. For example, it is possible that the drafters thought that a sales tax of 10% on a television should be equalized by a VAT of 10%, or that an individual filing his or her tax form online with respect to one product would be subject to a collection of tax on another product, even if it is not included in the filing. The point is that different products could indicate different tax surroundings, which could affect the competitive conditions, a potentially serious problem that must be resolved.

The AB in its analysis may be correct that the two phrases mean something different. But its narrow conclusion, specifying that the difference between the two phrases is only related to the amount of taxes, is too limited to be completely correct. The reason for the AB's focus on this point may be that the amount was the only issue raised by the parties.

6.1.8 Determining What Constitutes a Violation

From the above, some preliminary remarks can be made regarding when a violation can be said to exist. A complaining party alleging a violation of Article III can obtain the help of the WTO in one of two ways. For internal tax measures to be in violation of the first sentence of Article III:2, the Panel must find that (1) the taxed imported and domestic products are "like," and (2) the taxes applied to the imported products are "in excess of" those applied to domestic products, regardless of the amount of excess. For an internal tax measure to be in conformity with the second sentence, an additional factor is added. The Panel will determine if (1) the taxed imported and domestic products are either directly competitive with or substitutable for one another, (2) whether they are or are not "similarly taxed," and (3) whether different taxes are levied so as to afford protection to domestic production.[51]

6.1.8.1 Article III:4

> The products of the territory of any contracting party imported into the territory of any other contracting party shall be accorded treatment no less favorable than that accorded to like

[51]The steps are reproduced here, with modification, from Choi (2002, pp. 107, 110).

> products of national origin in respect of all laws, regulations and requirements affecting their internal sale, offering for sale, purchase, transportation, distribution or use . . . .

Section 4 of Article III is a general requirement, stipulating that contracting parties must not discriminate between imported goods and "like" domestic goods regarding "all laws, regulations and requirements" affecting the sales of imported products or any other issues related to the sales event. It does not explicitly use the word "discriminate," but instead states that imported products should not be treated less favorably, meaning that they are to be treated equally and afforded the same favorable treatment, if any.

The scope of Article III:4 "firstly depends on how broadly or narrowly one defines the 'likeness' of goods" (Lothar 2002, pp. 921–977). In addition, the other standard conditions must be met. The result is that three conditions must be satisfied in order to find a violation according to Article III:4: (1) "the imported and domestic products at issue are 'like products'"; (2) "the measure at issue is a 'law, regulation, or requirement affecting their internal sale, offering for sale, purchase, transportation, distribution, or use'"; and (3) "the imported products are accorded 'less favorable' treatment than that accorded to like domestic products."[52]

For a given tax law to be found to be in violation of this section, there must first be established a "likeness" between the products, a subject that has been a source of dispute. Second, there must be a law, regulation or requirement, the implementation of which would affect the sales of the imported products. This does not restrict potential triggers of a violation to those categories alone; indeed, other methods of violation could occur beyond the imposition of a law, regulation, and/or requirement. Other actions that could reasonably be included according to the wording of Article III:4 are measures, royal decrees, ministerial decisions or other government actions, or any action from any agency in a country if that action has a prohibited effect. Without this assumption of inclusion, it would be easy to label governmental action otherwise than as the three specific actions in the plain wording of the Article in an effort to escape violation. Finally, for a finding of a violation, a difference must be present between products that favor local products over imported products.

There is, understandably, some confusion in determining the meaning of "like products" in this context, because the term appears repeatedly throughout the General Agreement[53] and carries a different meaning each time. The Working Party Report on Border Tax Adjustments[54] recognized this issue, stating that the Contracting Parties have never developed a single general definition of "like product" for application to all provisions of the General Agreement. The Border Tax report states that:

[52]Appellate Body Report on Korea – Various Measures on Beef, Para. 133.

[53]18 times in the GATT.

[54]Report of the Working Party on Border Tax Adjustments, GATT B.I.S.D. II/18S/97 (1947), [/18].

> With regard to the interpretation of the term 'like or similar products', which occurs some sixteen times throughout the General Agreement, it was recalled that considerable discussion had taken place, but that no further improvement of the term had been achieved. The Working Party concluded that problems arising from the interpretation of the terms should be examined on a case-by-case basis. This would allow a fair assessment in each case of the different elements that constitute a 'similar' product. Some criteria were suggested for determining, on a case-by-case basis, whether a product is 'similar': the product's end-uses in a given market; consumers' tastes and habits, which change from country to country; the product's properties, nature and quality.

The Border Tax criteria, including a product's end-use in a given market, the nature, quality, and properties of the product, consumers' varying and tastes and habits that depend on nationality, circumstances, time, and place, govern interpretation of any relevant cases that arise under the WTO.

6.1.9 Concluding Remarks

Article III of the GATT, which has been the topic of much discussion, has been approached from various angles to interpret the exact intent of the drafters and the meaning of the portions of the text related to taxation. This chapter offered an overview of the GATT-tax relationship and the implications thereof, as well as highlighted potential problems. Of the many important issues under the GATT, the effort here was an exclusive focus on tax and tax-related issues. The author has presented the sections with the greatest current potential effect on tax issues, and has attempted to show the potential result of ignoring these provisions.

6.2 II. GATS and Tax

6.2.1 Introduction

The decision to negotiate multilateral trade in services is "of relatively recent origin" (Footer 1995, p. 453). Despite some early attempts, it was not until the Tokyo Round (1973–1979), on the initiative of the US government, that the service sector came under serious consideration (Footer 1995, pp. 453–454). From that time through 1995, different levels of negotiations were undertaken, culminating in the birth of the General Agreement on Trade in Services (GATS). This service agreement was finally negotiated during the Uruguay Round, launched in 1986 and becoming effective in 1995. The GATS is the first multilateral trade agreement regarding services, and is one of the major achievements of the Uruguay Round.

In general, the GATS is designed, as proclaimed by the agreement, to secure progressively higher levels of liberalization of trade in services through successive rounds of negotiations,[55] which are intended to promote the interests of all Members of the WTO and achieve an overall balance of rights and obligations.[56] Through liberalization of trade in services, the GATS will promote economic growth and the continued development of developing countries, as the GATT does through the liberalization of trade in goods, to "ensure that developing countries have more flexibility in pursuing economic integration policies, maintaining restrictions on balance of payments grounds, and determining access to and use of their telecommunications transport networks and services."[57] Certain elements of the GATT can found reproduced in the GATS, indicating that this agreement was likely inspired by essentially the same objectives.

One of the goals of the GATS is the liberalization of the laws and regulations that govern the service sector. This treaty plays a potentially crucial role not only in shaping the relationship between tax and trade, which is the subject of this study, but also in more broadly presenting "a new challenge to traditional conceptions of domestic sovereignty" (Paton 2003, p. 361).

The GATS is likely to increase the "deepening integration and globalization" (Ostry 1996) more now than ever. Since it touches upon traditionally sensitive areas, such as education and health care, it will be subject to careful scrutiny to ensure that local values and standards are not violated. Some sensitive sectors need to remain regulated domestically including, but not limited to, environmental protection, local public health, and maintenance of an acceptable level of economic welfare, all of which are very location-specific.

The GATS remains and will continue to be a "work in progress" (Steger 1998). It is a new, largely unexplored legal area that operates on a multilateral level and is built on unique grounds. One potentially important challenge will be the international taxation aspect of each country's domestic legal system.

6.2.2 *Scope*

The GATS does not offer any definition of "service" (see Abu-Akeel 1999, pp. 189, 190). Instead, Article I states that "any service in any sector" is covered by the GATS, with the exception of "services supplied in the exercise of governmental authority."[58] This provision provides the GATS with a very broad range of services potentially covered by it. Not only is the cross-border supply of services covered, but so are transactions involving the cross-border movement of capital and labor.

[55]GATS Article XIX.

[56]The GATS: Objectives, Coverage, and Disciplines, available at http://www.wto.org/english/tratop_e/serv_e/ gatsqa_e.htm.

[57]The GATS: Objectives, Coverage, and Disciplines.

[58]GATS Article I:3, b.

The GATS is similar in some aspects to the GATT, but different in many others. If a member schedules a service to be covered by the GATS, the MFN principle must be respected by all member nations regarding all services. The main fundamental difference between the two agreements is that the GATS is not obligatory agreement; thus, any member nation can exclude any portion it wishes and commit itself only in a limited way. This has led some to argue that GATS is "inherently weaker" (Sauvé and Robert 2000, p. 494) than the GATT, and that there is a high possibility that it will be "easier for government to undo . . . what has been agreed to in the GATS negotiation" (Sauvé and Robert 2000, p. 494).

6.2.3 Significance

The GATS will become one of the most important agreements in the WTO under which tax issues will gradually be exposed to a large extent. It seems only a matter of time before tax measures begin to be debated, argued, and disputed in earnest. The obvious reason is that the service sector continues to grow, resulting in serious economic implications (Nicolaides 1989, pp. 125, 127–128).

According to the WTO, services "represent the fastest growing sector of the global economy and account for two thirds of global output, one third of global employment and nearly 20% of global trade."[59] In the USA, eight out of ten jobs are in the service sector. The service sector accounts for 75% of the US GDP. Service exports totaled $340 billion in 2004 alone, or approximately 30% of the total value of US exports. Services account for over "70% of total employment and value added in OECD economies"[60] and for "almost all employment growth in the OECD area."[61]

These statistics do not take into account the fact that developing countries' measurements of service statistics may be less accurate because of a lack of information and the specialty resources needed to analyze such data. Developing countries are progressing, economically and otherwise, but their progress is not easy to quantify because of the lack of developed mechanisms to monitor changing circumstances. To get an idea of the magnitude of the growth of the services trade in recent years, one should consider that exports of services rose 6% over the year 2001–2002, an increase that represents approximately the same amount of growth over the 10-year period between 1990 and 2000. Furthermore, as barriers continue to diminish or be erected in the trade of goods sector, politicians are likely to try to use the service industry to find a way to reward their constituents, especially in light of the fact that the GATS is not as firm as the GATT and not as fully developed

[59]World Trade Organization, GATS – Fact and Fiction, available at http://www.wto.org/english/tratop<uscore>e/serv<uscore>e/gats<uscore>factfiction<uscore>e.htm.

[60]OECD Report, Growth in Service (2005), p. 1.

[61]OECD Report, Growth in Service (2005), p. 1.

legally as the GATT, offering room for manipulations without technical violation of the WTO laws.

6.2.4 *Modes of Supplies*

Four modes of supplying services are recognized under the GATS: cross-border trade, consumption abroad, commercial presence, and presence of natural persons. Article I, provides that for the purposes of the GATS Agreement, "trade in services is defined as the supply of a service:

(a) from the territory of one Member into the territory of any other Member;
(b) in the territory of one Member to the service consumer of any other Member;
(c) by a service supplier of one Member, through commercial presence in the territory of any other Member;
(d) by a service supplier of one Member, through presence of natural persons of a Member in the territory of any other Member."[62]

The first mode covers situations where services are provided from the territory of one Member to the territory of another Member. Examples of this kind of service include banking, legal services, or architectural services conducted by telecommunications or mail. The second mode, consumption abroad, covers situations where a service consumer moves and buys the service in another Member's territory. Examples include students and patients travelling to a foreign WTO member country. Commercial presence, the third mode, covers situations where a service supplier of one member establishes a presence in another member's territory. Examples include establishing a foreign office for a bank or law firm. Fourth, the presence of service providers covers situations where service providers of one member enter the territory of another member to provide a service. Examples of this kind include lawyers, accountants, or teachers.

The first mode, consumption abroad, makes it possible for non-resident services' suppliers to supply services cross-border into the member's territory. This is because there is no permanent establishment (PE),[63] meaning a fixed place of business through which the business of an enterprise is wholly or partly carried on.[64] If there is no PE, and no physical presence, there is no sufficient connection by which countries can impose tax on the non-resident service suppliers. For example,

[62]GATS article I, 2.

[63]On the concept of permanent establishment, see Skaar (1991); Russo (2005, with preface by Kees van Raad).

[64]US Income Tax Treaty Model, Article 5. Saudi Arabia tax department defined it as follows: "A permanent establishment of a nonresident in the Kingdom consists of the permanent place of activity of the nonresident through which it carries out business, in full or in part, including business carried out through an agent." http://www.zakat.gov.sa/en/NewIncomeTaxLaw/New-IncomeTaxLaw4_2.shtml.

if Ali, a physician from his country Saudi Arabia, provides medical consultations by means of phone or mail to his clients in China, there is no PE. The service itself "crosses" the border (Terry 2001, pp. 989, 1009). This kind causes less international tax problems due to the lack of the PE; thus, there is very little connection to China's tax system justifying imposition of the tax on him, in addition to the fact of enforceability.

The second service mode is where WTO Member's residents purchase services in the territory of another WTO's Member. Here, a student comes to study in the USA. Here, the service consumer, not the service, crosses the borders. In this instance, it is also unlikely that there will be any tax-trade or other problem with respect to the GATS, because the GATS' most important principle, the MFN and NT, aim to regulate the relation between members with respect to "services and service suppliers of any other Member."[65]

For example, if Harvard imposes a tax on education provided to Saudi students, there would be no GATS issue. Since the service provider, Harvard, and the service itself, education, are not "of any other member," there is no related issue to the GATS. This is reasonable because GATS, like other WTO agreements, does not regulate internal affairs of members dealing with their own citizens.

Thus, it seems that this type of service mode will never be an issue, because GATS is regulating issues surrounding the services and services' suppliers. When the service suppliers are locals in which there are no "other" members involved as service suppliers, there would be no MFN issue, because MFN speaks about equalizing treatment between services provided by one member with services provided by other members. The consumers are from the "other" WTO members, but the MFN is structured in a way that is just for regulating the sellers, suppliers, etc., not the buyers or the consumers. MFN requires service suppliers to be treated like local service suppliers; it does not require local service consumers to be treated like non-resident service consumers. Article II says, "each Member shall accord immediately and unconditionally to *services and service suppliers of any other Member* treatment no less favourable than that it accords to like services and service suppliers of any other country."[66] It seems difficult to imagine a situation where MFN can be applicable with respect to Harvard imposing tax or any other discriminatory treatment. If it were Tokyo University offering education service in the USA, then it would be another service mode, the commercial presence (mode three).

The same scenario is true for NT: "Each Member shall accord to services and service suppliers of any other Member," which in our case does not exist, because there are no service suppliers of any other country "in respect of all measures affecting the supply of services," which again does not apply to our Harvard

[65]GATS article II. Likewise, national treatment article speaks of the same issue, stating: "Each Member shall accord to services and service suppliers *of any other Member*, in respect of all measures affecting the supply of services, treatment no less favourable than that it accords to its own like services and service suppliers" GATS, article XVII.

[66]GATS article II.

example, because the service (education) is coming not from any other country, so that there is no "treatment ... less favourable than that it accords to its own like services and service suppliers."[67]

Outside the border, there is a possibility, however, that this mode can be raised and become an issue. Being outside the border of a WTO member, the MFN applies, but the NT will be hardly applicable. For example, as to MFN, it is possible to imagine that the USA passes a law that allow its citizens to use hotels in Jamaica, but prohibits and criminalizes them from using hotels in Cuba. As to market access, the USA may restrict the number of nights that US residents may stay in hotels in Cuba, while leaving the Jamaica tourist free to stay as long as he wishes. As to national treatment, it is conceptually a bit strange, but technically the rule requires that the USA treat Cuban hotels as well as it treats US hotels for purposes of the service issues covered in Article XVII of the GATS.

The third mode is where there is a commercial presence, or in tax terminology, where there is a PE. This kind of service involves the ability of non-resident service providers to set up a PE in another WTO member. Having a PE entails being subject to the tax law of any given country. For MFN, there is a requirement that all WTO members offer the same treatment to all PEs. MFN under the GATS requires that "each Member shall accord immediately and unconditionally to services and service suppliers of any other Member treatment no less favourable than that it accords to like services and service suppliers of any other country."[68] For tax purpose, if Saudi Arabia offers a no-tax treatment to China, a WTO member, it has to offer it to all WTO members, unless Saudi Arabia is taking advantage of other exceptions, such as the one included under Article II stating that "[a] Member may maintain a measure inconsistent with paragraph 1 provided that such a measure is listed in, and meets the conditions of, the Annex on Article II Exemptions."[69] As to NT, WTO members cannot do anything if there is a tax treaty, as Article XXII stated that any "Member may not invoke Article XVII [the NT article], either under this Article or Article XXIII, with respect to a measure of another Member that falls within the scope of an international agreement between them relating to the avoidance of double taxation."[70]

Mode four, the presence of natural persons, addresses the situation in which the foreign lawyers themselves enter the United States in order to offer legal services. MFN seems to be straightforward in asking that lawyers from one member be treated as the most favored member, getting the same treatment that any other

[67]GATS, article XVII. This mode also shows that sometimes there are cases where international law, be it tax or trade, misses (or ignores) an important regulatory component, in this case the consumers. Saudi students, consumers of services provided by WTO members, are not protected or regulated, which can lead to a discriminatory tax being applied to them. No tax treaty exists between Saudi Arabia and the US WTO agreements don't apply.

[68]GATS, article II (1).

[69]GATS, article II (2).

[70]GATS, article, XXII (3).

member is getting. For tax purposes, it can be different from country to country as to when a natural person should be subject to the tax system. In Saudi Arabia, for example, non-Saudi persons are subject to taxes if they are residents doing business in the Kingdom, partners in a resident partnership, or general partners in a resident company limited by shares; a natural person is a resident in Saudi Arabia, for tax purpose, if the person has a permanent place of abode in the Kingdom and is physically present in the Kingdom for not less than 30 days in the aggregate during the taxable year.[71] So, there must be a connection between the country and the person to trigger the tax rules. For NT, natural persons will be treated as citizens if there is no exception or a reservation has been made to exempt them from such treatment, as will be described later in this section.

6.2.5 Obligations

The GATS contains a general framework of obligations that apply to those scheduled services, and also contains other rules that are not obligatory concerning issues, such as market access and national treatment rules. Obligatory rules are contained in Part II (entitled "General Obligations and Disciplines"), which enunciates the unconditional obligations applicable to all services. The most notable of these obligations are the MFN and transparency principles.

Unlike GATT, GATS allows members to limit their commitment with respect to other articles. To do so, a member nation must declare its intention in what is called a specific commitment. Specific commitments are member country's commitments to market access and national treatment for specific sectors, for example healthcare or education.

6.2.5.1 Transparency

In addition to MFN, transparency applies to all services covered by the GATS. Any commitment can be easily violated or nullified if related rules and regulations can be hidden, and violations can only be documented if they are readily ascertainable. Thus, in virtually every agreement under the WTO, including the GATS, there is a noticeable emphasis on transparency.

Services, because of their potential sensitivity in areas such as healthcare, are typically subject to regulation. It would not be possible to achieve effective liberalization of trade in services without ensuring that suppliers of services can

[71]Tax Law, article 3 (a) Article 3 (b) for company residency stated that (b) A company is considered resident in the Kingdom during the taxable year if it meets any of the following conditions:
(1) It is formed in accordance with the Companies Law.
(2) Its central management is located in the Kingdom.

obtain the necessary information concerning all the rules and regulations framing the environment in which they operate. Thus, in order to guarantee transparency, as required by the GATS, governments must publish all relevant laws and regulations.[72] Accordingly, Article III requires member nations to "publish promptly (except in emergency situations), at the latest by the time of their entry into force, all relevant measures of general application which pertain to or affect the operation of this Agreement."[73]

Additionally, any other international agreements relating to trade in services to which a member nation is party are covered by the same obligation. Article III states that "[i]nternational agreements pertaining to or affecting trade in services to which a Member is a signatory shall also be published."[74] This indicates an application to bilateral tax treaties as well as multinational agreements by virtue of bilateral tax treaties' effect on trade in services.

There also must be continuing communication informing the GATS governing authorities "promptly and at least annually of the introduction of any new, or any changes to existing, laws, regulations or administrative guidelines which significantly affect trade in services covered by its specific commitments under this Agreement."[75] This is a continuing, not a one-time, requirement.

Each member nation must establish "one or more enquiry points to provide specific information to other Members,"[76] to provide information on laws and regulations affecting trade in services. This must be done within two years from the date of entry into force of the Agreement.

Of course, there is no way to truly force a country to publish anything that presents a potential risk to its domestic security, commercial interests, or public interests. Article III *bis*: provides that "Nothing in this Agreement shall require any Member to provide confidential information, the disclosure of which would impede law enforcement, or otherwise be contrary to the public interest, or which would prejudice legitimate commercial interests of particular enterprises, public or private."[77]

6.2.5.2 Specific Commitments

The national treatment principle is the most crucial standard, present everywhere in the WTO, including in the GATS, because services include some sensitive areas, such as healthcare or legal services. Thus, individual countries' commitments to open markets for foreign services and foreign service suppliers are determined

[72]GATS Article III.

[73]GATS Article III.

[74]GATS Article III at 1.

[75]GATS Article III at 3.

[76]GATS Article III at 4.

[77]GATS Article III at 4.

during negotiations among affected members. These commitments are then documented and appear in a package of "schedules," which show the type and extent of restrictions on the sectors, as well as new sectors being opened, the extent of market access allowed in those sectors, and any limitations on national treatment. These commitments are similar to tariff ceilings in the GATT; once these commitments are formed, they remain in place permanently and cannot be modified or withdrawn except by negotiations among those countries which are most affected; these nations have paid for the commitments and should be compensated for their demise. Thus, to be aware of a country's specific commitments, it is necessary to examine each country's schedules.

Commitments are usually split into two sections. The first is for "horizontal" commitments, which stipulate limitations that apply to all sectors included in the schedule. Horizontal commitments often refer to a particular mode of supply, notably commercial presence and the presence of natural persons. Any evaluation of sector-specific commitments must therefore take the horizontal entries into account. The second section of the schedule covers commitments, which apply to trade in services in a particular sector or subsector.[78]

To uncover GATS undertakings for any country, one must look to:

> three sources of GATS obligations: (1) the unconditional commitments to which all WTO Members are subject, mostly found in Part II of the GATS framework agreement; (2) the commitments found in Member States' Schedules of Specific Commitments to which the market access and national treatment obligations of Part III apply; and (3) the MFN exemptions lists submitted during the Uruguay Round negotiations, which excuse Members from granting MFN treatment in specified services sectors (Hopkins 2005, pp. 427, 437).

6.2.6 *GATS and Tax*

Since GATS covers services, it is most likely to affect income tax rules. Providing services usually will require some foreign presence (Hopkins 2005, pp. 427, 437), exposing the provider to the income tax laws in the domestically controlled area. This is not a new issue, but with the GATS application, international transactions involving services will likely become more difficult to administer than before. In the past, domestic authorities had almost absolute control over foreign presences, whether services or service-providing persons, but there now exists a set of international rules supervised by an international organization, stringent in the enforcement and application of its rules.

[78]http://www.wto.org/English/tratop_e/serv_e/guide1_e.htm.

6.2.6.1 Tax Negotiations in the GATS Treaty

The negotiations leading to the formation of the GATS illustrate the importance and sensitivity of international tax issues. The process of negotiation was difficult not only because negotiation is by its nature never easy, but also because when a discussion of taxes is involved, there is a necessary giving-up of at least some sources of revenue. Negotiations in fact did collapse (Dodwell 1993) as a result on several occasions and the media reported that negotiations were over, but each time the negotiators worked to reach an acceptable agreement, which can at best be characterized as distorted and vague for reasons that will be discussed later in this thesis. The first part of this section is an overview of the negotiations before the final agreement was reached. The second part addresses the reasons the ultimate agreement was insufficient.

6.2.7 The Dilemma

The major disagreement during the GATS negotiations was related to the national treatment concept, as articulated in Article 17 of the GATS. The problem is with a specific portion of text, which reads: "Each Member shall accord to services and service suppliers of any other Member, in respect of all measures affecting the supply of services, treatment no less favourable than that it accords to its own like services and service suppliers."[79] For tax purposes, this clearly means granting the same tax treatment to foreign service providers of the same or similar services. The treatment must not be "less favourable," which means that the different treatment must not "modif[y] the conditions of competition in favour of services or service suppliers of the Member compared to like services or service suppliers of any other Member."[80]

In other words, in theory and without reservations in the schedules, foreign service providers should be treated similarly to local service providers. This like treatment, required by Article XVII, includes tax treatment, because tax can clearly affect service providers' competition tremendously. If, for example, an income tax rate of 100% is imposed on accounting firms, no accounting firm is likely to be willing to operate in the 100%-tax region.

---

[79]GATS Article 17.

[80]GATS Article 17.

6.2.8 The US Resistance

During the negotiation of this Article, the United States noticeably tried to limit its application, although the USA was the leader in pushing the service agreement to its multilateral level. Most other countries were in support of this Article without major reservations. It is also surprising that the national treatment provision is not compulsory under the GATS. Governments are allowed to offer complete national treatment to foreigners, or they can choose to impose limitations on structuring the national treatment concept, since they retain the freedom to favor their own domestic service providers in their specific schedules. This is unlike trade in goods, as governed by the GATT, Article III of which requires national treatment to be applied without any additional controls once goods enter the country. This was a seemingly inconsistent action by the USA, because it was so firm regarding the exclusion of income tax from WTO supervision.

Despite the safety[81] measures inherent in the GATS, the United States nevertheless was not willing to risk any exposure to international supervision with regard to international taxation. Therefore, before the deadline for completing the entire Uruguay Round Agreement, the United States announced that it would not accept the inclusion of the national treatment obligation, and more specifically that it would not accept its application to income tax measures (Dodwell 1993).

The USA had two main goals in the tax negotiations, according to Leslie Samuels, Assistant Treasury Secretary for Tax Policy. The first was to ensure that domestic tax laws would have primacy, and the second was to leave in place existing bilateral tax treaties. The USA also demanded an exemption: "... to exempt itself from the obligation to provide national treatment for tax purposes[, which] provoked a storm among GATT negotiators" (Dodwell 1993, p. 3). The United States' argument was that income tax rules cannot easily be structured in a discriminatory manner, and thus need not to be included under the WTO. If they do exist, the USA argued, they are uncommon. Even if such discriminatory measures did occur, the USA contended that they could be settled in a different forum by alternative means, such as through diplomatic negotiations or the dispute settlement procedures included in income tax treaties.

In addition, the United States expressed concern that the application of the GATS to income tax measures "would upset the existing system of bilateral tax treaties, and could tie the hands of Congress in enacting new tax laws" (Williams 1993). This was expressed without evidence of how applying GATS could potentially harm existing treaties. In fact, as reported by the *Financial Times*, "no other country, including the 50 or so with double taxation agreements with the US, sees a

[81]Safety measures include the specific commitments concept involved in the GATS by which countries can choose how to commit themselves, which means countries can exempt income tax from national treatment.

threat to the existing system" (Williams 1993, p. 7). From the US position, a number of questions arise: Why should adding the income tax to the scope of the GATS not strengthen the existing system? How is it that the concern is limited only to the USA, while the rest of the world does not perceive it as a problem? Are there, in fact, any mechanisms for resolving disputes in tax treaties?

All of the 114 other member countries perceived no problems with including such measures under the GATS. Negotiators from these other countries expressed their frustrations (Nomani and Bahree 1993, A3), saying they had "no choice but to follow the US lead, leaving multinational companies vulnerable to tax discrimination wherever they are based" (Dodwell 1993, p. 7). That position was seen as putting "the whole round at risk" (Dodwell 1993, p. 7).

There were conflicting reports. Samuel told reporters that although some trade negotiators wanted to include taxes under GATS, tax authorities from other countries expressed agreement with the US position. There is no official record providing a complete and accurate portrayal of what really happened during negotiations, but it seems that the main objector was the USA, as it has been reported that former GATT Director Peter Sutherland[82] informed Samuels that "the United States is totally isolated in its position. All other 114 nations involved in the talks are against Washington's proposals" (see Green 1998, p. 139).

Rejection of the US position was reasonable, not only because it was desirable to hold the USA to an otherwise well-received and majority-approved principle, but also because there were indications that the USA was in the process of implementing certain tax rules that could potentially hurt international companies doing business inside the USA. This suspicion was substantiated when the United States announced in October 1994 that it was determined to increase taxes on foreign-controlled companies doing business in the USA because they were perceived to be reducing US taxes by using transfer-pricing methods. It is thus understandable that some countries could suspect that the United States' intention was to exempt income tax measures out of the national treatment obligation, because it intended to pursue discriminatory tax policies, particularly in the area of transfer pricing regulation. This conflict threatened to ruin not only the negotiations regarding trade in services, but also, more catastrophically, the entire Uruguay Round.

However, following three weeks of negotiations, a compromise was finally reached (Dodwell 1993, p. 3) on December 10, 1993. Under the compromise, tax measures that were inconsistent with the national treatment provision were vaguely excluded from the GATS. The United States gradually abandoned its extreme position and agreed that income tax measures be brought under the GATS, specifically under the national treatment obligation, with a broad exception as discussed below.

[82]GATT Director from 1993–1995. http://www.wto.org/english/thewto_e/dg_e/ps_e.htm.

6.2.9 The Final Agreement

A final agreement with respect to the taxation issue was reached, but with an important exception that represented the success of the USA in preserving its interests. The final language was very limited, first because opposition to the inclusion came from the world's most powerful economy, and second because the issue of international and multilateral governance in this context was new and unexplored.

The analysis of the legal text that follows will reveal that, although the drafters tried to limit Article 14 and its application, this was not an easy task. In fact, the application of the GATS to income tax issues could potentially apply. The final rules are not, at this stage, sufficiently clear; only future disputes and case-by-case application and interpretation will determine their meanings.

6.2.10 Relevant Legal Texts

6.2.10.1 Most Favoured Nation

GATS Article II puts forth a general obligation that applies to all services. It requires that "with respect to any measure covered by this Agreement, each Member shall accord immediately and unconditionally to services and service suppliers of any other Member treatment no less favourable than that it accords to like services and services suppliers of any other Member treatment no less favorable than that it accords to like services and services suppliers of any other country."[83] The MFN principle means that a member nation must treat all of its trading partners equally. Thus, under GATS, if a country allows a foreign-service supplier to participate in a given sector, equal opportunities in that sector should be offered to all WTO members' services providers.

In theory, MFN applies to all services, but some special temporary exemptions have been allowed. During the negotiation of the GATS, WTO members were given an opportunity to list any measures that are inconsistent with the Article II MFN principle as exemptions that become part of their GATS commitments. Article II states that member nations may maintain a measure inconsistent with MFN "provided that such a measure is listed in, and meets the conditions of, the Annex on Article II Exemptions."[84] Paragraph 6 of the referenced Annex provides that the MFN exemptions listed by a country in its schedule of specific commitments "in principle . . . should not exceed a period of 10 years" and at the same time it "in any event it shall be subject to negotiation in subsequent trade liberalizing rounds."[85]

---

[83]GATS Article II.

[84]GATS Article II, 2.

[85]Annex to Article II: 5 and 6.

Unlike the GATT, the GATS does not distinguish between direct and indirect tax. Nothing in this agreement can be understood to require that GATS distinguish between the two or apply the GATS to them differently. The agreement cannot be comprehended without accepting the notion that direct taxes are the subject of the GATS. Services are supplied via different modes. Mode one and two are more relevant to indirect taxation, since there no persons or entities involved. Services supplied by natural persons (mode four) or by a commercial establishment (mode three) are more clearly related to income taxes. This conclusion is reached by recognizing that the GATS definitions of services and measures are "very extensive" and by acknowledging the "well known effects of the income taxation on the private sector economic behavior."[86]

The term "measure" covers any action taken by any government institution. Likewise, it should cover any action undertaken by non-governmental entities "to which regulatory powers have been delegated."[87] A "measure" can take any form: law, regulation, royal decree, administrative decision or ruling, guideline, or even an unwritten enforceable practice supervised by any public body. Notably, the use of the term "affecting" rather than alternative terms such as "governing" or "regulating" implies that the scope of the GATS covers not only measures designed directly to regulate trade in services, "but also any other measures that might be designed to regulate other matters but which incidentally affect the supply of a service."[88]

Since tax rules are measures that can and do affect trade in services, taxation naturally falls under this Article. For example, if Saudi Arabia imposes a 50% income tax on all lawyers except those coming from France, a WTO member, who get a reduced tax rate of only 10%, then there exists: (1) a trade in service, (2) a measure affecting that trade, and (3) the treatment offered to French lawyers is favourable. Thus, Saudi Arabia either has to extend "immediately and unconditionally to service and services suppliers of any other member" as prescribed by Article II of the GATS. Alternatively, it will be violating the MFN. According to MFN, once tax measures are offered to one country, the host country will have to treat services and services suppliers of all other member nations no less favourably with regard to tax measures, unless there are exceptions or carve-outs explicit in the agreement as prescribed by Article II, (2). Otherwise, a violation can be found.

Although this is applicable in theory, tax measures under the GATS have been the subject of extensive debates and negotiations, with the result that MFN (like NT) has been limited in application to income tax measures. As pointed out earlier, member countries were allowed to list exemptions that are not to be covered by the MFN of the GATS, and many countries listed income tax measures.[89] Since the

[86]WTO and Direct Taxation, p. 36.

[87]GATS: Scope and Definition, available at http://www.wto.org/english/thewto_e/whatis_e/eol/e/wto06/wto6_11.htm.

[88]GATS: Scope and Definition.

[89]WTO and Direct Taxation, p. 36.

limitations are temporary, they will become inapplicable sometime in the future. The real limitation lies in the general exceptions of Article XIV, which provides, *inter alia*, that MFN can be violated if that violation is a result of employing a double taxation treaty[90] unless it is an "arbitrary," "unjustifiable," "disguised restriction" on trade in services.[91]

Thus, if Saudi Arabia and France have a tax treaty specifically prescribing that the French lawyers be subject to only 10% income tax, then under the exception of Article XIV, there will be no violation. Absent a tax treaty, a violation can be found, because this treatment does not seem to be aimed at collection or enforcing tax rules; rather, it is just mere favoritism that is not allowed under the GATS.

6.2.10.2 National Treatment

The general rule for the national treatment principle is expressed in Article 17. Although it is a fundamental issue in the international trade area, it is more limited in GATS than GATT.[92] Thus, NT applies to tax measures relating to service only to the extent provided for in the schedule of commitments. However, the power of this provision should not be underestimated, as it remains important for two reasons. The first reason is the linkage notion (see Trachtman 1998, p. 32): almost every country, during negotiations, links an offer of a commitment in sector X with the obtaining of favorable treatment in sector Y. Alternatively, country X may offer NT for service suppliers of country Y, if in exchange country Y offers a reduction of an applicable tariff. This becomes obvious when it is understood that nations deal with great pressure when negotiating newcomers and/or additional rounds. Hence, this provision can be used as a bargaining chip in the hands of the negotiators.

The second reason for the provision's importance is the long-term effect of a commitment. Countries may offer NT for services that are less important to them at the time of negotiation, but this level of importance may eventually change, and the types of services that are the subject of the commitment can increase in importance over time. Once NT is listed with respect to market access or for conditions or limitations, it remains in effect unless the terms of the commitment are re-negotiated.

Acknowledging these issues, the text of the Article states that:

1. ... each Member shall accord to services and service suppliers of any other Member, in respect of all measures affecting the supply of services, treatment no less favourable than that it accords to its own like services and service suppliers.
2. A Member may meet the requirement of paragraph 1 by according to services and service suppliers of any other Member, either formally identical treatment or formally different treatment to that it accords to its own like services and service suppliers.

---

[90]GATS Article XIV (e).

[91]GATS Article XVII and WTO and direct taxation p. 39.

[92]*See* The GATS: Objectives, Coverage and Disciplines, available at http://tsdb.wto.org/wto/JobNo4904.html.

3. Formally identical or formally different treatment shall be considered to be less favourable if it modifies the conditions of competition in favour of services or service suppliers of the Member compared to like services or service suppliers of any other Member.[93]

As previously mentioned herein, the first difference between the national treatment principle here and that found in GATT is that under the GATT national treatment it is applicable to all trade situations, while under the GATS each country commitment must be evaluated individually to determine if it accepts "explicitly" to apply this principle, to which sector, and with what limitations (Van den Bossche 2005, p. 367).

When examining the NT principle, there emerge three factors, which must be met before the principle is invoked. First, the measure at issue must affect services or service suppliers. Second, the measure must result in less favorable treatment for foreigners as compared to domestic services or providers. Third, the services or service suppliers between which differential treatment exists must be alike (Van den Bossche 2005, pp. 367–368).

Under the GATS, there is no requirement that countries treat service suppliers the same or provide *identical* treatment. Interestingly, *identical* treatment could be a violation of this Article if such treatment were to modify the competition balance. For example, identical treatment could alter the competition balance if foreign lawyers from China were required to speak local languages, or to memorize local folklore or local religious texts in order to practice law. For this reason, this Article insists on favoritism, "treatment no less favourable," rather than on the artificial, surface characteristics of the treatment itself. On the other hand, if a member nation grants different treatment to foreign services or providers than to their domestic counterparts that nevertheless results in no favoritism, there would be no breach of obligation.

For tax purposes, if a country is committed in its schedule of commitments to provide NT with respect to tax rules, then NT applies. In such a situation, country X, for example, would be required to offer treatment to foreign services and service suppliers that is no less favorable than that which it offers to its domestic services and service suppliers. If country Y imposes a tax on local banks that amounts to 2% interest income, it would be obligated to offer the same tax rate to other banks operating via one of the four modes. However, under Article XIV (General Exceptions, discussed below), to the extent that countries have made NT commitments in their schedules, these commitments apply to all tax measures, except where such measures are aimed at ensuring "equitable or effective" imposition or collection of direct taxes in respect of services or service suppliers of other member nations.[94] The only remaining limitation is the general overall limitation that member nations are prohibited from using tax measures in a manner that can be characterized as an "arbitrary," "unjustifiable," "disguised restriction" on trade in services.[95]

[93]GATS Article XVI.

[94]GATS Article XIV, D.

[95]GATS Article XVII.

Finally, for tax purposes, granting a tax treatment that is *more* favorable to foreigners compared to local services or service providers is *not prohibited* by the GATS, but it can nevertheless cause a problem: such reverse favorable treatment may be considered harmful to other countries, especially to the source country (for the benefit of the residence country where the activity takes place). This is a traditional case of a tax haven. Granting tax treatment that is more favorable to foreigners triggers what is called a "ring fenced"[96] situation, a situation where countries design their tax system in a way that is more favorable and limited to foreign residents, preventing domestic residents from sharing the favorable tax rules (Engel 2001, pp. 1525, 1559). The harm arises because these tax schemes are designed to foster exports and, therefore, are separated from the local economy, and take revenue from the source country. These taxation methods are "ring fenced," because they are set up by countries with a real domestic tax base that do not wish to see that base eroded by the tax concessions granted within the preferential regimes. There is a clear potential for conflict, but with the general exception Article in force, this issue should not present an immediate problem.

6.2.10.3 Article XIV: General Exceptions

Examining MFN and NT more closely, it becomes clear that GATS has a potentially very significant impact on tax measures, especially direct taxes, if no constraints are imposed. In fact, an application of the two principles together would signify an end to bilateral tax treaties and, in a broader sense, to the pure diplomatic era. This is clearly something for which the international community is not yet ready, thus Article XIV is inserted as a safeguard. Article XIV targets Articles II and XVII, the most important principles of the WTO. Article XIV is crucial because the full Agreement indicates that all tax issues would be included, until this Article dispels that notion. The Article is not especially clear, but what is clear is that the negotiators were trying very hard to carve out meaningful tax measures. This Article attempts to remove direct tax measures from the jurisdiction of the GATS. Has it succeeded in excluding all direct tax measures? The success of the negotiators' efforts will be evaluated in the following section, and will be revealed in the future as cases under GATS begin to emerge.

6.2.10.4 The Chapeau

Article XIV begins: "Subject to the requirement that such measures are not applied in a manner which would constitute a means of arbitrary or unjustifiable

[96] *See* OECD Announces Release of Harmful Tax Competition Report, 2000 WTD 124-10 (June 26, 2000); Primarolo Group's EU Harmful Tax Competition Report Identifies 66 Violative Regimes, 2000 WTD 50-1 (March 10, 2000).

discrimination between countries where like conditions prevail, or a disguised restriction on trade in services, nothing in this Agreement shall be construed to prevent the adoption or enforcement by any Member of measures."[97]

This is a typical WTO requirement: prohibiting "arbitrary," "unjustifiable," "disguised restriction," and the usual structure of requirements for permitting a limited violation under the WTO agreements.[98] This article is identical to Article XX of the GATT, which has been subject to many disputes and the evaluation of which may be helpful here in understanding the meaning of the GATS' Article's text. However, applicability is only indirect, since the context is different for services than goods. Nevertheless, it is enlightening to consider the direction of the AB with regard to this matter.

It should first be noted that this article is an exception and should be treated as such. The AB insisted on characterizing this clearly, saying that "the negotiating history of Article XX confirms that the paragraphs of Article XX set forth *limited and conditional* exceptions from the obligations of the substantive provisions of the GATT."[99] Under this Article, discrimination is acceptable if not abused; the AB has stated that "discrimination could be present in a 'measure' which it is being sought to justify under Article XX, and could be consistent with it, provided that it does not constitute 'the abuse of the exception provided for in Article XX.'"[100]

In another case, the AB held that "in order that the justifying protection of Article XX may be extended to it, the measure at issue must not only come under one or another of the particular exceptions – paragraphs (a) to (j) – listed under Article XX; it must also satisfy the requirements imposed by the opening clauses of Article XX."[101] Additionally, to examine whether a measure is applied in an unjustifiable,

[97]GATS article XIV.

[98]GATT Article XX: "Subject to the requirement that such measures are not applied in a manner which would constitute a means of arbitrary or unjustifiable discrimination between countries where the same conditions prevail, or a disguised restriction on international trade." TRIPS Article 4, D: (d) "... agreements related to the protection of intellectual property which entered into force prior to the entry into force of the WTO Agreement, provided that such agreements ... do not constitute an arbitrary or unjustifiable discrimination against nationals of other Members." Agreement on the Application of Sanitary and Phytosanitary Measures, Article 2: (3) "Members shall ensure that their sanitary and phytosanitary measures do not arbitrarily or unjustifiably discriminate between Members where identical or similar conditions prevail, including between their own territory and that of other Members. Sanitary and phytosanitary measures shall not be applied in a manner which would constitute a disguised restriction on international trade." Annex on Telecommunications, Article 5(d): "Notwithstanding the preceding paragraph, a Member may take such measures as are necessary to ensure the security and confidentiality of messages, subject to the requirement that such measures are not applied in a manner which would constitute a means of arbitrary or unjustifiable discrimination or a disguised restriction on trade in services."

[99]WTO Appellate Body Report: *United States – Import Prohibition of Certain Shrimp and Shrimp Products (Oct. 12, 1998), 38 I.L.M. 118, 123–124 [hereinafter US-Shrimp I]*. Para 157.

[100]WTO Panel Report, Argentina – Measures Affecting the Export of Bovine Hides and the Import of Finished Leather, WTO Doc. WT/DS155/R (Dec. 19, 2000) Para. 8.310.

[101]WTO Dispute Settlement Panel, United States Standards for Reformulated and Conventional Gasoline, WTO Doc., WT/DS2/R (Jan. 29, 1996) [hereinafter *US*-Gasoline] Para. 22.

arbitrary manner or is a disguised restriction, two requirements have been identified in the Panel and Appellate Body reports in *US-Shrimp and US-Shrimp* (Article 21.5): "First, whether a serious effort to negotiate has been made by the Member country adopting the measure, and second, whether the measure is flexible."[102] Conflicting interests are apparent, but the AB stated that "a balance must be struck between the *right* of a Member to invoke an exception under Article XX and the *duty* of that same Member to respect the treaty rights of the other Members."[103]

More recently the *Gambling* case has addressed the issue of exception. After Antigua and Barbuda brought a complaint against the United States, alleging that some of the US laws constitute a violation of the GATS' rules, the United States invoked the "public morals" clause of GATS. To invoke an exception, the chapeau requires that the measures be applied.

The AB discussed the meaning of the term "necessary," concluding that is something "that cannot be dispensed with or done without, requisite, essential, needful."[104] The AB in that case concluded that "a 'necessary' measure is, in this continuum, located significantly closer to the pole of 'indispensable.'"[105]

The Appellate Body also explained that "necessity" is "an *objective* standard."[106] In this regard, it said, while "a Member's characterization of a measure's objectives and of the effectiveness of its regulatory approach – as evidenced, for example, by texts of statutes, legislative history, and pronouncements of government agencies or officials – will be relevant in determining whether the measure is, objectively, 'necessary,'" a Panel "is not bound by these characterizations ... and may also find guidance in the structure and operation of the measure and in contrary evidence proffered by the complaining party."

The AB noted that there are "two factors that, in most cases, will be relevant to a panel's determination of the 'necessity' of a measure, although not necessarily exhaustive of factors that might be considered. One factor is the contribution of the measure to the realization of the ends pursued by it; the other factor is the restrictive impact of the measure on international commerce"[107] and that "the requirement, under Article XIV(a), that a measure be 'necessary' – that is, that there be no 'reasonably available', WTO-consistent alternative – reflects the shared understanding of Members that substantive GATS obligations should not be deviated from lightly."[108]

The Panel believed that the content of public moral concepts for Members could vary depending upon important factors, including cultural, ethical and religious

[102] http://www.wto.org/english/tratop_e/envir_e/envir_backgrnd_e/c7s3e.htm.

[103] Appellate Body Report on US-Shrimp, Para. 156.

[104] AB Korea, Para 160, citing Brown (1993, p. 1895).

[105] Appellate Body, Korea – Beef, Para. 160.

[106] AB gambling at 304.

[107] AB gambling at 306.

[108] AB at 308.

values.[109] In addition, the Panel admitted that WTO members should have some freedom "to define and apply for themselves the concepts of 'public morals' and 'public order' in their respective territories, according to their own systems and scales of values."[110]

Later, the AB analysis of the chapeau stated that it sets the rules as "does article XX of GATT."[111] Accordingly, the AB stated that, "like the Panel, we find previous decisions under Article XX of the GATT 1994 relevant for our analysis under Article XIV of the GATS."[112] There must be a violation of a general requirement. Then, the measure violating the rules must be designed to protect "public morals."[113] Finally, the measure must be necessary to do the job of protecting public morals.[114] In sum, "in order for a measure to be accepted as 'necessary' under Article XIV(a), the responding Member must have first '*explored and exhausted*' all reasonably available WTO-compatible alternatives before adopting its WTO-inconsistent measure."[115]

The AB went on to rely on the *Korean-Beef*[116] case where it established a balancing factor.[117] The "necessity test" has evolved into a weighing and balancing of three factors: (1) whether and the degree to which the common interests or values protected by the measure are vital and important; (2) whether alternative measures are "reasonably available" to accomplish the stated objective; and (3) whether alternative measures are less inconsistent with the Member's WTO obligations.[118] Then, there must be a comparison "between the challenged measure and possible alternatives . . . and the results of such comparison should be considered in the light of the importance of the interests at issue."[119]

The USA has, first, to prove that the three federal statutes were necessary to protect public morals; and second, to satisfy a legal balancing test found in the chapeau. With respect to the first, the AB concluded that the three federal statutes were necessary to protect public morals; "We see no error in the Panel's approach, nor in its finding ... that the Wire Act, the Travel Act, and the IGBA 'must contribute' to addressing those concerns."[120] As to the second, the AB determined that the USA did not meet the criteria in the chapeau. The AB found that the United

[109]Panel Report, para. 6.461.

[110]Panel Report, para. 6.461.

[111]AB, para 291.

[112]AB, para 291.

[113]AB, para 294.

[114]AB, para 294.

[115]AB, 315.

[116]Appellate Body Report, *Korea – Measures Affecting Imports of Fresh, Chilled and Frozen Beef*, WT/DS161/AB/R, WT/DS169/AB/R, adopted January 10, 2001, DSR 2001:I, 5.

[117]AB, para 305.

[118]AB, para 305–306.

[119]AB, 307.

[120]AB, 313.

States has failed to demonstrate that the prohibitions are applied equally to both foreign and domestic service suppliers; consequently, these measures fail to satisfy the requirements of the chapeau.[121] Thus, although the measures are accepted as protecting public morals, they were not necessary, because the USA allowed other US companies to do almost the same thing.

Essentially, in sum, the chapeau requires that all measures, income tax measures included, must not be imposed in such a manner as would constitute "arbitrary," "unjustifiable" or "a disguised restriction on trade in services." If such is found to be the case, then a violation of the NT obligation would be found, although on its face the measure might seem to fall under the Article XIV(d) exception.

Compared with GATT Article XX, it is reasonable to expect that if, for example, country X imposes a tax rate of 20% on all foreign banks operating under the GATS under the GATT XX Chapeau, but imposes a higher 80% tax rate on specific banks from country Y, despite the fact that the country Y banks operate under the same or similar conditions, the validity of such exception will be rightly questioned and will be likely found to be a violation of the GATS.

6.2.10.5 Measures Permitting Violation

Article XIV lists measures that permit a violation of the general rule, including any measure by a member, whether in the form of a law, regulation, rule, procedure, decision, administrative action, or any other form[122] that is not arbitrary, unjustifiable, or a disguised restriction. Countries can violate the GATS if the measures, *inter alia*, are:

d. inconsistent with Article XVII (NT article), provided that the difference in treatment is aimed at ensuring the equitable or effective (6) imposition or collection of direct taxes in respect of services or service suppliers of other Members . . .;
e. inconsistent with Article II, provided that the difference in treatment is the result of an agreement on the avoidance of double taxation or provisions on the avoidance of double taxation in any other international agreement or arrangement by which the Member is bound.[123]

Specific measures were also set forth aimed at ensuring the equitable or effective imposition or collection of direct taxes includ[ing] measures taken by a Member under its taxation system which:

(1) Apply to non-resident service suppliers in recognition of the fact that the tax obligation of non-residents is determined with respect to *taxable items sourced or located in the Member's territory*; or

[121] AB, 365–369.

[122] GATS Article 28, a.

[123] GATS Article XIV.

(2) Apply to non-residents in order to ensure the imposition or *collection of taxes* in the Member's territory; or
(3) Apply to *non-residents or residents* in order to prevent the *avoidance* or evasion of taxes, including compliance measures; or
(4) Apply to *consumers* of services *supplied in or from the territory of another* Member in order to ensure the imposition or collection of taxes *on such consumers* derived from sources in the Member's territory; or
(5) Distinguish service suppliers subject to tax on *worldwide* taxable items from other service suppliers, in recognition of the difference in the nature of the tax base between them; or
(6) Determine, allocate or apportion income, profit, gain, loss, deduction or credit of resident persons or branches, or *between related persons* or branches of the same person, in order to safeguard the Member's tax base

With respect to the national treatment provision, footnote (d) is relevant. The first measure, regarding non-resident service suppliers, applies to the presence of both natural persons (lawyers, for example) and commercial presences of establishments (law firms, for example). In this case, people or entities provide services within another member nation's territory. This is in "recognition of the fact that the tax obligation of non-residents is determined with respect to taxable items sourced or located in the Member's territory." The target for taxation in this case is the income generated from the service provided, which might be in the form of salary, fees, wages, compensations, or any other taxable income. Providing a service in another country makes the service supplier fairly subject to taxation by the nation, because the service supplier has "enjoyed the benefits of performing services within its borders" (Jeffrey 2006, p. 227). The reason for imposing such a tax on the service provider is because the service provided is sourced within the member nation's border, and thus is taxable inside that country.

The determination of the source of the taxable item or service is not an easy task. This provision merely recognizes what is an unclear international rule. This is, in fact, one of the most challenging issues associated with international taxation, because it is not easy to identify the definition of, or limitations associated with, "permanent establishment" in the case of business entities and "fixed base" in the case of individuals, especially when the performance of services is involved. The first question that arises in an international transaction is this: What level of activity will subject a foreign business to domestic income tax in another country? Answering this question is a difficult task, but "all we know is that pretty much any level of activity above and beyond a bare minimum is going to subject you to tax" (Byrnem 1996, pp. 695, 698).

The second measure (2) is aimed at ensuring the collection of taxes, and is applicable to non-residents with taxable income sourced inside the Member's territory. Pursuant to this measure, there is no requirement of a presence inside the member nation's territory; nevertheless, there exists taxable income arising from the occurrence of a taxable transaction attached to the member nation's tax system. This normally happens with services offered over the telephone, Internet, or through other means of communication. The GATS has distanced itself by not regulating such measures, instead leaving any disputes to be settled outside its jurisdictional sphere.

The third measure (3) applies to both non-residents and residents alike with respect to issues regarding compliance with tax evasion. Citation of this provision is minimally important, since there will be no dispute once a tax evasion has been determined to exist; inserting such a provision undermines the rest of the footnote by diminishing its overall importance.

Measure four (4) appears redundant, applying "to consumers of services supplied in or from the territory of another Member in order to ensure the imposition or collection of taxes on such consumers derived from sources in the Member's territory." This application affects services provided from outside the member nation's borders, such as online education. It targets consumers inside the member territory (citizens, non-citizen residents, or non-residents). A dispute is unlikely regarding the taxing of consumers located inside a country for consumption-related taxes that are sourced inside the same country. However, since this measure concerns the taxing of consumers, the measure is more likely an indirect tax, because it is linked to the consumption incidence. Indirect taxes do not fall within this provision's jurisdiction, given that the footnote about imposition or collection of "direct taxes" was defined in Article 28 to exclude consumption tax.

The fifth measure, in essence, is about the US tax system. It recognizes the legality of the worldwide tax system, allowing the USA to distinguish service suppliers accordingly.

Measure six concerns transfer pricing issues. It allows countries to intervene and restructure how related parties can conduct their dealings without violating the GATS, even if such restructuring involves some sort of discrimination.

Finally, the footnote gives member nations tremendous power by stating that all the tax terms or concepts mentioned in paragraph (d) of this Article, as well as those in the footnote, "are determined according to tax definitions and concepts, or equivalent or similar definitions and concepts, under the domestic law of the Member taking the measure."[124] The domestic authority is thus assured that the WTO will not interfere with domestic tax rules.

Paragraph (e) covers MFN. It allows members to act inconsistent with their MFN obligations if that inconsistency is the logical consequence of a tax treaty relating to the avoidance of double taxation "or provisions on the avoidance of double taxation in any other international agreement or arrangement by which the Member is bound." Although sovereignty is thereby preserved, this approach may be risky and could nullify the purpose of MFN altogether. It is imperative to remember that tax measures are a very powerful method by which governance of the service sector by the GATS can be changed.

Furthermore, it is not clear to what extent tax measures can be considered tax treaty measures exempt from MFN according to this provision if the measures are not related directly to the tax treaty. A related issue pertains to who should be

[124]GATS Article XIV.

responsible for deciding what the precise issue is, and whether a tax avoidance does or does not exist.[125] If two taxpayers are similarly situated but governed by different tax treaties, do different withholding tax rates comply with the MFN?[126] In Italy, for example, some costs related to tax havens, regardless of whether or not the affected nations are WTO members, are not deductible, while other costs are deductible when related to non-tax haven countries.[127] This has the potential to trigger a conflict-of-law problem between the OECD and the WTO, since the OECD identifies and fights such tax havens, while the WTO does not discriminate against them.

Other measures also may trigger concerns. One such measure relates to tax incentives. Countries sometimes grant tax incentives to special categories of taxpayers or activities, such as small businesses[128] or agriculture.[129] Assuming countries have not specified contrary exclusions in their commitments, there would remain an obligation to extend such tax incentives to other WTO members.[130]

6.2.10.6 Article XXII

As if the general exceptions were not enough to eliminate tax measures from control by the GATS, Article XXII increases the power of countries with respect to tax issues. Professor Green described this phenomenon, saying that the GATS "virtually eliminates [the risk] as a practical matter by severely limiting the jurisdiction of GATT panels over income tax measures" (Green 1998, p. 94). This Article reads, in part, as follows:

> 3. A Member may not invoke Article XVII, either under this Article or Article XXIII, with respect to a measure of another Member that falls within the scope of an international agreement between them relating to the avoidance of double taxation.[131]

Article XXIII deals with dispute settlement and enforcement. Thus, this provision eliminates the right of countries to come to the WTO under the GATS to complain about a violation. There remains, of course, the question of when the measure falls within the scope of the tax treaty, and on this subject the provision goes on to say:

> In case of disagreement between Members as to whether a measure falls within the scope of such an agreement between them, it shall be open to either Member to bring this matter

[125] WTO and Direct Tax, pp. 37 and 41.
[126] WTO and Direct Tax, p. 101.
[127] WTO and Direct Tax, p. 40.
[128] WTO and Direct Tax, p. 43.
[129] WTO and Direct Tax, p. 43.
[130] WTO and Direct Tax, pp. 43–44.
[131] GATS Article XXII, 3.

before the Council for Trade in Services. (11) The Council shall refer the matter to arbitration. The decision of the arbitrator shall be final and binding on the Members.

With respect to income tax treaties that were already in force on January 1, 1995, a dispute may be brought before the Council for Trade in Services only with the consent of both parties to the tax treaty[132] unless such a treaty includes provisions instructing the party countries to resolve the matter outside the scope of the GATS, which some nations have begun to do. The OECD's commentary on Article 25 of the OECD's Model Tax Convention suggests that this preemption may be accomplished by adding the following provision in new income tax treaties.

Although the GATS, through Article 22(3), tries to limit the jurisdiction of the Panel over income tax measures, there is room available for other possibilities. First, disputes relating to income tax measures may fall within the scope of income tax treaties that came into force after January 1, 1995, if there is not consent among the party nations. Second, an applicable tax treaty may have no provisions excluding the GATS.

Further, not every tax measure affecting service suppliers will be covered by income tax treaties. For example, as illustrated, the right to establish a partnership with a favorable tax pass-through treatment, as is common in the USA, is not covered by tax treaties. Nevertheless, it could affect the service suppliers in the importing counties. An "S" corporation, with its favorable limited liability and tax treatment under the US tax system, is a designation available only to US citizens. Clearly, certain measures that are not tax treaty issues may still affect the tax imposed on foreigners, and therefore may also affect their rights under the GATS.

Not every member nation is party to a tax treaty with every other member. This has the potential to create odd situations, because the outcome of a dispute between two members having a tax treaty with each other will be different from the outcome of a dispute between two members having no such treaty. This unintentional distortion may lead to confusion among nations, who will be required to deal with different outcomes based on whether the parties do or do not have a bilateral tax treaty. It may also encourage some countries to withdraw from tax treaties to which they are party if the Panel proves to be a more desirable resource for resolution of tax disputes. Moreover, there may arise a choice-of-law problem in which participants in international commerce are forced to rely on even less predictable outcomes. There may be circumvention of tax issues if nations are forced into the trade field in a way that gives the Panel jurisdiction, creating unfairness and distortion.

Another problem with this approach is that, absent a tax treaty between the member nations that are parties in the dispute, a Panel would still have to deal with the same issues that such treaties address. With the current procedures in place for appointing members to the Panel, tax rules have the potential to be mishandled. One critical aspect regarding invoking Article XVII is the examination of tax measures,

[132] GATS Article XXII, footnote 11.

but a difficulty arises regarding the determination of whether or not there is a "tax measure." There seems to be no clear way to identify such a measure.

In conclusion, GATS theoretically applies to all tax measures. Practically, however, numerous limitations exist. NT is subject to countries' individual schedules, general exceptions, and Article 22.3, all of which illustrate the difficulty of applying the GATS to direct tax measures. Nonetheless, the GATS is likely to pose a problem in the future.

6.3 Subsidies

6.3.1 Introduction

> Virtually every product and service moving in international trade is affected by a government action that could be considered a subsidy. (Southwick 1988, p. 1159)

Subsidies, generally speaking, occur when any help is provided by a government to the private sector, either to individuals or to corporations, in order to achieve particular goals. These goals may include stabilizing the price of certain commodities, encouraging production of certain types of goods or services, or helping certain groups, such as farmers, homeowners, mortgage companies (Hobbs 1978, p. 29), banks, or others for nation-specific reasons.

Offering subsidies under certain conditions can be economically sound. Some authorities claim that subsidizing the private sector alters the functioning of certain industries by diverting resources to facilitate the most efficient use (Kleiner 2002, p. 129). Other sources have claimed that not all subsidies pose a problem (Showalter 2004, p. 587, footnote 69). This chapter will not attempt to further evaluate this difficult issue, but rather will focus on the relationship between subsidies and taxation.

Whether subsidies are economically, socially, or legally acceptable or beneficial, fair or unfair, is irrelevant to the objectives of this thesis. What is relevant is the way in which subsidies can be structured through taxation, and how they can potentially violate the WTO rules. It is well established that the economic effects of tariffs can be duplicated almost exactly by structuring a destination-based consumption tax along with an equal-rate subsidy for domestic production (Avi-Yonah and Slemrod 2002, p. 535). Thus, tariffs may be considered disguised taxes, and because of their potential distortion of the trade environment, the WTO did put in place legal rules governing subsidies. The WTO rules on subsidies are encompassed in the Agreement on Subsidies and Countervailing Measures (SCM). The SCM is the third crucial agreement under which tax and trade interact.

The use of subsidies has always created some tension among nations, each trying to prevail both domestically and internationally at the expense of others by using its tax system and other economic and political tools to its own advantage. Before the 1994 Marrakesh Agreement, commentators admitted that one of the major problems facing international trade, particularly the GATT, was the absence of a mechanism "to deal effectively with subsidies" (Showalter 2004, p. 589). The international effort long ago began to combat this tactic.

Subsidies take many different forms. Money grants, interest-free loans, the use of public facilities, protection against foreign competition, and tax breaks are all actions that may be defined as subsidizing. There is no reason to expect subsidies to take one form over another, but many forms of subsidies used by governments may violate the WTO rules. The debate regarding what types of subsidies should be allowed has led to severe international disagreement. For example, the DISC, FSC, and ETI all addressed this issue over the 35-year period from 1971 to 2006. The major topics of debate during this time span were the ethical and legal boundaries that govern the use of taxes to subsidize certain activities in a way that violated GATT-WTO rules.

In fact, it could be argued that sometimes it is very hard to distinguish between taxes and subsidies at all, because taxes can be structured in a way that they may be considered subsidies, representing both an incentive and a burden. For example, if country Y offers a tax exemption for television producers, this exemption creates an incentive to produce this type of good, and is the equivalent of a subsidy for television producers. Countries can also offer favorable tax deductions for products that are exported or that need to be produced nationally in larger quantities.

The following discussion offers an overview of the SCM and an analysis of the relationship between subsidies and taxes, with a special focus on footnote 59 of the SCM.

6.3.2 SCM General

SCM is a product of GATT Article XVI, which prohibits governments from granting subsidies for the export of industrial products. The text reads: "Contracting parties shall cease to grant either directly or indirectly any form of subsidy on the export of any product other than a primary product which subsidy results in the sale of such product for export at a price lower than the comparable price charged for the like product to buyers in the domestic market."[133] Article XVI was fundamentally expanded by the SCM and included in the 1994 WTO.

The SCM agreement has two goals. First, because not every subsidy is a prohibited subsidy, the agreement "disciplines the use of subsidies." Second, because subsidies can cause economic damage to other nations, creating the possibility of retaliation, the agreement "regulates the actions countries can take to counter the effects of subsidies."[134]

---

[133]GATT Article XVI: 4.

[134]http://www.wto.org/english/thewto_e/whatis_e/tif_e/agrm8_e.htm#subsidies.

According to SCM, a subsidy has two basic elements. First, it is a financial contribution made by a government or any public body within the territory of a member nation. Second, a subsidy must confer a benefit.[135] This second element is likely included to ensure that not all government involvement is prohibited. Many government actions confer benefits, a reality recognized by the WTO jurisprudence; the Panel in *US – Export Restraints*, relaying the history of negotiations of the GATT, stated:

> This negotiating history demonstrates, in the first place, that the requirement of a financial contribution from the outset was intended by its proponents precisely to ensure that not all government measures that conferred benefits could be deemed to be subsidies . . . that only government actions constituting financial contributions should be subject to the multilateral rules on subsidies and countervailing measures.[136]

Financial contributions may take different forms. They may be made via income[137] or price support,[138] or may take the form of a direct transfer of money, as in a grant, loan, or equity infusion. Other financial contributions that can be characterized as subsidies include loan guarantees, forgiveness of debts to the government, or government provisions of goods and services.[139]

Once the scope of what constitutes a subsidy was thus established according to Article 1, Article 2 of SCM further limited the term. According to Article 2, a subsidy must be specific for the Agreement to apply. Only if the subsidy at issue is specific to a company, an industry, or a group of industries should the WTO exercise its jurisdiction.[140] There is no obvious reason for such a condition, but the official website of the WTO offers the following explanation: "The basic principle is that a subsidy that distorts the allocation of resources within an economy should be subject to discipline. Where a subsidy is widely available within an economy, such a distortion in the allocation of resources is presumed not to occur."[141]

6.3.3 Subsidies Categories

Subsidies play an important role in the development and growth of a country's economy. Most countries in the world grant subsidies in one form or the other. The Agreement on SCM permits such subsidies to be maintained so long as they are not specific; those which are available generally to all eligible recipients and which are

---

[135]SCM Article 1.

[136]Panel Report on US-Exports Restraints, Para. 65.

[137]SCM Article 1, a, (1).

[138]SCM Article 1, a, (2).

[139]SCM Article 1, a (1) i, ii, iii.

[140]SCM Article 2.

[141]*See* http://www.wto.org/english/tratop_e/scm_e/subs_e.htm.

governed by objective criteria for general infrastructure, for research activities, for the development of disadvantaged regions, and for the adaptation of existing facilities to new environmental requirements may not be actionable. All are, however, subject to certain limitations.

6.3.3.1 Specification

Obviously, not every subsidy is prohibited. Any positive action by a government can be considered a subsidy; even inactions might be considered subsidies. For example, taxing, spending on infrastructure, or regulation and enforcement of rights and contracts can all be considered subsidies, because they reduce the cost of doing business (Southwick 1988, p. 1159). These general subsidies "have such a widespread effect on production that countervailing duties, were they allowed in such cases, could be imposed on almost every product which enters international commerce."[142] Professor Trachtman makes his case regarding general subsidies by saying, "It would be legitimate – and necessary in order fully to redress 'subsidization' – to examine every public expenditure of an exporting country in order to determine to what extent it enhances the competitive capability of that country's firms" (see Trachtman 1993, p. 96). He describes this as a "proxy of intent" (Trachtman 1993, p. 97), referring to the specificity test incorporated in the SCM.

The Agreement specifically expresses disapproval of subsidies that distort trade, and specifically prohibits export subsidies and subsidies given to promote the use of domestic goods over imported ones. Countervailing measures can be taken against a subsidy causing injury to the domestic industry of other nations, such as the nullification or impairment of any benefits for, or serious prejudice to, the interest of other members.

The SCM divides subsidies into three categories: prohibited, actionable, and non-actionable.

6.3.3.2 Prohibited Subsidies

SCM Article 3 provides that subsidies contingent in law or in fact shall be prohibited, whether as the sole condition or one of several conditions imposed. Annex I of the SCM Agreement provides an illustrative list of what are deemed export subsidies. These include: (a) direct subsidies to an enterprise based on export performance; (b) currency retention schemes; (c) government mandated internal transportation charges on export shipments that are more favorable to domestic shipments; (d) subsidies on items used for production of exports; (e) tax breaks for export enterprises; (f)–(g) tax deductions directly and indirectly related to exports

[142]*See Carlisle Tire and Rubber Co. v. United States*, 564 F. Supp. 834, 838.

above those given to products consumed domestically; and (h) indirect taxes on goods or services used in the production of export products.

6.3.3.3 Actionable Subsidies

Actionable subsidies are those which are not problematic themselves, but which, if they result in any of the problems specified by the Agreement, may be countervailed. These are subsidies described in Article 1 that cause injury to the domestic industry of another member nation, nullify or impair a benefit accruing directly or indirectly to other member nations, or seriously prejudice the interests of another member nation.[143]

6.3.3.4 Non-actionable Subsidies

Non-actionable subsidies include all subsidies that do not fall into the categories of prohibited or actionable subsidies. Specifically, the Agreement on SCM describes non-actionable subsidies as subsidies which are not specific,[144] or those which, regardless of their specificity, fall under A, B, or C:

A. Assistance for research activities, not exceeding 75% of the costs of industrial research or 50% of pre-competitive development activity, provided that such assistance is limited to:

   - Costs of personnel
   - Costs of instruments, equipment, land and buildings used exclusively and permanently (except when disposed of on a commercial basis) for research activity
   - Costs of consultancy and equivalent services used exclusively for research activity, including both in research, technical know-how, patents, etc.
   - Additional overhead costs incurred directly as a result of the activity
   - Other running costs (such as those of materials supplied and the like), incurred directly as a result of the research activity[145]

B. Assistance to disadvantaged regions within the territory of a member given pursuant to a general framework of regional development and non-specific (within the meaning of Article 2) within eligible regions provided that the disadvantaged area is a clearly designated contiguous geographical area with a definable economic and administrative identity and is considered as disadvantaged on the basis of neutral and objective criteria.[146] The criteria shall include a

[143] SCM Article 5.

[144] SCM Article 1 (a).

[145] SCM Article 8.2 (a).

[146] SCM Article (b).

measurement of economic development which shall be based on at least one of the following factors:

- One of either income per capita or household income per capita, or GDP per capita, which must not be above 85% of the average for the territory concerned.
- Unemployment rate, which must be at least 110% of the average for the territory concerned as measured over a 3-year period; such measurement, however, may be a composite one and may include other factors.[147]

C. Assistance to promote adaptation of existing facilities to new environmental requirements imposed by law and/or regulations which result in greater constraints and financial burden on firms, provided that the assistance satisfies the following conditions. First, it must be a one-time, non-recurring measure. Second, it is limited to 20% of the cost of adaptation. Third, it does not cover the cost of replacing and operating the assisted investment, which must be fully borne by firms. Fourth, it is directly linked to, and proportionate to, a firm's planned reduction of nuisances and pollution, and does not cover any manufacturing cost savings which may be achieved. And finally, it is available to all firms which can adopt the new equipment and/or production processes.[148]

6.3.4 Tax and Subsidies

6.3.4.1 Article 3

Article 3 ultimately became the center of disputes relating to taxation. Article 3.1 states:

> [T]he following subsidies, within the meaning of Article 1, shall be prohibited:
>
> (a) subsidies contingent, in law or in fact, whether solely or as one of several other conditions, upon export performance, including those illustrated in Annex I;
> (b) subsidies contingent, whether solely or as one of several other conditions, upon the use of domestic over imported goods.

When a country offers a tax exemption on goods exported to be consumed abroad, it would normally be thought to be making a financial contribution by conferring a benefit. This should, on its face, be a prohibited subsidy, but is relieved of the prohibited designation by footnote 1 in Article 3, which states that "the exemption of an exported product from duties or taxes borne by the like product when destined for domestic consumption, or the remission of such duties or taxes in amounts not in excess of those which have accrued, shall not be deemed a subsidy."

---

[147]SCM Article (b).

[148]SCM Article 8.2 (c).

This footnote is a reference to so-called indirect taxes, specifically to the VAT employed by most EU members.[149] There has to date been no dispute regarding this understanding relating to the VAT; however, a different problem has been triggered by the income tax treatment exempting foreign income from taxation, a subject reviewed in footnote 59.

6.3.4.2 Footnote 59

A subsidy is given when "government revenue that is otherwise due is foregone or not collected."[150] Article 3.1(a) of the ASCM prohibits subsidies that are "contingent . . . upon export performance, including those illustrated in Annex I." Annex I (e) lists as an example of an export subsidy that is strictly prohibited "the full or partial exemption, remission, or deferral specifically related to exports, of direct taxes.(59)" Footnote 59 explains that:

> [t]he Members recognize that deferral need not amount to an export subsidy where, for example, appropriate interest charges are collected. The Members reaffirm the principle that prices for goods in transactions between exporting enterprises and foreign buyers under their or under the same control should for tax purposes be the prices which would be charged between independent enterprises acting at arm's length. Any Member may draw the attention of another Member to administrative or other practices which may contravene this principle and which result in a significant saving of direct taxes in export transactions. In such circumstances the Members shall normally attempt to resolve their differences using the facilities of existing bilateral tax treaties or other specific international mechanisms, without prejudice to the rights and obligations of Members under GATT 1994, including the right of consultation created in the preceding sentence. Paragraph (e) is not intended to limit a Member from taking measures to avoid the double taxation of foreign-source income earned by its enterprises or the enterprises of another Member.

The detail most relevant to this discussion is footnote 59's permission for members to take "measures to avoid double taxation." In essence, the footnote allows member nations to offer what otherwise would be characterized as prohibited exporting subsidies. In particular, the "fifth sentence of footnote 59" constitutes an exception to the legal regime applicable to export subsidies by explicitly providing that it is permissible to implement sanctions when measures have been taken "to avoid the double taxation of foreign-source income."[151] The footnote also emphasizes the importance of employing the "arm's-length" principle: allocating income among related parties as if they were independent enterprises dealing at arm's length. Tax principles are clearly involved in a trade agreement, including the problem of tax deferral, transfer pricing issues, arm's length principles, tax disputes, and tax treaties.

---

[149] *See also* Appellate Body Report on US – FSC, Para. 93.

[150] SCM Article 3.

[151] S.2.38.1 US – FSC, Article 21.5, Para. 132.

6.3.4.3 Tax Deferral

An important aspect of this footnote is the ambiguity of the language, a familiar feature not unusual in trade law, as opposed to tax law. The footnote states that, "deferral need not amount to an export subsidy where, for example, appropriate interest charges are collected." The sentence seems to be missing something after the word "where." "Where" appears to be intended to set conditions for the tax deferral to qualify as acceptable. Instead, the sentence continues with an example, saying that charging appropriate interest would render the deferral immune from any challenge alleging that it is a prohibited subsidy. The sentence stops abruptly and does not clarify the general rule, offering only an example that adds to the ambiguity of the sentence.

Is charging interest the only acceptable solution? Or must action be taken to make up for the deferral? There is no clear answer. The solution to tax deferral is not the imposition of a requirement that every country avoids employing this method; in fact, some countries find charging interest unconstitutional.

6.3.4.4 Transfer Pricing Issues

The second sentence of footnote 59 states that the WTO members "reaffirm the principle that prices for goods in transactions between exporting enterprises and foreign buyers under their or under the same control should for tax purposes be the prices which would be charged between independent enterprises acting at arm's length." This is risky, as the arm's length principle is not immune from challenge. Many arguments exist against its core logic, the most compelling being that it is counterintuitive to require related parties to deal as if they are unrelated, since their relationship is indisputable given their mutual attempt to reduce prices and profit in excess of what could be expected in dealings as unrelated entities. Large corporations, for example, merge with each other for the sake of reducing costs and increasing profits. They merge together knowing that they will each charge the other less than if they were unrelated, because when there is an acknowledged relationship, profits go to the same general balance sheet.

6.3.4.5 Tax Disputes

The fourth sentence deals with disputes. It asks the WTO members to "normally attempt to resolve their differences using the facilities of existing bilateral tax treaties or other specific international mechanisms, without prejudice to the rights and obligations of Members under GATT 1994, including the right of consultation created in the preceding sentence."

The meaning of "normally" is not clear. Is this an obligation, or is it an option to seek outside help before turning to the WTO? This uncertainty, coupled with the ambiguous phrase "other specific international mechanisms," makes a thorough and accurate understanding of this sentence difficult. Does it refer to the OECD, the WTO, or another institution? Or is it a diplomatic process? Representatives of the USA once raised the issue, saying that the EU "should have raised this matter in the Organization for Economic Cooperation and Development (OECD) or in the competent authority process under the relevant bilateral tax treaties."[152] These representatives then asked the Panel to dismiss the claims relating to transfer pricing issues. The EU responded with the seemingly unexpected answer that footnote 59 "is couched in hortatory language and it is left to the discretion of members whether to resort to such alternative mechanisms."[153]

6.3.4.6 Foreign Source Income

The last sentence of this footnote is the most crucial part. Recall that paragraph (e) specifically asserted that it would be an export subsidy, and strictly prohibited, the "full or partial exemption, remission, or deferral specifically related to exports, of direct taxes." The last sentence of footnote 59 clarifies this by saying that paragraph "(e) is not intended to limit a Member from taking measures to avoid the double taxation of foreign-source income earned by its enterprises or the enterprises of another Member." In other words, (e) would not prohibit the alleviation of double taxation on a foreign source.

Paragraph (e) adds a problem to that of the footnote. It states that it would be considered a prohibited subsidy to allow "the exemption ... specifically related to exports of direct taxes." The problem is with the word "related": how strong a relationship must be established to trigger this paragraph?

There are three problems with the fifth sentence of footnote 59. First, the statement, "double taxation of foreign-source income" is meaningless. There can be no international double taxation if there is no foreign source income, and if income is locally generated, then there is no double taxation in the international setting.

Second, there is a fundamental problem in identifying a "foreign source" in the international tax context. The use of this term here adds to the confusion and ambiguity of the trade agreement. The AB recognized this as a problem and attempted to resolve it, but that attempt was unsuccessful, in this author's opinion. The AB stated that "under footnote 59 to the *SCM Agreement*, the 'foreign-source income' arising in such a transaction is only that portion of the total income which is generated by and properly attributable to activities that do occur in a 'foreign' State." It is difficult, if not impossible, to make such a determination.

The AB seemed to realize the difficulty of distinguishing what is to be considered foreign income and what is not. To its great credit, the AB referred to international practice as follows: "Although there is no universally agreed meaning

[152]Panel Report, Para. 7.12.

[153]Panel Report, Para. 7.12.

for the term 'foreign-source income' in international tax law, we observe that many States have adopted bilateral or multilateral treaties to address double taxation entities. Here this sentence didn't add or explain much relating to this issue."[154]

The AB attempted to define double taxation by stating that it "occurs when the same income, in the hands of the same taxpayer, is liable to tax in different States."[155] But countries vary fundamentally in their definitions of income and taxable income, taxpayer, residency, and non-residency for tax purposes; bilateral tax treaties, therefore, offer a systematic tie-breaking solution in the case of individuals, but not businesses. It would be extremely difficult to force them to accept only one definition. Overall, the phrase is not the best possible outcome that can be achieved.

6.3.4.7 Footnote Status

An additional relevant consideration is the legal status of a footnote in deciding an international dispute. Why should a footnote to a law carry sufficient weight to determine the fate of a case? If the content of a footnote were crucial and fundamental to an agreement, that content should reasonably be expected to be contained in the body of the agreement. A footnote is not, after all, an amendment added later, thus justifying the content's placement in the footnote to distinguish the original text from that subsequently added.

In the WTO agreements, however, footnoting important elements of any text does not seem to be intended to undermine the footnotes' relevance or authority. The Panel and the AB have both considered footnotes to be important and authoritative. The Legal Division has suggested that "in WTO jurisprudence to date, footnotes have been considered by WTO panels and Appellate Body from a legal perspective to be an integral part of the text of the articles to which they are attached."[156]

In another document, dated May 12, 2004, the Division concludes, in answer to the question of whether the incorporation of a document by reference in a footnote would have the same legal effect as if the provisions of that document were incorporated in full, that "the legal effect of such a reference, whether in the main body of the Agreement or in a footnote, would obviously depend on the way the reference is written."[157] It is clear from the Secretariat's Notes that the Panel and the AB "have generally interpreted footnotes as a substantive part of the text, the

[154]Appellate Body Report on US – FSC, Article 21.5, Para. 141.

[155]Appellate Body Report on US – FSC, Article 21.5, Para. 137.

[156]*See* legal arguments in support of the African group proposal on the implementation of Paragraph 11 of the decision of August 30, 2003, IP/C/W/440 March 2005, section II, A, 3.

[157]*See* legal arguments in support of the African group proposal on the implementation of Paragraph 11 of the decision of August 30, 2003, IP/C/W/440 March 2005, section II, A, 3.

question of the status of footnotes *vis-à-vis* the text of an agreement has never been positively examined by a panel or the Appellate Body."[158]

Finally, the footnote approach therefore raises important concerns, which have not been fully addressed. Since there is a more straightforward and more legally acceptable alternative, that is, the direct amendment of the Agreement by inserting the needed texts, there is no strong justification for continuing to rely on footnotes.

6.3.5 Identifying the "Bad" Tax

Although the purpose of this section is to give an overview of subsidies as related to taxation, it is worthwhile to briefly discuss some of the more interesting statements offered by the AB relating to footnote 59 and tax as a subsidy in general.

Identifying the "bad" tax, or a tax that is used as an export subsidy, is not an easy mission. Sovereignty and complicated local tax rules penetrate the issue, transforming it into a very sensitive and complex dilemma. The AB attempted to isolate the tax-subsidy from other legitimate taxes, addressing first the issue of whether the tax is in fact a subsidy and then going on to discuss whether, if it is a subsidy, it is prohibited. The core provision is Article 1.1, which states that, *inter alia*, a subsidy is forgone government revenue "that is otherwise due."[159]

This "otherwise due" in the view of the AB implies a comparison with a "defined, normative benchmark."[160] The AB admitted that "it may be difficult to identify the appropriate normative benchmark for comparison ... because domestic rules of taxation are varied and complex."[161] To the credit of the AB, there seems to exist no other option but to pursue this "difficult" matter, because such is the AB's assigned duty. Exempting this issue from consideration under the WTO is the responsibility of the WTO members.

The AB went on to identify the bad tax. It stated that there must be a comparison between two taxing settings, the purpose of which is to "distinguish between situations where revenue foregone *is* 'otherwise due' and situations where such revenue is *not* 'otherwise due.'"[162]

This proved to be next to impossible, because each country has the right to tax whatever it wishes and exclude from taxation those things it feels should not be taxed, so long as the taxation decisions do not conflict with international obligations. The AB accepted this, stating that, "Members, in principle, have the

[158]*See* legal arguments in support of the African group proposal on the implementation of Paragraph 11 of the decision of August 30, 2003, IP/C/W/440 March 2005, section II, A, 3.

[159]SCM Article 1.1 (ii).

[160]In general, *see*, McDaniel (2001, p. 1621). *See* also Brauner (2005, pp. 304–305).

[161]Appellate Body Report on US – FSC, Article 21.5, Para. 89.

[162]Appellate Body Report on US – FSC, Article 21.5, Para. 89.

sovereign authority to determine their own rules of taxation."[163] The comparison "must necessarily be between the rules of taxation contained in the contested measure and other rules of taxation of the Member in question. Such a comparison enables panels and the Appellate Body to reach an objective conclusion ... as to whether the contested measure involves the foregoing of revenue that would be due in some other situation or, in the words of the *SCM Agreement*, 'otherwise due.'"[164] Is this resolution really attainable? Objective conclusion is an elegant idea, but the AB either forgot to explain or could not enunciate the meaning or criteria of objectivity. The AB explained, "... we believe that panels should seek to compare the fiscal treatment of legitimately comparable income to determine whether the contested measure involves the foregoing of revenue which is 'otherwise due', in relation to the income in question."[165]

A footnote to this statement contradicts the AB's final conclusion. The AB footnote states: "We recognize that a Member may have several rules for taxing comparable income in different ways. For instance, one portion of a domestic corporation's foreign-source income may not be subject to tax in any circumstances; another portion of such income may always be subject to tax; while a third portion may be subject to tax in some circumstances. In such a situation, the outcome of the dispute would depend on which aspect of the rules of taxation was challenged and on a detailed examination of the relationship between the different rules of taxation."[166]

This is an admission that different and legitimate taxing rules, as well as illegitimate taxing rules, are both possible. The outcome will depend on AB's own "detailed examination," which presents a question regarding the kind of detailed examination that will be undertaken. How can the AB, or the Panel, distinguish between countries that have three sets of taxing rules? In paragraph 103, the AB went on to say: "Where the taxpayer elects not to be taxed under the ETI measure, the United States taxes this income under the 'other' rules of taxation applicable to foreign-source income. *We see this as confirmation that, absent the ETI measure, the United States would tax the income under the 'otherwise' applicable rules of taxation we have used as our benchmark*."[167] This is perhaps the most important element of the paragraph, the very core of the problem. The AB sees any different rules as a "confirmation" of the prohibited subsidies, which is a mistaken view; sometimes countries have different rules for legitimate, nonfinancial goals. Thus, it is very hard to conclude that a subsidy exists exclusively from the finding of different taxing rules.

Overall, the AB's analysis is unacceptable. It is possible that the AB would attempt to define on its own the concepts of "objective" and "comparable income."

[163]Appellate Body Report on US – FSC, Article 21.5, Para. 89.

[164]Appellate Body Report on US – FSC, Article 21.5, Para. 89.

[165]Appellate Body Report on US – FSC, Article 21.5, Para. 91.

[166]Appellate Body Report on US – FSC, Article 21.5, Para. 91.

[167]ETI, Para. 103 [emphasis added].

As a result, the AB could compare corporate tax on interests from local banks as well as foreign banks, or between foreign banks in different jurisdictions. Taxing rules vary according to the circumstances, including time, location, and other geopolitical elements that can and do play significant roles when negotiating tax treaties. For example, deductions for interests could be permissible in the UK for a USA company, while the same deductions were not permissible for the same company in the Netherlands. In this hypothetical situation, the USA would have to treat the two nations differently because of different circumstances. An objective test or detailed examination by the AB would cause unknown and unpredictable results.

Clearly, it is very difficult to compare two taxes, even if they look similar. Nevertheless, that is essentially what the AB attempted to do, stating that, "if the measure at issue involves income earned in sales transactions, it might not be appropriate to compare the treatment of this income with employment income."[168] Apparently, the AB felt it was required to try to find an acceptable solution.

In a move that shows little concern for the reality of issues associated with international tax, the AB stated that footnote 59 of the SCM Agreement "permits a Member to take measures granting special fiscal treatment to 'foreign-source income' in order to alleviate a 'double taxation' burden on its taxpayer. Clearly, if the income benefiting from such special treatment could not be taxed twice in two different states, there would be no double tax burden to alleviate, and hence *no justification* for permitting an exception to the prohibition on export subsidies. Thus, the term 'foreign-source income' in footnote 59 refers to income which is susceptible of being taxed in two States."[169]

This is another instance of misinterpreting the international tax reality. The AB decided that if there is no double taxation, there is no justification for the exception that allows export subsidies. Sometimes, however, certain incomes may not be taxed at all in one state, while they are taxed in another. In such a situation, would the AB make tax exemption subsidies legally acceptable in one incidence where there is no susceptibility to double taxation, only to render them illegal in another incidence where double taxation is possible?

If the AB opted to rule in this way, it would have to establish different tax rules for each WTO member. It is not practical for any country to set a taxing rule for every other member country depending on whether or not the other country is taxing foreigners. Each country would be required to set 149 discreet taxing rules, one for each of the 149 members, and each rule would have to include regulations concerning taxing dividends, interests, intellectual properties, and other issues, depending upon the specific rules applicable to and applied by each country.

Even if the rules were similar with respect to all member countries, there is no reason to conclude that a country would maintain its taxation scheme; economic chaos would occur when a country suddenly decided to tax foreign income that had

[168]ETI, Para. 90.

[169]ETI, Para. 138.

not been subject to tax previously, or to eliminate taxation altogether. Each country has the right to set its own taxing rules as it sees fit, and has the authority to establish its own tax rules to fit its national policies.

The meaning of "foreign source" in this regard can vary. The meaning of "source" is likely to differ from place to place and with respect to different types of income. In the taxation arena, meanings are frequently difficult to determine, as they are likely to vary greatly according to context.

Apparently, the AB did not find this argument convincing; it ultimately stated that:

> one of the widely recognized methods of avoiding double taxation is the tax exemption method. Under this method, States may exempt income from taxation to avoid double taxation, irrespective of whether or not another State taxes the exempt income. The avoidance of double taxation is not an exact science. Indeed, the income exempted from taxation in the State of residence of the taxpayer might not be subject to a corresponding, or any, tax in a 'foreign' State. Yet, this does not necessarily mean that the measure is not taken to avoid double taxation of foreign-source income. Thus, we agree with the Panel, and the United States, that measures falling under footnote 59 are not required to be perfectly tailored to the actual double tax burden.

[170] If this is indeed the case and states are able to exempt at their will, regardless of other countries' tax systems, by, for example, employing a territorial tax system, then the previous sentence – "The term 'foreign-source income' in footnote 59 refers to income which is susceptible to taxation in two States" – is rendered meaningless.

Yet the AB continues with a different scenario relating to the interpretation of footnote 59: "Income must have links with a 'foreign' State such that it could *properly be subjected to tax in that State*, as well as in the Member taking the double taxation-avoidance measure."[171] Again, the AB seems to be unsure of what to do with income that originates in a foreign location. It oscillates between supporting an exemption of the income from tax, according to the exemption method, and requiring some sort of tax by two states. The AB seems to be hesitating to offer a precise recommendation.

The AB went on to say, most critically, that:

> [i]f footnote 59 were interpreted to allow a Member to grant a fiscal preference for *any* income that a Member chooses to regard as foreign-source, that reading would seriously undermine the prohibition on export subsidies in the *SCM Agreement*. That would allow Members, relying on whatever source rules they adopt, to grant fiscal export subsidies for income that may not actually be susceptible of being taxed in two jurisdictions. Accordingly, the term 'foreign-source income' as used in footnote 59 *cannot be interpreted by reference* solely *to the rules of the Member taking the measure to avoid double taxation of foreign-source income*.[172]

[170] ETI, Para. 146.

[171] ETI, Para. 147.

[172] Appellate Body Report on US – FSC, Article 21.5, Para. 140.

This last paragraph is very serious and dangerous to the sovereignty of the WTO members. If a member nation cannot rely on its own rules to explain what it means by foreign source income, then who should be responsible for such a determination? Should responsibility fall to another member nation? To the AB? To the WTO? If so, there should be an agreement to that end.

If the AB consisted of elected members of all the WTO countries, it might be appropriate to consider accepting their conclusion on this issue, since they would have been chosen from a group of elected people; however, the AB instead consists of a group of experts who do not necessarily have expertise in every field that comes before them. It is difficult to accept their interpretation of who should set the rules and give them meaning. The meaning of any rule most properly belongs to the one who creates it.

The AB did subsequently state that it does not have the necessary competence to decide such a case, acknowledging that it would need assistance from international tax resources in identifying what it means to be a foreign source. It stated:

> Although there is no universally agreed meaning for the term 'foreign-source income' in international tax law, we observe that many States have adopted bilateral or multilateral treaties to address double taxation .... Although these instruments do not define 'foreign-source income' uniformly, it appears to us that certain widely recognized principles of taxation emerge from them. In seeking to give meaning to the term "foreign-source income" in footnote 59 to the *SCM Agreement*, which is a tax-related provision in an international trade treaty, we believe that it is appropriate for us to derive assistance from these widely recognized principles which many States generally apply in the field of taxation.[173]

6.3.6 Conclusion

The SCM is undoubtedly an essential component of the WTO. As an agreement, it represents the point at which tax and trade collide, and where boundaries between the two become blurred. Identifying a subsidy and differentiating it from a tax are difficult tasks. The AB has struggled to draw an acceptable line and, so far, has been for the most part unsuccessful. Footnote 59 – notwithstanding its legal status – attempted to exempt certain types of taxes from prohibition by the SCM by stipulating that the Illustrative List does not prevent Members from taking measures to avoid double taxation of foreign-source income.

The FSC-ETI decision takes the WTO deep into the complexity of foreign-source income and double-tax treaties. The most interesting description of the WTO role in deciding tax issues was offered during the US appeal, in which the Panel established a new double taxation avoidance code. Depending on the resolution of future cases, WTO Panel Reports could challenge other tax practices, such as the

[173] Appellate Body Report on US – FSC, Article 21.5, Para. 141–143.

US export source rule, or resolve anomalies in the territorial systems practiced by European countries.

There is no international law "that requires nations to conform to a single tax system" (Peckron 2001, p. 21). Any country can choose the tax system that it prefers and that is best suited to its unique circumstances. There is no evident reason to prevent any country from adopting a system that incorporates elements of both worldwide and territorial tax systems, nor to prohibit any country from exempting certain types of income from taxation by employing the territorial system, while simultaneously employing a worldwide tax system for other activities. It is acknowledged by the AB that, "each Member is free to determine the rules it will use to identify the source of income and the fiscal consequences – to tax or not to tax the income – flowing from the identification of source."[174]

The AB suggests that it will ask for help from international tax resources because of the tax issues present in international trade treaties. This is the precise contention of this thesis: that it is necessary to "derive assistance from widely recognized" international tax resources.

References

Abu-Akeel AK (1999) Definition of trade in services under the GATS: legal implications. GW J Int'l L Econ 32:189, 190

Avi-Yonah RS (2001) Treating tax issues through trade regimes. Brook J Int'l L 26:1683

Avi-Yonah RS, Slemrod J (2002) (How) should trade agreements deal with income tax issues. Tax L Rev 55:533

Brauner Y (2005) International trade and tax agreements may be coordinated, but not reconciled. Va Tax Rev 25:251, 268

Brown L (1993) The new shorter Oxford English dictionary, vol II. Clarendon, Oxford

Byrnem PD (1996) Developing countries, tax treaties and the United Nations model tax convention. ILSA J Int'l Comp L 2:695, 698

Choi WM (2002) Overcoming the "aim and effect" theory: interpretation of the "like product" in GATT article III. UC Davis J Int'l L Pol'y 8:107

Dam WK (1977) The GATT law and international economic organization. The University of Chicago Press, Chicago

Dodwell D (1993) U.S. blocks international fair tax plan. Financial Times (London), October 28

Engel K (2001) Tax neutrality to the left, international competitiveness to the right, stuck in the middle with subpart F. Tex L Rev 79:1525, 1559

Footer ME (1995) The international regulation of trade in services following completion of the Uruguay round. Int'l Law 29:453

Gifford WC (1978) Permanent establishment under the non-discrimination clause in income tax treaties. Cornell Int'l L J 11:51

Green RA (1998) Antilegalistic approaches to resolving disputes between governments: a comparison of the international tax and trade regimes. Yale J Int'l 23:79

Hobbs CD (1978) The welfare industry. Heritage Foundation, Washington, DC

[174] Appellate Body Report on US – FSC, Article 21.5, Para. 139.

Hopkins RW (2005) Liberalizing trade in legal services: the GATS, the accountancy disciplines, and the language of core values. Ind. Int'l Comp L Rev 15:427, 437

Hudec RE (1998) GATT/WTO constraints on national regulation: requiem for an "aim and effects" test. Int'l Law 32:619

Jackson JH (1997) The world trade system: law and policy of international economic relations, 2nd edn. MIT Press, Cambridge MA

Jeffrey D (2006) Taxing the international athlete: working toward free trade in the Americas through a multilateral tax treaty. NW J Int'l L Bus 27:227

Kleiner M (2002) Marc export subsidies: bananas, airplanes and the WTO: prohibited export subsidies. U Miami Int'l Comp L Rev 10:129

Lachica E (1992) International, p. A8. The Wall Street Journal, March 13

Lansing P, Rose EC (1984) The granting and suspension of most-favored-nation status for nonmarket economy states: policy and consequences. Harv Int'l L J 25:329

Lennard M (2002) Navigating by the stars: interpreting the WTO agreements. J Int'l Econ L 5:21

Lennard M (2005) The GATT 1994 and direct taxes: some national treatment and related issues. In: Lang M, Herdin J, Hofbauer I (eds) The WTO and direct taxation. Kluwer, The Hague

Lidstone (1962) Liberal construction of tax treaties – an analysis of congressional and administrative limitations of an old doctrine. Cornell L Q 47:529, 537–538

Lothar E (2002) De facto discrimination in WTO law: national and most-favored-nation treatment – or equal treatment. J World Trade 36(5):921–977

Luja RHC (1999) WTO agreements versus the EC fiscal aid regime: impact on direct taxation. Intertax 27(6–7):211

McDaniel P (2001) The pursuit of national tax policies in a globalized environment: principal paper: trade and taxation. Brooklyn J Int'l L 26:1621

Mintz JM (2001) Most favored nation: building a framework for smart economic policy. C.D. Howe Institute, Toronto

Nicolaides P (1989) Economic aspects of services: implications for a GATT agreement. J World Trade 23:125, 127–128

Nomani AQ, Bahree B (1993) GATT team push final efforts to set global trade pact as deadline looms. The Wall Street Journal A3, December 9

O'Brien JG (1978) The non-discrimination article in tax treaties. L Pol'y Int'l Bus 10:545

Ostry S (1996) Sylvia globalization and the world trading system – the deeper integration policy agenda. In: 14th International Trade Law Seminar, Canadian Bar Association and Department of Justice Canada

Paton PD (2003) Legal services and the GATS: norms as barriers to trade. New Eng J Int'l Comp L 9:361

Peckron HS (2001) Uniform rules of engagement: the new tax regime for foreign sales. Hastings Int'l Comp L Rev 25:1, 21

Rädler AJ (1998) Most favoured nation concept in tax treaties. In: Lang M (ed) Multilateral tax treaties: new developments in international tax law. Kluwer, The Hague

Russo R (2005) The attribution of profits to permanent establishments: the taxation of intra-company dealings. IBFD, Amsterdam

Sauvé P, Robert M (eds) (2000) GATS 2000: new directions in services trade liberalization. Brookings Institution, Washington, DC

Showalter JM (2004) A cruel trilemma: the flawed political economy of remedies to WTO subsidies disputes. Vand J Transnat'l L 37:587

Skaar AA (1991) Permanent establishment: erosion of a tax treaty principle. Kluwer, Deventer

Snyder RC (1948) The most-favored-nation clause: an analysis with particular reference to recent treaty practice and tariffs. King's Crown, New York

Southwick JD (1988) The lingering problem with the specificity test in United States countervailing duty law. Minn L Rev 72:1159

Steger D (1998) Dispute settlement – World Trade Organization, 3.13 GATS. United Nations, New York

Steinberg RH (2004) Judicial lawmaking at the WTO: discursive, constitutional, and political constraints. Am J Int'l L 98:247

Terry LS (2001) GATS' applicability to transnational lawyering and its potential impact on U.S. state regulation of lawyers. Vand J Transnat'l L 34:989, 1009

Trachtman JP (1993) International regulatory competition, externalization, and jurisdiction. Harv Int'l L J 34:47

Trachtman JP (1998) Trade and ... problems, cost–benefit analysis and subsidiarity. Eur J Int'l L 9:32

Trebilcock M (2004) The national treatment principle in international trade law. In: American Law and Economics Association 14th annual meeting, Working paper 8. http://law.bepress.com/alea/14th/art8

Tsai ES (1999) "Like" is a four-letter word – GATT article III's "like product" conundrum. Berkeley J Int'l L 17:26, 28

Van den Bossche P (2005) The law and policy of the world trade organization: text, cases and materials. Cambridge University Press, Cambridge

Williams F (1993) Warning to U.S. over tax demands. Financial Times (London), November 24

Part III
The Future

Chapter 7
The Tax Agreement Option

The problem is that international trade negotiators do not understand direct tax.

(Jones 1999, p. 1)

There can be little doubt that the World Trade Organization shall and should deal with the interface between trade and other global issues.

(Nichols 1996, pp. 295, 327)

After the First World War, "international economic relations were developing rapidly, but cross border transactions were impeded by overlapping tax claims."

(Ault 1992, p. 567)

7.1 Introduction

Part I, Chap. 1, showed that there is a theoretical problem due to the fragmentation between direct and indirect taxes. This issue has generated a substantial cost, because the isolation of tax regime has created a problem that has kept growing. Chapter 2 then explored the tax-related cases. The DISC keeps coming up again and again, and no one knows when this costly set of ongoing disputes will come to an end, in the meantime wasting human capital, distracting focus from other important issues, and weakening the WTO more and more. Without a solution, the WTO will continue to suffer, as it has been for almost 40 years, with no satisfying resolution. Chapter 2 also drew attention to some potential problems related to tax rules that may violate WTO rules.

Chapters 1 and 2 supported including tax rules under the WTO. Chapter 3 presented another dimension: namely, that Saudi Arabia's religiously rooted tax system will not be easy to govern under the WTO. As in other societies, some social values are attached to the tax rules or mixed in with them; thus, the chapter argued that it is risky to try to regulate social values from Geneva. Instead, the message of Chap. 3 was that the WTO should leave room for countries to move according to their local needs and pressures. Part I ended with a complicated problem: On one hand, tax affects trade and should be brought under the WTO to guarantee that it is not abused to nullify trade agreements; and on the other hand, tax regulations sometimes are socially motivated so that they are hard to change even if they are violating international norms. There is a danger that countries with total tax freedom, and no mechanism to ensure that taxation is not merely disguised as religious or otherwise domestically motivated, could easily violate fundamental international trade rules that are in conflict with the WTO members' agreements.

Part II analyzes the problem, which excellent scholars have tackled, as reviewed in Chap. 4. Some professors have argued for excluding tax from any trade measure,

T. Althunayan, *Dealing with the Fragmented International Legal Environment: WTO, International Tax and Internal Tax Regulations*,
DOI 10.1007/978-3-642-04678-0_7, © Springer-Verlag Berlin Heidelberg 2010

as exemplified by Robert Green. Some, like Professor Brauner, have argued for the creation of an international tax organization just like the WTO. Some scholars have landed in the middle, suggesting that taxes that overlap and clash with trade should be controlled by the WTO, as illustrated by Professor McDaniel. The insights of these legal scholars inform, and form the basis of, the following proposals. This study attempts to avoid their shortfalls and build upon their strengths. Major concerns raised by them, whether implicitly or explicitly, are answered in the next chapter.

Chapter 5 started with the concept of sovereignty. It analyzed it, explored its meaning and origin and its application to international law in different contexts, including the international tax regime. This same chapter reviewed the European tax experience to examine the practicalities of dealing with tax issues on an international level. Then, Chap. 5 ended with a short visit into history to demonstrate that the two fields of tax and trade are *not* fundamentally in conflict with each other in a way that would make it impossible for a single organization, such as the WTO, to supervise. Valuable lessons can be learned from history, some of which will also be discussed in the suggested solution.

Chapter 6 moved to the present, analyzing important WTO agreements. As discussed, tax issues are addressed in the WTO agreements, affecting and affected by the WTO rules. Specifically, tax issues arise in the GATT, GATS, and SCM; they can present a barrier to international trade if not addressed.

Part III, the future, suggests a solution to this complicated problem. Chapter 7 addresses the suggested solution. The best method to solve the problem is to bring tax issues under the WTO umbrella in a thoughtful way that will not upset fundamental domestic values, but at the same time will govern the issues "softly"; this will put the tax issues in the light of day so there is no room for disguising or manipulating the system by using unjustified reasons. This chapter will present the ultimate recommendation of this study: the tax agreement option. The author will include a discussion of why such an option could succeed, especially under the WTO; what factors should be taken into account in order to avoid potential failure, the possibility of which was demonstrated by the GATT-ITO; and why a "soft law" approach is likely to be the best fit for this option.

7.2 Tax Agreement Features

The tax agreement is a platform governing all tax-trade related issues on the one hand, while on the other hand leaving countries unthreatened and with as much freedom as possible to decide their own fundamental internal tax issues, even if it means violating international norms. This solution is based on a fundamental factor supported historically: "soft law" approach with maximum flexibility and limited visibility. The proposal is a framework within which different countries can negotiate, discuss, and settle their differences, with settlement when necessary assisted by an independent third party – the DSB. The system must have so-called "soft" teeth to ensure compliance and enforcement in the event of non-compliance. The best approach is not one single set of rules, but rather concerted cooperation in certain tax matters, with soft dispute settlement mechanisms, firstly. Secondly, this tax agreement must be backed by a consensus based on the old-GATT mechanism, requiring unanimous consensus to adopt a ruling.

This proposed approach has the advantage of being realistic, allowing countries the marginal freedom needed to satisfy their fundamental local needs. Such a system would also substantially simplify an approach to tax issues that has become muddled over time due to the steadily increasing inflexibility of the bilateral treaty network, and this simplification would provide an incentive for countries to buy this "tax agreement" idea.

Safeguards are built into this proposal. First, it allows countries to schedule exceptions to particular disciplines. This will make regulation less rigid, thereby allowing countries to more easily accept the solution, because members are less likely to feel threatened by the rules contained under this tax agreement. Giving countries the right to pull out of the agreement at their discretion, or to object to any ruling conforming to its provisions, is similar in effect to the right to have a reservation[1] in the context of a multilateral treaty. This approach has proved beneficial to the effectiveness of other treaties, and should have the same effect on a tax treaty. Allowing such reservations "will encourage wider acceptance of treaties" (Gamble 1980, p. 372), and is likely to simultaneously ease the fears of nations that arise when faced with a potential attack on sovereignty.

There is a second safeguard: Even if an individual state accepts or is "forced" to accept certain tax rules that later turn out to be in conflict with its internal needs, and those rules are subject to dispute, under this proposal WTO members would have the right to veto any interpretations or applications that infringe upon their rights or do not fit their local needs, a space for countries to deal with unanticipated circumstances as well as guaranteeing against powerful states' misuse of the agreement. This safeguard would be built into the system, and would be very helpful to weaker or developing countries in the event they came to feel pressure in resisting any ruling. The safeguard would also protect a nation like Saudi Arabia from feeling compelled to change its religious tax system.

This suggestion is based on "soft adjudication," encouraging nations to disseminate information, share problem-solving responsibilities, and ensure that trade agreements are not misused. The proposed solution is not strictly binding. With more than 2,500 bilateral tax treaties that share very similar substantive principles, this particular proposal is likely to be successful, because the basic foundation already exists.

[1]The Vienna Convention on the Law of Treaties defines a reservation as "a unilateral statement, however phrased or named, made by a State, when signing, ratifying, accepting, approving or acceding to a treaty, whereby it purports to exclude or to modify the legal effect of certain provisions of the treaty in their application to that State." UN Doc. A/CONF.39/27, Art. 2(1)(d) (1969).

The following discussion will investigate in greater detail the most significant aspects of the proposal. The discussion will attempt first to introduce and support the idea of multilateral tax treaty because ultimately, this is part of the suggestion. It will also explain why this multilateral tax treaty ought to be under the WTO. Thirdly, from a procedural point of view, it will review the soft law concept to illustrate the point that softly treating this issue is the best way to achieve the necessary delicate balance.

7.3 Multilateral Tax Treaty's Previous Suggestions

Previously, similar suggestions have been advanced. The international tax community has attempted many times to introduce multilateral tax treaties, either through the introduction of subject matter-based taxation, such as a transfer pricing multilateral agreement, or through the creation of a multilateral tax treaty among a limited number of similar countries.

For example, Professor Seligman originally suggested that a small-scale international tax treaty be created among countries sharing basic structural principles. He suggested that the USA, the UK, Holland, and Germany should enter into an agreement dealing with international double taxation, a "multilateral compact" (Seligman 1928, p. 70). Gradually, other countries would accept this compact. The same consideration would apply to a multilateral agreement between France and Italy, and countries sharing comparable views of taxation. Ultimately, "a few such multilateral compacts would be preferable to a heterogeneous multiplicity of bilateral agreements" (Seligman 1928, p. 70).

Another modified version of this suggestion would involve a multilateral approach based exclusively on subject matter. Some have argued for a multilateral tax treaty regarding the issues of international athletes,[2] e-commerce taxation (Sweet 1998, p. 1949),[3] transfer pricing issues,[4] and other single-subject matters (see Loukota 1998, pp. 85, 98–99, 103; see also Williams 1991, p. 167). Along the same lines, a tax agreement could be created with a focus exclusively on tax discrimination. Once success has been achieved on this experimental single issue, other subjects could be brought in gradually and with less hesitation, given the increased assurance that the method is operable and effective.

[2]Evans (1995, pp. 297, 304, discussing use of bilateral tax treaties and arguing for implementation of a multilateral tax treaty with respect to international athletes); *see also* Dunlop (2006, p. 227).

[3]Sweet writes "perhaps the next 'miracle' in the evolution of the international tax system will be the development of a network of multilateral tax treaties to deal with, inter alia, the taxation of E-commerce" (Sweet, 1998, p. 2008).

[4]*See* Organization For Economic Co-Operation and Development, *Transfer Pricing Guidelines For Multinational Enterprises and Tax Administrations* (2001); *see*, also, Convention on the Elimination of Double Taxation in Connection with the Adjustment of Profits of Associated Enterprises, 90/436/EEC, 1990 O.J. (L 225) 10, (July 23, 1990).

In 1929, the League of Nations Fiscal Committee, relying in part on Professor Thomas Adams' report relating to transfer pricing issues, recommended the adoption of a multilateral convention on double taxation, stating that a multilateral approach "would materially encourage the movement to reduce double taxation by uniform law – a method which in important respects is obviously superior to the method of reducing double taxation through the instrumentality of bilateral conventions."[5] Adams recognized that a multilateral, rather than bilateral, approach to tax treaties was more desirable, noting that "it is entirely practicable for the great nations of the world to get together and adopt a uniform multilateral treaty by which double taxation could be eliminated, except for these items of bond interest and dividends," but was unable to convince individual governments of the benefits of such an approach at that time.

In 1933, another report was issued by the League based on the advice of Carroll (1978, p. 11), but was never promulgated as an official model. After the draft was circulated, 33 governments responded *favorably* to the text. However, only a small number of governments expressed an immediate desire to become party to a multilateral convention along the lines of the 1933 Draft Convention.[6] In 1978, the UN's Group of Experts, appointed to examine tax issues in 1967, stated during the summary of its deliberations that "for the time being it did not seem feasible to initiate preparatory work for the conclusion of a multilateral agreement that could cover all the controversial issues involved in transfer pricing."[7]

Yet, there was no success. The current system is slow-moving compared to the speed and development of the world economy. This reality requires a new perspective; it "will require the multilateral tax treaty negotiation process to be much more efficient than the process associated with 'slow-moving' and change-resistant bilateral tax treaties" (Sweet 1998, p. 2010). Existing tax-treaty structures "were largely conceived in the days of a 'brick-and-mortar' industrial economy" (Tillinghast 1996, p. 456). In addition, tax treaties are "time-consuming to negotiate and impossible to update on a regular basis" (Tillinghast 1996, p. 455). Tanzi argues that globalization is putting tax systems under substantial pressure and that the coordinating role of the OECD "falls far short of what it needs to be on a worldwide scale … There is no world institution with the responsibility to establish desirable rules for taxation and with enough clout to induce countries to follow those rules. *Perhaps the time has come to establish one*" (Tanzi 1995, p. 140, Emphasis Ta).

---

[5]Report to the Council on the Work of the Second Session of the Committee, Held in Geneva from May 22nd to 31st, 1930, League of Nations Doc. C.340.M.140.1930.II. (1930), *available at* http://www.law.duke.edu/shell/cite.pl?10±Duke±J.±Comp.±&±Int'l±L.±43#F64.

[6]Report to the Council on the Fifth Session of the Committee, Held at Geneva from June 12th to 17th, 1935, League of Nations Doc. C.252.M.124.1935.II.A.

[7]U.N. Department of Economic and Social Affairs, Report of the Group of Experts on Tax Treaties Between Developed and Developing Countries on the Work of its Seventh Meeting, U.N. Doc. ST/ESA/79, U.N. Sales No. E.78.XVI.1 (1978).

7.4 Tax Convention Models

Perhaps the most important factor encouraging and facilitating the introduction of a tax agreement into the WTO is the reliance of most bilateral tax treaties on a single model: the OECD model. This is crucial, because it helps ease the anxiety when speaking about multilateralizing tax issues. The OECD model is based on a set of shared international tax rules that share fundamental concepts and values. "Virtually all of these are based on a single model treaty ... the OECD ... and therefore exhibit a high degree of uniformity" (Thuronyi 2003, p. 1641). In fact, the OECD Model "has almost acquired the status of a multilateral instrument."[8] These factors unite to make the OECD model something established, trusted, and unlikely to present unwanted surprises.

David Rosenbloom described this network of tax treaties as a "triumph of international law in the field of taxation" (Rosenbloom 1999, pp. 137, 164). Even those skeptical of the benefits of a multilateral tax treaty can acknowledge the benefits of the OECD model. Jones argued that having a multilateral tax treaty in the EU would not succeed due to "the present state of diversity of tax system," but presented the following observations:

> [A]re we really all that far away from having a multilateral treaty today? ... [C]an one not equally regard the OECD Model Treaty as a template for a multilateral web of treaties? (Jones 1999, p. 6)

The international community recognizes a set of rules that have been applicable to a varying extent since the 1920s. The UN tax model and the US model share a number of basic principles that have come to serve as common bases for more than 2,500 bilateral income tax treaties (Arnold et al. 2002, p. 65)[9] currently in force throughout the world.

This network of treaties is "largely similar in policy, and even in language" and "constitutes an international tax regime, which has definable principles that underlie it and are common to the treaties."[10] The core issues have been in place for long time, and as such are a reliable foundation on which to build. Graetz noted that "it is remarkable that not only the fundamental structure of the system for taxing international income [exists] today, but also many of the core concepts used to implement that structure" (Graetz 2001, pp. 1359–1360).

In addition to this general structure, other basic principles have been in place for some time to help with implementation. The most important of these principles in

---

[8]American Law Institute, Federal Income Tax Project – International Aspects of United States Income Taxation II: Proposals on United States Income Tax Treaties 3 (1992).

[9]Also see the OECD news section claiming that the its Model Tax Convention, "used by OECD and other countries as a basis for the negotiation, application and interpretation of bilateral tax treaties, of which there are now more than 2500 in force around the world." http://www.oecd.org/document/11/0,2340,en_2649_33747_35318475_1_1_1_1,00.html.

[10]Avi-Yonah, *Tax Competition*, p. 5. John M. Olin Center For Law and Economics (2007).

the context of the suggested tax agreement is the anti-discrimination principle. From an equality point of view, this principle "has strong implications for a prohibition of tax discrimination against international commerce" (Graetz 2001, pp. 1359–1360). It is, however, important to note that equality in the international setting does not necessarily lead to identical treatment since the "concept of equality, by itself, cannot be a guide to international policy, because the very idea of sovereign nations implies some differences in the treatment of domestic and foreign interests. What is needed is a set of principles on which to base limitations on that sovereignty" (Graetz 2001, pp. 1359–1360).

However tax treaties are structured, there must be a sufficient link between the taxes and the taxing country. It is not always easy to establish such a link; there is always the question of what constitutes that appropriateness that satisfies the "minimum of reasonableness" and what is considered "sufficient" (Mann 1999, pp. 12–15). This uncertainty has led some scholars to raise doubts about the coherence of some international tax issues; Asif Qureshi noted that there is a general consensus about the "need for a more coherent international tax system."[11]

7.5 Why Have Tax Treaties Not Been Combined Previously?

If tax treaties are in fact so similar, why have they not been combined before? Arguably, their shared principles should have led to uniformity among tax treaties; since such uniformity was not achieved, it is reasonable to assume that there is something fundamentally wrong with the idea of bringing tax issues to a multilateral setting under the WTO. This is a legitimate concern worthy of a separate, independent study; this author will briefly offer possible reasons for the lack of uniformity.

Professor Richard Vann argued that the current bilateral tax OECD Model is inappropriate for dealing with existing challenges and new issues that have recently arisen or are likely to arise, including thin capitalization, foreign currency conversion, and finance leasing. He suggested that an international organization structured along the lines of the WTO would provide the needed flexibility to handle difficult new international tax issues (Vann 1991, pp. 151, 157–160). Richard Mitchell observed that, "tax treaties are like dinosaurs in the modern world of international trade ... bilateral in a world of multilateral trade agreements" (Mitchell 1997, pp. 209, 210). David Williams, in examining these problems, advocated a "piecemeal multilateral approach," whereby "some part of the content of double taxation agreements could be standardized" to be a partial solution to these problems (Williams 1991, pp. 166–167). The subject of controlled foreign corporations is a

[11]Qureshi, p. 8.

further example of a situation in which the bilateral treaty system is no longer equipped to adequately handle (Rigby 1991, p. 301).

Realistically, there has been no significant attempt to combine them under one multilateral treaty; "although the United States and most of the EU countries coordinate tax treaty policy though the OECD, there has not been a serious movement toward a multilateral tax treaty" (Mason 2005, pp. 65, 121). This is expected, taking into account the fact that the development of the international tax regime has emerged in circumstances that have forced its bilateral nature. Tax treaties were bilateral from the start, for unascertainable reasons. This beginning and subsequent acceptance of the structure may have locked the system. Since countries have become accustomed to the flexibility of working on tax issues within the bilateral framework, and because there exists neither an urgent need to change the framework nor a practical alternative, this norm would be difficult and likely resistant to change. This does not mean this bilateral nature is the best or second-best option. But basically, that's what happened.

Further, strategically, at some point, especially in a less globalized world, there is a need to "preserve one's negotiating position" (Jones 1999, p. 3). This leads to unsound policies; "the more outrageous the provisions of internal law, the better the starting position for negotiating treaties" (Jones 1999, p. 3). One could imagine a powerful state introducing "a crazy tax system with the knowledge that other countries will come running to its door asking for a treaty in familiar form, which it will willingly give the other state, subject, of course, to some concessions on the part of the other state, which it does not mind giving because its system was designed to allow for this" (Jones 1999, p. 3). Under these circumstances, the best approach to negotiating a tax treaty would be to impose as many high withholding taxes on foreigners as possible in order to pressure other countries to develop tax treaties (Jones 1999, p. 3).

Additionally, "bilateral tax treaties are easier to renegotiate in order to realign treaty benefits" (Altman 2006, p. 380, discussing Green article). Due to the differences in nations' economic and political environments, it is reasonable for countries to approach negotiations differently. It is also conceivable that tax treaties could be used to achieve political goals or to reflect political dynamics among nations, which can sometimes be too narrow.

Nerveless, the suggested tax agreement under the WTO must take these realities into account, focusing on the basic principles rather than attempting to incorporate the vastly diverse details that arise depending on specific bilateral relations. The suggested tax agreement should allow for bilateral tax negotiation, while at the same time aiming to incorporate this into a multilateral setting, similar to what happens in other WTO negotiations.[12] Put differently, the bilateral approach has its benefits, but it is not the best approach, given the potential of what the multilateral approach can offer.

[12]See, for example, GATS negotiation.

7.6 Changed Circumstances

Although the original bilateral regime served reasonably well for many years, it is no longer capable of doing so, or at least it is not the best possible scenario. Undeniable and unavoidable modern issues force the international community to change its methods from those that were sufficient previously. The causes are numerous; the most important of which "are easily identified: increased mobility of capital (and people), the continuous de-construction and re-assembly of transaction forms, and the evolution of commerce from transactions in tangible goods to services and electronic-based (or at least electronically-acquired) products. All have contributed to increasing dissonance in international tax results" (Reinhold 2004).

Worldwide real-time instant communication, coupled with a standardization of major financial regulations, does, and will continue to, have an impact on international regulations, including taxation. It is also important to consider that the "use of the derivative financial instruments to bundle or unbundle economic interests, synthesize securities or confer the economic equivalent of the ownership of property without actually transferring that ownership raises treaty issues that require resolution" (Tillinghast 1996, p. 256; see also Warren 1993, p. 460). The reason for this complexity, as observed by Mukadi, is that specific categories of income "can't be objectively attributed to any one jurisdiction, due to multiple contributions that aren't always precisely assessable and to different national-source factors" (Mukadi 2001, p. 1713).

The revolution currently occurring in electronic commerce is another factor in support of the WTO tax agreement. Cooperation and mutual assistance are no longer optional, but have become a necessary step to ensure that "international policies regarding the Internet and electronic commerce are consistent and do not lead to multiple or discriminatory taxation of electronic commerce or the Internet."[13] It is foreseeable that the next imperative step in the evolution of the international tax system will be the development of a network of multilateral tax treaties to deal with, *inter alia*, the taxation of e-commerce. A tax agreement will help ease the potential difficulties emerging from e-commerce trade and taxation.

In addition, the increasing influence of international organizations, such as the IMF, the World Bank, and the WTO, has had an undeniable impact on the international economy, and presents an opportunity to explore a multilateral tax approach. The United Nations encouraged the creation of a multilateral tax treaty, stating that the "creation of a network of bilateral tax treaties based on a common model will be an important step on the way leading to the eventual conclusion of a world-wide multilateral tax convention for the avoidance of double taxation."[14]

---

[13] Joseph Guttentag, Deputy Assistant Treasury Secretary for International Tax Affairs, "Statement at Finance Committee Hearing on Internet," 137 DTR L-1 (July 17, 1998).

[14] United Nations Model Double Taxation Convention Between Developed and Developing Countries 12 (1980).

Modern attempts at multilateral tax treaties, even on a regional basis, have enjoyed limited success at best, so "there exists a growing set of regional tax treaties, but these involve culturally and geographically close countries with similar tax systems" (Mason 2005, p. 121). One example of such a situation is the Nordic Convention,[15] first signed in 1983, the last version of which came into force at the end of 1997. Additionally, foreign ministers from the members of the South Asian Association for Regional Cooperation (SAARC) signed a limited-scope multilateral tax treaty in Dhaka on November 13, 2005 (Nishtar 2005, p. 571);[16] the Andean effort occurred in 1971. Furthermore, the Multilateral Convention on Mutual Administrative Assistance in Tax Matters was signed by the member states of the Council of Europe and the OECD member states in 1988[17] to provide administrative assistance in tax collection and service documents through the transfer of information; it was of particular importance "because it is the first multilateral tax treaty to which the United States is a party" (Dunlop 2006, p. 248).

A WTO-tax related problem is triangular (or quadruple) taxation, the situation in which more than one country is in a position to claim that a single taxpayer is a resident of that country or has a taxable presence therein; alternatively, in some situations no nation can claim an individual or entity as subject to its own domestic taxation (Brauner 2003, p. 293). A multilateral approach would provide a means for "resolving qualification disputes and triangular cases, a multilateral tax treaty would solve problems arising from the bilateral nature of the current treaty network" (Mason 2005, p. 115).

The advantage of the tax proposal in terms of its simplicity over the current bilateral tax regime is also apparent, and is "an extension of its efficiency gains" (Brauner 2003, p. 297). A tax agreement under the WTO is likely to solve many of the existing complexities surrounding bilateral tax treaties. It would reduce the number of tax treaties and would reduce the cost of doing business. Investors would need to spend less time and money "seeking information about the different tax systems that might apply to any of their enterprises, and less resources would be spent on tax planning or on the compliance requirements of different countries. Information would be more accessible and cheaper, reducing administrative and enforcement costs" (Brauner 2003, p. 295). This would help achieve the WTO goals. It seems also a reasonable development, as D'Amato argued that, "if we look at the matter mathematically, a multilateral convention among ten states is the

[15]*See* Convention Between the Nordic Countries for the Avoidance of Double Taxation With Respect to Taxes on Income and on Capital, Sept. 23, 1996, Den.–Faroe Is.–Fin.–Ice.–Nor.–Swed., 98 TNI 9-25, Jan. 14, 1998, *available at* LEXIS, TNI File. Three of the parties to the Nordic Convention are EU Members: Denmark, Finland, and Sweden.

[16]The nations of the South Asian Association for Regional Cooperation (SAARC) are Bangladesh, Bhutan, India, Maldives, Nepal, Pakistan, and Sri Lanka.

[17]Council of Europe-Organisation for Economic Co-operation and Development Convention on Mutual Administrative Assistance in Tax Matters, Jan. 25, 1988, 90 T.N.I. 26-52, Europ. T.S. No. 127, *available at* http://conventions.coe.int/Treaty/en/Treaties/Html /127.htm.

equivalent of forty-five similarly worded bilateral treaties among the same ten states" (D'Amato 1971, p. 164).

Sharing information is perhaps even more important from the perspective of government officials, and combining tax and trade information in one place makes information-sharing more efficient. Bilateral tax treaties currently incorporate such measures, but the proposed multilateral approach would be an enormous enhancement, "allowing tax authorities in several countries to build cases cooperatively against tax evaders who seek to exploit information asymmetries that occur in cross-border situations."[18] Sharing information would enhance the international community's ability to combat tax competition and tax havens; Avi-Yonah asserted that with regard to tax competition, "a multilateral solution is therefore essential if the fundamental goals of taxation are to be preserved" (Avi-Yonah 2000, pp. 1575, 1675). A multilateral tax approach surely "would give unprecedented opportunities for coordinated action" (Mason 2005, p. 118) by as many as 151 WTO members, who together could discover and fight tax avoidance or fraud. And they already have a well-established and accepted informative unit, which is the policy review.

Avi-Yonah has shown that there are clear indications of the existence of a set of international tax laws, customary in nature,[19] supporting the idea that the time for creation of a multilateral tax treaty has arrived. Several of the necessary underlying principles have already been established and have gained wide acceptance; "source, residence, and citizenship are the currently existing bases for the imposition of an income tax in [an] international setting" (Kaufman 1998, p. 148). Avi-Yonah also writes that "[n]ot only can tax lawyers talk to each other across national boundaries and understand what each is saying (the terminology is the same), but the need to face similar problems in taxing income has led jurisdictions with different starting points to reach quite similar results."[20] This proposal is simply a codification of an already established customary international law. Customary practices reach the status of international law when, for an extended period of time, "a large number of the states within the international system suppose these practices establish appropriate guidelines for the relations of states" (Schwarzewnberger 1967, pp. 32–33).

The ultimate implication is that as circumstances change, countries' attitudes toward the use of a multilateral tax approach will change. An impending shift from a purely bilateral approach to a more multilateral approach must be acknowledged, especially when taking into account that even the multilateral approach under the WTO has managed to preserve the bilateral component needed to structure negotiations to comply with the specific needs of different parties to such negotiations. The

[18]D'Amato (1971, p. 164), citing US Model Treaty, note 18, art. 26, 1 Tax Treaties (CCH) P 210.26 (exchange of information and administrative assistance); OECD Model Treaty, note 17, arts. 26 (exchange of information), 27 (assistance in the collection of taxes), 1 Tax Treaties (CCH) P 200.26-27.

[19]Avi-Yonah, International Tax Law, at 168. *See also* Ault (1992, p. 565); Rosenbloom and Langbein (1981, p. 359); Wang (1945, p. 73).

[20]Avi-Yonah, International Tax Law, p. 168.

need is clear for an introduction of a more disciplined approach to international tax issues, a mechanism that is stronger than what currently exists, but still maintains a regard for the sensitive nature of this issue and the need for a careful and gradual approach.

With circumstances since the present system's inception having changed over time and continuing to evolve, a new and different approach to dealing with tax issues should be expected. However, change should take place slowly and piecemeal. Similar evolutions have occurred with other regimes. David Spencer argued that "[i]t is clear how significant multilateral regulatory cooperation on global financial law issues has been since 1980, when the degree of such ... cooperation that would develop could not have easily been foreseen" (Spencer 1997, pp. 353, 383–384) without the help of the OECD, the Basle Committee, and the International Organization of Securities Commissions (Spencer 1997, p. 384).

What currently exists as a structure for handling international tax is not working as it should. The only acceptable model, the OECD, is becoming increasingly questionable with regard to its solution to major international tax problems. Vann argued that the OECD model is "reaching an impasse" and that apportionment on a multilateral basis is required to deal with multinational corporate groups (Vann 1991, pp. 157–160). Bilateral dealings are no longer able to survive successfully "in ... thrivingly multilateral world dealings." This OECD bilateral approach appears "anomalous in an era where taxpayers have become global and many other regulatory areas increasingly are being dealt with globally by governments" (Thuronyi 2003, p. 1641).

Finally, the fact that nations are at least somewhat comfortable with the OECD model will aid the introduction of the tax agreement option, since one of most difficult aspects of the development process, an agreement on general principles, has been overcome.

7.7 WTO Suitability

If multilateralism is the appropriate solution, why is the WTO the appropriate forum? If it is true that a multilateral approach is both desirable and possible, and that there exists less fear regarding sovereignty issues, should international tax issues be handled under the WTO, or should they be determined in an altogether different arena, as some scholars have suggested? The main arguments *against* the WTO are as follows: first, the WTO does not currently have sufficient staff resources to take on such a role; second, the WTO may be overwhelmed by an issue as sensitive as taxation, given that it is already responsible for the handling of numerous difficult-to-manage issues. Adding further responsibility, especially in the form of difficult issues such as tax, anti-trust, or environmental regulations, could lead to "overloading" (Jackson 2007, p. 132) the WTO. Jackson raised the point that the WTO's "extraordinary tight resources" make stretching the institution beyond its capacity unwise. Jackson admitted that some subjects are important for the WTO to face, but that they should perhaps "be deferred for some future evolution" (Jackson 2007, p. 132). In addition, there is the related concern that the WTO lacks sufficient tax expertise to take on international taxation issues.

Although there exist undeniable obstacles, these do not *inherently*, in principle, conflict with the present proposal. This proposal suggests that there is an urgent need to introduce the issue of taxation into the body of issues for which the WTO is responsible, but does not advance the unworkable solution of introducing a tax agreement today, or sooner than it can conceivably be handled. This author recognizes that it would be meaningless to introduce an issue as critical as taxation into an organization that is lacking the resources needed to handle that issue appropriately. The organization itself, and its members, must be willing to commit to this initiative and to plan for long-term implementation, financially and otherwise, recognizing and accepting its attendant costs, the need for the engagement of additional tax experts, and the necessary devotion of increased resources to handle tax issues.

One simple solution would be to allocate a just-sufficient portion of the WTO budget to creating a new tax department and to hiring an adequate number of tax experts to sit on the WTO's panels and policy review councils, and to participate in discussions of other relevant departments. Drafters of international agreements have long recognized this sort of approach. For example, the drafters of the GATS, in the Financial Annex, Article 4, stated: "Panels for disputes on prudential issues and other financial matters shall have the necessary expertise relevant to the specific financial service under dispute." The suggestion is clear: that it is responsible and necessary to ask for tax experts to sit on a panel if the issue before it involves tax problems; presence of such experts may be by default or at the request of disputing members, as was the case in the DISC (Hudec 1988, p. 1455).

There are a number of reasons to argue for the WTO to take on the responsibility of resolving international taxation issues and disputes. One is to help build a bridge between the two regimes. Although there is an overlap between the tax and trade regimes, the issue of isolation raises questions: "One of the baffling aspects of international commerce is the wall that separates taxation and trade" (Rosenbloom 1994, p. 539). Rosenbloom writes that "[It is unknown why] none of the US experts in international taxation with whom I have become acquainted over the years lays claim to a solid understanding of international trade ... I suspect the situation there is basically the same: Neither discipline takes much cognizance of the other" (Rosenbloom 1994, p. 593). This is what the tax agreement attempts to do: build a bridge between the two related regimes (Rosenbloom 1994, p. 598).[21]

Another reason for bringing international trade-related tax issues to the WTO is the fact that a tax can nullify WTO rules if left unsupervised by the WTO. A major goal of international tax policy is "the reduction of impediments to international

[21]He contends that bringing the two regimes together in any format without a clearer articulation of the benefits is unwise, because "international tax laws should depend upon well-developed tax policies and not illusory analogies and characterizations drawn from other fields" (Rosenbloom 1994, p. 598).

commerce" (Warren 2001, p. 169), and this goal should be accomplished in a way that "necessarily include[s] consideration of the appropriate relationship of taxation to the international trade regime, which did not exist in the 1920s" (Warren 2001, p. 169). Taxation schemes can nullify trade agreements, as we have seen in previous chapters, even though it is well established that the fundamental goal of tax treaties is "to promote international movement and exchange of persons, goods, services, and capital and international trade and investment by removing tax barriers."[22]

Tax is certainly a candidate as the next major barrier to international trade unless the tax issues are treated. As international trade barriers continue to fall or diminish, tax issues are good candidates for manipulation unless a multilateral tax agreement is introduced under the supervision of the WTO. It is important to recall that tax issues have been somehow within the international trade regime from the beginning, as DISC cases illustrate, disputed and reviewed more effectively through GATT than through any other means and resolved more readily under a multilateral agreement than through bilateral tax treaty, or as Hudec wrote, "where bilateral diplomacy had failed" (Hudec 1990, p. 72).

If tax issues are indeed handled under the WTO, and if tax and trade are as closely related as this work has argued, then the best proposition would be not to separate tax from trade totally, an action that is impossible on even a purely practical level, because such a move would be likely to create a choice-of-law problem; the availability of two potentially quite different decisions by two separate organizations would undoubtedly lead to increased confusion in international commerce.

Moreover, having tax issues under the supervision of a new organization would involve unnecessary costs associated with building that new organization. The WTO is the result of a long process that started with the negotiation of the ITO, GATT, and finally, the WTO. Building an international tax organization from scratch for all countries will not be as efficient as building a new department within an already established organization.

The OECD is a potential competitor with the WTO for oversight of a multilateral trade agreement. A major problem with the OECD is that the problem this study is addressing is not interactional taxation *per se*; rather it is the interaction, clash, and overlap between the interactional taxation and international trade, an issue that can lead to unwanted results because of the fragmentation between the two regimes. So, any argument that can be advanced for the OECD also applies to the WTO. But, not every argument that can be used in favor of the WTO can be used by the OECD. There are several issues that make it harder to obtain the level of trust held by the WTO, such as stringent limitations in OECD membership. Also, the OECD is known to represent mainly rich countries, unlike the WTO where developing countries are increasingly becoming empowered, an issue that makes the WTO a

[22]American Law Institute, Federal Income Tax Project: International Aspects of United States Income Taxation II, Proposals on United States Income Tax Treaties 1 (1992).

better environment in which to handle sensitive and difficult issues such as taxation.

The WTO provides the best environment in which nations may engage in negotiations. The organization's environment is one in which "possibility" exists, where "sovereignty" and "sensitivity" are less revered, although this does not mean that there is respect for sovereignty inside the WTO. Its success as a forum for negotiation is impressive even with its shortfalls – after all, there is no perfect system. That 151 members of the WTO could reach a point of agreement on a wide variety of trade and tariff issues is a reality that encourages the proposal of a consensus-based tax agreement. As discussed, sovereignty arguments hold little water, because the WTO has proven that once countries are given an appropriate environment in which to succeed in meeting domestic goals, they are willing to give up some domestic powers in return. With respect to tax matters, it is possible to reach an internationally acceptable consensus (Graetz and O'Hear 1997, pp. 1106–1107) that can be implemented into the WTO.

The WTO has inspired a sense of trust[23] that is of fundamental importance in handling international matters; such trust in the organization is imperative to the success of an international proposal and must be the first and most important thing considered. Although with limited membership, the same is true for the OECD; the trust inspired by nations in the organization made them "increasingly prepared to accept the OECD's leadership in resolving other areas of international tax policy concern, including binding multilateral mechanisms in limited areas such as transfer pricing arbitration" (Cockfield 2006, p. 136).

In addition, the WTO already has established a structure of negotiating international matters. Major powers are currently actively working within the WTO framework, and meeting with success thus far; hence, the introduction of the tax agreement within the WTO would be easier in terms of ensuring acceptance than the alternative creation of an entirely new and separate international organization. While the change in approach may be difficult for nations to become accustomed to initially, this would undoubtedly be a better way of handling international issues than bilaterally without transparency.

With the world becoming ever smaller politically, socially, and financially, trade and tax issues can impact more than the two countries involved in a single tax-trade dispute. A dispute between the USA and the UK – for example, if the USA was offering tax subsidies to a company to offset some of its operational costs in a way that would affect its British competitors – would affect not only those two nations, but would also impact other WTO members, potentially in a way that is more significant than its the effect on the USA or the UK. Situations like this, which occur frequently under the current regime, further support the argument for bringing international tax treaties under WTO jurisdiction.

[23]Problems could be expected, of course, as the Doha Round illustrated, but that does not mean the WTO has not earned the trust of many.

Religion and social values, as illustrated by the tax system in Saudi Arabia, should be treated in a way that reflects a long-term vision, admitting the existence of globalization while at the same time coping with its challenges in a way that does not jeopardize the benefits of having a smaller world. Religious tax, as we have seen, can be potentially in conflict with WTO rules, which can lead to a decision condemning Saudi tax rules. This is risky. Allowing Saudi Arabia to use its religious tax system, even if it results in unwanted discrimination, is a more realistic approach than holding the country to international standards; this harmonizing approach is risky, because countries will refuse to obey the offending international organization authority, obey superficially with reluctance (DISC), or withdraw from the organization altogether, a backfiring result that is not what the rules are for.

WTO already decides tax related cases. It is bringing more attention to sophisticated tax concepts and theories. Tax economists can be employed to carry out tax studies to clarify difficult issues, such as the effects of direct and indirect taxes. or territorial and worldwide tax. They could (though unlikely) reach the same old results, or they could release new findings; in any event, they would add to the knowledge of the Panel and AB, which would be reflected in the rulings.

With the right to retain reservations, countries' fears should be allayed, since WTO members would have the power to block any ruling. Knight stated that, "it can be asserted that the permissive use of reservations encourages adherence to multilateral treaties and thus encourages universality, an objective of the current law of the sea negotiations" (Knight 1975, p. 5). According to the International Law Commission:

> [A] power to formulate reservations must in the nature of things tend to make it easier for some States to execute the act necessary to bind themselves finally to participating in the treaty and therefore tend to promote a greater measure of universality in the application of the treaty. Moreover, in the case of general multilateral treaties, it appears that not infrequently a number of States have, to all appearances, only found it possible to participate in the treaty subject to one or more reservations.[24]

7.8 Subjects for Inclusion

The question of which issues to include is a political decision and its comprehensive answer is not the goal of this project, because the proposed tax agreement is not intended to provide comprehensive rules. Rather, this proposal offers a set of guidelines and a forum in which tax officials can meet with one another, as well as with trade officials, to develop a common language, agree on terminology, and come to a consensus on interpretations.

---

[24]Reports of the International Law Commission on the Second Part of its 17th Session and on its 18th Session, [1966] 2 Y.B. Int'l L. Comm'n 169, 205-06, UN Doc. A/6309/Rev.1 (1966).

In the proposed environment, success will be attainable through the creation of "sufficient comfort with a multilateral structure such that there will be a shift away from bilateral treaties toward wider participation in a multilateral treaty."[25] Ideally, this will lead to the development of a tax agreement consisting of subject matter that includes "those issues not addressed currently in treaties; and possibly increasing the uniformity of countries' domestic rules and definitions."[26] Although this proposal is not intended to be broad enough in scope to cover everything that should be included in the tax agreement, a decidedly political question, some discussion of associated points may be helpful in guiding such a determination.

Discrimination is the main issue related to taxation under the WTO, given that the WTO is about preventing discrimination, or minimizing it as much as possible. This concept has been interpreted in a variety of ways, but one reasonable definition with respect to tax matters was presented by the ECJ, which stated that "a member state commits tax discrimination when it treats similar tax situations differently (or different tax situations the same) based on a criterion, such as tax residence, that is likely to disadvantage non-nationals" (Mason 2007, p. 19). It may be gathered from this explanation that disfavoring non-residents with respect to tax is the main concern of the ECJ.

Fighting discrimination is the focus of this proposal, as it has been the focus of the OECD tax model. With respect to individuals, under Article 24(1) of the OECD Model Treaty, business carried on directly in the source state by a resident of the treaty partner cannot be subject "to any taxation or any requirement connected therewith, which is other or more burdensome than the taxation and connected requirements to which nationals of that other State [are subject] in the same circumstances." This is an unambiguous equality requirement: the rate of tax imposed, the requirement to comply, and "the method of taxation (for example, net basis taxation) must be the same" (Ault 1992, p. 569).

With regard to entities, Article 24(3) of the OECD provides that enterprises based in the source state, the capital of which is owned by residents of the treaty partner, cannot be subject to taxation that is "less favourably levied in that other State than the taxation levied on enterprises of that other State carrying on the same activities." The OECD Model Treaty Commentary "makes explicit, this provision is based on the classical view of the separation of corporation and shareholder, and does not restrict the source state's right to tax resident state shareholders" (Ault 1992, pp. 569–570).

This antidiscrimination attitude also exists in the WTO. For example, Article III of the GATT provides, *inter alia*, that the products imported into a WTO member "shall not be subject, directly or indirectly, to internal taxes or other internal charges of any kind in excess of those applied, directly or indirectly, to like domestic products." GATS Article XXII states that if a service is in the schedule, and conditions are met, a WTO member "shall accord to services and service suppliers

[25]Ring, p. 1700.

[26]Ring, p. 1700.

of any other Member, in respect of all measures affecting the supply of services, treatment no less favourable than that it accords to its own like services and service suppliers." "No less favorable" and "not in excess" are both phrases that are aimed at combating discrimination against products and producers, including discrimination associated with taxation issues. Thus, it seems "reasonable to argue that, in analogy to equal treatment among persons and as a matter of good international manners . . . a rule of 'nondiscrimination' should prevail" (Ault 1992, p. 675, citing Musgrave 1969, p. 247).

National treatment, a deeply rooted WTO concept, is another tax issue that is relevant to the trade regime, since "one original purpose of the national treatment obligation is to prevent circumventions and frustrations of tariff concessions, given that discriminatory internal taxes could neutralize the effect of tariff reductions. In the relationship between imports and domestic goods, the tariff is origin-based by definition so that only an openly discriminatory tax or one with appreciably asymmetric impact can achieve the same or similar effect" (Ehring 2001).

An antidiscrimination campaign is ongoing internationally, with the ECJ and the US Supreme Court having reached similar conclusions with respect to tax issues, rendering "similar decisions on factually similar tax discrimination cases. For example, both courts have held that:

- Host states must allow as a deduction expenses related to the generation of host-state taxable income, but host states need not allow unrelated expenses.
- Host states may not categorically deny non-resident individuals the benefit of deductions for personal expenses or exemptions" (Mason 2007, p. 18).

Both courts concluded "that imposition of higher tax rates upon a nonresident taxpayer for no reason other than the taxpayer's non-residence is a classic case of discrimination, identified as such by both the ECJ and the U.S. Supreme Court" (Mason 2007, p. 19). Thus, there seems a general consensus to prohibit discrimination.

7.9 WTO Tax Department

In addition to devoting special attention to discrimination, the tax agreement should, logistically, lead to development of a department or a unit in charge of tax issues. This department should do the following:

- Offer an international tax forum in which countries' policy makers and experts can exchange ideas on tax matters, holding conferences, workshops, and the like to assist with the creation of a constructive dialogue to deal with international tax issues affecting trade.
- Create a place where conflicts can be mitigated by discussion, negotiation and mediation.

- Provide a platform for (quick) friendly third party opinion or tax arbitration if needed when conflicts between countries or among groups of countries arise – in addition to having the option to take the issues to the DSB.
- Collect and publish relevant tax statistics and information for all WTO members.
- Prepare an annual tax report describing main trends, identifying problems, and pointing toward feasible solutions to these problems. Highlight emerging problems and (possible) solutions, and emphasize countries' best international tax practices.
- Review tax policy and rules of all members. Conduct a review over tax developments similar to the IMF surveillance on macroeconomic developments. Such a process of surveillance could be conducted: (a) at the country level; (b) at the regional level; and (c) at the world level. The modus operandi of the IMF could provide a useful guide for the new organization (Tanzi 1998, p. 384).
- Provide technical assistance, especially to developing countries, if needed, in tax policy and tax administration, taking into account the goal of creating less fragmentation.
- Link to development issues in formulating tax policies to improving tax administration.
- Provide an equal voice to developing and developed countries for tax cooperation negotiations (Horner 2001, p. 179).

Under no circumstances should this unit be involved in recommending changes in countries that do not have significant cross-border spillovers affecting WTO agreements. It is reasonable to expect that incorporation of the tax agreement into the WTO would deal with discrimination issues, since this subject is a common feature and mutual concern of tax and trade regimes. There is a developed and well-established body of jurisprudence relating to discrimination in the tax arena that can offer guidance in setting the most effective set of rules.

This unit also should be in charge in reviewing tax issues that are exempted or vetoed to make sure that they have opted out because of legitimate concerns. Thus, there should be a procedural requirement that any member wishing to take a policy that is not compatible with the tax agreement must demonstrate that there is a conflict with a widely shared social, religious, or developmental domestic value.[27] Any finding should be reviewed by affected parties before announcing the results, allowing additions by any member to the report, so everyone knows what is at stake.

7.10 Possible Counterarguments

Two powerful issues have been raised occasionally in support of the idea of excluding taxes from the WTO, necessitating more clarification. One is the notion

[27]See a similar suggestion for social exemption made by Rodrik (2007).

that international taxation is diplomatically driven, while the WTO is legally oriented (Warren 2001, p. 147). The second is the idea that international taxation is bilaterally based, while WTO is a multilateral agreement (Warren 2001, p. 147), and that it would thus be difficult to reconcile the two systems, trade and tax, under one organization such as the WTO. In this author's opinion, this is an oversimplification.

The WTO is both diplomatic and a bilateral-multilateral treaty. The major difference between trade and tax is the forum in which trade is discussed. The WTO provides a forum where trade matters are discussed openly, and where a system of equal voting rights exists, although the power some nations can have over others makes the construct admittedly imperfect. International tax matters, on the other hand, have no world forum; instead, they fall under the umbrella of the OECD, which has only limited membership, and the UN, which has demonstrated no effects on tax so far. This may change if tax issues are allowed to be treated under the WTO, as advanced herein.

7.11 The WTO Is Not Purely Legal Organization

The first argument generally made in comparing the WTO and the tax regime is that the WTO is a legal system, and as such, is diplomatically very constrained. If true, this is clearly not a suitable construct when dealing with tax issues, which are sensitive by virtue of their relationship to the sovereignty of individual nations, and thus require diplomacy. However, this notion is not entirely accurate. WTO is neither purely a legal nor a diplomatic system.

As the first issue commonly raised when comparing the WTO and the tax system, the idea of a legalistic-diplomatic division between the two has led some scholars to argue for excluding tax issues from the WTO (Green 1998). However, even some legally sound cases do not appear in the WTO simply because they are diplomatic or political in nature, and thus associated with a higher level of nation-specific tension (Hudec 1980, pp. 145, 159, discussing "wrong cases"). These so-called "wrong" cases could be defined as those that "might overwhelm the system because of political considerations" (Davey 2003). Such cases are difficult for a panel to decide, and if and when the panel did issue a decision regarding such a dispute, that decision would likely be very controversial, decreasing the likelihood that a losing party would observe the decision. Such situations have the potential to ultimately damage the legitimacy of the WTO.

The general belief has, to some extent, been that governments "should never bring legal complaints against trade measures that have so much domestic political support that, no matter how WTO-illegal they are, it is simply politically impossible to change them" (Hudec 1980, pp. 145, 159). In a footnote to a law review article, Professor Robert Hudec offered a brief background of this belief that is relevant to the tax issues discussed in this study:

> The 'wrong case' idea was introduced at a time when the GATT dispute settlement system had a great deal less political acceptance than it does today, and when governments were more concerned about the dangers of placing too much stress on the system by trying to litigate legal claims other governments could not accept. The emergence of a more powerful dispute settlement system has kept that idea on the shelf for several years ... I must admit that there remain many issues on which governments are still unwilling or unable to submit to legal claims. (Hudec 2002, p. 213)

The WTO legal rules are intended to offer countries the freedom necessary to meet their individual diplomatic needs or requirements brought on by unexpected local political pressures. The exceptions for national security[28] and public morals[29] give countries the needed space to act in a way that remains acceptable. Further, the opt-out clause articulated by Article XXXV[30] of the GATT and by Article XIII[31] of the WTO[32] offers countries a one-time opportunity to utilize this option,[33] which allows nations to choose not to extend trade benefits to another nation, and also to

[28]GATT Article XX.

[29]GATT Article XX.

[30]This article reads: Non-application of the Agreement between Particular Contracting Parties 1. This Agreement, or alternatively Article II of this Agreement, shall not apply as between any contracting party and any other contracting party if: (a) the two contracting parties have not entered into tariff negotiations with each other, and (b) either of the contracting parties, at the time either becomes a contracting party, does not consent to such application. 2. The Contracting Parties may review the operation of this Article in particular cases at the request of any contracting party and make appropriate recommendations.

[31]This article reads:Article XIII: Non-Application of Multilateral Trade Agreements between Particular Members 1. This Agreement and the Multilateral Trade Agreements in Annexes 1 and 2 shall not apply as between any Member and any other Member if either of the Members, at the time either becomes a Member, does not consent to such application. 2. Paragraph 1 may be invoked between original Members of the WTO which were contracting parties to GATT 1947 only where Article XXXV of that Agreement had been invoked earlier and was effective as between those contracting parties at the time of entry into force for them of this Agreement. 3. Paragraph 1 shall apply between a Member and another Member which has acceded under Article XII only if the Member not consenting to the application has so notified the Ministerial Conference before the approval of the agreement on the terms of accession by the Ministerial Conference. 4. The Ministerial Conference may review the operation of this Article in particular cases at the request of any Member and make appropriate recommendations. 5. Non-application of a Plurilateral Trade Agreement between parties to that Agreement shall be governed by the provisions of that Agreement.

[32]Jackson (1997, pp. 60–61). *See also* Ezrahi (1999, p. 123, suggesting elimination of the clause because "the opt-out clause suffers from general inadequacies in terms of its potential for abuse"); Kontorovich (2003, p. 283).

[33]It is interesting to note that the USA has used it the most among all WTO members. Paragraph 320 of the WTO analytical index cite only the USA "The United States invoked Article XIII:1 with respect to Romania, Mongolia, Kyrgyz Republic, Georgia, Moldova and Armenia. As of 31 December 2002, the United States had revoked its invocation of Article XIII with respect to Romania, Mongolia, the Kyrgyz Republic and Georgia. El Salvador invoked Article XIII with respect to China on 5 November 2001 and Turkey invoked it with respect to Armenia on 29 November 2001." The index, Volume, 1. 97. http://www.wto.org/english/res_e/booksp_e/analytic_index_e/wto_agree_04_e.htm#articleXIIIA.

offer the option of extra distance between countries that are unwilling to deal with each other for any of a variety of sometimes sensitive reasons (Kontorovich 2003, p. 283). Moreover, Article XIX of GATT gives a contracting party the right to suspend an obligation in whole or in part when "serious injury" is likely to result to the domestic producers of the party facing the harm.[34] These all reflect the notion that the WTO can accept norms that are not strictly in agreement with its rules.

The flexible structure of the agreement is clearly intended to retain the ability to cope with different circumstances and unexpected situations that are certain to arise; this flexibility serves to preserve national sovereignty and local values. In *International Fruit*, the ECJ noted, with regard to the GATT, that: "the principle of negotiations undertaken on the basis of 'reciprocal and mutually advantageous arrangements' is characterized by the *great flexibility* of its provisions, in particular those conferring the possibility of derogation, the measures to be taken when confronted with exceptional difficulties and the settlement of conflicts between the contracting parties."[35]

This concept was illustrated clearly during the early existence of the GATT. Hudec (1990, p. 69) explained that the first cases brought under the GATT were resolved through the inclusion in the process of not only the Plaintiff and the Defendant in the particular dispute, but independent parties as well. Such use of a panel is best accomplished with low visibility and with ample room to retreat, given the unpopularity of new and more far-reaching international law in many areas of the world (Hudec 1990, p. 76). Less visibility by involving a working party is less threatening and more easily accepted, since there is no appearance of a decision being imposed upon a nation, a particular concern with regard to the USA (Hudec 1990, p. 78).

Any legal process involving international matters requires time to achieve acceptance. Thus the evolution of the GATT from a purely political system based on negotiation among parties to a more legally binding dispute settlement system did not seem to be an accident, but rather looked like a natural gradual process. This does not, of course, mean that trade matters under the WTO are resolved by purc legal means as domestic disputes; a mix of political and legal issues and approaches is still involved. The author of this work agrees with Nichols that WTO panels "are not courts and are not meant to be courts" (Nichols 1996, pp. 295, 326), which implies that the WTO should be sensitive to the specific issues of each individual case presented to it and flexible in its approach to cases based on their particular circumstances.

Countries obey international law because they see it authoritative at some level. This accepting, non-authoritative attitude could be considered unnecessary, a result of excessive anxiety or unwarranted caution; a conceivable argument is that legal issues should be treated in a regimented way, with clear-cut opinions and definitive

[34]GATT, art. XIX(1)(a).

[35]Joined Cases 21 to 24/72, *International Fruit Co. v. Produktschap voor Groenten en Fruit,* 1972 E.C.R. 1219, 1227, 2 C.M.L.R. 1, 22 (1975).

outcomes. This approach is acceptable, even necessary, in the domestic environment, but in the international arena, where enforcement of dispute settlement decisions depends mainly on states' willingness to obey the law, a legal ruling disguised in "soft diplomatic clothes" is a promising approach to resolving sensitive disputes.

The tax agreement option can best be developed by recognizing that subjecting tax issues to a WTO dispute mechanism would not be a purely legal solution, especially when in combination with the consensus requirement. The WTO contains rules that offer to nations the freedom necessary to suspend some rights for variety of reasons,[36] which will further affect the process. Thus, although such a tax agreement option would be stricter than a purely diplomatic option, it would nevertheless reflect the pragmatic nature of the WTO and would accommodate nations' perceived and actual needs.

7.12 The WTO Is Not a Purely Multilateral System

The WTO is commonly described as a multilateral system, which is assumed to be in conflict with the nature of the international tax system (Brauner 2005, pp. 263–262). This categorization is incorrect, as the WTO is not purely multilateral. In addition to the fact that each member nation has the right to refuse to extend its commitments to any other member if it so wishes,[37] the negotiation process highlights aspects of the organization that are more bilateral in nature.

When a country desires to become a member of the WTO, it must negotiate with other members the conditions of its admission, including tariff rates and service commitments. Prospective members do not negotiate with all member nations at one time, so the process can be a long one. For example, China's membership negotiation process took 15 years,[38] and Saudi Arabia's process took 12 years. Russia is still negotiating membership (see Åslund 2006), a process that has been ongoing since 1993. Furthermore, the opt-out clause further illustrates this bilateral nature, offering members the option to altogether avoid dealings with a particular country.

Clearly, the process of attaining membership in the WTO, and the conditions according to which a country is admitted into the organization, are set bilaterally by individual member countries, and not by the organization as a whole as part of a

[36]Article XX, for example, offer countries the right to violate the WTO if the violation is for reasons related to public morals, health, or national security.

[37]Article XIII of the WTO.

[38]China was one of the original contracting parties of GATT in 1948, but did not participate actively; in 1986, China applied for "resumption" of its membership; it was granted full membership in 2001. Halverson writes: "No country has endured as lengthy an accession process to the GATT/WTO as China, nor has any country acceding to the WTO been asked to take on as many concessions as the price for admission" (Halverson 2004, pp. 319, 323).

multilateral process. Thus, although WTO obligations are ultimately extended to all member countries, and become multilateral duties even for those nations that did not participate in the membership negotiations, both obligations and rights are developed and negotiated bilaterally, in the working party.

The WTO provides a forum where trade matters are discussed openly, with a system of equal voting in theory, even though in reality this is not the case always. International tax matters, on the other hand, have no world forum. Instead, they are handled by the OECD, which has limited membership, and by the United Nations, which has not yet demonstrated any impact on the tax arena, a situation that may change if tax issues are allowed to be handled under the WTO.

The WTO is flexible enough to accommodate a variety of tax issues, both those currently existing and those that may potentially arise, and is positioned to handle exceptional or urgent needs should the handling of such become necessary. A tax agreement under the WTO would offer countries the right to refuse to extend privileges to other members if they so desire, preserving the bilateral nature of the tax regime; in the event that no agreement was reached, countries could simply abstain from extending their tax treaties benefits to any member.

7.13 Political Concerns

7.13.1 Developed Countries

It is crucial to recognize that the proposed tax agreement must have the support of major economic powers, including the USA and the EU, as well as the major developing countries, such as China, India and Brazil. This is by no means a rigid condition, because the proposal is not mandatory, so countries objecting to the idea could simply elect not to join such an agreement. Nevertheless, the support of the major powers would increase the likelihood of acceptance of the proposal by other potential parties.

The USA is more likely to be willing to accept this proposal because of the disadvantages it has under the current system. DISC/FSC cases are representative of how the USA feels about the differentiation of indirect and direct taxes, as well as territorial and the worldwide tax system. The United States has been wounded not only financially, but also prestigiously from losing case after case regarding the same issue, regardless of the changes it makes to correct the defect. Also, it has nothing to lose. If anything goes wrong, or if there is an immense political pressure, it has a veto power, which the USA is not shy to use.

It would be a hard case to sell for the EU, however, especially if the focus is on the EU/USA relationship. Narrowly, the EU members have relatively less to lose with respect to taxation, so there is compelling reason to accept this proposal. In fact, they probably will lose from this proposal, because it would give the USA the legitimacy needed to cover its disputed taxing schemes.

However, the EU has something to gain, which is to stop the furious cycle of disputes between the EU and the USA. The losses of the USA in the tax cases came at a high cost and the price seems to be particularly high because the USA kept, and will keep, chasing the EU with different cases until it gets its "revenge" which is due, in part, to its perception of unfairness. Thus, the benefit to the EU is a cessation of costly disputes on various fronts. A tax agreement for the EU will be appealing if the cost of other cases is high enough, and the possibility that other cases and "revenge" cases will be fewer. Otherwise, there is less incentive politically in the WTO to engage in negotiating a proposal focusing on the EU/USA relationship.

However, looking at the matter more broadly, the benefits listed previously to bringing tax matters under the WTO, as well as making them multilateral, are worth consideration. They are well thought-of issues that in the long term would benefit the EU. The existence of the WTO is already benefiting the EU; otherwise it would not be as active as it is now. This is an indication that some worthy causes are there even if they can't be quantified. To retain these benefits, and possibly to enlarge them, inserting a tax agreement with soft adjudication is another strengthening block for this beneficial institution. Thus, accepting and negotiating this agreement is a positive step. And after all, if things get out of control for whatever reason, and EU influence isn't effective; the EU has veto power.

7.13.2 Developing Countries

Another issue relevant to the cost of introducing this tax agreement is the subject of developing countries. New policies, when implemented, normally result in "winners" and "losers," but the goal of a policy should be to maximize the benefits and cost-effectiveness for all parties. The WTO, a globalized organization, is no exception; "globalization produces winners and losers, both among countries and within them."[39]

Developing countries would be weak, with or without the tax agreement; these nations have nothing to lose. On the other hand, a new, integrated tax policy could open opportunities for new businesses to take advantage of and, consequently, provide economic benefits to all countries.

In fact, bringing international tax issues within the WTO would allow weaker nations to raise important international tax and trade issues, directly or indirectly, individually or collectively, much more powerfully than they are currently able to do with the bilateral approach already implemented under the tax regime. This very issue was raised under the GATT, in which a less developed country asked: "Why has the MFN dealt only with trade in goods and not with the rights of businessmen?" (Nurkse 1961, p. 62).

---

[39]The World Bank, 2001, p. 1.

The least developed nations are also extremely poor; "their 614 million people suffer some of the most intensive deprivation in the developing world. More than 40% live on less than US $1 a day. Life expectancy is 25 years lower than in the industrialized countries" (Oxfam 2001, pp. 2–4). Some suggest that the solution to this problem of poverty can be found in offering immediately "duty-free and quota-free access for all products exported by LDCs to industrialized-country markets, and adequate technical assistance to enable LDCs to seize increased export opportunities" (Oxfam 2001, p. 4). No conflict exists between this tax agreement and the developing countries' major demands: to open the market and stop subsidizing products for which they have a comparative advantage.

Putting an international body in charge of setting applicable rules and resolving the disputes adds weight to the proposal, specifically as a deterrent to violation of the rules, since countries are likely to adhere to established rules for fear of acting against the WTO. This is likely to be more effective than other procedures because "anticipatory compliance may even be a more compelling example of the WTO's power, as it shows that the WTO reaches even into the U.S. political process, a process perceived to be largely inviolable by foreign powers. The sovereignty issues surrounding anticipatory compliance are further compounded by the ability of other sovereign states to use the WTO system as a vehicle to give them influence in the U.S." (Kimble 2006, p. 97).

Developing countries would find it easier to achieve results that they would be unlikely to achieve independently outside the WTO. With developed, more economically and politically powerful nations fighting over imposition and interpretation of rules, the least developed countries are poised to benefit, because anything taken from the powerful at the resolution of a dispute will translate to something shared by the rest of the parties to an agreement, the most and the least powerful alike.

Inaction is an obvious option, but developing and weak countries would continue to face the pressures of big business enterprises dealing with them in private. Since the primary goal of business enterprises is maximization of profits, developing and presenting applicable rules out in the open lessens the opportunity for such enterprises to deal with governments in a secretive manner.

Governments are more transparent than businesses, with more wide-spread knowledge of governmental information and a checks-and-balances system in most countries. Political parties other than those in power, NGOs, international agencies, and the media, are keen to expose political issues and to take advantage of any mistakes. Thus, negotiation with governments under the WTO umbrella could be more fair to nations worldwide than a bilateral negotiation or complete inaction with regard to business taxation. If the system proves too costly for developing nations to bear, under the tax agreement option they could either pull out of the agreement or veto decisions, as well as participate in developing the tax agreement into one that reflects their needs and wants. Structuring this tax agreement on soft law will ensure a minimum safeguard against unexpected incidences.

7.14 Soft Law Compliance

> Accomplishments of the GATT jurisprudence, "if not unique, are at least rare in the history of international legal institutions." (Hudec et al. 1993, p. 353)

> State behavior merely reflects state interests. So what? The point is not that states act against their interests – who would seriously believe that? (Keohane 1998, p. 703)

7.14.1 Success of the Proposal

It could be argued that if individual countries can choose their own rules, or can stop a particular decision, a uniform code is ineffective and altogether unnecessary. Why link any issue with the WTO if countries will not change how they act in response to the issue? This may be true if the current approach were to remain the same; however, countries are currently negotiating and dealing bilaterally, which is a non-transparent mechanism that could lead to unfair deals.

One potential objection to the tax agreement option is that this tax agreement only adds to the burdens currently borne by the WTO; because it is not obligatory, the tax agreement option may be viewed as having no "teeth," based on "soft law" that allows WTO members to join freely, with restrictions if desired, and to stop any undesirable rulings. If nations have the ability to stop any ruling that does not fit their individual criteria, what benefit can be had from creating additional rules and complicating further an already burdened system?

The short answer to this undeniably legitimate concern is that evidence has shown that nations are willing to comply with international law rules in most instances, even though there is no specific enforcement mechanism beyond the voluntary willingness of nations to obey such rules. In fact, the strength of the tax agreement suggestion lies in the very notion of non-obligation, since the associated freedom and flexibility will make nations feel less threatened in accepting the option; since the nations will participate in shaping the rules, the feeling of community that arises in the rule-making process is likely to induce countries to comply with the resulting rules. As a result, the tax agreement is likely to have an impact that gradually will evolve to be a body of respected international law that is difficult to violate, and that is backed by an international organization that supervises the creation, amendment, and enforcement of the rules.

A more in-depth answer to the dilemma can be found in a survey of the literature; the cited works are all generally in agreement of the potential effectiveness of soft international law based on mentoring, reporting, and negotiating, law based on partnership rather than coercion. Koh argued that states can be socialized toward obedience, and not merely to enhanced compliance (Koh 1997, p. 2599). He identified a process involving interstate activity, transnational relations, and domestic law and politics, linked together in a system that promotes internalization of international law (Koh 1998, pp. 623, 629).

7.14.2 Soft Law Effectiveness

Henkin stated that "almost all nations observe all principles of international law and almost all of their obligations almost all the time" (Henkin 1979, p. 47). There is a set of international law rules that are respected regardless of why they are observed; a fact that even skeptics acknowledge. Morgenthau, a prominent critic of international law, noted that "to deny that international law exists as a system of binding legal rules flies in the face of all the evidence" (Morgenthau 1954, pp. 249–252). Why nations so behave is a "perplexing" (Koh 1997, p. 2599) question, but facts empirically confirm this statement (Koh 1997, p. 2599).

Admittedly, the current era faces very different issues from those that affected the past. First, with the decline of national sovereignty, nations are today increasingly willing to give up some domestic powers. The current ease of communication and transportation makes the concept of national sovereignty even less important; "the collapse of the public–private distinction; the rapid development of customary and treaty-based rules; and the increasing interpenetration of domestic and international systems" (Koh 1997, p. 2604) are additional features that support the argument that this new era is likely to be more open to the present proposal in conjunction with the decrease in importance attached to the concept of sovereignty.

The probable reason that nations do obey international law is that they feel it is in their domestic self-interest to do so, regardless of the definition of "interests."[40] It is a repeated game, so the chances of cheating and getting away with it are absent. Of additional importance is the fact that nations, through the actions of their politicians and advisors, will obey international law if they see it as fair and if they participate in its development. Franck asserts that powerful nations "obey powerless rules" (Franck 1990, pp. 3, 242), even though those rules are not enforced, because they are encouraged to comply when the "legitimate rule pulls toward compliance" (Franck 1990, p. 242), where "compliance pull" is the notion that legitimacy has "the power to pull toward compliance those who cannot be compelled" (Franck 1990, p. 23).

Keohane described what he called the "exclusion from the club," or pressure arising from potential exclusion from an accepted group. He argued that "governments decide that they can make mutual gains through coordinating their policies – finding a set of 'focal points' on which they can all agree," such as finding "common ground on procedures for interpreting and adjudicating disputes on issues involving international trade." Gradually, this club's "standards become the only standards. Members of the club adhere to these rules since they have an interest in coordination. Non-members, on the other hand, find themselves in a dilemma, since maintaining their non-standardized practices will not only deny them the benefits of

[40]Koh provided five reasons, including self-interests: (1) Reasons of power and coercion (2) Reasons of self-interest (3) Reasons of liberal theory, both rules and identity (4) Communitarian reasons (5) Legal process reasons.

coordination but may well lead to conflicts with members of the club – conflicts in which the non-members will be quite isolated" (Keohane 1998, p. 704). Once such a system begins, it grows and increases in popularity, ultimately transforming to a "club." This club is very similar to the WTO, an environment in which non-members struggle to become members even though there is no meaningful gain to be achieved by membership in the club.

An additional argument in support of soft law, especially in the context of international taxation, is that "enforcement measures or sanctions" are more expensive, and that they disturb systems such as the proposed code more than consultation, negotiation, or persuasion, methods which are more likely to be successful in dealing with complicated international tax issues. Incentives ("carrots") can induce states to cooperate, and are more effective than "sticks" (Downs et al. 2000, p. 465), or punishments for non-compliance. Soft law not only enables states to reach agreements more efficiently, but state compliance with soft law agreements is in many ways a better option than compliance under the "hard law" (Joyner 1998, p. 401). Soft law enables officials to minimize their losses. Trachtman has offered an additional, more practical view, arguing that compliance with international law will always be tempered by the realities of state self-interests; and that's the reason Professor Trachtman suggested that "soft law" agreements are essential to attract and preserve powerful states as members by allowing them to avoid circumstances in which they perceive no alternative other than patent noncompliance, arguing that "hard law is not necessarily good law" (Trachtman 1999, p. 655).

Florini (1996, pp. 363, 365) offered additional insight with the notion of "cultural inheritance" as a more suitable basis for compliance. Florini presented a theory of international compliance that is based on a comprehensive analogy to evolutionary biology. This Darwinist view, which contends that "law can grow and evolve" (Cotterrell 2006, p. 103), is as likely an explanation as the "club-exclusion" argument presented by Keohane. Club rules or cultural norms can be binding to the extent that compliance is based thereon. This observation provides a foundation on which to build a system to address tax issues within the WTO, a system that is based on "cultural inheritance" from the OECD, customary international tax law rules, network of bilateral tax treaties and other established international tax principles.

Compliance has also occurred because compliance with international law can strengthen the reputations of complying countries. The "potential compliance is thus, to some degree, bounded by the importance of reputation within particular issue-areas of international relations, but admittedly reputation is less important in issue-areas of 'high politics,' such as armed conflict, and territory, than in issue-areas of 'low politics,' such as economics and radio frequencies or environmental protection" (Guzman 2002, p. 1823). The rational choice theory supports the notion that states are motivated to comply by a desire to preserve their reputations (Huang 2002, p. 237).

It is reasonable to expect that states would inherently coordinate efforts and cooperate in international matters, because it is hard (not efficient, not possible or very expensive) to accomplish things individually. If agreement among international participants can be accomplished peacefully and with as little resistance as possible, there is no reason to choose an option potentially associated with increased difficulty or additional cost. The main aspect that should be recognized and ensured is fairness, which is not easily obtained; however, countries at some time will seek the independent, unbiased expertise of international judicial opinions in order to resolve factual ambiguities and to preserve decisions for future coordination, supporting the theory that fairness can be achieved through adjudication, which works by clarifying ambiguous conventions or facts (Tom and Adams 2004, p. 1229).

One theory of "new institutionalism" argues that developing transnational networks of domestic bureaucracies, courts, and administrative agencies, along with other government officials and entities, are increasingly becoming the primary agents for the spread of new normative and legal regulations (James and Olsen 1998, p. 943). This idea was previously advanced by Nye and Keohane, who explicitly distinguished "transgovernmental" activity from the broader category of transnational activity, defining "transgovernmental relations" as "sets of direct interactions among sub-units of different governments that are not controlled or closely guided by the policies of the cabinets or chief executives of those governments" (Keohane and Nye 1974, pp. 39, 43). They need, of course, a forum in which they can negotiate and discuss relevant ideas and settle differences.

Slaughter supports this notion, arguing that the key actors with respect to compliance are not states, but rather individuals, institutions, organizations, and other components of civil society (Slaughter 1995, p. 503). She explained that it is really the so-called informal links between counterpart state officials that transcend national boundaries, as these are important resources for enhancing nations' capacity for compliance and building upon the natural propensity of states toward voluntary compliance (Slaughter 2000, pp. 1103–1124). Accepting this argument literally seems to argue against including tax under the WTO, and for that matter against any international organization; however, international organizations are created, *inter alia*, to settle differences that can and do emerge from state officials' different prospective and ideas regarding disputed or misunderstood issues. The benefit of this argument is that it shows that having a forum, a place where informal meetings and discussions between counterpart state officials can take place, is essential to clarify misunderstandings, or explain different perspectives, leading to the creation of interactional cooperation.[41]

Slaughter emphasized also that there is currently a movement to regulate international issues by voluntary codes of conduct "adopted by corporate and other private actors, as well as emerging bodies of transgovernmental law, such as the rules and principles adopted by securities regulators, central bankers, environmental officials and others" (Slaughter et al. 1998, pp. 367, 383). These are networks "of national government officials exchanging information, coordinating

[41] I thank Professor Alford for this comment.

national policies, and working together to address common problems" (Slaughter 2003, pp. 1041, 1042).

Slaughter, together with Tulumello and Wood, also wrote that:

> specialized governmental officials in particular agencies have long been seconded to international institutions; the difference here is the conscious creation of a forum for national government officials to come together in their national capacities but under the auspices of an international institution. The result may be less friction between national and international institutions and more integrated implementation of international rules and norms. (Slaughter et al. 1998, pp. 392–393)

This is a compelling view of international law. International organizations are built by people who believe, at least to some extent, in the rules and their benefits. These are the people are who are in charge, meeting to discuss the rules from their introduction, arguing before dispute resolution panels, and ultimately selling the organization and rules to their own communities.

Finally, Keohane summarized the concept as follows: "States indeed do comply with international law most of the time. This observation gains the assent of a variety of authors – political scientists as well as international lawyers – who may agree on little else. Governments do not agree to binding international law unless they anticipate that they, and other major players, will comply with it" (Keohane 1998, pp. 699, 702).

7.15 Compliance Under Trade Law

The issue of voluntary compliance has been addressed in the context of international trade law. The early days of the GATT illustrated that soft law can help encourage obedience of international law. Obtaining compliance under the GATT was a remarkable success. The sense of community associated with the GATT appears to have had a strong influence on compliance with the trade rules, resulting from "a flexible and ad hoc strategy of law-enforcement based on *partnership* rather than traditional, repressive means of law-enforcement, such as unilateral sanctions or reprisals[;] reporting, monitoring, fact-finding, and consultation designed to reduce conflict and tension between states are the best tools for compliance assistance" (Beyerlin and Marauhn 1997). Ehrmann argued that a "partnership method" for managing international compliance is, overall, a better approach to international rules, with consultation and negotiation, rather than sanctions, employed to resolve compliance disputes (Ehrmann 2002, p. 377).

In an empirical study, Professor Robert Hudec (1993) showed that in most instances, GATT members obey panel rulings and carry out their obligations. Moreover, "even non-complying nations gradually come back into compliance over time with previously violated international legal norms" (Koh 1997, p. 2609, footnote 2). One example is that of the USA in the DISC case: after postponing the ruling for 17 years, the USA came to a settlement under which it changed domestic law and removed the DISC rules.

Hudec analyzed GATT cases from 1948 through 1989, including 207[42] total complaints, defined as any public invocation of GATT procedures for issuing legal rulings in a dispute between governments (Hudec et al. 1993, p. 3). Strikingly, he found out that "90% ended with a positive outcome" (Hudec et al. 1993, p. 10). In addition, "about two-thirds of all positive results involved optimal or almost optimal results" (Hudec et al. 1993, p. 17), a statistic which indicates great success, given that those results were achieved without resorting to strict adjudicative means. Hudec noted that the GATT's "accomplishments to this point, if not unique, are at least rare in the history of international legal institutions" (Hudec et al. 1993, p. 97).

It is worth emphasizing that governments evaluated in the above-referenced study were objectively reasonable and sensitive to delicate issues when raising their claims. This is illustrated by the high percentage of rulings in favor of the complainant. Seventy-seven percent (Hudec et al. 1993, p. 9) of complainants were successful, indicating that the governments paid careful attention to the legal grounds on which they based their claims. The system was neither abused nor misused to achieve illegitimate goals; this success continued from 1948 until 1980s – almost 30 years of a satisfying rate of success.

There were also, of course, impasses. In some instances, countries did not comply; in others, compliance was the result of a threat. Of the analyzed complaints, seven resulted in negative outcomes of which "five were cases in which the ruling was followed by impasse, and two were cases in which an arm-twisting restriction achieved its intended result, the ruling notwithstanding" (Hudec et al. 1993, p. 10). Interestingly, these cases[43] started only after 1983. Nonetheless, even taking these failures into account, the overall success rate during the 1980s remained high; according to Hudec, positive outcomes were at a mere 83% (Hudec et al. 1993, p. 97). Indeed, a failure of 10% in an international setting could be a sign of success and that was only after 1983. In other words, for more than 30 years, "the success rate for cases with rulings of violation was 100%" (Hudec et al. 1993, p. 20).

There are several possible explanations for the increase in negative outcomes. One is that those particular cases were "hard cases." It is possible that the same outcome would have occurred had those cases been disputed under the WTO if the outcome was particularly difficult to accept for political reasons. The worse

[42]"In 55 of the 207 complaints, complaints were withdrawn or abandoned without any ruling having been made, or without any settlement or concession having been achieved" (Hudec 1993, p. 6).

[43]The seven cases with negative outcomes after rulings of violation were: 1. United States: Prohibition on Imports of Tuna and Tuna Products from Canada, BISD 29th Supp. 91 (1983). 2. United States: Imports of Sugar from Nicaragua, BISD 31st Supp. 67 (1985). 3. Canada: Countervailing Duty on Boneless Manufacturing Beef, GATT Doc. SCM/85 (1987). 4. United States: Section 337 of the Tariff Act of 1930, BISD 36th Supp. 345 (1990). 5. European Community: Antidumping Regulation on Imports of Parts and Components, BISD 37th Supp. 132 (1991). 6. United States: Antidumping Duties on Stainless Pipes and Tubes from Sweden, GATT Doc. ADP/47 (1990). 7. Canada: Restriction on Imports of Ice Cream and Yoghurt, BISD 36th Supp. 68 (1990).

compliance record belongs to the United States, the country that most frequently resisted the legal rulings of the dispute settlement process. In fact:

> four of the fourteen rulings of violation made against the United States ended with a negative outcome – two with a failure to comply and two with compliance only after the complainant had acceded to arm-twisting demands. All four negative outcomes occurred in the 1980s, leading to a negative-outcome rate of 29% for the entire forty-two year period, and a 40% rate for the 1980s alone .... The United States has by far the worst compliance record in any time period. The United States forced negative outcomes in 36% of all valid complaints against it over the entire forty-two year period, and in 50% of the valid complaints filed against it in the 1980s. (Hudec et al. 1993, pp. 41–42)

The second least-compliant nation has historically been Canada. "Canada, the defendant that litigates a higher percentage of complaints against it than any other, comes in with the second worst compliance record. Canada had only eight rulings of violation with known results. Canada's refusal to follow two rulings, both in the 1980s, leads to an overall negative-outcome rate of 25%, and a rate of 29% for the 1980s alone" (Hudec et al. 1993, p. 42).

The positioning of the two nations as first and second in terms of poor compliance records illustrates that lack of compliance is not necessarily always a power issue; the USA is undoubtedly politically and financially powerful, but Canada is hardly second thereto in the international community. In other words, something more profound than a mere thirst for power and consequent misuse of the system is at work.

One explanation is that the internal environment of a particular country forces the country to act in a certain way. Hudec offered two additional possible explanations for why some of the cases evaluated produced negative outcomes. He wrote that:

> the huge increase in the number of complaints filed during the 1980s indicates that a major change in government attitudes toward dispute settlement was taking place. The fact that governments were using dispute settlement much more frequently testifies that they had much greater confidence in the legal system. This confidence, in turn, would tend to elicit more ambitious complaints as well – complaints attacking trade measures with powerful domestic political support, measures that might have been left in peace in earlier decades. A higher incidence of such ambitious complaints could well explain, at least in part, a higher incidence of legal failure .... A second possible consequence of increased volume would be increased visibility of the decision-making process, and this increased visibility, in turn, would likely have an effect upon the manner of decision-making. Placed under a spotlight, panels would tend to adopt a more objective, legally sound approach to decision-making, because in the end that is the only basis on which a critical public audience will accept an adjudicatory decision. This more objective technique of decision-making would tend to produce more findings of violations in hard cases, in contrast to the tendency of earlier, more "diplomatic" panels to avoid confrontations by vague decisions that skirt a direct finding. (Hudec et al. 1993, p. 22)

Failures are unavoidable. Arguably, even if international tax rules face difficulties at times, such difficulties would most likely be temporary and specific to a single location, time or circumstance. Not only adjudicative bodies, but also law schools, as well as regulatory, political, and executive bodies around the world "will be paying increasing attention to WTO law, both as written and as interpreted by WTO panels. They will also be paying attention to who is paying attention, often receiving international law through the medium of foreign law" (Slaughter 2000, p. 1124).

The fact that the system might sometimes be ill-equipped to deal with difficult issues is inevitable. From a developmental point of view, "any newborn legal system is going to begin this way" (Hudec et al. 1993, p. 32), but such obstacles can be beneficial, as they are likely to inform and strengthen the system, similar to the way in which a virus may sicken the human body but ultimately strengthens the natural immunization system of the body. Hudec wrote that:

> success builds confidence, and confidence stimulates greater demands upon the system .... Governments became more aggressive in selecting complaints to bring, and decision-makers, now in the open, began to give direct answers to hard questions. Legal systems must take these risks if they are to become effective. Governments have to be challenged, and the challenges will almost inevitably cause some failures by demanding too much too soon. The failures themselves are not the problem. The trick is to keep improving the system in order to overcome those failures." (Hudec et al. 1993, p. 25)

7.16 Government Procurement Agreement Experience

Governments acquire goods and services as inputs into the production of public goods and services. Such purchases account for a substantial share of total demand for goods and services domestically and internationally. For some nations, after being closed for a long time, governments have opened procurement markets to some degree, if not entirely, under the WTO's Agreement on Government Procurement. This agreement is a good example to mention, because it is an agreement that mixes internal political issues with finical issues as well as international trade rules, as suitably comparable to the suggested tax agreement.

It was called plurilateral because it is an optional agreement, and was first negotiated during the Tokyo Round in 1976. Later, during the Uruguay Round, effort was put into broadening the coverage to purchases by sub-central government entities and to the services sectors. Following these negotiations, the Agreement on Government Procurement was signed in Marrakesh on April 15, 1994.

The main purpose of these agreements is to open up as much of this business as possible to international competition, guaranteeing fair, transparent, and non-discriminatory conditions of international competition.[44] It is not an easy agreement and surely "the process likely will require at least a generation to mature" (Yukins and Schooner 2007, pp. 529, 530). Its significance, however, is too much to be dismissed. It is estimated to have increased the international procurement business an estimated ten-fold. During fiscal year 2007, the United States federal procurement market alone will account for approximately $400 billion.[45]

---

[44] It does not apply to every governmental actions; it applies only to contracts that cross a threshold, which is 182,000.

[45] Acquisition Advisory Panel, Report of the Acquisition Advisory Panel to the Office of Federal Procurement Policy and the United States Congress 1 (Draft Final Report, Dec. 2006).

Three observations are to be taken from this short overview. The first is to note that the number of members to this agreement has increased. In January 1, 1996, the agreement was signed by 26 signatories,[46] and it increased to 40 WTO members by 2007.[47] What started as a small number ten years ago has doubled by 2007. This is a 100% increase, not a small increase. Thus, a small agreement can evolve if proven effective.[48]

Second, the member countries to this agreement are diverse. For example, although developing countries are considered weak and will not be part of such an agreement, they seem to have some interest in the agreement. For example, China is already a member. Argentina, Colombia, Sir Lanka, and Turkey are observing, and seem willing to participate at a later point, if not immediately. Thus, there seems an indication that the agreement is attracting considerable attention from different countries.

Thirdly, there is a political aspect to the evolvement of this agreement. This agreement originally came from earlier European directives in the 1970s (see Verdeaux 2003, p. 721). Since the USA is an attractive market as well as the EC, both sought to open other procurement markets to their business. For example, in 1993, after the USA announced its intention to ban the purchase of European-made equipment by US federal agencies, the EC modified some rules to allow US business to enter the market. The US government later withdrew the threat (see Verdeaux 2003, p. 721). Over time, this evolution, driven by a desire to eliminate discriminatory rules, formed the basis for the WTO agreement on government procurement.

From the above discussion we can see that there is no reason why a tax agreement cannot be just like a government procurement agreement. A tax agreement where the USA and the EU can negotiate would be a starting point to proceed toward creating an international setting where tax-trade issues can be managed. Such an agreement would be a guideline and supervise non-discriminatory and transparent rules, as much as possible. As developing countries participate in the

---

[46]Canada, the European Union with its fifteen Member States, Hong-Kong China, Iceland, Israel, Japan, Korea, Lichtenstein, Norway, Singapore, Switzerland, and the United States; *see* Verdeaux (2003, pp. 713, 716).

[47]Government Procurement: General Overview. http://www.wto.org/english/tratop_e/gproc_e/overview_e.htm.

[48]Current members are: Canada; the European Communities, including its 27 member States; Hong Kong, China; Iceland; Israel; Japan; Korea; Liechtenstein; the Kingdom of the Netherlands with respect to Aruba; Norway; Singapore; Switzerland and the United States. Nineteen other WTO members with observer status include: Albania, Argentina, Armenia, Australia, Cameroon, Chile, China, Colombia, Croatia, Georgia, Jordan, the Kyrgyz Republic, Moldova, Mongolia, Oman, Panama, Sri Lanka, Chinese Taipei and Turkey. In addition, four intergovernmental organizations, namely the International Monetary Fund (IMF), the International Trade Centre (ITC), the Organization for Economic Co-operation and Development (OECD), and the United Nations Conference on Trade and Development (UNCTAD) also have observer status in the WTO Committee on Government Procurement, which administers the Agreement (Government Procurement: General Overview, http://www.wto.org/english/tratop_e/gproc_e/overview_e.htm).

government procurement agreement, there is also a possibility they will participate and benefit from a tax agreement. This path may not be easy and it could take generation to mature as well.

7.17 Summary

The ultimate realization is that soft law can be a success story. Under the GATT, with its ability to stop any ruling, for a losing party to accept panel findings is a very powerful indication that countries do accept the rulings of an independent body, in this case the panel, even if that ruling is adverse to their own interests or preferences. Nations are, it seems, able to accept rulings of which they are not truly convinced, a lack of conviction that may be presumed since if one party were convinced by its opponent's point of view, it would be unlikely to waste time litigating the case.

Arguments for and against the application of soft law are unlikely to end any time soon. Why nations do or do not obey international law is not the primary concern of this study. Instead, it should be acknowledged and accepted that soft law is usually obeyed and that compliance can be achieved, as illustrated by the GATT experience.

There is no reason to doubt that international tax can be more sensitive to soft law, the ramifications of which are decided independently by individual states in one of two ways: (1) by accepting the tax agreement as it is or modifying it with reservation; or (2) by voting for or against a ruling if and when a dispute does arise. With this foundation, it remains important to remember that soft law is not meaningless law; rather, it is law that gradually can attain cultural acceptance with the help of state officials, NGOs, local courts, and the like. Simply put, soft law can be effective in increasing compliance, yet it is not a threat and causes minimal or no political damage, offering the needed policy, social, and internal space within a transparent framework.

In sum, for solving the theoretical problem of direct vs. indirect tax, the prospect of a multilateral tax agreement will bring more attention to the WTO, which will bring this issue to the front to be discussed thoroughly. It could lead to more studies, more negotiations, or any other action. The importance is that the differentiation will be discussed. This will be reflected in the Panel as well as the AB rulings.

As for actual cases, the tax agreement will stop "wrong" or very sensitive cases. The DISC, FSC, ETI, have all been costing too much effort and have lasted for much too long. The USA is not doing this just to violate the WTO. It is doing it because it is under an internal pressure that is hard to defeat. The WTO cannot upset the USA. It can pressure it, but only to an extent before it breaks its bones. Once the Americans feel their interest and pride has been undermined by the WTO, there is a risk that the USA will pull out of the organization or just ignore it. Once the USA is out or not as effective, the organization will not function as it should. When such a huge market segment and powerful economy exits from the WTO, the organization's effectiveness will be compromised.

In religious or other social values, the tax agreement will guarantee not only a peace of mind for countries, but also guarantee that even these kinds of tax cases will not be brought for disputes in the WTO. Saudi Arabia's religious tax will not be an issue for the Kingdom or for any Islamic government wishing to implement some religious element into its system. That's also true for other social issues, such as taxes related to labor or environment issues, for example.

The soft jurisdiction works against abusing the veto. The old-GATT proved the success of softly adjudicating international trade. A major objection would be that under the old-GATT, and because of its litigation mechanism, GATT members did bring only hard-core legal issues, issues that were very clear violations and issues that were worth litigation. This should not be an objection; indeed, it should be the goal. This is why it was a success: because the cases were clear and worth it. This is what is needed under the tax agreement, cases that are clear violations and worth litigating. WTO is an organization where sovereign states settle their disputes. Its existence can be at risk if it is open to litigation of all issues, minor and major issues alike.

The tax agreement option is a challenge: developers must tread carefully at first, but the construct has the potential to grow and flourish. It is, of course, possible that difficult cases will arise, potentially leading to disappointment in the system; however, if governments continue to support and improve the system, over time it can be transformed into a strong body of international legal rules. The introductory phase will achieve a balance between governing all tax issues on one the hand, and allowing countries to retain the sovereignty they desire on the other by not infringing upon or threatening that sovereignty. At the same time, the tax agreement option will likely encourage countries to follow multinational rules, inspiring trust by taking into account the circumstances surrounding any tax legislation, particularly the historical backgrounds and the cultural values attached to taxation that vary so greatly among countries.

References

Altman ZD (2006) Dispute resolution under tax treaties. IBFD, Amsterdam

Arnold BJ, Sasseville J, Zolt E (2002) Summary of the proceedings of an invitational seminar on tax treaties in the 21st century. Can Tax J 50(1):65

Åslund A (2006) Russia's WTO accession. Testimony at the hearing on EU economic and trade relations with Russia, Committee on International Trade, European Parliament, Brussels, November 21, 2006. Peterson Institute for International Economics. http://www.iie.com /publications/papers/paper.cfm?ResearchID=686

Ault HJ (1992) Corporate integration, tax treaties and the division of the international tax base: principles and practices. Tax L Rev 47:565

Avi-Yonah RS (2000) Globalization, tax competition, and the fiscal crisis of the welfare state. Harv L Rev 113:1575, 1675

Beyerlin U, Marauhn T (1997) Law-making and law enforcement in international environmental law after the 1992 Rio conference research project. Erich Schmidt, Berlin
Brauner Y (2003) An international tax regime in crystallization. Tax L Rev 56:259
Brauner Y (2005) International trade and tax agreements may be coordinated, but not reconciled. Va Tax Rev 25:251
Carroll MB (1978) Global perspectives of an international tax lawyer. Exposition, Huntsville, NY
Cockfield A (2006) The rise of the OECD as informal 'World Tax Organization' through national responses to e-commerce tax challenges. Yale J L Technol 8:136. http://ssrn.com/abstract=916555
Cotterrell R (2006) Roger, law, culture and society: legal ideas in the mirror of social theory. Ashgate, Aldershot
D'Amato A (1971) The concept of custom in international law. Cornell University Press, Ithaca, NY
Davey WJ (2003) Resolving U.S.–European trade disputes through law: is the WTO dispute settlement mechanism effective? http://eucenter.wisc.edu/Publications/davey_13Feb03.pdf
Downs GW, Danish KW, Barsoom PN (2000) The transformational model of international regime design: triumph of hope or experience. Colum J Transnat'l L 38:465
Dunlop J (2006) Taxing the international athlete: working toward free trade in the americas through a multilateral tax treaty. NW J Int'l L Bus 27:227
Ehring L (2001) De facto discrimination in WTO law: national and most-favored-nation treatment – or equal treatment? http://www.jeanmonnetprogram.org/papers/01/013201.html
Ehrmann M (2002) Procedures of compliance control in international environmental treaties. Colo J Int'l Envtl L Pol'y 13:377
Evans SC (1995) U.S. taxation of international athletes: a reexamination of the artiste and athlete article in tax treaties. Geo Wash J Int'l L Econ 29:297, 304
Ezrahi AM (1999) Opting out of opt-out clauses: removing obstacles to international trade and international peace. Law Pol'y Int'l Bus 31:123
Florini A (1996) The evolution of international norms. Int'l Stud Q 40:363, 365
Franck TM (1990) The power of legitimacy among nations. Oxford University Press, New York
Gamble JK (1980) Reservations to multilateral treaties: a macroscopic view of state practice. Am J Int'l L 74:372
Graetz MJ (2001) The David R. Tillinghast lecture: taxing international income – inadequate principles, outdated concept, and unsatisfactory policy. Brooklyn J Int'l L 26:1357
Graetz MJ, O'Hear MM (1997) The "original intent" of US international taxation. Duke L J 46:1021, 1106–1107
Green RA (1998) Antilegalistic approaches to resolving disputes between governments: a comparison of the international tax and trade regimes. Yale J Int'l 23:79
Guzman AT (2002) A compliance-based theory of international law. Cal L Rev 90:1823
Halverson K (2004) China's WTO accession: economic, legal, and political implications. BC Int'l Comp L Rev 27:319, 323
Henkin L (1979) How nations behave. Columbia University Press, New York
Horner FM (2001) Do we need an international tax organisation? Tax Notes Int'l 24:179
Huang PH (2002) International law and emotional rational choice. J Leg Stud 31:237
Hudec RE (1980) GATT dispute settlement after the Tokyo round: an unfinished business. Cornell Int'l L J 13:145, 159
Hudec RE (1988) Reforming GATT adjudication procedures: the lessons of the DISC case. Minn L Rev 72:1443
Hudec RE (1990) The GATT legal system and world trade diplomacy, 2nd edn. Butterworth, New Hampshire
Hudec RE (1993) Enforcing international trade law: the evolution of the modern GATT legal system. Butterworth, Salem, NH
Hudec RE (2002) Free trade, sovereignty, democracy: the future of the World Trade Organization. World Trade Rev 1(2):211–222

Hudec RE, Kennedy DLM, Sgarbossa M (1993) A statistical profile of GATT dispute. Settlement cases: 1948–1989. Minn J Global Trade 2(1):1–113

Jackson JH (1997) The world trade system: law and policy of international economic relations, 2nd edn. MIT Press, Cambridge, MA

Jackson JH (2007) Sovereignty, the WTO and changing fundamentals of international law. Cambridge University Press, Cambridge

James G, Olsen J (1998) The institutional dynamics of international political orders. Int'l Org 52:943

Jones JFA (1999) Are tax treaties necessary? Tax L Rev 53:1

Joyner C (1998) Recommended measures under the Antarctic treaty: hardening compliance with soft international law. Mich J Int'l L 19:401

Kaufman NH (1998) Fairness and the taxation of international income. Law Pol'y Int'l Bus 29:145

Keohane RO (1998) When does international law come home? Hous L Rev 35:699, 702

Keohane RO, Nye JS (1974) Transgovernmental relations and international organizations. World Polit 27:39, 43

Kimble TP (2006) Anticipatory compliance with WTO rules and the erosion of U.S. sovereignty. Quinnipiac L Rev 25:97

Knight HG (1975) The potential use of reservations to international agreements produced by the third United Nations conference on the law of the sea, policy issues. Ocean Law 1:5

Koh H (1997) Why do nations obey international law? Yale L J 106:2599

Koh H (1998) Bringing international law home. Hous L Rev 35:623, 629

Kontorovich E (2003) Reconciling political sanctions with globalization and free trade: the Arab league boycott and WTO accession: can foreign policy excuse discriminatory sanctions? Chi J Int'l L 4:283

Loukota H (1998) Multilateral tax treaty versus bilateral treaty network. In: Lang M, Herdin J, Hofbauer I (eds) Multilateral tax treaties: new developments in international tax law. Kluwer, The Hague

Mann FA (1999) Further studies in international law. Clarendon, Oxford

Mason R (2005) U.S. tax treaty policy and the European court of justice. Tax L Rev 59:65, 121

Mason R (2007) In search of internal consistency: tax discrimination in the EU. Colum J Transnat'l L 46:72

Mitchell R (1997) United States–Brazil bilateral income tax treaty negotiations. Hastings Int'l Comp L Rev 21:209, 210

Morgenthau H (1954) Politics among nations: the struggle for power and peace. Alfred Knopf, New York

Mukadi NJ (2001) International income – the last remaining tax issue triggered by international business. Tax Notes Int'l 22:1713

Musgrave RA (1969) Fiscal systems. Yale University Press, New Haven, CT

Nichols PM (1996) Extension of standing in World Trade Organization disputes to non government parties. U Pa J Int'l Econ L 17:295

Nishtar A (2005) Central cabinet approves multilateral tax treaty. Tax Notes Int'l 37:571

Nurkse R (1961) Pattern of trade and development. Oxford University Press, Oxford

Oxfam (2001) Rigged trade and not much aid: how rich countries help to keep the least developed countries poor. http://www.oxfam.org.uk/what_we_do/issues/trade/ downloads/rigged_trade.pdf

Reinhold RL (2004) Some things that multilateral tax treaties might usefully do. Tax Lawyer 57(3):661

Rigby M (1991) A critique of double tax treaties as a jurisdictional coordination mechanism. Australian L F 8:301

Rodrik D (2007) How to save globalization from its cheerleaders. Working paper series RWP07-038. John F. Kennedy School of Government, Harvard University

Rosenbloom HD (1994) What's trade got to do with it? Tax L Rev 49:593

Rosenbloom HD (1999) International tax arbitrage and the international tax system. Tax L Rev 53:137, 164
Rosenbloom HD, Langbein SI (1981) United States treaty policy: an overview. Colum J Transnat'l L 19:359
Schwarzewnberger G (1967) A manual of international law, 5th edn. Oceana, Dobbs Ferry, NY
Seligman ERA (1928) Double taxation and international fiscal cooperation. Macmillan, New York
Slaughter AM (1995) International law in a world of liberal states. Eur J Int'l L 6:503
Slaughter AM (2000) Judicial globalization. VA J Int'l L 40:1103
Slaughter AM (2003) Global government networks, global information agencies, and disaggregated democracy. Mich J Int'l L 24:1041
Slaughter A, Tulumello A, Wood S (1998) International law and international relations theory: a new generation of interdisciplinary scholarship. Am J Int'l L 92:367, 383
Spencer DE (1997) OECD information exchange recommendations are a significant first step in resolving tax evasion. J Int'l Tax'n 8:353, 383–384
Sweet JK (1998) Formulating international tax laws in the age of electronic commerce: the possible ascendancy of residence-based taxation in an era of eroding traditional income tax principles. U Pa L Rev 146:1949
Tanzi V (1995) Taxation in an integrating world. Brookings Institution, Washington, DC
Tanzi V (1998) The impact of economic globalization on taxation. Bull Int'l Fiscal Doc 52:384
Thuronyi V (2003) Comparative tax law. Kluwer, Deventer
Tillinghast DR (1996) Tax treaty issues. U Miami L Rev 50:455
Tom G, Adams R (2004) Adjudicating in anarchy: an expressive theory of international dispute resolution. Wm Mary L Rev 45:1229
Trachtman JP (1999) Bananas, direct effect and compliance. Eur J Int'l L 9:655
Vann RJ (1991) A model tax treaty for the Asian-Pacific region? Bull. Int'l Fiscal Documentation 45:151, 157–160
Verdeaux J (2003) Public procurement in the European Union and in the United States: a comparative study. Pub Cont L J 32:713, 716
Wang KC (1945) International double taxation of income: relief through international agreement 1921–1945. Harv L Rev 59:73
Warren AC (1993) Financial contract innovation and income-tax policy. Harv L Rev 107:460
Warren AC (2001) Income tax discrimination against international commerce. Tax L Rev 54:131
Williams DW (1991) Trends in international taxation. International Bureau of Fiscal Documentation, Amsterdam
Yukins R, Schooner SL (2007) Incrementalism: eroding the impediments to a global public procurement market. Geo J Int'l L 38:529

Chapter 8
Conclusions

> *The only way to save globalization is not to push it too hard.*
> Rodrik 2007, p. 31

This study was devoted to the understanding of the current conflict between trade and tax in an international setting. This author's conclusion is that there is a need for a soft mechanism to supervise taxation in its interaction with international trade under the WTO if WTO agreements are to be respected and not nullified. This work has demonstrated the strong need for a coordination mechanism that does not currently exist, and for which the need for it is rising; the most efficient way to reach this goal is through the WTO.

The decline of trade barriers has been a major international accomplishment, due mainly to the establishment of the WTO, which requires members to refrain from discriminatory or protectionist actions, including those using taxation instruments. Tax and trade regimes have been isolated from one another, although international taxation and the WTO trade agreements are in fact closely related, sharing a goal of facilitating international commerce, exchanging goods and services, and easing movement of capital and persons.

Tax plays major societal roles within nations that are not necessarily in harmony with international trade theory. As a result, two conflicting points of view have emerged from discussions and analyses of the regimes. From one perspective, taxation can affect trade so fundamentally as to nullify trade agreements. From the other point of view, tax affects the very lives of the people and can be associated with deep values that are hard to manage on an international level.

This study examined the two fields of tax and trade together in a comprehensive way, including a survey of the existing literature and an analysis of the historical development of the individual regimes, as well as studying the specific case of the Saudi Arabia religious tax system. This study for the first time has analyzed the WTO when it interacts not only with international taxation issues, but also with religious taxation, as is the case in Saudi Arabia. The author has attempted to conduct a thorough analysis of the current separation and the need for coordination within the WTO itself.

Balancing local needs with global requirements is a condition of unparalleled importance for the continuing growth of globalization of international trade. If the

T. Althunayan, *Dealing with the Fragmented International Legal Environment: WTO, International Tax and Internal Tax Regulations*,
DOI 10.1007/978-3-642-04678-0_8, © Springer-Verlag Berlin Heidelberg 2010

WTO attempts, or is seen to be attempting, to change fundamentally rooted values in any given nation, the phenomenon of growth could see the beginning of its end. Ultimately, in light of historical factors and academic arguments, this study proposed a novel framework to handle international tax issues, to resolve the existing and potential tensions between international tax and international trade.

In the end, this study suggested a soft mechanism for settling this problem, introducing soft regulation, guidance, and back-up by a soft jurisdiction that can be vetoed by the losing party. This soft law will guarantee meeting international standards most of the time, while at the same time addressing urgent and deep local values that cannot be expected to change. This flexibility will offer the WTO members the freedom needed to face difficulties or meet fundamental values while at the same time protecting a globalizing world from collapse; because if local values clash with international views, the sustainability of the system will be questionable.

The future of the WTO with regard to tax matters depends on how to deal with sensitive issues – issues ranging from using taxes as trade barriers to the imposition of religious taxation. It is better for the WTO with respect to tax rules to "recognize that sometimes countries need their own maneuvering room than to leave such a possibility outside the scope of the rules" (Rodrik 2007, p. 26). There is an urgent need to understand more fully the role that local values, such as religion, ethics, education, and forces other than law, as preserved by the west, can play in achieving certain objectives that can only be reached through formal law as understood in the west (Alford 1986a, pp. 915, 971).

Mistakes arising in the context of taxation issues are, in the opinion of the author, likely to cost the organization a high price. For example, if the WTO allows tax rules to damage trade commitments, then many agreements will become null and meaningless. On the other hand, if the WTO becomes involved with every tax issue related to trade, even if a particular tax issue is related only remotely or accidentally, such involvement could imperil the WTO's existence and credibility.

Soft jurisdiction is the most suitable approach to dealing with sensitive issues in different sovereign states in an international setting. The WTO needs to approach tax issues cautiously, because it is almost impossible to have a "grand theory" fitting all situations. This is an idea that was raised by Professor William Alford when he wrote that it is "incumbent upon all of us in the field of comparative law – and particularly those of us who focus upon non-Western legal systems – to resist the pressure, often emanating from well-meaning colleagues, to approach distant cultures armed with or in search of 'grand theory'" (see Alford 1986b, pp. 945, 946).

One obligation upon us as international law scholars is to point to directions where legal order can be preserved as much as possible from within each country, and yet not imposed upon them, and which will help build a peaceful friendly bridge between local and the international factors that are important to shaping the global order. A tax agreement is an attempt to do just that.

References

Alford W (1986a) The inscrutable occidental? Implications of Roberto Unger's uses and abuses of the Chinese past. Tex L Rev 64:915, 971

Alford W (1986b) On the limits of "grand theory" in comparative law. Wash L Rev 61:945, 946

Rodrik D (2007) How to save globalization from its cheerleaders. Working paper series RWP07-038. John F. Kennedy School of Government, Harvard University